The Cooke siste

MANCHESTER
1824

Manchester University Press

Politics, culture and society in early modern Britain

General editors

PROFESSOR ANN HUGHES
PROFESSOR ANTHONY MILTON
PROFESSOR PETER LAKE

This important series publishes monographs that take a fresh and challenging look at the interactions between politics, culture and society in Britain between 1500 and the mid-eighteenth century. It counteracts the fragmentation of current historiography through encouraging a variety of approaches which attempt to redefine the political, social and cultural worlds, and to explore their interconnection in a flexible and creative fashion. All the volumes in the series question and transcend traditional interdisciplinary boundaries, such as those between political history and literary studies, social history and divinity, urban history and anthropology. They thus contribute to a broader understanding of crucial developments in early modern Britain.

Already published in the series

The Cooke sisters

Education, piety and politics
in early modern England

GEMMA ALLEN

Manchester
University Press

Published by Manchester University Press
Altrincham Street, Manchester M1 7JA, UK
www.manchesteruniversitypress.co.uk

British Library Cataloguing-in-Publication Data is available

Library of Congress Cataloging-in-Publication Data is available

ISBN 978 0 7190 9977 9 *paperback*

First published by Manchester University Press in hardback 2013

This paperback edition first published 2016

Printed by Lightning Source

Contents

Figures

Acknowledgements

This book is the product of numerous debts and the generosity of many individuals and institutions. It started life as a doctorate, which was supervised by Felicity Heal with patience, enthusiasm and encouragement. Her shrewd comments have benefited my research enormously and I am immensely grateful for her ongoing support. The helpful observations of my doctoral examiners, Susan Doran and James Daybell, have improved my research considerably and they have been kind enough to advise and guide me ever since my viva. Susan Brigden, Pauline Croft, Cliff Davies, Diarmaid MacCulloch and Rosemary O'Day have also generously read part or all of the text and their recommendations have been invaluable. Many other scholars have been generous in offering references, comments and guidance, including John Craig, Ken Fincham, Melissa Franklin Harkrider, Ian Green, Steve Gunn, Peter McCullough, Martin Ingram, Paulina Kewes, Lynne Magnusson, Marjorie McIntosh, Glyn Redworth, Tracey Sowerby, Phil Withington and Alison Wall. Sections of this book have been presented to seminars and conferences in Oxford, Cambridge, York, Plymouth, Bristol and Baltimore and I appreciate the valuable feedback offered by those audiences. I could not have completed this project without the financial support of the Arts and Humanities Research Council. I am also indebted to Jesus College, both for generous research grants and for providing a wonderful home for my graduate studies. Since then, I have benefited immensely from the presence of encouraging colleagues in Oxford. At Lincoln College, Susan Brigden, Perry Gauci and Alana Harris supported me through the fraught, final stages of the doctoral thesis. As the thesis turned into a book, Adrian Gregory, Michael Finch, Lynda Mugglestone, David Sim and Stephen Tuck have proved wonderful colleagues at Pembroke College and I have learnt a great deal from them all. I would like to thank the series editors, Anne Hughes, Peter Lake and Anthony Milton, for their support of this book and the staff at Manchester University Press, particularly Emma Brennan. David Stenton, John Holland, Simon Price, Ida Toth and David Butterfield have all kindly assisted with the classical translations. Any infelicities that remain are, of course, my own.

Chapter 2 uses material previously published as '"a briefe and plaine declaration": Lady Anne Bacon's 1564 translation of the *Apologia Ecclesiae Anglicanae*', in P. Hardman and A. Lawrence-Mathers (eds), *Women and Writing, c.1340–c.1650: The Domestication of Print Culture* (Boydell and Brewer, 2010), pp. 62–76, which is reprinted here with kind permission. I am most grateful to the Duke of Sutherland for permission to quote from the Ellesmere Manuscripts in his private collection and to the Marquess of Salisbury for permission to reproduce the portrait of Mildred Cooke Cecil. I am also grateful for the assistance I have received from numerous archivists and librarians, but I wish to thank especially Robin Harcourt

Acknowledgements

Williams and Vicki Perry at Hatfield House, Mary Robertson at the Huntington Library, Carl Peterson of Colgate University, Eddie Smith of Westminster School and in particular all the staff of Lambeth Palace Library, on whose time I have been most demanding.

My friends have shown me great kindness – and tolerant understanding – during this long project, most especially Dunlaith Bird, Rachele De Felice and Freyja Cox Jensen, who have commiserated and encouraged in equal measure.

It seems fitting that a book so concerned with sisterhood, marriage and motherhood should finally acknowledge my gratitude to my family. I owe a huge debt to my mother and sister, Vanessa and Francesca Allen, for all their support during the writing of this book. My husband, Edward Arnold, has lived with the Cooke sisters in our midst now for many years and has shown boundless patience throughout. He has accompanied me on research trips, discussed ideas, read chapters and, above all, seen me through the ups and downs of the project which has finally culminated in what I call my 'Cooke book'. The book is for them, with love and thanks.

Abbreviations

Apologie	J. Jewel, *An Apologie or answere in defence of the Churche of Englande*, trans. Anne Bacon (1564). *STC* 14591.
Ascham Letters	R. Ascham, *Letters of Roger Ascham*, trans. M. Hatch and A. Vos, ed. A. Vos (New York, 1989).
Ballard	G. Ballard, *Memoirs of Several Ladies of Great Britain*, ed. R. Perry (Detroit, 1985).
BL	British Library, London.
BN	Bibliothèque Nationale, Paris.
Bodl.	Bodleian Library, Oxford.
CP	Hatfield House, Hertfordshire, Cecil Papers.
CS	Camden Society.
CSP, Foreign	*Calendar of State Papers, Foreign Series, of the reign of Elizabeth I, 1558–1603*, ed. J. Stevenson (23 vols, 1863–1950).
CSP, Spain	*Calendar of Letters and State Papers relating to English affairs preserved principally in the Archives of Simancas, 1558–1603*, ed. M.A.S. Hume (4 vols, 1892–99).
CUL	Cambridge University Library, Cambridge.
Folger	Folger Shakespeare Library, Washington DC.
HALS	Hertfordshire Archives and Local Studies, Hertford.
Hatfield	Hatfield House, Hertfordshire.
Haynes	S. Haynes, *A Collection of State Papers ... left by William Cecil, Lord Burghley* (1740).
HJ	*Historical Journal.*
JEH	*Journal of Ecclesiastical History.*
LMA	London Metropolitan Archives, London.
LPL	Lambeth Palace Library, London.
NA	National Archives, London.
NAL	Bibliothèque Nationale, Paris, Nouvelles acquisitions latines.
ODNB	A.R. Matthew (ed.), *The Oxford Dictionary of National Biography* (Oxford, 2004).
PAPS	*Proceedings of the American Philosophical Society.*
Reconciliation	*A Way of Reconciliation of a good and learned man touching the Trueth, Nature, and Substance of the Body and Blood of Christ in the Sacrament*, trans. Elizabeth Cooke Hoby Russell (1605). *STC* 21456.
SP	State Papers, National Archives, London.
Spedding	J. Spedding (ed.), *The Letters and the Life of Francis Bacon, including all his occasional works* (7 vols, 1861–74), I.

Abbreviations

STC   *A Short-Title Catalogue of Books Printed in England, Scotland, and Ireland and of English Books Printed Abroad, 1475–1640,* compiled by A.W. Pollard and G.W. Redgrave, revised and enlarged by W.A. Jackson, F.S. Ferguson and K.F. Pantzer (3 vols, 1986–91).

TRHS   *Transactions of the Royal Historical Society.*

Urwick   W. Urwick, *Nonconformity in Herts. Being Lectures upon the Non-Conforming Worthies of St Albans and Memorials of Puritanism and Nonconformity in all the Parishes of the County of Hertford* (1884).

Vives   J.L. Vives, *Vives and the Renascence Education of Women,* ed. F. Watson (New York, 1912).

Wing   *A Short-Title Catalogue of Books Printed in England, Scotland, Ireland, Wales and British America and of English Books Printed in Other Countries, 1641–1700,* compiled by D. Wing (4 vols, New York, 1982–98).

Note on conventions

The original spelling of documents has been retained, but u/v and i/j have been modernised and abbreviations have been silently expanded. Punctuation has been modernised where necessary and insertions to the text of a manuscript have been noted by ^^. Conjectured reconstructions, in the case of damaged manuscripts, are shown in square brackets. Quotations are provided in the original language and, where necessary, a translation follows in parentheses, except when quoting from translated sources. Quotations from Scripture are from the Geneva Bible (1560). Dates are Old Style, except that the year has been taken to begin on 1 January. Publications with Greek and Latin titles are given only in the latter language, but all other titles are reproduced in their original languages. The place of publication is London, unless otherwise stated.

The sisters are referred to throughout primarily by their first names to avoid confusion between natal and marital surnames.

Introduction

During the early years of her marriage, Mildred Cooke Cecil translated a sermon of St Basil the Great from its original Greek into English. She translated his belief that every man should use his particular gifts to further 'the chirche of the living god', because 'in this chirche, which is as a large house, be not onely vessels of all sortes, as of goolde, silver, woode & earthe, but also, all maner of craftes'.[1] To Mildred, her classical education provided her with a craft, which she could use to further the evangelical faith through the act of translation. Yet her text must also be seen within the context of the patronage networks of Edwardian England. Mildred presented her work to Anne Seymour, the duchess of Somerset. Recently married to William Cecil, then an up-and-coming administrator, Mildred acknowledged herself as a client, a 'humble servant & dettor', to the duchess; Anne Stanhope Seymour, then married to Edward Seymour, Protector Somerset, was one of the most powerfully connected female patrons in the country. By the accession of Elizabeth I, everything had changed. Mildred, now the wife of the Queen's Principal Secretary, was herself an influential member of the political networks of Elizabethan England. However, the issues revealed through her work of translation, namely those of education, piety and politics, still dominated her life and would continue to do so. How these themes interacted and impacted upon the lives of Mildred and her sisters is the major focus of this book.

Mildred was the first child born in 1526 to Sir Anthony Cooke and his wife, Anne Fitzwilliam. She was followed by four brothers and four sisters: Anne was the next girl, born in 1528 or 1529, followed by Margaret (c.1533), Elizabeth (c.1540) and Katherine (c.1542). Their father never attended university and was largely self-taught; his greatest claim to posthumous reputation is that he provided both his sons and his daughters with a thorough humanist education, in both classical and modern languages.[2] It has long been suggested that Anthony Cooke acted as a tutor to Edward VI, yet it is more probable that he was employed as a reader after the retirement of Richard Cox in 1550.[3] There has also been a persistent belief that Anne assisted her father in tutoring the young king, but there is no contemporary evidence for this assertion.[4]

Mildred was the first sister to marry, becoming the second wife of William Cecil in December 1545. Motherhood proved difficult to achieve and no children were born for the first nine years of the marriage; of her five children, only Anne and Robert survived to adulthood. Mildred was certainly involved in the early education of her children, for her husband described her as a 'matchless mother' governing Robert Cecil's education as 'so zealous and excellent a tutor'.[5] The marriage was a happy one; Cecil described his wife as 'dearest above all' on her monument in Westminster Abbey.[6] Mildred's influence grew with her husband's rising status, first as Principal Secretary and later as Baron Burghley and Lord Treasurer. Mildred was particularly politically active in the 1560s and 1570s, although there is evidence of her continued role as an intermediary to her husband well into the last decade of her life. William and Mildred were married for forty-three years, until Mildred's death on 4 April 1589.

Mildred's marriage was influential in determining her sisters' matches, for in February 1553 Anne Cooke was married to Cecil's friend, Nicholas Bacon, as his second wife, after a proposal by Walter Haddon had been rejected.[7] On the accession of Mary I, Anne was instrumental in securing pardons for her husband and her brother-in-law, William Cecil, through her service to the new Queen.[8] The Bacons' fortunes rose with the accession of Elizabeth in 1558, as Nicholas Bacon was made a privy councillor and Lord Keeper of the Great Seal shortly after. A translator of sermons by the Italian evangelical Bernardino Ochino in her youth, Anne continued her scholarly pursuits after her marriage, as shown by her 1564 translation into English of John Jewel's *Apologia Ecclesiae Anglicanae*, a project endorsed by her husband's political circle. The marriage brought multiple pregnancies, but only two of Anne's children survived into adulthood, Anthony and Francis Bacon. John Walsall, the Bacons' household chaplain, praised the couple's care in 'demeaning your selves in the education of your children'; however, it is after Nicholas Bacon's death in 1579 that there is the most evidence of Anne's maternal influence, in the form of the vast body of surviving letters exchanged between Anne and her then adult son Anthony.[9] During Anne's thirty-one year widowhood, her godly religious beliefs are also most clearly apparent, as she took on a more active role in advancing the 'right Reformation', both in Hertfordshire and beyond, before her death in August 1610.[10]

Elizabeth and Margaret were the next sisters to marry after Anne, in a joint ceremony on 27 June 1558. Elizabeth had been living with the Cecils in Wimbledon since her father left for Continental exile in 1554, and there she met her first husband, Thomas Hoby.[11] His elder half-brother, Sir Philip Hoby, was a close friend of William Cecil's and the men were no doubt influential in arranging the match. The couple were well suited intellectually; Thomas Hoby published his translation from Italian of Castiglione's *The Courtyer* in 1561 and it is likely that Elizabeth undertook her translation from Latin of John Ponet's *Diallacticon* at a similar time, although it remained unpublished until 1605.[12] Thomas Hoby was knighted in 1566 and sent as the Elizabethan ambassador to France, accompanied by his wife and their growing family. Thomas

Hoby's sudden death in Paris in July 1566 left a pregnant Elizabeth to organise transporting her children back to England, events which she immortalised in neo-classical funerary verse. Tragedy struck again in 1571, when her two daughters died of the sweating sickness, leaving Elizabeth with her two sons, Edward and Thomas Posthumous Hoby, the latter having been born after the death of his father. Rumours had circulated in 1569 that Cecil had arranged for Elizabeth to marry the imprisoned duke of Norfolk, Thomas Howard, following the Northern Rising, but in the end Elizabeth remained a widow until marrying John, Lord Russell, heir to the earldom of Bedford, in December 1574.[13] After the birth of two daughters, Bess and Anne, a longed-for son and heir to the earldom, Francis, was born in 1579, but died the following year. Elizabeth was again widowed after Lord Russell's early death in 1584, and the following year she was plunged into an inheritance battle on behalf of her Russell daughters, which she again recorded in Latin and Greek commemorative verse. Elizabeth's legal claims for her daughters were eventually rejected in 1593, yet her efforts on their behalf did not cease.[14] She was active in securing for them positions as Maids of Honour to the Queen and in arranging the marriage of her daughter Anne Russell to Henry Somerset, Lord Herbert, the eldest son of the earl of Worcester in 1600; Elizabeth had previously been instrumental in securing the marriage of her son Thomas Posthumous Hoby to Margaret Dakins Sidney in 1596. Elizabeth's political networks are also most apparent during her second widowhood, as she exchanged letters with Lord Burghley, Robert Cecil and the earl of Essex, as well as hosting the Queen at Bisham in 1592. As her political contacts declined at the start of the seventeenth century, Elizabeth became increasingly isolated, as demonstrated by her eventual defeat in 1606 in her legal battle over rights to Donnington Castle. Elizabeth died on 3 June 1609, survived by three of her seven children.

Less is known about the other Cooke sister who married alongside Elizabeth in June 1558. Margaret served Mary I at court and her father, though in exile, was concerned that she was still unwed in 1557. He wrote to his son-in-law Cecil in March, and it may have been through the latter's means that Margaret came to marry Sir Ralph Rowlett in June of the following year.[15] Margaret died shortly after the wedding and she was buried on 3 August 1558.[16]

The marriage of the youngest sister, Katherine, was the only match over which William Cecil exercised less initial influence. On Easter Day in April 1564, Cecil noted in his diary that 'H. Killigrew wrote to me an Invective for my misliking of his Mariadg with my Sister, Catharyn Cook'.[17] His reasons for opposing the match are unknown, but they may have included Henry Killigrew's closeness to the earl of Leicester.[18] Cecil's concerns, however, were not enough to stop the match and the couple married on 4 November 1565. Four daughters were born at intervals amongst Henry Killigrew's diplomatic missions to Scotland, Germany and France. There is little surviving evidence regarding Katherine's activities during her marriage, bar her composition and receipt of a limited number of neo-Latin verses; her relationship with the godly preacher Edward Dering is revealed through his extant letters. Katherine predeceased her husband, on 27 December 1583.

The sisters have long received brief individual mention in the biographies of their male relatives. The manuscript 'Anonymous Life' of Burghley, written within five years of his death and possibly by his secretary Michael Hickes, described Mildred as a 'wise, & vertuous Gentlewoman ... excellently lerned'.[19] In the early seventeenth century, William Camden characterised the sisters primarily in terms of their father, Sir Anthony Cooke, 'whom having brought up in Learning, both Greek and Latine, above their Sex, he married [them] to men of good Account'.[20] In the first biography of Anne's son Francis Bacon, published in 1657 by his chaplain, William Rawley, Anne was described as a 'choice lady, and eminent for piety, virtue and learning; being exquisitely skilled, for a woman, in the Greek and Latin tongues'.[21]

Yet there is also a trend of scholarly disapproval of the sisters by those historians writing on their male relatives. Thomas Birch's 1754 *Memoirs of the reign of Queen Elizabeth* described Anne as having a peevish and severe temper, suggesting that such a temperament worked to make her less effective in advising her sons.[22] James Spedding, writing in 1861 on Francis Bacon, characterised Anne as an admirable mother throughout her son's youth, yet was more critical of her behaviour by the 1590s; she was described as 'just beginning to fail ... in the power of self-command'.[23] The twentieth century brought more overt disapproval, particularly of Mildred. Conyers Read argued that while Burghley showed 'respect and admiration' for his wife, he 'wonders whether Burghley's conjugal relations lacked warmth'.[24] He added, unnecessarily surely, that 'If we may judge from her portrait, she lacked feminine charm'. Read even wrongly suggested that there was a silence in her political and religious activities from 1570 onwards: 'Burghley may have whispered in her ear that she was doing more harm than good'.[25] Ian MacFarlane, in his study of the neo-Latin poet George Buchanan, wrote of Mildred that 'some have thought she confused scholarship and tedium', although he provided no evidence as to who these contemporary detractors might be.[26] Other recent scholarship on the Cookes' husbands and sons has been less condemnatory of the sisters, yet still gives little consideration to the political and religious roles they played alongside their male relatives.[27]

The sisters have, however, received considerable attention in their own right. Early works presented them as exemplars for women to follow, in a tradition which Natalie Zemon Davis has termed that of the 'women worthies'.[28] In the early eighteenth century, John Strype described Mildred as 'singularly excellent a woman', and all the sisters were presented in the same manner in their individual biographies in George Ballard's 1752 *Memoirs of Several*

Ladies ... Celebrated for their Writings.[29] It is only in the last three decades that the sisters have received more thoughtful attention. Literary scholars have been predominant amongst the recent work on the sisters, primarily treating them individually rather than as a group. A variety of studies have considered different aspects of their writings in English, in particular focusing on their contribution to various different genres of writing.[30] The sisters have been less well served by historians, with the exception of work on Mildred Cooke Cecil.[31] Yet to date there has been no large-scale and systematic study on all four sisters that draws upon the full range of surviving evidence, across all of their own writings, including those in classical languages, as well as more traditional historical sources.[32] It is only by uncovering and analysing a more comprehensive source-base for all the sisters that we can ask – and answer – key questions about the nature and utility of the Cooke sisters' humanist education, about the extent of their religious and political agency and about its relationship to their unusual degree of learning. In order to address these questions, the book that follows draws on the entire extant body of the Cooke sisters' correspondence. Their letters exist in remarkable numbers for the period.[33] Of those letters written by the sisters themselves, Anne's and Elizabeth's survive in the greatest numbers. Over a hundred letters written by Anne are still extant within the papers of her son Anthony Bacon, held at Lambeth Palace Library; the majority of Anne's letters therefore date from after Anthony's return to England in 1592. Over sixty of the letters penned by Elizabeth also still exist, dating from 1566 through to 1608, and the majority of this correspondence survives in the Cecil Papers at Hatfield House. Detailed analysis of this correspondence informs this study, which also draws on further important and previously untapped letters in a variety of other archives.[34] In comparison to that of her sisters, the absence of Mildred's correspondence is striking and unexplained; certainly we know that she received many letters which are no longer extant.[35] Only five letters composed by Mildred survive, including the dedicatory epistle appended to her translation of St Basil the Great. Two further letters are in Greek and an additional letter in Latin is in another's hand.[36] The fifth has previously been known only in printed form, however, I have discovered the existence of Mildred's original letter, written in her own handwriting.[37] This has importantly allowed the authenticity of her hand to be established for the first time, revealing her translation of St Basil to be in her own handwriting.[38] This discovery also has implications for the identification of her marginalia within the extant volumes from her library. There is a greater survival of letters written to Mildred, with a significant cluster dating from the Anglo-Scottish negotiations of 1560; I have also discovered previously unknown letters written to Mildred from Ireland in 1568.[39] Only one letter still survives in the hand of Katherine Cooke Killigrew.[40] However, four letters written to Katherine by the evangelical preacher Edward

Dering are printed within his *Certaine godly and comfortable Letters*.[41] No letters written either by or to Margaret Cooke have survived. Alongside their letters, the sisters' other literary works in English and classical languages have been analysed, including verse, dramatic interludes and translations, as well as their iconographical representations in portraits and on monuments. More traditional sources, such as ecclesiastical registers and household accounts, have also yielded significant material. This range of evidence allows important deficiencies in our knowledge of the sisters to be addressed for the first time, yet the extant material is still unevenly spread across their lives and the book that follows is therefore not a collection of standard biographies. Instead the central concerns of this book are those most strongly reflected in the surviving evidence: the Cooke sisters' education, their piety and their politics.

The sisters' education deserves closer attention than the imprecise panegyric it has so far received, since it sheds light both on their distinctive experience and on wider issues of early modern female learning. Girls in this period were educated in the home, and therefore the extant source material through which to investigate their educational provision is scarcer than that generated by their male contemporaries in scholarly institutions. Scholarship on early modern female education has thus long concentrated on prescriptive texts, written by male pedagogues such as Juan Luis Vives; previous evaluations of the Cooke sisters' education have similarly relied on the prescriptive context.[42] From this basis, emphasis has been placed on the restrictions upon early modern women's reading, termed by Jacqueline Pearson as a form of 'policing'.[43] This study goes beyond the limitations of that approach, instead offering a reconstruction of the sisters' education through the texts they owned and read, both during their youth and in their later lives. In reconstructing the reading of the sisters, the study relies upon a distinctive methodology. It draws not only upon the evidence of ownership marks and book inventories, but upon a diverse range of sources, including letters and portraits, which allows the breadth of their studies as female humanists to be appreciated fully for the first time. The study therefore provides much needed information on sixteenth-century female book-ownership. Kevin Sharpe has lamented of the early modern period as a whole that 'Nearly all the readers about whom we have information are male'.[44] It has even recently been asserted that 'few women developed libraries of their own'.[45] To ignore the precise nature of the reading of this group of female humanists is to ignore the role of sixteenth-century women in the history of the book; the paucity of research on women's reading in this period compares with the ever-growing body of literature on female writers during this century.[46] The reconstruction of the Cooke sisters' reading provides important information to place against the larger body of work on seventeenth-century women's libraries, most notably that of Heidi Brayman Hackel on Lady Anne Clifford and the countess of Bridgewater, David McKitterick on Elizabeth Puckering and Paul Morgan on Frances Wolfreston.[47]

Beyond reconstructing the nature of their learning, this study is concerned with the question of whether there was any practical utility to a humanist education for women. Writing from a prescriptive viewpoint, previous scholarship has perceived the aims of a female humanist education to be focused only on training women to make good marriages and become godly mothers.[48] For early modern men, a humanist education instead provided training for their political and civic careers, the implications of which have been stressed by historians of political culture; Markku Peltonen, for example, has argued that the Elizabethan male elite shared a belief in the 'classical humanist' notion of the *vita activa*, the virtuous active life.[49] Early modern women have been seen as excluded from using their education in that way, with the practical implications of female humanist education being explored only for Elizabeth I.[50] Anthony Grafton and Lisa Jardine have argued that the pursuit of humanist learning by fifteenth-century Italian women was not designed for political ends. They maintain that classical education for these women was seen as an accomplishment, akin to needlework, rather than as providing any constructive training.[51] Maria Dowling concluded that for early sixteenth-century English female humanists 'education did not give them egress into public life'.[52] Mary Ellen Lamb, writing on the Cooke sisters, has suggested that for early modern women a humanist education was 'merely a way of keeping them busy'; she has argued that, unlike for their male contemporaries, a classical education for women was not a means of exerting power and influence.[53]

This book challenges these views concerning the practical use of humanist learning for early modern women. Here the public nature of the sisters' writings in the genres of verse and translation is illuminating. The act of translation offered the Cooke sisters the chance not only to bolster their political networks, but also to contribute to strengthening the faith of their contemporaries, particularly with Anne Cooke Bacon's widely disseminated 1564 translation of Jewel's *Apologia Ecclesiae Anglicanae*. Female translation has long been viewed as a 'defective' activity, revealing little of the woman's direct agency.[54] Earlier work on Anne's translation of the *Apologia* has thus viewed it as an example of the silencing of women's voices within a patriarchal society.[55] Detailed analysis of the text instead reveals Anne's involvement with religious issues of national importance to the reformed faith, in line with the priorities of her privy councillor husband and her brother-in-law William Cecil. Her sister Elizabeth instead used her classical education to write Latin and Greek verse, which allowed her to utilise ancient ideas to legitimate her acts of female mourning. Through writing neo-classical verse, she could advance her self-image as a learned woman and speak clearly about her experience of widowhood. The sisters' letters also provide more clarity on the impact of their education, particularly their letters of political and religious counsel. Timothy Elston's work on the writings of Vives has indicated that the Spanish humanist, like Thomas More, thought that women educated to humanist principles could find a role in offering counsel to men, yet there has been no consideration of whether this was a practical reality.[56] The Cookes were aware of the vulnerability of their counsel and thus used their humanist training as a means to legitimate their epistolary advice. In order to achieve this, they strategically utilised rhetorical appeals to their own political and religious experience, whilst they also made considerable reference to their classical and scriptural learning in their correspondence. This allowed them to conceal, emphasise and legitimate their epistolary counsel, particularly through recourse to their reading in the form of *sententiae*, the quotation of pithy maxims. Thus, through their letters, we are able to explore the sisters' responses to their reading; whilst their extant marginalia are not comparable to those of Gabriel Harvey or John Dee, the use of *sententiae* reveals that, like their male contemporaries, they transformed their reading to practical purpose.[57] Analysis of the sisters' religious and political counsel in their correspondence also makes a significant contribution to the study of early modern women's letter writing. It has become increasingly apparent in recent research that early modern women were often skilled letter writers. Attention has largely focused on the petitionary letter, focusing on the 'strategies' used by women when constructing such letters in order to persuade.[58] This detailed analysis of the Cooke sisters' letters of counsel demonstrates that references to reading were another type of persuasive strategy employed by women in their letter writing.

The sisters' letters also allow a reconstruction of their political and religious networks, particularly their wide-ranging political activities as intermediaries for diverse clients. This analysis builds on the work of Barbara Harris on the late fifteenth and early sixteenth centuries, which revealed the 'careers' of aristocratic women in that period and proposed that these activities should be incorporated into a broader definition of early modern politics.[59] It also contributes to recent research on Elizabethan women's interest in the dissemination of news and intelligence.[60] However, this study makes an important departure from previous work. Writing on the archival issues for the study of early Tudor women, Harris has admitted that it is 'difficult to discern ... aristocratic women's impact – if any – on the problems and policies that form the subject of traditional political history'.[61] The surviving evidence on the Cooke sisters, however, allows an exploration of their contribution to Elizabethan diplomacy, the Queen's marriage and the political divisions of the 1590s, providing another perspective on these key issues. This study continues to emphasise the role of the family as a motivating factor for women's political activities, although its focus on 'high politics' suggests that the range of female political roles considered as motivated by kin advancement has often been perceived too narrowly. The sisters' family connections remained at the centre of their religious networks. These were the connections they relied upon when acting as brokers for godly figures, yet here there is also evidence of family networks operating in more complex ways, with the sisters working together, both as religious intermediaries and in opposition to their husbands. The sisters are also shown as religious patrons in their own right, with a particular focus on Anne Cooke Bacon's control of clerical advowsons in the area of Hertfordshire surrounding her Gorhambury estate.

There is therefore a spatial dimension to this exploration of the sisters' activities. Previous work on early modern female political and religious agency has tended to focus on the location of the great household or, particularly, the court.[62] The study of the Cooke sisters reveals female concern in other political arenas and locations, for example their interest in Parliament and in British issues. This book furthermore highlights for the first time the political relevance of the Elizabethan diplomatic wife, accompanying her husband's resident embassy. The parish context also receives much-needed attention. There has to date been little research on the role of elite women in godly networks in the localities, as compared to male Puritan gentry patrons, although Melissa Franklin Harkrider's recent work on Katherine Willoughby's advancement of reform in Lincolnshire is a notable exception.[63] By delineating Anne's clerical patronage in Hertfordshire, this study firstly places the activities of godly sixteenth-century women alongside past research on male Puritan gentry patrons in this period, as explored for example in the work of Bill Sheils and Patrick Collinson; and secondly highlights the continuities with seventeenth-century female Puritan patrons, such as Lady Joan Barrington.[64] Whilst the exploration of the sisters' political and religious networks often reveals parallels with the activities of their less learned elite female contemporaries, their humanist education still provided a particular focus to their activities, offered as additional examples of the utility of the sisters' learning.

By exploring contemporary views of the sisters, this study considers the interaction between women and learning in sixteenth-century England more widely. Scholars have long associated high levels of education for early modern women with negative stereotypes. J.R. Brink has commented that an educated woman in this period was 'for the most part an oddity, labeled "unnatural" by women as well as men'.[65] Mary Ellen Lamb has argued that female learning in sixteenth-century England was perceived as a 'threat'. For a woman to assert her learning in public was to leave herself open to accusations of foolishness, vanity, impiousness and a lack of chastity.[66] Even overtly positive associations, for example with warrior maidens or chaste beauties, have been questioned as having negative connotations, although Jane Stevenson has suggested that there was increasing acceptance of the learned European woman by the seventeenth century.[67] The range of language used in descriptions of the Cooke sisters is important for understanding the nature and form of ideas about women's education and agency in the early modern period. Yet ultimately this book suggests that such representations are dependent on the perceived political power of the female scholar; only during the widowhoods of Elizabeth and Anne, when that power and influence starts to wane, are they open to critique as educated women.

The study of the Cooke sisters thus has important implications. Recent scholarship has emphasised the contexts and conditions for women's agency and subordination in this period. Early modern domestic patriarchy was not a blanket system of male authority and female subordination, but instead part of flexible 'grids of power' in which multiple factors affected authority, such as status and age.[68] This book presents education as a way in which individual women could negotiate the patriarchal restrictions placed upon them by early modern society, allowing an opportunity to explore the interaction between social position and an inherently masculine educational authority. The study of the Cookes also reveals the impact of life-cycle and age upon female agency. Marriage was an empowering state for the sisters, in terms of both learning and their patronage power. Writing on fifteenth-century Italian female scholars, Margaret King has argued that a choice had to be made between scholarship and marriage, suggesting that 'The community of marriage, it seems, inhibited the learned woman from pursuing studious interest'.[69] This was not the case with the Cooke sisters: they continued their studies long after their marriage ceremonies. Likewise, it was marriage which ensured the sisters' roles in the political and religious networks of Elizabethan England and marriage that ensured the positive representations of the sisters' learning. Widowhood proved to be a more contested time for Anne and Elizabeth. It undoubtedly allowed them opportunities, for example in exercising independent ecclesiastical patronage; Elizabeth was particularly active as an intermediary in the political networks of the 1590s and Anne fashioned a role for herself as a biblically sanctioned godly widow. Yet it also brought increased vulnerability, as both sisters found their authority questioned as aged widows, increasingly bereft of political contacts. The sisters' lives reveal the shifting and unstable nature of sixteenth-century women's agency, as their influence was at all times embedded in and interacting with the relationships with the men in their lives.

This study also highlights the need for the sisters' activities to be incorporated into the existing political and religious historiographies. The precise nature of the piety and ecclesiastical patronage of a small number of Henrician courtly women has received close attention in research on the spread of evangelical religion, yet study of these issues for elite women in the Elizabethan period is less well served, notwithstanding important research by Susan Wabuda and Melissa Franklin Harkrider.[70] This book greatly expands the picture of late sixteenth-century female piety unbounded by the walls of the household. The evidence of the Cooke sisters' political activities also contributes to scholarship on later Tudor political culture, where attention has increasingly focused on the background of political actors in order to understand better their perception of and responses to the challenges facing the Elizabethan regime. Whilst significant recent research has emphasised the importance of gender to Elizabethan political culture, through exploring the responses of the Protestant male elite to a female monarch, there has been little consideration of the actual roles of noble and gentry women.[71] Throughout this study, the sisters' relationships with the powerful men in their lives receive attention, considering, for example, how Mildred's involvement in diplomatic circles mirrors the concerns of her privy councillor husband, William Cecil. Furthermore, this study builds on increasing interest in the educational background of political actors and their use of language; Stephen Alford, for example, has explored the importance of William Cecil's education in his political career.[72] This book highlights the need for that approach to be extended to women, by demonstrating the centrality of the Cookes' linguistic skills to their political agency. There are further implications for the existing understanding of later sixteenth-century politics. Concerns over the future of the Protestant nation for men within the ruling elite have been shown as central to Elizabethan political culture.[73] The analysis of Anne's translation of the *Apologia* and of Elizabeth's activities as a diplomatic wife in Paris in 1566 demonstrates the importance of these issues to this group of women. Mildred's own involvement in her husband's intelligence-gathering networks that stretched to Scotland and Ireland in the 1560s and 1570s reveals her concern with 'British' diplomacy and complements Stephen Alford's work on William Cecil's vision of England as the hub of a Protestant British Isles.[74] Through its study of the Cooke sisters, this book therefore highlights the need to incorporate the role of elite women into the discussion of Elizabethan political culture. Without understanding the opportunities and restrictions placed upon these women, we fail to understand fully the nature of early modern politics.

NOTES

1 British Library (BL), Royal MS 17 B.XVIII, fos 10v–11r. The translation is signed 'Mildred Cicill', so must have been written sometime after her marriage in 1545; *ibid.*, fo. 2v.

2 Marjorie McIntosh suggests that Cooke started serious study in the 1530s and may have pursued his education at much the same time as his children. See M.K. McIntosh, 'Sir Anthony Cooke: Tudor humanist, educator, and religious reformer', *Proceedings of the American Philosophical Society (PAPS)*, 119 (1975), 235, 237, 240.

3 *Ibid.*, 241.

4 The idea that Anne tutored Edward VI was apparently first recorded by William Rawley,

the chaplain of her son Francis, in 1657, yet I would suggest it is Rawley's phrasing which has led to this confusion and that, in fact, he was describing her father's activities. Rawley wrote of Bacon, 'His mother was Anne, one of the daughters of Sir Anthony Cook; unto whom the erudition of Edward the Sixth was committed'. See W. Rawley, 'Life of Bacon', in *The Works of Francis Bacon*, ed. J. Spedding, R.L. Ellis and D.D. Heath (14 vols, 1861–79), I, p. 3. For restatements of Anne's role in tutoring the king, see, for example, G. Ballard, *Memoirs of Several Ladies of Great Britain*, ed. R. Perry (Detroit, 1985) (Ballard), p. 195 and D. du Maurier, *Golden Lads: A Study of Anthony Bacon, Francis and their Friends* (1975), p. 15.

5   W. Cecil, *The Counsell of a Father to his Sonne, in ten severall Precepts* (1611), single-page sheet.

6   Inscription on Mildred's tomb, Chapel of St Nicholas, Westminster Abbey, London. Translation by Margaret Stewardson from an unpublished text held at Westminster Abbey Library.

7   For the Haddon courtship, see chapter 6.

8   For Anne's role in securing pardon for her husband and brother-in-law, see chapter 4.

9   J. Walsall, *A Sermon Preached at Pauls Crosse by John Walsal, one of the Preachers of Christ his Church in Canterburie* (1578), sig. A5v.

10 BL, Lansdowne MS 43, fo. 119r: 26/02/1585.

11 For their courtship, see T. Hoby, *The Travels and Life of Sir Thomas Hoby, Kt of Bisham Abbey*, ed. E. Powell (*Camden Miscellany* 10, Camden Society (CS), 3rd series, 4, 1902), pp. 126–7.

12 B. Castiglione, *The courtyer of Count Baldessar Castilio divided into foure bookes*, trans. T. Hoby (1561). For Elizabeth's translation of Ponet's *Diallacticon*, see chapter 2 below.

13 Both De Spes, the Spanish ambassador, and Fénélon, the French ambassador, reported such a scheme, in June and October 1569 respectively. See *Calendar of Letters and State Papers relating to English affairs preserved principally in the Archives of Simancas, 1558–1603*, ed. M.A.S. Hume (4 vols, 1892–99) (*CSP, Spain*), vol. *1568–1579*, p. 167; B. de Salignac Fénélon, *Correspondance diplomatique* (7 vols, Paris, 1838–40), II, p. 304.

14 For the inheritance battle, see chapter 2 below.

15 Hatfield House, Hertfordshire, Cecil Papers (CP) 152, fo. 8r: 27/03/1557. For Mary I's gift to the bride, see National Archives, London (NA), LC 5/31, fo. 107r. For Rowlett, see S.T. Bindoff, *The House of Commons, 1509–1558* (3 vols, 1982), III, pp. 223–4.

16 H. Machyn, *The Diary of Henry Machyn, Citizen and Merchant Taylor of London, from A.D. 1550 to A.D. 1563*, ed. J.G. Nichols (CS, old series, 42, 1848), pp. 169–70.

17 W. Murdin (ed.), *A collection of state papers ... from the year 1571–1596* (1759), p. 755.

18 It should also be noted that Killigrew had been a travelling companion of Thomas Hoby in Italy in 1549. See A. Miller, *Sir Henry Killigrew: Elizabethan Soldier and Diplomat* (Leicester, 1963), pp. 97, 100.

19 The so-called 'Anonymous Life' is printed in F. Peck, *Desiderata curiosa: or, a collection of divers scarce and curious pieces* (2 vols, 1732–35), I, p. 7. For more on the 'Anonymous Life' see S. Alford, *Burghley: William Cecil at the Court of Elizabeth I* (2008), pp. 336–40.

20 W. Camden, *The history of ... Princess Elizabeth* (1688), p. 218. Camden's work was actually commissioned by Mildred's husband, Burghley, as an official history of Elizabeth's

reign. For more on Camden's commission, see S. Alford, *Burghley*, pp. 345–7. David Lloyd's *Statesmen and Favourites of England*, first published in 1665, followed Camden's account in describing the sisters in relation to their father and their husbands. Lloyd also included some additional and often inaccurate details; for example, Lloyd wrongly suggested that Anthony Cooke educated his daughters for fear he would have no sons. See D. Lloyd, *State-worthies: or, the statesmen and favourites of England from the Reformation to the Revolution*, ed. C. Whitworth (2 vols, 1766), I, p. 251.

21 Rawley, 'Life of Bacon', p. 3.

22 T. Birch, *Memoirs of the reign of Queen Elizabeth from the year 1581 till her death* (2 vols, 1754), I, p. 11.

23 J. Spedding (ed.), *The Letters and the Life of Francis Bacon, including all his occasional works* (7 vols, 1861–74), I (Spedding), p. 116.

24 His evidence was the meditation Burghley wrote upon the death of his second wife, which Read felt read 'too much like an *oraison funèbre*, not quite enough like a *cri de coeur*', ignoring Burghley's personal testimony of his 'harty love' for his wife. C. Read, *Lord Burghley and Queen Elizabeth* (1960), p. 448. For a discussion of Burghley's 'harty love' for his wife, see chapter 6.

25 Read, *Lord Burghley*, p. 446.

26 I.D. MacFarlane, *Buchanan* (1981), p. 329.

27 See, for example, S. Alford, *The Early Elizabethan Polity: William Cecil and the British Succession Crisis, 1558–1569* (Cambridge, 1998); Alford, *Burghley*; R. Tittler, *Nicholas Bacon: The Making of a Tudor Statesman* (1976); L. Jardine and A. Stewart, *Hostage to Fortune: The Troubled Life of Francis Bacon, 1561–1626* (1998); P. Hammer, *The Polarisation of Elizabethan Politics: The Political Career of Robert Devereux, Second Earl of Essex, 1585–1597* (Cambridge, 1999).

28 N. Zemon Davis, '"Women's History" in transition: the European case', *Feminist Studies*, 3 (1976), 83.

29 J. Strype, *Annals of the Reformation and Establishment of Religion ... during Queen Elizabeth's happy Reign* (4 vols in 7, Oxford, 1824), III. ii, p. 125; Ballard, pp. 195, 200. This was still the dominant tone in early twentieth-century biographical sketches. See, for example, M.B. Whiting, 'Anne, Lady Bacon', *Contemporary Review*, 122 (1922), 497–508; M.B. Whiting, 'The learned and virtuous Lady Bacon', *Hibbert Journal*, 29 (1931), 270–83; M. St Clare Byrne, 'The mother of Francis Bacon', *Blackwood's Magazine*, 236 (1934), 758–71; M. St Clare Byrne, 'The first Lady Burghley', *The National Review*, 103 (1934), 356–63.

30 See, for example, M.E. Lamb, 'The Cooke sisters: attitudes toward learned women in the Renaissance', in M.P. Hannay (ed.), *Silent But for the Word* (Kent, Ohio, 1985), pp. 107–25; L. Schleiner, *Tudor and Stuart Women Writers* (Bloomington, Ind., 1994), pp. 30–51; A. Stewart, 'The voices of Anne Cooke, Lady Anne and Lady Bacon,', in D. Clarke and E. Clarke (eds), *This Double Voice: Gendered Writing in Early Modern England* (Basingstoke, 2000), pp. 88–102; L. Magnusson, 'Widowhood and linguistic capital: the rhetoric and reception of Anne Bacon's epistolary advice', *English Literary Renaissance*, 31 (2001), 3–33; P. Phillippy, *Women, Death and Literature in Post-Reformation England* (Cambridge, 2002), pp. 179–210; K. Mair, 'Anne, Lady Bacon: A Life in Letters' (PhD thesis, Queen Mary, University of London, 2009); E.Z. Kolkovich, 'Lady Russell, Elizabeth I and female political alliances through performance', *English Literary Renaissance*,

39 (2009), 290–314; L. Magnusson, 'Imagining a national church: election and educa-tion in the works of Anne Cooke Bacon', in J. Harris and E. Scott-Baumann (eds), *The Intellectual Culture of Puritan Women, 1558–1680* (Basingstoke, 2010), pp. 42–56. Just before this manuscript went to press, three new pieces were published on Elizabeth and Anne: P. Phillippy, 'Living stones: Lady Elizabeth Russell and the art of sacred conver-sation', in M. White (ed.), *English Women, Religion, and Textual Production, 1500–1625* (Aldershot, 2011), pp. 17–36; P. Demers, '"Neither bitterly nor brablingly": Lady Anne Cooke Bacon's translation of Bishop Jewel's *Apologia Ecclesiae Anglicanae*', in *ibid.*, pp. 205–18; C. Laoutaris, 'The radical pedagogies of Lady Elizabeth Russell', in K. Moncrief and K. MacPherson (eds), *Performing Pedagogy in Early Modern England: Gender, Instruc-tion, and Performance* (Aldershot, 2011), pp. 65–86.

31 P. Croft, 'Mildred, Lady Burghley: the matriarch', in P. Croft (ed.), *Patronage, Culture and Power: The Early Cecils* (2002), pp. 283–300; P. Croft, 'The new English church in one family: William, Mildred and Robert Cecil, 1547–1612', in S. Platten (ed.), *Anglicanism and the Western Christian Tradition* (Norwich, 2003), pp. 163–88; J. Stevenson, 'Mildred Cecil, Lady Burleigh: poetry, politics and protestantism', in V. Burke and J. Gibson (eds), *Early Modern Manuscript Writing: Selected Papers from the Trinity/Trent Colloquium* (Aldershot, 2004), pp. 51–73; C. Bowden, 'The library of Mildred Cooke Cecil, Lady Burghley', *The Library*, 7th series, 6 (2005), 3–29.

32 A doctoral thesis by Sheridan Harvey and an MPhil thesis by Susan King were both based on an extremely restrictive body of source material: S. Harvey, 'The Cooke Sisters: A Study of Tudor Gentlewomen' (PhD thesis, Indiana University, 1981); S. King, 'The Daughters of Sir Anthony Cooke (1505–1576) of Gidea Hall, Essex' (MPhil thesis, Birmingham University, 1998).

33 For a survey of the survival of other Tudor women's letters, see J. Daybell, *Women Letter-Writers in Tudor England* (Oxford, 2006), pp. 32–47.

34 For example, this study considers the letters of Anne Bacon in the Harleian manuscripts at the British Library, as well as those she sent to Theodore de Bèze, which have received no attention in previous work, focused primarily on correspondence held in Lambeth Palace Library. See, for example, Stewart, 'The voices of Anne Cooke'; Magnusson, 'Widowhood and linguistic capital'; Mair, 'Anne, Lady Bacon'; Magnusson, 'Imagining a national church'. Similarly, this book draws upon letters by Elizabeth Russell which were not included in Elizabeth Farber's 1979 doctoral edition of her correspondence, for example those held at the Bodleian Library, the Lincolnshire Archives, Mertoun House in Roxburghshire and the Surrey History Centre as well as at the Folger Shake-speare Library (Folger) in the United States. See E. Farber, 'The Letters of Lady Elizabeth Russell (1540–1609)' (PhD thesis, Columbia University, 1977).

35 See chapter 4.

36 BL, Lansdowne MS 104, fo. 156r: n.d.; fo. 158r: n.d.; NA, State Papers (SP) 10/15, fo. 178a: n.d.

37 Bodleian Library, Oxford (Bodl.), Carte MS LVI, fo. 475r: 26/10/1573. For the letter in printed form, see Ballard, pp. 190–1.

38 BL, Royal MS 17 B.XVIII.

39 Bodl., Carte MS LVIII, fo. 218r: 20/01/1568; fo. 664r: 29/08/1568.

40 NA, SP 12/155, fo. 178r: 18/11/1582.

41 E. Dering, *Certaine godly and comfortable Letters* (1614), sigs C3r–C7r.

42 See, for example, Harvey, 'The Cooke Sisters', pp. 63–102.

43 J. Pearson, 'Women reading, reading women', in H. Wilcox (ed.), *Women and Literature in Britain 1500–1700* (Cambridge, 1996), p. 81. See also, for example, A.T. Friedman, 'The influence of humanism on the education of girls and boys in Tudor England', *History of Education Quarterly*, 25 (1985), 57–70; H. Smith, 'Humanist education and the Renaissance concept of women', in H. Wilcox (ed.), *Women and Literature in Britain 1500–1700* (Cambridge, 1996), pp. 9–29; K. Vosevich, 'The education of a prince(ss): tutoring the Tudors', in M. Burke *et al.* (eds), *Women, Writing, and the Reproduction of Culture in Tudor and Stuart Britain* (New York, 2000), pp. 61–76.

44 K. Sharpe, *Reading Revolutions: The Politics of Reading in Early Modern England* (2000), p. 297.

45 Pearson, 'Women reading, reading women', p. 82.

46 David McKitterick made a similar complaint in 2000, which is unfortunately still true of research today. See D. McKitterick, 'Women and their books in seventeenth-century England: the case of Elizabeth Puckering', *The Library*, 7th series, 1 (2000), 363–4.

47 H. Brayman Hackel, 'The Countess of Bridgewater's London library', in J. Andersen and E. Sauer (eds), *Books and Readers in Early Modern England* (Philadelphia, 2002), pp. 138–59; H. Brayman Hackel, *Reading Material in Early Modern England: Print, Gender and Literacy* (Cambridge, 2005), pp. 222–55; McKitterick, 'Women and their books', 359–80; P. Morgan, 'Frances Wolfreston and "Hor Bouks": a seventeenth-century woman book-collector', *The Library*, 6th series, 11 (1989), 197–219.

48 R. Warnicke, 'Women and humanism in England', in A. Rabil (ed.), *Renaissance Humanism: Foundations, Forms and Legacy* (3 vols, Philadelphia, 1988), II, p. 47; Smith, 'Humanist education', pp. 9–29.

49 M. Peltonen, *Classical Humanism and Republicanism in English Political Thought, 1570–1640* (Cambridge, 2004). See also Alford, *Early Elizabethan Polity*, pp. 14–24.

50 See, for example, Vosevich, 'The education of a prince(ss)', pp. 70–72; L. Shenk, 'Turning learned authority into royal supremacy: Elizabeth I's learned persona and her university orations', in C. Levin, J. Carney and D. Barrett-Graves (eds), *Elizabeth I: Always Her Own Free Woman* (Burlington, 2003), pp. 78–96; L. Shenk, *Learned Queen: The Image of Elizabeth I in Politics and Poetry* (Basingstoke, 2010); N. Mears, *Queenship and Political Discourse in the Elizabethan Realms* (Cambridge, 2005), pp. 74–78. Jane Stevenson has instead highlighted the teaching and medical roles a humanist education allowed some early modern European women to adopt, primarily from the seventeenth century onwards. See J. Stevenson, *Women Latin Poets: Language, Gender and Authority, from Antiquity to the Eighteenth-Century* (Oxford, 2005), pp. 423–4.

51 L. Jardine and A. Grafton, *From Humanism to the Humanities: Education and the Liberal Arts in Fifteenth and Sixteenth-Century Europe* (1986), p. 56.

52 M. Dowling, *Humanism in the Age of Henry VIII* (1986), p. 242.

53 Lamb, 'The Cooke sisters', p. 124.

54 See, for example, *ibid.*, p. 116; P. Parker, *Shakespeare from the Margins: Language, Culture, Context* (1996), pp. 139–40.

55 See Lamb, 'The Cooke sisters', p. 124; A. Stewart, 'The voices of Anne Cooke', p. 89.

56 T. Elston, 'Transformation or continuity? Sixteenth-century education and the legacy of Catherine of Aragon, Mary I, and Juan Luis Vives', in C. Levin, J. Carney and D. Barrett-

Graves (eds), *High and Mighty Queens of Early Modern England: Realities and Representations* (Basingstoke, 2003), p. 21.

57 L. Jardine and A. Grafton, '"Studied for action": how Gabriel Harvey read his Livy', *Past and Present*, 129 (1990), 30–78; W. Sherman, *John Dee: The Politics of Reading and Writing in the English Renaissance* (Amherst, 1995).

58 See, for example, J. Daybell, 'Scripting a female voice: women's epistolary rhetoric in sixteenth-century letters of petition', *Women's Writing*, 13 (2006), 3–20; J. Daybell, *Women Letter-Writers in Tudor England* (Oxford, 2006), pp. 250–64. See also L. Magnusson, 'A rhetoric of requests: genre and linguistic scripts in Elizabethan women's suitors letters', in J. Daybell (ed.), *Women and Politics in Early Modern England, 1450–1700* (Aldershot: 2004), pp. 51–66.

59 B. Harris, 'Women and politics in early Tudor England', *The Historical Journal (HJ)*, 33 (1990), 259–81; B. Harris, *English Aristocratic Women, 1450–1550* (Oxford, 2002).

60 J. Daybell, 'Suche news as on Quenes hye wayes we have mett': The news and intelligence networks of Elizabeth Talbot, Countess of Shrewsbury (c. 1527–1608)', in J. Daybell (ed.), *Women and Politics in Early Modern England, 1450–1700* (Aldershot, 2004), pp. 114–31; Daybell, *Women Letter-Writers*, pp. 152–7; J. Daybell, 'Women, news and intelligence networks in Elizabethan England', in R.J. Adams and R. Cox (eds), *Diplomacy and Early Modern Culture* (Basingstoke, 2010), pp. 101–19; Mears, *Queenship and Political Discourse*, pp. 54–55, 110–13.

61 B. Harris, 'The view from my lady's chamber: new perspectives on the early Tudor monarchy', *Huntington Library Quarterly*, 60 (1997), 243.

62 The literature is extensive, but for court politics see, for example, Harris, 'The view from my lady's chamber'; Harris, *English Aristocratic Women*; H. Payne, 'Aristocratic women, power, patronage and family networks at the Jacobean court, 1603–1625', in J. Daybell (ed.), *Women and Politics in Early Modern England, 1450–1650* (Aldershot, 2004), pp. 164–80; H. Payne, 'The Cecil women at court', in P. Croft (ed.), *Patronage, Culture and Power: The Early Cecils, 1558–1612* (2002), pp. 265–82; N. Mears, 'Politics in the Elizabethan Privy Chamber: Lady Mary Sidney and Kat Ashley', in J. Daybell (ed.), *Women and Politics in Early Modern England, 1450–1700* (Aldershot, 2004), pp. 67–82. For women's religious agency at court see, for example, S. James, *Kateryn Parr: The Making of a Queen* (Aldershot, 1999); D. Durant, *Bess of Hardwick: Portrait of an Elizabethan Dynast* (1999); E. Ives, *The Life and Death of Anne Boleyn* (Oxford, 2004).

63 M. Franklin Harkrider, *Women, Reform and Community in Early Modern England: Katherine Willoughby, Duchess of Suffolk and Lincolnshire's Godly Aristocracy, 1519–1580* (Woodbridge, 2008).

64 W.J. Sheils, *The Puritans in the Diocese of Peterborough, 1558–1610* (Northampton Record Society, 30; Northampton, 1979), pp. 102–18; P. Collinson, 'Magistracy and ministry: a Suffolk miniature', in P. Collinson, *Godly People* (1983), pp. 445–66; D. Willen, 'Godly women in early modern England: Puritanism and gender', *Journal of Ecclesiastical History (JEH)*, 43 (1992), 561–80.

65 J.R. Brink, 'Introduction', in J.R. Brink (ed.), *Female Scholars: A Tradition of Learned Women before 1800* (Montreal, 1980), p. 5. See also P. Labalme, 'Introduction', in P. Labalme (ed.), *Beyond Their Sex: Learned Women of the European Past* (New York, 1980), pp. 4–6.

66 Lamb, 'The Cooke sisters', pp. 114–15. See also L.A. Pollock, '"Teach her to live under

obedience": the making of women in the upper ranks of early modern England', *Continuity and Change*, 4 (1989), 241.

67 L. Jardine '"O Decus Italiae Virgo", or the myth of the learned lady in the Renaissance', *HJ*, 28 (1985), 815–6; M. King, 'Book-lined cells: women and humanism in the early Italian Renaissance', in P. Labalme (ed.), *Beyond Their Sex: Learned Women of the European Past* (New York, 1980), pp. 66–90; Stevenson, *Women Latin Poets*, p. 412–13.

68 For a discussion of various social hierachies in early modern Britain, see M. Braddick and J. Walter, 'Grids of power: order, hierarchy and subordination in early modern society', in M. Braddick and J. Walter (eds), *Negotiating Power in Early Modern Society: Order, Hierarchy and Subordination in Britain and Ireland* (Cambridge, 2001), pp. 1–42. For other considerations of female negotiations of patriarchal restrictions, see, for example, M. Ezell, *The Patriarch's Wife: Literary Evidence and the History of the Family* (Chapel Hill, 1987); A. Wall, 'Elizabethan precept and feminine practice: the Thynne family of Longleat', *History*, 75 (1990), 23–38; B. Capp, 'Separate domains? Women and authority in early modern England', in P. Griffiths, A. Fox and S. Hindle (eds), *The Experience of Authority in Early Modern England* (1996), pp. 117–45; L.A. Pollock, 'Rethinking patriarchy and the family in seventeenth-century England', *Journal of Family History*, 23 (1998), 3–27.

69 King, 'Book-lined cells', p. 69.

70 S. Wabuda, 'Shunamites and nurses of the English Reformation: the activities of Mary Glover, niece of Hugh Latimer', in W.J. Sheils and D. Wood (eds), *Women in the Church* (Studies in Church History, 27; Oxford, 1990), 335–44; Harkrider, *Women, Reform and Community*. For women's patronage at the Henrician court, see, for example, Ives, *Life and Death of Anne Boleyn* and James, *Kateryn Parr*.

71 See, in particular, A.N. McLaren, *Political Culture in the Reign of Elizabeth I: Queen and Commonwealth, 1558–1585* (Cambridge, 1999); Mears, *Queenship and Political Discourse*, pp. 73–103.

72 Alford, *Early Elizabethan Polity*.

73 See, for example, P. Collinson, 'The monarchical republic of Elizabeth I', *Bulletin of the John Rylands Library*, 69 (1987), 394–424; P. Collinson, 'The Elizabethan exclusion crisis and the English polity', *Proceedings of the British Academy*, 84 (1995), 51–92; Alford, *Early Elizabethan Polity*.

74 Alford, *Early Elizabethan Polity*.

Chapter 1

'Nouzeled and trained in the studie of letters': reading and learning

In mid-sixteenth-century England, many figures celebrated the achievements of the nation's few female humanists. 'It is nowe a common thing to see young virgins so nouzeled and trained in the studie of letters, that they willingly set all other vayne pastimes at naught for learninge's sake,' wrote Nicholas Udall in 1548, praising those women 'not onelye geven to the studie of the humaine sciences and of straunge tongues, but also so thoroughlye experte in holy scriptures'.[1] John Coke continued in a similar vein in 1551, writing 'we have dyvers gentylwomen in Englande, which be not onely well estudied in holy Scrypture, but also in Greek and Latyn tonges as maystres More, mastryes Anne Coke, Maystres Clement, and others'.[2] The Cooke sisters were not only lauded alongside their learned female contemporaries, as in the above extract, but they also received their own praise. Walter Haddon described a visit he made to the Cooke household. 'While I stayed there,' he wrote, 'I seemed to be living among the Tusculans, except that the studies of women were flourishing in this Tuscany.'[3] The Cooke household was therefore acclaimed as a little academy, in which the female children were educated alongside their brothers. The sisters have been similarly celebrated in scholarly work, up to the present day; the eighteenth-century historian George Ballard argued that the education of the sisters made them 'the wonders of the age'.[4] Yet both contemporary panegyric and later research are vague as to the precise nature of the education of these women. This chapter will reconstruct the sisters' education through the texts they owned and read, both during their youth and in their later lives.

Early modern humanist learning was bibliocentric; both model curricula compiled by pedagogues and the statutes of educational institutions in this period conceived the education they provided in terms of set texts to be read by the student.[5] Beyond prescriptive discussions of texts, knowledge of the books read by Cooke sisters' learned female contemporaries is, however, vague. Roger Ascham outlined Princess Elizabeth's reading of religious and classical texts, as discussed later in this chapter, and there is evidence that Lady Jane Grey read Cicero, Demosthenes, Livy and Plato as well as Bullinger's *De matrimonii*, but beyond these texts references to her reading are more imprecise.[6] The inventory made on the death of her sister, Lady Mary Keys, reveals ownership of books in French and Italian, but the main body of her library was composed of religious works.[7] The reconstruction of the Cooke sisters' libraries therefore provides much-needed detailed evidence regarding the reading of sixteenth-century women. Whilst Mildred Cooke Cecil's extant volumes have previously been collated, by looking at all the sisters we can say far more about their reading practices, revealing the continuities between their interests and developing a wider picture of their reading, particularly through analysis of their extant marginalia.[8] Moreover, this chapter contextualises the evidence of the sisters' reading; it evaluates it against the prescription for both their male and female contemporaries, as well as discussing the role of the sisters themselves in directing their reading. Finally, in reconstructing the reading of the sisters, the chapter relies upon a distinctive methodology. It draws not only upon the evidence of book inventories and ownership marks, but upon a diverse range of sources, including letters and portraits, which in turn allow the breadth and depth of the sisters' studies as female humanists to be appreciated fully for the first time.

'NOW WHAT BOOKS OUGHT TO BE READ': THE PRESCRIPTION OF TEXTS

From the late medieval period through to the sixteenth century, reading was often perceived as a positive activity for gentlewomen within a household context, through which their thoughts could be kept occupied.[9] 'Not that I disapprove the ideas of those who plan to protect their daughters' honour by teaching them the domestic arts,' wrote Erasmus in 1521, 'but nothing so occupies a girl's whole heart as the love of reading.'[10]

Reading material was carefully prescribed and delineated through pedagogical treatises and conduct books, in a process which has been characterised as the 'policing' of women's reading.[11] The most significant works of prescription for early sixteenth-century women are those of Juan Luis Vives. In his *De institutione foeminae christianae* (1523), he followed St Jerome in prescribing that nothing should be read by women except that which encourages the fear of God: 'Now what books ought to be read, everybody knoweth, as the Gospels and the Acts and the Epistles of the Apostles and the Old Testament, St. Jerome, St. Cyprian, Augustine, Ambrose, Hilary, Gregory, Plato, Cicero, Seneca and such others.'[12]

In his *De officio mariti* (1529), Vives argued that certain classical authors were an important supplement to the religious texts, for 'A woman hath very great need of this moral part of philosophy'.[13] Aristotle and Xenophon were recommended, as they wrote on 'how men should rule and govern their house and family, and of the education and bringing up of children'.[14] Plutarch was also set, alongside more recent works, such as the *De ingenius moribus* by Paolo Vergerio (c.1392) and Francesco Filelfo's *De educatione liberorum* (1493). These works would teach the precepts of daily life and simple medical treatment. Such a list of authors was thought to be sufficient for most women 'to live commodiously and religiously'.[15] However, Vives recognised that some women might want to read poetry, in which case he suggested the Christian poets, either in Latin or in translation. He also praised the Greek poets, such as Callimachus and Sappho, asking 'What can be told more pleasant, more sweet, more quick, more profitable, with all manner of learning than these poets?'[16]

For the Princess Mary, destined to be a governor, Vives went beyond these texts. In *De ratione studii puerilis* (1523), Vives argued that Mary would need to learn grammar, aided by Antonio Mancinelli's *Thesaurus*, Thomas Linacre's *Grammatical Compendium*, Melanchthon's *De constructione* and Erasmus's *Colloquies*.[17] The latter was also helpful for providing vocabulary.[18] A Latin and an English dictionary should accompany all her reading.[19] In order to be able to converse in Latin, the distichs of Dionysius Cato, the sentences of Publilius Syrus and of the Seven Wise Men, early Greek philosophers, should be learnt from Erasmus's *Colloquies*.[20] Vives also stipulated authors whose works 'inculcate not only knowledge, but living well'. Many of these authors are the same as those prescribed in Vives's other works, yet for the Princess he included some dialogues by Plato, 'especially those which concern the government of the State'. Erasmus's other works were also recommended, in the form of his *Institutio principis christiani*, the *Enchiridion* and his biblical *Paraphrases*. Thomas More's *Utopia* was also a set text. History was prescribed as a subject for the Princess, in contrast to Vives's prescriptions for other women: 'With no great trouble she can learn history from Justinus, Florus and Valerius Maximus'. Alongside those Christian authors recommended for women in *De institutione*, Vives also suggested that the Princess should read the 'heathen' poets, particularly Lucan, Seneca and some parts of Horace.[21]

The breadth of Vives's list of acceptable reading for women was in some ways revolutionary; even for non-royal women, he went beyond religious works to include classical verse and works of moral philosophy. Yet for female readers other than the Princess Mary, he provided some limits. Firstly, he laid out a schedule for women's reading. A woman might read continually on holy days, but both then and especially on working days, she should read only after her household responsibilities had been discharged.[22] Secondly, even for women following his prescriptions, Vives offered a warning: women might need to ask the guidance of men in understanding the texts he had recommended, for otherwise women would misrepresent the 'profit' of their reading.[23] He was clear on what texts should not be read by non-royal women: 'as for the knowledge of grammar, logic, histories, the rule of governance of the commonwealth, and the art mathematical, they shall leave it unto men'. Eloquence was also noted as 'not convenient nor fit' for such women.[24] A particular area of exclusion was tales of romance. He argued that his native stories such as Amadis of Gaul, Tristan and Isolde and the Celestina should be prohibited, as well as romances from other countries. Unsuitable translations, such as Boccaccio's *Decameron*, should also be excluded, 'which books but idle men wrote unlearned, and set all upon filth and viciousness, in whom I wonder what should delight men but that vice pleaseth them so much'.[25] Particular disapproval was reserved for Ovid: 'Plato casteth out of the commonwealth of wise men which he made, Homer and Hesiod the poets, and yet have they none ill thing in comparision with Ovid's books of Love ... Therefore a woman should beware of these books, like as of serpents or snakes.' Such texts would lead a woman into sin like Eve. If a woman desired to read such romantic material, or indeed read approved texts 'with an ill will', she should be kept from any reading at all by her father and her friends, 'so by disuse, forget learning, if it can be done. For it is better to lack a good thing than to use it ill'.[26]

DIRECT PRESCRIPTION OF TEXTS FOR THE COOKE SISTERS

The sisters had more immediate sources of recommendations for their reading, at least during the early years of their education. Like other young early modern elite women, the Cooke sisters' education took place within a household setting.[27] Burghley stated after his wife's death that Anthony Cooke was the only tutor of his daughters. He referred to Mildred's 'singular knowledge of the Greek and Latin tongues, which knowledge she received solely at the hands of her father who instructed her'.[28] Anthony Cooke never attended university and was largely self-taught; Marjorie McIntosh suggests that Cooke started serious study in the 1530s and may have pursued his education at much the same time as his children.[29]

Cooke had his sons and daughters educated together, reading the same texts. In a copy in the original Greek of Moschopulus's *De ratione examinandae orationis libellus* (Paris, 1545), Anne wrote the following inscription: 'My father delyvered this booke to me and my brother Anthony, who was myne elder brother and scoolefellow with me, to follow for wrytyng of Greke.'[30] The inspiration for Anthony Cooke's sponsorship of female education is unknown. McIntosh suggests that it may have been as simple as his daughters showing more intellectual promise than his sons.[31] Cooke would also have been aware of the model in the More household. By Mary's reign, he was in contact with European humanists who favoured the education of women; however, by then the childhood education of his daughters was largely completed. Whilst in exile during the reign of Mary, he became close to the Strasbourg humanist, Johann Sturm, who also strongly supported women's education.[32] Coelius Secundus Curio dedicated his edition of John Cheke's work on Greek pronunciation to Cooke in 1555. Curio was another well-known exponent of female education, tutoring his own daughters; three years later he would edit the works of Olympia Morata.[33]

Whether or not these figures discussed the ideal reading material for women with Cooke, it is clear he would have been a central figure in directing the sisters' reading during their youth. His influence over their early reading material can be shown through the contents of their adult libraries. Many of the sisters' volumes have connections to their father's own intellectual concerns. The sisters had a lifelong fascination with the early Church Fathers and Anthony Cooke would appear to be influential in their interest in these theologians. He translated St Cyprian's *De dominica oratione* from Latin into English and presented the translation to Henry VIII in 1541.[34] The translation of Cyprian demonstrates his reading of Chrysostom, for he compares the linguistic styles of the two writers in the dedication. He also translated St Gregory Nazianzen's *Theophania*, which he presented to Elizabeth I in 1560.[35] Caroline Bowden has shown both that Mildred owned a copy of the 1583 edition of Peter Martyr Vermigli's *Loci Communes* and that the author was an acquaintance of her father whilst Anthony Cooke was in exile in Strasbourg.[36] However, there is a closer connection between their father and this particular volume. Mildred had been presented with her copy of *Loci Communes* by the editor, Robert Masson, minster to the French Stranger Church in London.[37] Masson dedicated not only his 1576 edition of the work to her father, Anthony Cooke, four months before Cooke's death, but also posthumously dedicated the 1583 edition to him. The prefatory letter printed in both editions also mentions the virtue and wisdom of Cooke's four daughters and these connections were presumably the reason behind Masson's presentation of the volume to Mildred.[38]

Their mother, Anne Fitzwilliam Cooke, was also instrumental in directing her daughters' education. In dedicating her second set of translations of Ochino's sermons to her mother, Anne Cooke describes her mother's 'many, and moste Godly exhortacyons' which came as if from 'the minister of God'. Anne acknowledges her mother's 'chyfe delight, to rest in the destroynge of man hys glorye, and exaltynge wholy the glory of God', adding therefore,

> I have taken it in hande to dedicate unto youre Ladyship this smale number of Sermons (for the excelent fruit sake in them conteined) proceding from the happy spirit of the santified Barnardyne, which treat of the election and predestinacion of God, wyth the rest ... a perteyning to the same effect to the end it might appere, that your so many worthy sentences touching the same, have not utterly ben without some note in my weake memory.[39]

Her mother clearly had a role in the spiritual and moral upbringing of her daughters, directing them towards reading religious works. However, there was a limit to their mother's influence over their studies. In defending her decision to translate the sermons, Anne references her mother's previous dislike of her Italian studies, which was clearly disregarded by Anne: 'it hath pleased you, often, to reprove my vaine studye in the Italyan tonge, accompting the sede thereof, to have bene sowen in barayne, unfruitful grounde (syns God thereby is no whytte magnifyed)'.[40]

While their father may have been the sisters' main tutor, other teachers were also employed in directing their education. Dr William Turner, dean of Wells, wrote to William Cecil in May 1551, referencing a candidate for the mastership of Wells Cathedral School, one John Ακανθίνος, the surname being the Greek for sharp or thorny.[41] This was the tutor's actual surname, Thorne, for one John Thorne was schoolmaster of Wells School from 1551 to 1553.[42] Turner described Thorne as 'sumtyme scoolmaster unto your bedfelow', suggesting he may have previously acted in the capacity of tutor to Mildred and her sisters. Certainly Thorne was an evangelical, for Turner wrote to Cecil that he supported Thorne's suit for the mastership, as the current incumbent was one of 'very corrupt and evel jugement', who had already been imprisoned in the Marshalsea for his beliefs.[43] It is unknown what reading Thorne would have prescribed for the sisters, but it is likely that it would have included religious works.

The sisters continued their studies after marriage and then, too, they had tutors who would have influenced their choice of reading. Mildred, for example, continued to perfect her Greek skills, as is shown by a letter written in 1564 from London by Karel Utenhove to Jean Morel, describing 'lecturing on Thucydides' to Mildred.[44] Utenhove's letter not only provides evidence of the reading material he worked on with Mildred, but also that she was attending the lecture with 'other English people who have a reputation for learning', presumably men, as they are not thought remarkable enough to be mentioned by name. After her marriage, Mildred also pursued her Greek studies with Giles Lawrence, the regius professor of Greek at Oxford University, at some time during the 1560s. Lawrence and Mildred read the works of St Basil and St Gregory Nazianzen together.[45] Lawrence was well pleased with his student, testifying that 'she equalled, if not overmatched, any of the same Profession in that Language'.[46]

The sisters' husbands would presumably have influenced their choice of reading. Facing arrest and perhaps execution in 1553, William Cecil wrote to Mildred with various requests if he should die, beginning by exhorting her to 'fear and love God', adding that she should 'spend hir tyme as muche as she may in studying and reading the Scripture'.[47] In his poem dating from the Marian period, Nicholas Bacon described reading classical literature with

Anne, namely 'your Tullye (Cicero) and my Senecke', which would suggest that he would have urged her to greater familiarity with the works of Seneca.[48]

MILDRED CECIL AND FEMALE INTEREST IN PRESCRIBED READING

Mildred herself was also personally interested in which authors constituted the ideal humanist curriculum, as evidenced by her involvement in the publication of two letters by Roger Ascham and Johann Sturm. In April 1550, Ascham wrote to the Strasbourg humanist and rector of the city's Protestant Gymnasium, Johann Sturm. The latter had visited England in 1549, at the invitation of Martin Bucer, although he and Ascham never met in person. Sturm replied to Ascham's letter five months later; however, by then Ascham had left for Germany with Richard Morison, so did not receive the letter until later in the year. In February of the following year, Morison wrote to William Cecil and, after warning Mildred that any Greek letters she wrote to Ascham would be forwarded to Sturm, he added the following message: 'Mister Aschamm hath al ready donn her errand to hym, & I do belive, yow & she shal shortly see their Letters in printe.'[49] The two letters of Ascham and Sturm were published in Strasbourg in 1551, included in Conrad Heresbach's *De laudibus Graecarum literarum oratio* as *Epistolae Duae de Nobilitate Anglicana*. It had been assumed that Sturm had arranged the printing in his home city, largely without input from Ascham, however Morison's acknowledgement of Mildred's sponsorship of the work questions that interpretation.[50]

Mildred's interest in the publication of these letters is particularly significant because of their content. Ascham's initial letter was written in praise of humanist learning. Whilst one motivation for the letter was to inspire Sturm to further publications, the letter is also notable for articulating Ascham's pedagogical beliefs. In his letter, he argues that he places the reading of the Scriptures above all else: 'I have resolved to build the tabernacle of my life and studies above all on the reading of the Scriptures, and I have in mind to join Plato, Aristotle, Demosthenes, and Marcus Cicero to the rest of my labors ... For these books contain the arts and sound learning, and they profit and enrich human life.'[51] He suggests that Aristotle surpasses all these authors in learning and judgement, particularly in his *Rhetoric*. However, he acknowledges that Aristotle's dialectic, his 'subtle system of logic', lacks sufficient examples to appeal to all readers, therefore he believes passages should be found to illustrate his rules from the Socratic dialogues of Plato and Xenophon. He supplements Aristotle's rhetorical principles with examples from Demosthenes, Cicero, Thucydides, Livy and other works of oratory and history. Ascham argues that readers should be instructed neither purely in 'bare principles', nor in just reading orators and historians, 'so that the course of study may seem neither unprofitably impeded by obscurity nor boldly led astray by deception'.[52] Ascham also places importance on the study of the Church Fathers, 'where they themselves do not wander from the Holy Scriptures'. He tells Sturm that the English favour the Latin writings of Augustine, adding 'I would not yield to you in your preference for the Greeks Basil and Chrysostom, except that I love you very much.'[53]

In his letter of response, Sturm also discusses the ideal reading for young scholars, asking 'is it permissible to read indiscriminately from any one period, or should there be some discrimination of times, periods, and abilities?'[54] He approves of the Greeks' choice to teach Homer to young students and the use of Virgil by Roman teachers. Yet he questions the benefit in conservative curricula of using Cato's distichs or the works of Aquinas, Jean Gerson or Merlin Cocca. Instead he argues that, from the first, children should read those authors who were both eloquent and learned; for this reason he ranks Chrysostom ahead of Augustine, for the latter, whilst more erudite, was less fluent and eloquent. Sturm's argument is that 'the order in which authors are read makes a very great difference'.[55]

A second theme in these two letters is the praise of female scholarship. Ascham lauds the learned women of England, stating 'We now have many honorable women who surpass the daughters of Thomas More in all kinds of learning. Amongst them the shining star, not so much for her brightness as for the splendor of her virtue and her learning, is my lady Elizabeth, sister of our King.'[56] In his response, Sturm too praises female education: 'What in our times can be more desirable than that the families of the rulers and the nobility bring forth talented people in both sexes who delight in learning, cultivate and pursue it, and achieve a full knowledge of literature, the arts, and the sciences?'[57] Sturm suggests that elegance of speech, based in humanist learning, should indeed become the marker of nobility, following the example set by Princess Elizabeth: 'It will have such effect that young girls, maidens and mature women will be deemed noble not only by virtue of antiquity of their families, but also by virtue of the elegance of their learning and speech.'[58]

Ascham's letter even includes a detailed description of Princess Elizabeth's reading and curriculum:

> She has read almost all of Cicero with me and most of Titus Livy. From these two authors alone she has drawn her knowledge of Latin. She has always begun the day with the New Testament in Greek, and then read selected orations of Isocrates and the tragedies of Sophocles. For I thought that from these she would derive linguistic purity and intellectual acuity so that for the rest of her noble life she would be well-prepared for every blow of fortune. For religious instruction she added Cyprian and the Commonplaces of Melanchthon to the foundations of the Scriptures, as well as others of a similar nature, from whom she can drink in purity of doctrine along with elegance of speech.[59]

25

Mildred's interest in the publication of these letters reveals that she wanted the two scholars' advocacy of female scholarship more widely disseminated.[60] It also confirms that she was concerned with the ideal humanist curriculum, and particularly in the type of reading that should be undertaken, by both male and female students. This questions the scholarly assumption that the prescription of women's reading in this period was necessarily limiting and subjugating.[61] Mildred's role in this publication reveals that whilst her father may have directed her childhood reading, she would have personally composed her adult library with great care.

RECONSTRUCTING THE SISTERS' LIBRARIES

There are greater methodological problems in reconstructing the libraries of early modern women than with those of their male counterparts. References to books in wills and probate inventories only survive for widowed or single women; the books of married women were often subsumed into their husbands' libraries, either during their own lifetime or upon their death.[62] In order to establish the reading practices of early modern women, scholars therefore need to be more creative and to use evidence from a diverse range of sources. Ownership marks are the most useful evidence of women's libraries, but portraits, commonplace books, letters and diaries all provide references to women's reading practices.[63] In order to reconstruct the reading of the Cooke sisters, it will be necessary to explore many varied types of evidence. Such a methodology is distinctive in studies on the libraries of individual early modern women. Whilst there have admittedly been calls for work drawing on varied source material, existing research has primarily focused on the unusual examples, either where inventories exist or where a woman's books still remain extant as a collection.[64]

Such a methodology is not without its drawbacks. Firstly, evidence of book ownership can often be frustratingly non-specific. Anthony Cooke left his daughters some of his books in his will in 1576: 'I will that of my bookes my daughter of Burghleigh shall have Twoe volumes in latyne and one in greeke, suche as she will choose of my gyfte. And after her choice, that my daughter Bacon shall have other volumes in latyne and one in greeke, such as she will chose.'[65] Cooke repeated this bequest of two Latin books and one Greek book for Elizabeth and Katherine. He then left the remainder of his library to his son Richard and his grandson Anthony. His remembrance of his daughters for his choicest classical volumes once again demonstrates Cooke's encouragement of his daughters' humanist learning. However, there is no way of establishing which books from their father's library the sisters each chose.[66] Another similarly frustrating piece of evidence concerns Elizabeth sending a 'litle booke' to Mary Talbot, the countess of Shrewsbury, from which she could find out 'what my religion is, and the grownds therof'. It is, however, possible to speculate as to the nature of the volume. Mary, who had turned to Catholicism, was advised to 'Rede it', for in her letter Elizabeth urges she should not be 'like the Deafe Adder that stoppeth her eares and refuseth the voyce of the Charmer'. The reference to the deaf adder comes from Psalm LVIII.4–5, so while it cannot be conclusively proved, it seems likely that the gift was of Scripture itself; such a conclusion is reinforced by Elizabeth's own testimony regarding the volume, for she urges Mary 'to here seke and follow his woord and will, in all obedience according to his woorde, and not after men's traditions and fansyes'.[67]

A major source for this reconstruction will be references to their reading, either explicit or unacknowledged, within the Cookes' own writings, particularly their letters. Using *sententiae* (quoted axioms) as evidence of reading can, however, be problematic. Printed collections of *sententiae* became increasingly popular during the sixteenth century. One of the Cooke sisters' contemporaries, Mary Fitzalan, later the duchess of Norfolk, presented her father, Henry Fitzalan, the earl of Arundel, with three manuscript volumes of *sententiae* before and after her marriage in 1554.[68] One of the manuscript volumes initially appears as evidence of a huge body of reading, including authors such as Theognis, Pythagorus and Euripides. The *sententiae* in the volume were, however, not collected by Mary herself; rather, they were drawn from Stobaeus's *Florilegium* and then translated from Greek into Latin.[69] It is probable that the Cookes were aware of such volumes. Mildred, for example, owned the 1532 edition of Callimachus's *Hymns*, which also contained the *Gnomologia*, a collection of moral extracts from Greek authors, many of which were later incorporated into Stobaeus's *Florilegium*.[70] Anne certainly knew of the collection of *sententiae* by Publilius Syrus, for she cited one in a letter to her son Anthony.[71] Elizabeth also used a motto from Alciato's *Emblemata* in a letter of her own.[72] However, when the Cookes used *sententiae* in their letters and other writings, they did so usually with an awareness of context within the original source, confirming their familiarity with the text itself. In addition, they did not always slavishly follow the exact wording of the original author, suggesting they were often recalling the *sententia* from their memory of the original text.[73] In those cases where it is unclear as to whether the *sententia* is drawn merely from popular usage, rather than personal reading, then I have not discussed the text as part of the sisters' libraries. Elizabeth, for example, used the phrase 'mens sana in corpore sano' (a healthy mind in a healthy body) in one of her letters, but it cannot be ascertained whether she knew the quotation from its original context in Juvenal's *Satire X*, or from its widespread application.[74]

Marks of ownership appear in many of the books owned by the Cooke sisters. The most basic are signature marks, although even these are not unproblematic evidence.[75] Mildred's name is appended to many of her texts still at Hatfield House, although, now that I have established the authenticity of her hand, it is clear that Mildred herself did not always write her name in the front of her own books. The Latin inscription 'Mildreda Burghleya' on the title-page of Roger Ascham's *Apologia*, for example, is actually written in her husband's hand, rather than her own.[76] This would in part explain the difference in spelling between so many of the ownership marks appended to her volumes. Even though Mildred did not personally autograph all her own books, it does not follow that they were not important volumes for her; the texts were closely associated with Mildred and thus were marked as distinct from or within her husband's library. Comparison of the sisters' extant signature marks thus sheds light on their marital relationships. The ownership marks in Anne's books reveal that she had a greater desire to distinguish her personal volumes from those of her husband, as compared to her sister Mildred. Four of Anne's texts bear her autograph and the date '1558', however they also all bear earlier ownership markings, either her name before marriage, or an earlier date.[77] It would appear that Anne purposely marked her personal books as her property in 1558 in order to distinguish them from her husband's library. While there is no evidence that either sister stored her volumes in a separate book closet, for Anne, it seems that it was more important to prevent her books from being subsumed into the library of Nicholas Bacon.[78]

Similarly problematic to the study of their reading is the fact that the sisters would have had access to their husbands' libraries and writings, suggesting a hinterland of texts beyond their personal libraries. William Cecil was a voracious purchaser of books; for example, between 1553 and 1555 he added eighty-six volumes to his library.[79] Nicholas Bacon and Thomas Hoby were similarly learned. Thomas Hoby, for example, published his manuscript translation of Castiglione's *The Courtyer* after his marriage to Elizabeth, spending thirteen weeks in London arranging the printing, so it is likely that Elizabeth would have read this text in either manuscript or published form.[80]

Difficult questions also arise regarding book dedications. Mildred, Anne and Elizabeth all received many dedications and it is likely that they would have been presented with a copy of at least some, if not all, of these works. The question is whether they would have read these works or, at the very least, been pleased to incorporate them into their libraries. Geoffrey Fenton, who had served with Thomas Hoby in Paris in 1566, dedicated his *Actes of Conference in Religion* (1571) and *Monophylo* (1572) to Elizabeth, and in these cases it is likely she would have been happy to receive copies of the works.[81] Thomas Drant's *A Medicinable Morall* (1566), consisting of 'two bookes of Horace his satyres' and the 'wailyngs of the prophet Hieremiah' translated into English, was dedicated to both Anne and Mildred.[82] However, Drant's text is not a straightforward translation. He replaced Horace's fifth satire of the first book, the 'Iter Brundisium', with his own original poem, consisting of a dialogue between two papists,

Pertinax and Commodus. The dialogue must be read in the context of the Vestiarian Controversy, for Drant argued that non-conformists were akin to papists in trying to destroy the cohesion of the Church of England.[83] Would Mildred and Anne have been pleased to be associated with this text and, if they were presented with a copy, would they have considered it part of their library? Such methodological difficulties mean that works dedicated to the sisters are not discussed here as part of their reading material, unless there is other evidence suggesting their personal appreciation of the works.

Ultimately, it is difficult to assign with certainty close readership of a particular volume without marginalia in the reader's hand. Heidi Brayman Hackel has suggested that early modern women left very little by way of annotation or marks of readership in their volumes, due to the practicalities of female reading and due to the patriarchal expectation of female silence in public spaces; she argues that this would have included the margins of their books, as texts would have circulated around households.[84] There are exceptions, however. Elizabeth Cooke Hoby Russell's daughter-in-law Lady Margaret Hoby annotated her religious reading.[85] Lady Anne Clifford's copy of *A Mirror for Magistrates* contains notes written in her hand, which form a diary of Clifford's reading of the volume.[86] Marginalia in books owned by the Cooke sisters are harder to establish. As I have been able to determine Mildred's hand for the first time, certain annotations, for example in her copy of Erasmus's *De conscribendis epistolis* or in her copy of Callimachus, now at Westminster School, are revealed as not her own.[87] However, there appears to be evidence of marginalia left in three books belonging to Mildred, Anne and Elizabeth and, in those instances, it is possible to establish both their understanding of the texts and their intellectual engagement with other readers in their households through the margins of their books.[88]

THE COOKE SISTERS' LIBRARIES: RELIGIOUS TEXTS

Scripture was at the centre of the sisters' libraries; Anne testified that it was the 'infallible towchstone' of all believers and Elizabeth urged Mary Talbot, as has been discussed, that all men must 'seke and follow his woord'.[89] Portraits of both Anne and Elizabeth reveal them holding small pocketbooks, which may have been Bibles or prayer books.[90] The precise version of the Bible owned by a particular reader is often difficult to specify; however, it is known that Mildred owned the third edition of Robert Estienne's Greek New Testament (1550).[91] She also possessed a copy of Johannes Herwagen's 1545 fourth edition of the Greek Bible, with a preface by Melanchthon, which she was given by the diplomat Sir Thomas Smith and later presented to Lancelot Andrewes.[92] Pauline Croft has suggested that Mildred was involved in the production of the 1572 revision of the Bishops' Bible, which presumably would have meant she had access to a copy of the 1568 version, as well as earlier biblical translations into English, including Tyndale and Coverdale.[93] Mildred also owned Christopher Plantin's rare eight-volume polyglot Bible, which she presented to St John's College, Cambridge, in 1580 and which contained parallel texts in Hebrew, Greek, Latin, Syriac and Chaldean.[94] Although Mildred owned the text for four years before presenting it to St John's College, Caroline Bowden has questioned whether she ever read the book herself.[95] Certainly she would have been able to use the Greek and Latin sections of the text, and very probably the Hebrew section as well.[96] Furthermore, William and Mildred must have had enough familiarity with the text to be pleased with the quality of this edition by Plantin; Burghley bought Plantin's 1580 edition of the Hebrew Old Testament.[97] Like her sister, Anne similarly owned the third edition of Robert Estienne's Greek New Testament (1550), which she recorded in Greek as being a gift from her brother-in-law, William Cecil, in 1552.[98] She also owned the Geneva Bible, as she followed its division into chapter and verse in a letter to the earl of Essex.[99] Elizabeth's letters reveal that she had a Latin Bible, as her scriptural citations are in that language.[100] Although she incorporated much scriptural translation into her translation of Ponet's *Diallacticon*, she provided her own rendering of the passages, rather than following any existing version of the Bible in the vernacular.[101]

Anne also owned a copy of Erasmus's *Paraphrase of the Gospel of St John*. She acquired the text before her marriage, as it is marked firstly in Anne's own hand with the name 'Anne Cooke', without a date, and then subsequently with 'ABacon, 1558'.[102] The inclusion of Erasmus's *Paraphrase* in the sisters' religious reading is not surprising. Vives had suggested it as a suitable text for Princess Mary to read and there was much support at court for an English translation of the work, even before Henry VIII's death. Anne's ownership of the text may also suggest her awareness of female literary and religious activities at court. Katherine Parr was a consistent supporter of the translation project, even requesting her step-daughter Mary to translate the *Paraphrase of the Gospel of St John*.[103] Moreover, whilst the first volume of the translated New Testament *Paraphrases* was published under the patronage of Katherine Parr, the second volume was sponsored by Anne Stanhope Seymour, the duchess of Somerset and patron of Mildred Cecil.[104]

The activities of this courtly circle seem also to lie behind Mildred's choice of prayer book. She owned the *Psalmi seu Precationes* (Psalms and Prayers) of John Fisher, bishop of Rochester.[105] Fisher was executed for his allegiance to the Roman Catholic faith in 1535, and so Mildred's use of his work for her daily devotions has been seen as evidence for the continued use of Catholic books in the later sixteenth century.[106] However, the initial publication of Fisher's work in April 1544 was overseen by Queen Katherine Parr, as her first literary patronage project.[107] She then went on to provide the first English translation of the work, which ran to eighteen editions between 1544 and 1608. Parr even distributed richly bound copies of her work to various members of her circle.[108] It would appear that Mildred's personal copy of the Latin text is not the first printing, sponsored by Katherine Parr.[109] However, given both her husband's closeness to Parr and the popularity of her English version of the work throughout the sixteenth century, it is likely that she was aware of Parr's patronage of the work and was possibly introduced to it through her means. Certainly, Parr's involvement with the work reveals that, although the text was conceived by a Catholic author, its contents, comprising prayers for godly wisdom, for the protection of enemies and for assurance of confidence in God, were not seen as unsuitable for reformed believers.[110] Another text belonging to Mildred formed the basis of Parr's 1545 *Prayers or Meditations*, namely Thomas à Kempis's *De imitatione Christi*. Mildred, however, owned the 1563 version of Kempis's work, published in Basel and edited by Sebastian Castellio from impure, ecclesiastical Latin into classical.[111]

Anne owned at least one book of psalms. She sent a 'litle psalme Boke in meeter' to her son Anthony in March 1597, which, as it is specified as a little volume, may have been one of the smaller versions of Sternhold and Hopkins.[112] Anne would have owned at least one other version of the Psalms and a prayer book, for she organised Bible readings, followed by prayers and the psalms, both morning and evening at Gorhambury during her widowhood.[113] She also owned at least one copy of Theodore de Bèze's meditations on the Penitential Psalms. Bèze had dedicated the French edition of his meditations to Anne in 1581 and the English translation of the following year bore the same dedication.[114] Whether she owned a copy of those editions is unknown; however, she was presented with a copy of the 1593 edition.[115] Mildred also owned a verse paraphrase of the psalms by Apollinaris, the fourth-century bishop of Laodicea, in Homeric hexameters.[116] Mildred's interest in Apollinaris's paraphrase of the psalms may have been inspired by his correspondence with St Basil, one of the Church Fathers, who was an important author for Mildred.

Burghley testified upon his wife's death to her long interest in the Greek Church Fathers: 'She was conversant with sacred literature, and the writings of holy men, especially those Greeks such as Basil the Great, Chrysostom, and Gregory Nazianzus, and others of their ilk.'[117] St Basil was clearly a favourite author for both Mildred and Anne. Anne owned a copy of St Basil's *Opera Graeca* (Basel, 1551) and she wrote on the first page, in Greek, that the book was a gift from her husband, Nicholas, in 1553.[118] Mildred owned Basil's *Orationes de moribus XXIIII* in Greek, which are a cento of extracts from Basil's writings made in the latter half of the tenth century by Simeon Metaphrastes, as well as a copy of the works of St Basil's brother, Gregory of Nyssa, which developed his elder sibling's theology.[119] She also owned a Greek volume of the letters of St Basil and St Gregory Nazianzen, entitled *Basilii Magni et Gregorii Nazanzeni*,

Epistolae Graecae. The text was not Mildred's sole property, for it is bound with the joint binding of 'William Myldred Cecyll' in gold; however, the inscription on the title-page, 'Mildredae Ceciliae', is in Mildred's own hand, indicating its greater significance to her.[120] Mildred must also have either owned or had access to a volume containing Basil's sermons, as she translated his sermon on Deuteronomy xv.9 around 1550.[121] The source for her lost translation, 'a peece of Chrisostome out of Greeke into English', may have been her copy in the original Greek of St John Chrysostom's *De orando Deum*, his writings on prayer; this 1551 edition of Chrysostom was published at the same time that Mildred produced her other two known translations.[122]

There is evidence of the sisters' understanding of their reading of St Basil. The volume of letters of St Basil and St Gregory Nazianzen owned by William and Mildred Cecil contains marginalia in Greek. Robin Alston has suggested that the notes might be those of William Cecil; however, comparison with his Greek hand in his private memorandum book reveals this not to be the case.[123] Instead, it appears that the marginalia are in Mildred's own hand. The most substantial annotation occurs alongside a letter of Basil to Gregory Nazianzen from the beginning of Basil's monastic retirement. As with Mildred's markings throughout the volume, the notes here are simply references of key words in the text, but they highlight Mildred's interest in certain sections of the letter. She is not concerned with the initial section of the letter, detailing Basil's sponsorship of the monastic life and the need to shun the cares of the world, such as those of marriage, for piety. Mildred's marking begins when Basil discusses the importance of study of the Scriptures, a section in which he argues that the lives of saintly men are offered as exempla for imitation. Where Basil notes that Joseph is a symbol of chastity, Mildred has marked in Greek the name 'Joseph' and 'chastity'; where Basil advances Job as an example of fortitude, she has marked those two words.[124] Mildred also noted the start of Basil's discussion of prayer, with 'prayer' added in Greek, for Basil goes on to argue that through prayer man makes himself into a temple to God.[125]

Anne's copy of St Basil's *Opera Graeca* also contains some marginalia in her Greek hand. The majority of the notation reflects Mildred's practice of recording key subjects and it also reveals the sisters' shared intellectual interests. A particular cluster of Anne's notes occur in the margins of St Basil's homily on Deuteronomy xv.9, the sermon Mildred translated for the duchess of Somerset. Anne made detailed notes in Greek by what she labelled Basil's discussion of 'craftsmen of all types in the church of God', before listing the different types of craftsmen in the margin and noting the section of the sermon on 'each of their habits'.[126] Mildred's treatment of this passage has been discussed in the introduction to this book, but Anne's marginalia reveal that she too was concerned with Basil's belief that every man had a craft they could use to further 'the chirche of the living god'.

There is further evidence of how the sisters' read St Basil. Mildred presented a volume of St Basil to Lady Jane Grey in 1552. In her accompanying Greek letter, apparently inscribed in the book itself, Mildred states that, whilst she has read many of the ancient authors and theologians, 'yet of no one has the perusal been more pleasing and agreeable to me than of Basil the Great, excelling all the Bishops of his time, both in the greatness of his birth, the extent of his erudition and the glowing zeal of his holiness'.[127] Mildred argues that reading Basil 'will raise the soul, grovelling below and set on earthly things, to God the Almighty and the remembrance of heavenly things'. Mildred thus suggests to Jane that, whilst this gift might seem 'small and trifling' if only the ink and paper were considered, 'if you consider the profit [it is] more valuable than gold and precious stones'. She admits to Jane that the writings of Basil have been important to her throughout her youth, so she hopes they will be equally 'agreeable and delightful' to her.

It is striking how many of the sisters' early Church texts are first editions, as are many other works in their libraries. Anne's copy of Basil's *Opera Graeca* (Basel, 1551) is the first edition. Mildred's edition of the letters of Basil and Gregory Nazianzen was also the first published version. Edited by Vincent Opsopoeus, its status was highlighted by the inclusion of 'nunquam antea edite' (never before put forth) within its title. Mildred also owned the 1544 edition of Eusebius's Greek work of preparation for the gospel, *Pamphili evangelicae praeparationis*.[128] This was again the first published edition, made from an unpublished manuscript in the French Royal Library at Fontainebleau. A manuscript in the Royal Library was again the source of Robert and Charles Estienne's 1551 first edition of the original Greek works of Justin Martyr, another volume in Mildred's library.[129] She also owned Grynaeus's *Orthodoxographa* (2nd edition, Basel, 1569).[130] The work was a collection of early Church writings, both New Testament Apocrypha and minor orthodox writers, some of whom were again being published for the first time.[131] Through the medium of print, Anne and Mildred had access to works formerly accessible only in manuscript form, which, as women outside of educational institutions, they would not previously have been able to read.

Through their reading of these first editions of early Church authors, the sisters would have been exposed to often controversial ideas. In his collection, *Orthodoxographa*, part of Mildred's library, Grynaeus's approach was to offer the writings of the early Church to all Christians throughout the world, viewing these authors as a conciliatory force within Christianity. Such a view accords with the efforts of early apologists of the Church of England, such as John Jewel, who turned to the early Church to defend Protestantism from accusations of dissension and who was translated into English in 1564 by Mildred's sister Anne. From her copy of Justin Martyr, Mildred could have learned of his view that pagan authors, such as Socrates and Heraclitus, could be Christian without justification by faith, which created a storm of contro-versy in Europe.[32] Clement of Alexandria, whilst rejecting polytheism, built on Justin's argument that the ideals of Greek literature and philosophy could be accommodated within the Christian church.[33] His work, *Paedagogus*, was closely read by Elizabeth Cooke Russell, as revealed by her inclusion of a segment in her translation of Ponet's *Diallacticon*, not in the Latin original.[34] *Paedagogus* was written for new converts to Christianity and counselled them as to how to live according to Christian ideals. Clement's *Paedagogus* also included prescriptions on the role of women, limiting them to the role of housekeeper and to the physical space of the house.[35] However, *Paedagogus* is part of trilogy of works by Clement; the third text, *Stromata*, discusses female philosophers, arguing that women should read classical philosophy in order for them to learn virtue and better withstand the tribulations of life.[36] It is attractive to speculate that Elizabeth read the other works in Clement's trilogy.

Mildred also owned a copy of Niels Hemmingsen's *Commentarius in epistolam Pauli ad Ephesios*, published in London in 1576. The question whether Mildred read the text cannot be conclusively answered; the extensive marginalia in the volume are not in her hand.[37] However, the inclusion of this volume within her library is suggestive. Hemmingsen's commentary on St Paul's letter to the Ephesians takes an anti-Calvinist stance, arguing that predestination is condi-tional on faith.[38] Caroline Bowden has suggested that Mildred's connection to the volume is through her daughter, Anne Cecil de Vere, to whom Abraham Fleming's English translation of Hemmingsen's commentary was dedicated in 1580; Bowden suggests that Fleming must have known of the 'importance of learning and religion to the women of the Cecil family'.[39] That may be true, but there is a more significant link. A year later, in 1581, Anne Cecil de Vere received another book dedication, this time of an anonymous translation of John Chrysostom's commentary, again on Paul's letter to the Ephesians. Fincham and Tyacke have noted that both these texts contain indices which highlight an anti-Calvinist interpretation of the biblical text, with Hemming-sen's commentary discussing 'election conditionall', whilst the index to Chrys-ostom's work states 'the cause of election [by God] is not our labour but his love, who respecteth our vertue by his grace'.[40] Fincham and Tyacke argue that these dedications suggest that Anne may have been seen as a conduit to influence her father and brother. The existence of Hemmingsen's commen-tary in her mother's library is at the very least evidence of Mildred's exposure to such anti-Calvinist arguments, alongside her daughter. Mildred's copy of Chrysostom's commentary on Paul's letter to the Ephesians was instead in its original Greek.[41]

The sisters' libraries also show their interest in current religious controver-sies. Jerónimo Osório da Fonseca (Osorius), then a Portuguese priest, wrote an epistle to Elizabeth I urging her to recognise the break from Rome as an error and therefore to advance the Catholic religion in England as her first duty as monarch; the epistle was printed and widely circulated in Europe in 1563. William Cecil decided that Osorius must be answered and chose Walter Haddon to write the reply.[42] Haddon's answer was printed in Paris in 1563; Osorius, by then a bishop, published a reply in 1567. The controversy by this time had ensured the fame of Osorius's style and Elizabeth Russell owned a copy of his most famous work, a Portuguese history, entitled *De rebus Emmanuelis Regis Lusitaniae invictissimi.*[43] The religious debate continued and Haddon's further response, left unfinished at his death in 1571, was completed by John Foxe. Mildred owned a copy of the completed Haddon/Foxe work, entitled *Contra Hieron. Osorium.*[44] Her sister Elizabeth also owned another of Foxe's anti-papal tracts, a Latin work published anonymously in 1580 as *Papa Confutatus.* Elizabeth was obviously perceived as an influential reader, for she received a presentation copy of the work.[45]

There is also evidence within Mildred's library that the sisters shared interests in contemporary religious debates. Mildred owned a copy of Roger Ascham's *Apologia ... pro caena Dominica, contra Missam.*[46] The work was completed in manuscript at a much earlier date, probably in 1547, but was not printed until 1577. Personal connections with the late Ascham might explain the volume's inclusion in Mildred's library, although another explanation may be that Mildred's sister Elizabeth was undertaking her translation of Ponet's *Diallacticon* during this period, another Edwardian work on the nature of the Eucharist, which may have influenced her sister's continued interest in the debate.[47] Mildred also owned a copy of John Whitgift's *The defense of the Aunswere to the Admonition against the Replie of Thomas Cartwright*, published in 1574.[48] As we shall see, her sister Anne was closely involved with figures involved in the original Admonition to Parliament and, together with Elizabeth, attempted to protect Cartwright's supporters in this controversy; Mildred herself was associated in the early 1570s with Edward Dering, who was a notable supporter of Cartwright's works, particularly his *Replie* to Whitgift's earlier *Answer to the Admonition.*[49]

THE *STUDIA HUMANITATIS*

In addition to their religious texts, the sisters' other volumes show that their education covered the five-part *studia humanitatis*, extolled by sixteenth-century educationalists and taught in the grammar schools, which consisted of grammar, poetry, rhetoric, moral philosophy and history.[50] The basics of Latin grammar would have been covered early in their education. Although we have no evidence as to what Latin grammar books they used during the first stages of their classical education, Anne and Elizabeth later recorded their early familiarity with Terence, whose works were used by elementary students during this period as examples of phrases and syntax.[51] There is more evidence of the method by which the sisters learnt Greek. Anne owned the first edition of Moschopulus's *De ratione examinandae orationis libellus*, published by Robert Estienne in December 1545 from manuscripts in the French Royal Library.[52] This textbook contains twenty-two Greek passages, which Moschopulus subjects to syntactical and lexical analysis; a major source for the passages in the text was the scholia of Aristophanes.[53] Mildred owned a copy of Suidas's Greek lexicon, which she later donated to St John's College, Oxford; Vives recommended that male students should keep this dictionary close at hand when starting to work on Greek texts.[54] There is no evidence of which basic works the sisters turned to when learning Hebrew, although there were alphabets and grammars for elementary students on the market.[55] After scholars had mastered the basics, they would move onto the Bible in Hebrew. The sisters may also have relied upon their father's texts; Anthony Cooke was a close acquaintance of the Hebrew scholar Ralph Cavelarius, and the family home, Gidea Hall, was inscribed with Hebrew quotations, indicating their father's knowledge of the language.[56] Anne and Katherine both seem to have had at least some knowledge of the language. Anne used a few Hebrew characters in a letter to the earl of Essex, and the epitaph written for Katherine by Andrew Melville notes her knowledge of Hebrew.[57]

The sisters were familiar with the poets used to support the early development of their male contemporaries' classical language skills.[58] Virgil was held by early modern educationalists to be the foremost poet, and a later letter by Elizabeth demonstrates her detailed knowledge of his *Aeneid*.[59] Thomas Elyot argued that reading Ovid's *Fasti* was necessary 'for the understanding of other poets', whilst Hesiod, although not 'so high in philosophy', was delightful for his fables.[60] Mildred read verse by both Ovid and Hesiod, namely the former's *Fasti* and the latter's *Works and Days*.[61] She also used a phrase from *The Greek Anthology* in one of her poems, indicating her familiarity with that ancient collection of Greek and Christian verse.[62] Both Anne and Elizabeth read Horace. Anne was at the very least familiar with his *Odes* and *Epistles*, whilst Elizabeth's later letters reveal her knowledge both of his *Satires* and his *Epistles*.[63]

The sisters read classical poets beyond those of the grammar school curriculum. Mildred owned Zacharias Kallierges's 1515 edition of Pindar's 'Victory Odes', which focus on the festivals and games in the Hellenic calendar.[64] This was the first Greek text ever published in Rome and was printed only two years after the Aldine Press's first edition of Pindar's *Odes*. A line written by Elizabeth for her own tomb borrows directly from the early Latin poet Ennius:

Nemo me lacrimis decoret, neque funera fletu,
faxit cur? vado per astra Deo.[65]
(Let no one honour me with tears, nor should my funeral be performed with weeping. Why? I go through the stars to God.)

If Elizabeth had directly read Ennius's poetry, then she must have had access to the first edition of his work and that of several other Latin poets, such as Pacuvius and Caecilius, published in 1564 by Robert Estienne in Geneva as the *Fragmenta Poetarum Veterum Latinorum*.[166]

Mildred owned Christian poetry, thought by Vives to be particularly suitable for women who wished to read verse. As discussed above, her name is appended in Greek letters to the paraphrase of the Psalms by Apollinaris. Published in Paris in 1552, this was again the first edition of the work. Her edition of the *Hymns* of Callimachus is not the first edition, nor the 1513 Aldine edition; she owned the 1532 version, published by the Froben press, which was considered far superior, as it was not only a more complete edition, but it also contains the scholia and preface of the Czech Greek scholar and close friend of Erasmus, Sigmund Gelen.[167]

Alongside the reading of classical texts, three handbooks were central to the grammar school curriculum for rhetoric and composition: Aphthonius's *Progymnasmata* and Erasmus's *De duplici copia verborum et rerum* and *De conscribendis epistolis*. Mildred owned all three of these texts.[168] She donated her Greek copy of Aphthonius's *Progymnasmata* to Westminster School in 1585.[169] Sixteenth-century schoolboys usually had access to a Latin translation of the text by Rudolph Agricola, although it is characteristic that Mildred owned the work in the original Greek.[170] The *Progymnasmata* contained a series of composition exercises which ultimately taught students how to compose orations.[171] It is therefore likely that Mildred, and perhaps her sisters, learnt the technique *in utramque partem*, arguing both sides to find a solution to a problem. The most common method of learning this was to follow the rhetorical exercises of the *Progymnasmata*. Stephen Alford has demonstrated how influential this technique was upon the thinking of William Cecil in the 1560s and it is possible that Mildred used the same method in her political activities.[172] Mildred's copy of the *Progymnasmata* also contained Hermogenes' *Ars Rhetorica*, which was a key text for sixteenth-century Arts candidates studying rhetoric at the universities.[173] Mildred would have been able to develop her rhetorical skills through studying her copy of the orations of Demosthenes, as her name is appended to Vincent Obsopoeus's selections from Demosthenes' orations.[174] Mildred also owned Aldus Manutius's *Orationes horum rhetorum* (Venice, 1513), which she later presented to Westminster School.[175] This volume is the first edition of most of the Attic orators, including orations by Aeschines and Isocrates. Richard Morison testified to Mildred's knowledge of Isocrates' oration 'On Peace' in a letter from 28 April 1551. After an extensive quotation from chapter 72 of the oration, he wrote: 'I have moch a do, not to adde that that foloweth, but my lady Cicil, can easely spie my theft, and so see, what I myght a stolen more'.[176]

For Philosophy, the writings of Cicero, particularly his *De officiis*, were central to the curriculum of sixteenth-century educationalists; Mildred's husband supposedly carried *De officiis* with him at all times.[177] Mildred surely knew Cicero's writings, as her sisters, Anne and Elizabeth, were certainly familiar with his works. Elizabeth quoted from her reading of Cicero's *De officiis* in her letters, suggesting a close knowledge of the text.[178] If Elizabeth's citation of Ennius in her commemorative verse did not stem from direct knowledge of his poetry, then she must have learnt the verse through its quotation in Cicero's *Tusculanae disputationes*.[179] As discussed above, Anne's detailed knowledge of Cicero was celebrated by her husband, Nicholas, along-side his familiarity with Seneca.[180] Whilst there is no direct evidence of the particular texts of Cicero which were read by Anne, it is significant that the *sententiae* on the walls of their home at Gorhambury were drawn from the same two authors, Cicero and Seneca.[181] Although the manuscript version of the *sententiae* which Nicholas presented to Lady Jane Lumley states that they were 'Selected by Him owt of Divers Authors', it is surely more likely that the *sententiae* reflected the combined interests of both Anne and Nicholas; the former in Cicero and the latter in Seneca. The Ciceronian *sententiae* are drawn from *De officiis*, *De amicitia* and probably from *De finibus*, so it is likely that Anne was at the very least familiar with these texts.[182] The Senecean *sententiae* were primarily drawn from the *Epistulae morales* and Anne's later letters reveal her wider knowledge of that work, for she quoted from the text to her son Anthony.[183] Her correspondence also reveals her reading of Seneca's *De ira*.[184] This was a key work for the sixteenth-century male humanist, for it extolled one of the primary qualities of a *vir civilis*, a statesman: that of clemency.[185] Anne was interested in poetry which followed this moral outlook. Her familiarity with Horace's doctrine of the golden mean is demonstrated by a translation of his ode on that subject by her husband, Nicholas, who 'turned [it] at the desier of my Ladye his Lordship's wyfe'; the ode is famous for its espousal of the Aristotelian view that excellence lies between two extremes.[186]

Little is known of the reading of the youngest Cooke sister, but Katherine Cooke Killigrew did read Plato's *Laws*, as can be demonstrated from a reference in a letter to her brother-in-law, Lord Burghley.[187] In Elyot's *The boke named The Governour*, Plato was thought to be a moral philosopher 'above all other' necessary for young noblemen to read.[188] Lady Jane Grey read Plato's work on the afterlife, *Phaedo*, and the Princess Mary was encouraged by Vives to read his works on the state, such as *The Republic* and *Laws*.[189] Katherine's reading of Plato on law-making and governance is significant, as she had no obvious outlet for the knowledge gained from this text as a woman beyond the throne.

Mildred appears to have had an interest in Aristotle's natural philosophy, which would have constituted required reading for her male contemporaries taking a Masters degree at the universities.[190] Her library contains Johannes Velcurio's commentary in three books on Aristotle's *Physics*.[191] Velcurio's work interpreted classical natural philosophy within a Protestant mindset. When discussing the taxonomy of causes, Aristotle had compared nature to other causes, such as luck; Velcurio, however, interpreted all natural causes as deriving from God's providence.[192]

The ancient Greek historians also formed part of the sisters' libraries. Mildred owned a copy of Dionysius of Halicarnassus's *Antiquitatum Romanarum* and she donated volumes of Eusebius's *Historia ecclesiastica* to Westminster Abbey Library and to Christ Church, Oxford.[193] She also gave texts of both the histories of Herodotus and Thucydides to Westminster School. Mildred presented the school with a volume of the Greek scholia, the marginal glosses, upon Thucydides's histories.[194] The origin of Mildred's volumes of Eusebius and Dionysius of Halicarnassus is significant. In 1544, the French printer Robert Estienne turned to publishing Greek works and he printed a series of eight first editions; the first two of this series were the Eusebius and Dionysius of Halicarnassus owned by Mildred Cecil, published respectively in 1544–46 and 1546–47.[195] Similarly her 1544 edition of Flavius Josephus was again the first published version of his works in Greek, printed in Basel by Froben and Episcopius.[196] Her sister Elizabeth was also interested in the ancient historians, owning a copy of Herodotus's *Historia*.[197] Sir John Harrington further implied Elizabeth's familiarity with the Greek historian Theopompus in a letter, with his reference to the latter's tale of Herostratus.[198]

BEYOND THE *STUDIA HUMANITATIS*

Drama found a place in the sisters' libraries. Anne's letters reveal her close knowledge of the comedies of Terence, including *Eunuchus* and *Phormio*, and Elizabeth demonstrated her familiarity with his play *Adelphoe*.[199] As mentioned above, Terence was central within the curriculum of sixteenth-century schoolboys, particularly in the elementary stages of Latin tuition. However, many elements of his plays would seem to indicate they were unsuitable for reading by women. One of the central characters in *Eunuchus*, for example, is a courtesan and the plot also revolves around a rape after the eunuch is replaced by a virile young man. Both St Augustine and, more contemporaneously, Vives had warned against the evil effects of the immorality of this tale upon young male readers.[200]

Mildred's library instead contained Greek tragedies, by Aeschylus, Euripides and Sophocles.[201] Anne may also have been familiar with at least one of Seneca's tragedies; whilst there is no direct evidence of her reading his dramas, her husband's personal motto, *mediocria firma* (the middle way is the surest), derives from a chorus in Seneca's *Oedipus*. Sir John Harrington also implied the familiarity of her sister Elizabeth with that tragedy, instead in the form of Sophocles' *Oedipus Coloneus*.[202] A letter written by Elizabeth in 1597 further mentioned the tragedy *Hercules Furens*, either referring to Euripides' original or Seneca's later version.[203]

There is evidence that both Elizabeth and Mildred studied logic and dialectic, which for their male contemporaries normally formed part of the reading for an Arts degree at the universities.[204] Elizabeth studied logic before her first marriage in 1558, shown by a copy in the original Greek of Aristotle's *Organon*, marked as the property of 'Ελιξαβετα κοκα' (Elizabeth Cooke); its existence at Hatfield House would suggest that she continued her studies whilst staying with the Cecils, during her father's Marian exile.[205] The *Organon* comprises of Aristotle's following works: the *Categories*, *Prior Analytics*, *On Interpretation*, *Posterior Analytics*, *Sophistical Refutations* and *Topics*. There are some marginalia in the text, in the same Greek hand as Elizabeth's signature on the front of the volume.[206] As with Mildred and Anne's marginalia, she noted down in Greek the themes discussed at various points in the text, such as 'body' and 'atom', although she did not write any independent observations in the margins of the volume.[207]

There is also evidence that Mildred pursued an interest in dialectic after her marriage, for a copy of Cornelius Valerius's *Tabulae totius dialectices* is marked with her name and the date, 1575.[208] Valerius was a Louvain scholar and his volume of dialectic was designed to present a simplified version of classical thinking on the subject, accompanied by a companion volume on rhetoric. This was again another work used by university students during the sixteenth century, appearing frequently on Oxford and Cambridge book lists.[209]

It is possible that Mildred was interested in mathematics in her later years. She owned Henry Billingsley's 1570 translation of Euclid's work on geometry, one of the most influential textbooks on mathematics in the period. According to the inscription on the title-page, 'Mildred Burghley, anno domini 1579', it would appear that Mildred was starting to develop an interest in mathematics in the last decade of her life.[210] Caroline Bowden has rightly suggested that the translation, prefaced by John Dee, was designed to instill mathematical skills in 'unlatined Studentes', for example common artificers.[211] But surely, this then begs the question, why was such a book in Mildred's personal library? She would have been quite capable of reading Euclid in the original and Mildred owned no other texts translated into English, bar Arthur Golding's 1565 rendering of Caesar's *Martiall Exployte*; in that case there was a personal connection between Mildred and the translator, as Golding had been living in Cecil House since the end of 1564.[212] I would suggest that Mildred's ownership of Billingsley's translation of Euclid again stems from a personal connection. Billingsley's earlier translation of Peter Martyr Vermigli's *Most learned and fruitfull Commentaries ... upon the Epistle of S. Paul to the Romanes* (1568) was dedicated, as was Vermigli's original Latin work, to Mildred's father, Sir Anthony Cooke.[213]

This is not to argue that Mildred or her sisters did not study mathematics. Little tuition in mathematics was provided for sixteenth-century boys.[214] However, some of the Cookes' learned female contemporaries did study mathematics, notwithstanding that Vives disapproved of the study of mathematics by women.[215] Margaret More and Margaret Giggs were taught mathematics by Nicholas Kratzer.[216] Elizabeth I also owned copies of works by Euclid.[217] Elizabeth Russell's later letters provide the strongest evidence that the sisters did at the very least have training in basic mathematics. A letter to her brother-in-law, Lord Burghley, from May 1593, for example, is filled with her calculations as to the financial standing of her daughters and Burghley's rough notes on the reverse of the letter reveal the complexity of the reckoning.[218]

Mildred's library contained several medical texts. Early modern women were excluded from receiving a medical education from the universities, although some had access to medical texts written in the vernacular.[219] All of Mildred's texts were written in classical languages, including the complete works of Galen in both the original Greek and in Latin, as well as Linacre's translation into Latin of Galen's *De sanitate tuenda*.[220] Her possession of Fernel's *Medicina* is not as surprising as Caroline Bowden has suggested.[221] With a few exceptions, Fernel's text was largely dependent on Galenic principles, in keeping with Mildred's other medical texts. Mildred was renowned amongst her female contemporaries for her medical knowledge. When the son of the countess of Bedford was ill in 1557, possibly from the ague, his mother told William Cecil she was not afraid to 'pute hym to my Lady your wyfe's order'.[222] In her volume of the letters of St Basil and St Gregory Nazianzen, Mildred even noted a section of a letter of St Basil to Eusebius, where Basil describes the symptoms of a fever.[223] Her sister Anne was also conversant with the classical principles of medicine, suggesting that she had undertaken similar reading. She told Anthony that the gout had been named 'pulvinaria morbi [the disease of the Gods' cushions] because it lyketh softeness & ease'.[224]

Modern languages found a place within the sisters' reading. As previously discussed, Anne's study of Italian was disapproved of by her mother. However, in order to translate Ochino's sermons into English, she must have had access to the first two volumes of the first edition of his collected sermons, his *Prediche*, printed in Geneva from 1548. Mildred may not have known Italian, as she owned Boccaccio's *Le Philocope* in French. Vives had argued that unmarried women should not read 'the hundred fables of Boccaccio', his *Decameron*.[225] Mildred instead owned the 1555 French translation of Boccaccio's *Filocolo*, translated by Adrien Sevin. Considered the first prose novel in Italian literature, Boccaccio's work was based on the popular romance of Florio and Biancifiore. Although the reading of romances was frowned upon for sixteenth-century women, Mildred was married by the time she autographed the text with her name and the date '1564', which would have lessened the perceived threat from the text.[226] Jean Bodin also presented Mildred with a copy of his *Les Six Livres de la République* in 1581, which again may indicate her French language skills.[227] Mildred's sister Elizabeth is likely to have had skill in French, testified to by the diverse friendship networks she developed during her husband's embassy to Paris in 1566, although there are no extant French volumes connected to her.[228]

Katherine is the only sister for whom the ownership of a manuscript volume can now be established. She was presented with a volume of verse by the neo-Latin Scottish poet, George Buchanan, sometime after 1579.[229] Katherine had many connections with Buchanan's circle. He had become a firm friend of her husband by the year of their marriage, in 1565.[230] One of Buchanan's early students and a lifelong friend was Andrew Melville, whose friendship with Katherine is demonstrated by an epitaph he wrote upon her death.[231] Only a small number of the poems in Katherine's manuscript volume had already been published at that time.[232] The manuscript contains verses on Katherine's own family members, such as Buchanan's fourth verse on her sister Mildred and an epitaph on her brother-in-law Nicholas Bacon.[233] Reading the volume's poetry on their wider intellectual circle, including verses on Karel Utenhove, Roger Ascham and Johann Sturm, would have highlighted to Katherine her place and that of her sisters within a European humanist community, all the more so due to Buchanan's lauding of female scholars in poetry in her manuscript, including Camille de Morel and her own sister Mildred.[234] Katherine's manuscript also contains many politicised pieces, including verses on both Mary and Elizabeth Tudor.[235] The manuscript itself shows that Katherine was recognised as possessing a good understanding of the rules of poetry, for the scribe included notes on metre and on Buchanan's choice of language.[236]

Mildred and Anne possessed shorter manuscript works. In 1571, Giles Fletcher dedicated and presented to Mildred a manuscript version of four of his eclogues, which were the first Latin pastorals to be written in England.[237] Anne owned a short manuscript meditation by Percival Wyborn, designed to assist her religious worship during her widowhood.[238] Whilst Elizabeth may not have owned a manuscript copy of Sir John Harrington's *A New Discourse of a Stale Subject, called the Metamorphosis of Ajax*, according to Harrington's own testimony she had portions of the work read to her in draft form and was presented with a copy of the octavo pamphlet upon its publication in 1596.[239] As the Ajax of the title was a pun on a privy, namely 'a jakes', the work had a strong vein of scatological humour, indicating the breadth of Elizabeth's reading matter.[240]

CONCLUSION

The evidence gathered here is most probably only a portion of the sisters' reading, as it is impossible to reconstruct their entire libraries. Yet this chapter provides far more clarity on the nature of the Cookes' education and, as the first detailed recreation of the reading of female scholars from this period, it also sheds much-needed light upon the wider practices of the humanist education of women. It reveals that the Cookes' reading went far beyond even the wide body of texts prescribed by Vives for Princess Mary. Rather than using their learning purely to read religious works, as has previously been suggested of early modern women's reading, the Cookes were familiar with an extensive variety of classical and modern texts, including those, such as Terence and Boccaccio, which were often thought unsuitable for women. The evidence suggests not only that their reading was comparable to that of their learned contemporaries, such as Lady Jane Grey and the Princess Elizabeth, but that the breadth of their reading, encompassing, for example, logic and dialectic, surpasses our current understanding of the reading of sixteenth-century female humanists in England.

It also highlights the need for scholars not to view the prescription of texts in a wholly negative light, purely as a limitation upon women's reading. Mildred Cecil's involvement with the publication of Ascham and Sturm's letters suggests her own interest in the prescription of texts as a potentially positive force for female education. The chapter furthermore reveals the opportunities awarded by this methodology for the reconstruction of the libraries of elite women. Drawing on a variety of sources, such a methodology is not without its difficulties; however, in the case of the Cooke sisters, it allows an appreciation for the first time of the breadth and depth of their learning. As befits women who were educated outside of an institution, their learning was unbounded by specific time-frames and took place throughout their lives.

It is important to note that so many of the texts owned by the sisters were first editions, revealing the impact that print had on the education of women. Outside of the university system, print allowed them access, within the household, to authors previously available only in manuscript form and confined to male readers within educational institutions. Their extant marginalia, although limited, reveal that they were not silenced in the margins of their texts, as suggested by Heidi Brayman Hackel. The existence of the majority of their marginalia in Greek, whilst appropriate to the Greek texts upon which they were commenting, does, however, suggest that their interaction with other readers through the margins of their books was limited to the highly educated within their households. The nature of the sisters' extant marginalia, which highlighted themes in their reading, instead indicates that they were more likely making separate notes on their reading in commonplace books.[241]

Finally, their libraries reveal in more depth the knowledge and skills which they gained from their reading. It was this learning that made the Cooke sisters 'the wonders of the age' and provided them with the tools to influence others through their translations, verse, letters and even conversations.

NOTES

1 N. Udall, 'To the most virtuous ... Quene Katherine', in D. Erasmus, *The first tome or volume of the Paraphrase of Erasmus upon the Newe Testamente* (1548), sigs Aaa1r–v.

2 J. Coke, *The debate betweene the Heraldes of Englande and Fraunce* (1550), sig. K1r.

3 M.K. McIntosh, 'Sir Anthony Cooke: Tudor humanist, educator, and religious reformer', *PAPS*, 119 (1975), 240. For Haddon's treatise, see G. Haddon, *G. Haddoni Legum Doctoris ... lucubrationes* (1567), sig. R2r.

4 Ballard, p. 189.

5 For four early modern grammar school statutes, starting in 1523, see P. Mack, *Elizabethan Rhetoric* (Cambridge, 2002), p. 13.

6 For Princess Elizabeth's reading, see N. Mears, *Queenship and Political Discourse in the Elizabethan Realms* (Cambridge, 2005), pp. 75–6. For Lady Jane Grey, see J.S. Edwards, '"Jane the Quene": A New Consideration of Lady Jane Grey, England's Nine-Days Queen' (PhD thesis, University of Colorado at Boulder, 2007), pp. 48–53.

7 The classical works owned by Lady Mary Keys, namely Demosthenes and Isocrates, were in translation, respectively in English and French. See NA, SP 12/124, fo. 86r: 01/06/1578.

8 C. Bowden, 'The library of Mildred Cooke Cecil, Lady Burghley', *The Library*, 7th series, 6 (2005), 3–29. Bowden did not engage with Mildred's marginalia, as she could not confirm the authenticity of her hand.

9 C. Meale and J. Boffey, 'Gentlewomen's reading', in L. Hellinga and J.B. Trapp (eds), *The Cambridge History of the Book in Britain, III, 1400–1557* (Cambridge, 1999), p. 526.

10 D. Erasmus, *The Correspondence of Erasmus*, ed. R.A.B. Mynors *et al.*, *Collected Works of Erasmus*, 8 (Toronto, 1988), p. 297.

11 J. Pearson, 'Women reading, reading women', in H. Wilcox (ed.), *Women and Literature in Britain 1500–1700* (Cambridge, 1996), p. 81.

12 J.L. Vives, *Vives and the Renascence Education of Women*, ed. F. Watson (New York, 1912) (Vives), pp. 56, 62.

13 *Ibid.*, p. 204.

14 *Ibid.*

15 *Ibid.*, p. 205.

16 *Ibid.*, pp. 60, 147.

17 *Ibid.*, p. 142.

18 *Ibid.*, p. 143.

19 *Ibid.*, pp. 145, 147.

20 *Ibid.*, p. 144.

21 *Ibid.*, p. 147.

22 *Ibid.*, pp. 62–3.

23 *Ibid.*

24 *Ibid.*, pp. 205–6.

25 *Ibid.*, p. 59.

26 *Ibid.*, pp. 61–2.

27 In the second set of Ochino's sermons translated by Anne Cooke, the editor highlighted that Anne's education was based at home, being 'a maiden's that never gaddid farder then hir father's house to learne the language'. See B. Ochino, *Fourtene sermons ... concernynge the predestinacion and eleccion of god*, trans. A.C. (?1551), sig. A2v.

28 Burghley's words are drawn from Mildred's tomb, Chapel of St Nicholas, Westminster Abbey, London. Translation by Margaret Stewardson from an unpublished text held at Westminster Abbey Library. John Clapham also suggested Cooke was his children's tutor in his *Certain Observations*, written after the death of Elizabeth I. J. Clapham, *Certain Observations*, ed. E. Plummer Read and C. Read (Philadelphia, 1951), p. 84.

29 McIntosh, 'Anthony Cooke', 240.

30 The above quotation is included in an anonymous cutting held by Essex Record Office: Sage 773. I have located its original context as a note by a 'J.H. Mn' on 'Lord Bacon's Mother', included in *Notes and Queries*, 95 (1857), 327, however I have not been able to locate Anne's volume of Moschopulus.

31 McIntosh, 'Anthony Cooke', 239.

32 *Ibid.*, 244. For a list of Cooke's continuing correspondence with Sturm during the 1560s, see M.K. McIntosh, 'The Cooke Family of Gidea Hall, Essex, 1460–1661' (PhD thesis, Harvard University, 1967), p. 339.

33 J. Cheke, *Joannis Cheki Angli De pronuntiatione Graecae potissimum linguae disputations cum Stephano Vuintoniensi Episcopo*, ed. C.S. Curio (Basel, 1555); McIntosh, 'Anthony Cooke', 244; J. Stevenson, *Women Latin Poets* (Oxford, 2005), p. 261. See chapter 6, below, for Morata's connections with Mildred.

34 NA, SP 6/12, fos 14r–31r. See also chapter 2, below, for more on Cooke's translations.

35 BL, Royal MS 5 E.XVII.

36 Bowden, 'The library of Mildred Cooke Cecil', 19.

37 Hatfield House, Hertfordshire (Hatfield): P.M. Vermigli, *Loci communes D. Petri Martyris Vermilii*, ed. R. Masson (1583), title-page. Anne owned a copy of the 1576 edition of *Loci Communes* although, unlike Mildred's 1583 edition, it bears no inscription from Masson. Kingston Lacey House, Dorset: P.M. Vermigli, *Petri Marytis Vermilii, Florentini praestantissimi nostra aetate theologi, Loci communes*, ed. R. Masson (1576).

38 R. Masson, 'Antonio Coko', in Vermigli, *Loci communes* (1576), sig. *4v; R. Masson, 'Antonio Coko', in Vermigli, *Loci communes* (1583), sig. B2r.

39 *Fouretene sermons*, sigs A3r–A4r.

40 *Ibid.*, sigs A3r–v.

41 Both Jane Stevenson and Charles Knighton conjecture that the Greek suggests that the tutor's name was sharp or thorny, although both are unable to make a positive identification of the schoolmaster. See J. Stevenson, 'Mildred Cecil, Lady Burleigh: poetry, politics

and protestantism', in V. Burke and J. Gibson (eds), *Early Modern Manuscript Writing: Selected Papers from the Trinity/Trent Colloquium* (Aldershot, 2004), p. 55; *Calendar of State Papers, Domestic, 1547–1553*, ed. C.S. Knighton (1992), p. 195.

42 N. Orme, *Education in the West of England, 1066–1548* (Exeter, 1976), pp. 89–90.

43 NA, SP 10/13, fo. 39r: 22/05/1551.

44 Utenhove cited and translated in Stevenson, 'Mildred Cecil', p. 58.

45 These authors are noted in Lawrence's observations for Mildred on particular modes of expression in ancient Greek. See BL, Lansdowne MS 98, fos 211r–241v: n.d.

46 J. Strype, *The Life and Acts of Matthew Parker* (4 vols, 1711), IV, p. 404.

47 BL, Lansdowne MS 104, fo. 3r: 13/06/1553.

48 N. Bacon, *The Recreations of His Age* (Oxford, 1919), p. 27.

49 NA, SP 68/6, fo. 28v: 03/02/1551.

50 For Sturm's primary role in the publication of the letters, see R. Ascham, *Letters of Roger Ascham*, trans. M. Hatch and A. Vos, ed. A. Vos (New York, 1989) (*Ascham Letters*), pp. 156, 157, 168.

51 *Ibid.*, p. 159.

52 *Ibid.*, p. 162.

53 Mildred's favour of these Fathers, particularly of Basil, as described below, aligns her with Sturm, rather than Ascham, in this debate over the Church Fathers.

54 *Ascham Letters*, p. 173.

55 *Ibid.*, p. 175.

56 *Ibid.*, p. 166.

57 *Ibid.*, p. 169.

58 *Ibid.*, p. 176.

59 *Ibid.*, p. 167.

60 Ascham went on to discuss Mildred's own achievements in his next letter to Sturm on 14 December 1550. See chapter 6 for his description of Mildred.

61 See Pearson, 'Women reading, reading women', pp. 81–2.

62 H. Brayman Hackel, 'The Countess of Bridgewater's London library', in J. Andersen and E. Sauer (eds), *Books and Readers in Early Modern England* (Philadelphia, 2002), p. 138; H. Brayman Hackel, *Reading Material in Early Modern England: Print, Gender and Literacy* (Cambridge, 2005), p. 214. For a study based on the evidence from wills, see P. Clark, 'The ownership of books in England, 1560–1640: an example of some Kentish townsfolk', in L. Stone (ed.), *Schooling and Society* (Baltimore, 1976), pp. 95–111. For studies based on inventories and wills, see E. Leedham-Green, *Books in Cambridge Inventories* (2 vols, Cambridge, 1986); and E. Leedham-Green and R.J. Fehrenbach, *Private Libraries in Renaissance England: A Collection and Catalogue of Tudor and Early Stuart Book-Lists* (6 vols, Marlborough, 1992–2004).

63 For studies that use other types of manuscript testimony to reconstruct early modern women's reading, see, for example, R. Wray, 'Recovering the reading of Renaissance Englishwomen: deployments of autobiography', *Critical Survey*, 12 (2000), 33–48; S. Roberts, *Reading Shakespeare's Poems in Early Modern England* (Basingstoke, 2003); J. Donawerth, 'Women's reading practices in seventeenth-century England: Margaret Fell's *Women's Speaking Justified*', *The Sixteenth Century Journal*, 37 (2006), 985–1005.

64 A notable exception is James Carley's research on the books of Henry VIII's wives: J. Carley, *The Books of King Henry VIII and his Wives* (2004), pp. 107–42. Heidi Brayman Hackel argues that a multi-facted evidential approach is necessary to understand fully early modern women's reading and although her own study on Lady Anne Clifford relies primarily on the evidence in the Great Picture commissioned by Clifford, it also draws on wider evidence of the countess's reading material; her work on the countess of Bridgewater's library relies on an extant inventory list. See Brayman Hackel, 'Countess of Bridgewater's London library', pp. 138–59; Brayman Hackel, *Reading Material*, pp. 222–55.

65 NA, PROB 11/59, fo. 72r.

66 For example, none of the volumes bearing the sisters' ownership marks also bears their father's earlier mark, nor do they reference this bequest in any of their extant letters.

67 Lambeth Palace Library, London (LPL), Talbot 3203, fo. 410r: n.d. [after 1590].

68 BL, Royal MS 12 A.I–III.

69 BL, Royal MS 12.A.I. See R. Ellis, 'Translation for and by the young in 16th-century England: Erasmus and the Arundel children', in G. Iamartino, M. Maggioni and R. Facchinetti (eds), *Thou Sittest at another Boke ... English Studies in Honour of Domenico Pezzini* (Milan, 2008), p. 60.

70 Westminster School: Callimachus, *Cyrenaei Hymni* (Basel, 1532) [Greek].

71 Anne quoted 'Nimia familiaritas parit contemptum' (Too much familiarity breeds contempt). LPL 651, fo. 210r: 20/08/1595.

72 Elizabeth quoted 'quae supra nos nihil ad nos' (what is above us does not pertain to us). CP 25, fo. 51r: 24/02/1596.

73 See, for example, Anne's quotation from Terence's *Eunuchus*: 'yow learned in terence long ago, sic luxuriantur Famuli cum absunt Domini' (in this way the servants grow indulgent when the masters are absent); LPL 650, fo. 130r. Terence's original line instead is 'perstrepunt, ita ut fit domini ubi absunt' (chattering away, as happens when the master is absent); Terence, *Eunuchus*, trans J. Barsby (2001), p. 381 [III.v.600].

74 CP 53, fo. 88r: 07/1597.

75 Gold-tooled initials in the binding can also be problematic as evidence. The auctioneer Bernard Quaritch suggested that a copy of Richard Day's *A Booke of Christian Prayers* (1578) previously belonged to Mildred, due to the 'M.C.' in the binding. However, by 1578 Mildred was already Lady Burghley and therefore she had 'M.B.' tooled on the covers of her books, for example the Aeschylus at Westminster School or the Galen at Christ Church, both donated in 1586. I would suggest that as the prayer book in question is bound in what Quaritch admitted was the 'favourite style' of Matthew Parker's bookbinder, then the 'M.C.' may instead stand for M[atthew Parker] C[antuariensis]. See B. Quaritch, *Examples of Book-Binding and Volumes bearing Marks of Distinguished Ownership* (1897), p. 9.

76 Hatfield: R. Ascham, *Apologia doctissimi viri Rogeri Aschami Angli pro caena Dominica, contra Missam* (1577), title-page.

77 Pierpont Morgan Library, New York: St Basil the Great, *Opera Graeca quae ad nos extant omnia* (Basel, 1551) [Greek], first unpaginated leaf; Folger: D. Erasmus, *Paraphrasis in Evangelium secundum Joannem* (Basel, 1523), title-page; Essex Record Office: Sage 773; Sotheby's, *The Library of the Earls of Macclesfield removed from Shirburn Castle ... Bibles 1477–1739* (2006), pp. 38–9.

78 Other early modern women were similarly motivated to distinguish their books from

those of their husband. Frances Wolfreston (1607–77) inscribed her volumes with 'Frances Wolfreston hor book' and Heidi Brayman Hackel notes that another seventeenth-century woman inscribed her copy of Culpepper's *Directory for Midwives* with 'Elizabeth Hunt her Book *not* his'. See P. Morgan, 'Frances Wolfreston and "Hor Bouks": a seventeenth-century woman book-collector', *The Library*, 6th series, 11 (1989), 197, 211; Brayman Hackel, *Reading Material*, pp. 214–15. For examples of early modern women's book closets, see *ibid.*, pp. 41–3, 246.

79 CP 143, fos 91r–92r.

80 BL, Egerton MS 2148, fo. 180r.

81 Fenton's past service suggests he could be sure that his translation of a conference held at Paris, attempting to mediate between Catholic and Protestant extremists, would appeal; likewise, *Monophylo*, with its classical and religious material and an extended dedication to Elizabeth, should have been well received. See C. Clarke, 'Patronage and Literature: The Women of the Russell Family, 1520–1617' (PhD thesis, Reading University, 1992), pp. 341, 344, 346.

82 *A medicinable morall, that is two books of Horace his satyres*, trans. T. Drant (1566).

83 N. Mukherjee, 'Thomas Drant's rewriting of Horace', *Studies in English Literature, 1500–1900*, 40 (2000), 1–20.

84 H. Brayman Hackel, '"Boasting of silence": women readers in a patriarchal state', in K. Sharpe and S. Zwicker (eds), *Reading, Society and Politics in Early Modern England* (Cambridge, 2003), pp. 101–21; Brayman Hackel, *Reading Material*, pp. 203–13.

85 A. Cambers, 'Readers' marks and religious practice: Margaret Hoby's marginalia', in J.L. King (ed.), *Tudor Books and Readers: Materiality and the Construction of Meaning* (Cambridge, 2010), pp. 211–31.

86 S. Orgel, 'Marginal maternity: reading Lady Anne Clifford's *A Mirror for Magistrates*', in D. Brooks (ed.), *Printing and Parenting in Early Modern England* (Aldershot, 2005), pp. 267–90. Anne Clifford also left some annotations in her copy of *Barclay His Argenis* (1625). See Brayman Hackel, *Reading Material*, pp. 236–37.

87 Hatfield: D. Erasmus, *Opus de conscribendis epistolis* (Antwerp, 1564); Westminster School: Callimachus, *Cyrenaei Hymni* (Basel, 1532). This opposes the view of David Selwyn regarding the marginalia in Mildred's volume of Erasmus's *De conscribendis epistolis*. See Bowden, 'The library of Mildred Cooke Cecil', p. 20.

88 In addition, Mildred's letter to Lady Jane Grey with a volume of St Basil, discussed later, was apparently written in the book itself. The location of Elizabeth's copy of Foxe's *Papa Confutatus* is now unknown, but it was offered for sale in 1848 by the bookseller Thomas Rodd. According to the auction note, Elizabeth also wrote some Latin verses on the back leaf of the book. See *Catalogue of Books in Theology, Ecclesiastical History and Canon Law ... On Sale, at the Prices affixed by Thomas Rodd* (1848), p. 148.

89 BL, Lansdowne MS 43, fo. 120r; LPL Talbot, 3203, fo. 410r.

90 Portrait of Anne Bacon attributed to George Gower in a private collection and anonymous portrait of Elizabeth Russell, Bisham Abbey, Buckinghamshire.

91 For example, all the libraries in Jayne's sample contained a Bible, although the precise version is rarely given. See S.R. Jayne, *Library Catalogues of the English Renaissance* (Berkeley, 1956). E. Nares, *Memoirs of the Life and Administration of Lord Burghley* (1831), p. 365; Humanities Research Center, University of Texas, Austin: *Novum Jesu Christi D.N. Testamentum* (Paris, 1550) [Greek].

92 Pembroke College, Cambridge: *Divinae Scripturae, Veteris ac Novi Testimenti, omnia* (Basle, 1545) [Greek].

93 P. Croft, 'Mildred, Lady Burghley: the matriarch', in P. Croft (ed.), *Patronage, Culture and Power: The Early Cecils* (2002), pp. 290–1.

94 St John's College, Cambridge: *Biblia Sacra Hebraice, Chaldaice, Graece et Latine* (8 vols, Antwerp, 1569–72).

95 Bowden, 'The library of Mildred Cooke Cecil', p. 18.

96 Her sisters Anne and Katherine both had some knowledge of the Hebrew language, as is discussed below.

97 This two-volume work also now belongs to St John's, Cambridge; however, it was not directly donated by Burghley himself.

98 Sotheby's, *Library of the Earls of Macclesfield*, pp. 38–39.

99 CP 128, fo. 68r: 23/12/n.y.

100 See chapter 3 for Elizabeth's use of biblical citation in Latin.

101 See chapter 2 for Elizabeth's biblical translation.

102 Folger: Erasmus, *Paraphrasis in Evangelium secundum Joannem*, title-page.

103 S.E. James, *Kateryn Parr: The Making of a Queen* (Aldershot, 1999), pp. 227–33.

104 J.N. King, 'Patronage and piety: the influence of Catherine Parr', in M.P. Hannay (ed.), *Silent But for the Word* (Kent, Ohio, 1985), p. 49.

105 This text owned by Mildred has not been located. The first reference to her possession and use of this text occurs in J. Strype, *Annals of the Reformation* (4 vols in 7, Oxford, 1824), III, ii, p. 129. See also Ballard, p. 189.

106 Bowden, 'The library of Mildred Cooke Cecil', p. 13.

107 James, *Kateryn Parr*, p. 204.

108 *Ibid.*, p. 206.

109 Both Strype and Ballard record the title of Mildred's volume to be *Psalmi seu Precationes Johannis Episcopi Rossensis*. If their precise wording of the title is correct, then it would appear that Mildred owned a version of the work printed in Cologne by Arnold Birckman: *Psalmi seu precationes Joannis [Fisher] episcopi Roffensis* (Cologne, 1561).

110 James, *Kateryn Parr*, p. 201.

111 Hatfield: T. à Kempis, *De Christo imitando, contemnendisque mundi vanitatibus libellus authore Thoma Kempisio ... interprete Sebastiano Castellione* (Basel, 1563).

112 LPL 656, fo. 47r: 18/03/1597. For versions of Sternhold and Hopkins, see H. Hamlin, *Psalm Culture and Early Modern Literature* (Cambridge, 2004), p. 39.

113 LPL 649, fo. 37r: 22/02/1593.

114 T. de Bèze, *Chrestienes meditations sur huict pseaumes du prophete David composees et nouvellement mises en lumiere par Theodore de Besze* (Geneva, 1581); T. de Bèze, *Christian meditations upon eight Psalmes of the prophet David*, trans. I.S. (1582).

115 See chapter 5 for the presentation of the volume.

116 Balliol College, Oxford: Apollinaris, *Apollinarii interpretatio Psalmorum, versibus heroicis* (Paris, 1552) [Greek].

117 Memorial inscription, Westminster Abbey. Translation by Margaret Stewardson.

118 Pierpont: Basil, *Opera Graeca*.

119 Hatfield: St Basil the Great, *Orationes de moribus XXIIII* (Paris, 1556) [Greek]; Westminster Abbey Library: Gregory of Nyssa, *Opus admirandum Gregorii Nysseni antistitis de hominis opificio* (Basel, 1567) [Greek and Latin].

120 BL: St Basil and St Gregory Nazianzen, *Epistolae Graecae* (Haguenau, 1528) [Greek].

121 BL, Royal MS, 17 B XVIII.

122 Hatfield: St John Chrysostom, *De orando Deum libri duo* (Louvain, 1551) [Greek]. See chapter 2 for more on Mildred's translations.

123 R.C. Alston, *Books with Manuscript: A Short Title Catalogue of Books with Manuscript Notes in the British Library* (1994), p. 31. For Cecil's Greek hand, see BL, Lansdowne MS 118, fo. 83v.

124 BL: Basil and Gregory, *Epistolae Graecae*, sig. B3v.

125 *Ibid.*, sig. B4v.

126 Pierpont: Basil, *Opera Graeca*, sig. M4r.

127 NA, SP 10/15, fos 178a, 178c.

128 Westminster Abbey Library: Eusebius, *Pamphili evangelicae praeparationis lib. XV* (Paris, 1544) [Greek].

129 Westminster Abbey Library: Justin Martyr, *Opera Graeca* (Paris, 1551) [Greek].

130 St John's College, Oxford: *Monumenta S. Patrum orthodoxographa*, ed. J.J. Grynaeus (2 vols, Basel, 1569).

131 I. Backus, *Historical Method and Confessional Identity in the Era of the Reformation* (Leiden, 2003), pp. 253–4.

132 R. Price, 'Are there holy pagans in Justin Martyr', in E. Peters and E. Livingstone (eds), *Studia Patristica*, 31 (1997), 167.

133 H. Chadwick, *The Cambridge History of Later Greek and Early Medieval Philosophy* (Cambridge, 1967), p. 168.

134 *A Way of Reconciliation of a good and learned man touching the Trueth, Nature, and Substance of the Body and Blood of Christ in the Sacrament*, trans. Elizabeth Cooke Hoby Russell (1605) (*Reconciliation*), sig. D3r.

135 D. Kinder, 'Clement of Alexandria: conflicting views on women', in E. Ferguson (ed.), *Christianity and Society* (1999), pp. 215–16.

136 *Ibid.*, p. 215.

137 Hatfield: N. Hemmingsen, *Commentarius in epistolam Pauli ad Ephesios* (1576). Bowden had previously speculated whether the marginalia might be in Mildred's hand; Bowden, 'The library of Mildred Cooke Cecil', 20–1.

138 K. Fincham and N. Tyacke, *The Altars Restored: The Changing Face of English Religious Worship, 1547–c.1700* (Oxford, 2007), p. 82. For more on Hemmingsen's theology, see P. White, *Predestination, Policy and Polemic* (Cambridge, 2002), pp. 90–1.

139 Bowden, 'The library of Mildred Cooke Cecil', 18.

140 Fincham and Tyacke, *Altars Restored*, p. 83.

141 Cambridge University Library (CUL): St John Chrysostom, *Divi Joannis Chyrsostomi in omnes Pauli apostoli epistolas accuratissima vereque aurea et divina interpretatio* (Verona, 1529) [Greek].

142 L.V. Ryan, 'The Haddon-Osorio controversy (1563–1583)', *Church History*, 22 (1953), 143.

143 BL: Osorius, *De rebus Emmanuelis Regis Lusitaniae invictissimi* (Cologne, 1576). Roger Ascham's *The Schoolmaster* recorded contemporary interest in Osorius's Ciceronian style of writing. See R. Ascham, *The Schoolmaster*, ed. L.V. Ryan (New York, 1967), p. 110. See also pp. 91, 111.

144 Hatfield: W. Haddon, *Contra Hieron. Osorium, eiusque odiosas insectationes pro evangelicae veritatis necessaria defensione, responsio apologetica* (1577).

145 The bookseller Thomas Rodd noted that Elizabeth's volume was a presentation copy, with her arms emblazoned on the first leaf: *Catalogue of Books in Theology*, p. 148.

146 Hatfield: Ascham, *Apologia*.

147 For the dating of Elizabeth Cooke Russell's translation *Diallacticon*, see chapter 2.

148 Hatfield: J. Whitgift, *The defense of the Aunswere to the Admonition against the Replie of T[homas] C[artwright]* (1574).

149 See chapter 5, below, for more on these networks.

150 Q. Skinner, *Reason and Rhetoric in the Philosophy of Hobbes* (Cambridge, 1996), p. 23.

151 LPL 650, fo. 130r; Terence, *Eunuchus*, III.v.600. LPL 654, fo. 43r; Terence, *Phormio*, IV.i.9. Mertoun House, Roxburghshire, Ellesmere MS EL 45: 28/06/1597; Terence, *Adelphoe*, II.iv.269.

152 Essex Record Office: Sage 773.

153 J. Keaney, 'Moschopulus and Harpocration', *Transactions and Proceedings of the American Philological Association*, 100 (1969), 204–5.

154 Vives, p. 249. For the donation of Suidas, see Burghley House Muniments, 49/5/2. I am grateful to Dr Eddie Smith, archivist at Westminster School, for a copy of this document.

155 G. Lloyd-Jones, *The Discovery of Hebrew in Tudor England* (Manchester, 1983), pp. 248–58.

156 For Ralph Cavelarius, see McIntosh, 'Anthony Cooke', p. 242, n. 60. Although Gidea Hall was demolished in 1720, Morant records the Hebrew inscriptions: P. Morant, *The History and Antiquities of the County of Essex* (2 vols, 1823), I, ii, p. 66.

157 CP 128, fo. 68r; Ballard, p. 207. Melville's epitaph is presumably the source for Ballard's assertion that Katherine knew Hebrew; he remained silent as to her sisters' proficiency in the language. See Ballard, p. 205.

158 For sixteenth-century grammar school statutes with prescribed reading of Latin and Greek poets, see Mack, *Elizabethan Rhetoric*, p. 13. See also T. Elyot, *The Book Named The Governor*, ed. S.E. Lehmberg (1962), pp. 30–3.

159 CP 179, fo. 92r: 10/1599.

160 Elyot, *The Book Named The Governor*, pp. 32–3.

161 For her quotation from Ovid's *Fasti*, see Bodl., Carte MS LVI, fo. 475r. For Hesiod's *Works and Days*, see CUL Ii.v.37, sig. 5r; J. Stevenson and P. Davidson, *Early Modern Women Poets* (Oxford, 2001), p. 20. Mildred's familiarity with Hesiod's poem, *Works*

and Days, is striking, as Vives noted that the text reveals Hesiod as a poet who is hostile to women. See J.L. Vives, *The Education of a Christian Woman: A Sixteenth Century Manual*, trans. C. Fantazzi (Chicago, 2000), p. 328.

162 CUL Ii.v.37, sig. 5r; Stevenson and Davidson, *Early Modern Women Poets*, p. 20.

163 For Anne, see LPL 651, fo. 326r. for Horace, *Epistles*, I.18.86 and Bacon, *Recreations*, pp. 14–15 for Horace, *Odes*, II.10. For Elizabeth, see CP 175, fo. 92r. for Horace, *Satires*, I.4.85; CP 179, fo. 92r. for Horace, *Epistles*, I.10.24; and CP 175, fo. 118r. for Horace, *Epistles*, I.4.8–11.

164 Westminster Abbey Library: Pindar, *Olympia, Pythia, Nemea, Isthmia* (Rome, 1515) [Greek].

165 E. Ashmole, *The Antiquities of Berkshire* (3 vols, 1719), II, p. 470. Bar the last phrase, 'vado per astra Deo', the couplet is drawn from Ennius. His epigram ends with the phrase, 'Volito vivus per ora virum', which translates as 'I fly, alive on the lips of men'. Instead Elizabeth removed the pagan sentiment and added a Christian conclusion to her epitaph, which she also presents in Greek on the tomb. For Ennius, see *The Remains of Old Latin*, ed. E.H. Warmington (4 vols, 1935), I, pp. 402–3.

166 R. and H. Stephanus (eds), *Fragmenta poetarum veterum Latinorum quorum opera non extant* (Paris, 1564).

167 T. Dibdin, *An Introduction to the Knowledge of the Rare and Valuable Editions of the Greek and Latin Classics*, 4th edn. (1827), p. 366; W. Smith, *Dictionary of Greek and Roman Mythology and Biography* (1870), I, p. 572.

168 For her copies of Erasmus, see Hatfield: D. Erasmus, *De duplici copia verborum ac rerum* (1573); D. Erasmus, *Opus de conscribendis epistolis* (Antwerp, 1564).

169 Burghley House Muniments, 49/5/2. Although the reference in Burghley's list is not clear as to which edition of the text Mildred owned ('Comentarii in Aphthonii progymnasmata cum commentariis in Hermoginis Rethorica. Graece.'), it would seem likely it was Crispini's 1570 edition, *Aphthonius, Hermogenes, & Dionysius Longinus, praestantissimi artis rhetorices magistri*, published in Geneva.

170 Mack, *Elizabethan Rhetoric*, p. 27.

171 *Ibid.*, pp. 27–8.

172 S. Alford, *The Early Elizabethan Polity: William Cecil and the British Succession Crisis, 1558–1569* (Cambridge, 1998), pp. 17–20. For Mildred's political activities, see chapter 4.

173 Mack, *Elizabethan Rhetoric*, pp. 51–2.

174 Hatfield: *Castigationes ac diversae lectiones in orationes Demosthenis*, ed. V. Obsopoeus (Nuremberg, 1534) [Greek and Latin]. She must have acquired this text sometime before her husband's elevation to the peerage in 1571, as she marks her name on the title-page as Mildred Cecil.

175 Westminster School: A. Manutius, *Orationes horum rhetorum* (Venice, 1513) [Greek].

176 NA, SP 68/6, fo. 213v.

177 H. Peacham, *The Compleat Gentleman* (1634), p. 44.

178 CP 175, fo. 92r; Cicero, *De officiis*, I.i.3. Other sixteenth-century Englishwomen were also encouraged to read *De officiis*; Roger Ascham, for example, also turned to Cicero when urging Anne Herbert to improve her Latin, sending her a copy of *De officiis* in 1545. See *Ascham Letters*, p. 75.

179 Cicero, *Tusculanae disputationes*, I.xv.34.

180 Bacon, *Recreations*, p. 27.

181 For the *sententiae*, see E. McCutcheon, *Sir Nicholas Bacon's Great House Sententiae* (Amherst, Mass., 1977).

182 *Ibid.*, p. 36.

183 LPL 650, fo. 331r; Seneca, *Epistulae morales ad Lucilium*, XXV.2.

184 LPL 660, fo. 151r; Seneca, *De ira*, I.i.4.

185 Skinner, *Reason and Rhetoric*, p. 78.

186 Bacon, *Recreations*, p. 14; Horace, *Odes*, II.10. See also the commentary in Horace, *Vatis amici: Horace Odes II*, trans. D.A. West (Oxford, 1998), p. 69.

187 NA, SP 12/155, fo. 178r: 18/11/1582. Her letter to Cecil used Plato's phrase 'the orphan and the desolate', in *Laws*, XI.927.

188 Elyot, *The Book Named The Governor*, p. 39.

189 For Lady Jane Grey reading Plato, see Ascham, *The Schoolmaster*, pp. 35–6.

190 P. Dear, 'The meanings of experience', in K. Park and L. Daston (eds), *The Cambridge History of Science, III: Early Modern Science* (Cambridge, 2006), p. 107.

191 Hatfield: J. Velcurio, *Commentariorum libri iiii. In universam Aristotelis Physicen* (Lyons, 1573). Velcurio's text-book also drew upon the works of other classical authors, such as Cicero's *De natura deorum* and Aulus Gellius's *Noctae Atticae*. See L. Daston and M. Stolleis, *Natural Law and the Laws of Nature in Early Modern Europe* (Aldershot, 2008), p. 107.

192 *Ibid.*, p. 109.

193 St John's College, Oxford: Dionysius, *Antiquitatum Romanarum lib. X* (Paris, 1546–47) [Greek]; Westminster Abbey Library: Eusebius, *Ecclesiasticae historiae libri decem* (Paris, 1544) [Greek]. For the volume of Eusebius donated to Christ Church, see Burghley House Muniments, 49/5/2.

194 Burghley House Muniments, 49/5/2.

195 See J. Sandys, *A Short History of Classical Scholarship* (Cambridge, 1915), p. 217.

196 Westminster Abbey Library: F. Josephus, *Flavii Josephi Antiquitatum Judaicarum libri XX* (Basel, 1544) [Greek and Latin].

197 Windsor Castle Library: Herodotus, *Herodoti Halicarnassei Historia, sive historiarum libri IX* (Geneva, 1570) [Greek].

198 BL, Lansdowne MS 82, fo. 186r: 14/08/1596.

199 LPL 650, fo. 130r; Terence, *Eunuchus*, III.v.600. LPL 654, fo. 43r; Terence, *Phormio*, IV.i.9. Ellesmere MS EL 45; Terence, *Adelphoe*, II.iv.269.

200 H. Norland, *Drama in Early Tudor England, 1485–1558* (1995), pp. 81, 98. Thomas Elyot, however, argued that young men should be exposed to vice in ancient writers, for example Terence, so that 'they being thereof warned may prepare themself to resist or prevent occasion'. Elyot, *The Book Named The Governor*, p. 48.

201 Westminster School: Aeschylus, *Tragoediae VII* (Paris, 1557) [Greek]; Burghley House Muniments, 49/5/2.

202 BL, Lansdowne MS 82, fo. 186r: 14/08/1596.

203 CP 30, fo. 26r: 27/01/1597.

204 Logic was a central component of the university curriculum at Oxford and Cambridge during the sixteenth century, with Aristotle's *Organon* remaining a key text in the statutory requirements for the first two years of the BA degree. See E.J. Ashworth, 'Traditional logic', in C.B. Schmitt *et al.* (eds), *The Cambridge History of Renaissance Philosophy* (Cambridge, 1988), p. 143; E.J. Ashworth, 'Text-books: a case study – logic', in L. Hellinga and J.B. Trapp (eds), *The Cambridge History of the Book in Britain, III, 1400–1557* (Cambridge, 1999), p. 381; Elyot, *The Book Named The Governor*, p. 34.

205 Hatfield: Aristotle, *Organon* (Basel, 1545) [Greek], title-page.

206 Unfortunately, none of Elizabeth's letters includes her Greek hand for further authentication.

207 Hatfield: Aristotle, *Organon*, sig. A5r.

208 Hatfield: C. Valerius, *Tabulae totius dialectices* (Cologne, 1573), title-page.

209 Peter Mack notes that the *Tabulae totius dialectices* is found much more frequently in university book lists than Valerius's companion work on rhetoric, *In universam bene dicendi rationem tabula*. See Mack, *Elizabethan Rhetoric*, p. 66.

210 Colgate University Library: Euclid, *The elements of geometrie* (1570). I am grateful to Carl Peterson for providing me with images of the volume.

211 Bowden, 'The library of Mildred Cooke Cecil', 16.

212 Hatfield: Caesar, *The eyght bookes ... conteyning his martiall exploytes*, trans. A. Golding (1565).

213 P.M. Vermigli, *Most learned and fruitfull Commentaries ... upon the Epistle of S. Paul to the Romanes*, trans. H. Billingsley (1568).

214 Elyot's *The boke named the Governour* has no place for mathematics within the curriculum and the most popular textbook was Robert Recorde's extremely elementary *Arithmetick* (1540). See S. Gaukroger, *Francis Bacon and the Transformation of Early-Modern Philosophy* (Cambridge, 2001), p. 25.

215 Vives, p. 205.

216 J. Guy, *A Daughter's Love: Thomas and Margaret More* (2008), p. 67.

217 Mears, *Queenship and Political Discourse*, p. 76.

218 NA, SP 12/245, fos 36r–v: 05/1593. Another piece of evidence of Elizabeth's mathematical skill is her acceptance of calculations of the rents owed to her in the city of Carlisle, dating from December 1587, revealed by her signature to the paper. See NA, SP 12/206, fo. 117r: 05/1597.

219 Lady Grace Mildmay, for example, read John de Vigo, *The Most Excellent Worke of Chirurgerye*, trans. B. Traheson (1543) and W. Turner, *A Newe Herball* (1551). Lady Margaret Hoby's medical reading included T. Bright, *A Treatise of Melancholie* (1586) and a herbal text, probably J. Gerard, *The Herball or Generall Historie of Plantes* (1597). See L.A. Pollock, *With Faith and Physic: The Life of a Tudor Gentlewoman* (1993), pp. 97, 170; M. Hoby, *The Diary of Lady Margaret Hoby, 1599–1605*, ed. J. Moody (Stroud, 1998), pp. 18, 28. For more on early modern women and medical texts, see E. Furdell, *Publishing and Medicine in Early Modern England* (Rochester, NY, 2002), pp. 93–112.

220 Christ Church College, Oxford: Galen, *Opera omnia* (Basel, 1538) [Greek]; Galen, *Opera omnia* (Venice, 1562–63); Hatfield: Galen, *De sanitate tuenda, libri sex, Thoma Linacro Anglo interprete* (Lyons, 1559).

221 Hatfield: J. Fernel, *Medicina* (Paris, 1554). Bowden, 'The library of Mildred Cooke Cecil', p. 16. Bowden suggests that as a compilation of autopsies, Fernel's text was an 'unusual choice for a layperson not intending to practise medicine professionally'. However, his work offered a complete medical overview and was one of the most popular medical texts of the sixteenth century. See N.G. Siraisi, *History, Medicine and the Traditions of Renaissance Learning* (Ann Arbor, 2007), p. 124; J. Daintith *et al.*, *Biographical Encyclopedia of Scientists* (2 vols, Abingdon, 1994), II, p. 285.

222 CP 152, fo. 17r: 09/08/1557.

223 BL: Basil and Gregory, *Epistolae Graecae*, sig. C2v.

224 LPL 653, fo. 303r: 14/08/n.y.

225 Vives, p. 59.

226 Hatfield: G. Boccaccio, *Le Philocope* (Paris, 1555), title-page.

227 Hatfield: J. Bodin, *Les six livres de la République* (Lyons, 1580).

228 See chapter 4 below.

229 Bibliothèque Nationale, Paris (BN), Nouvelles acquisitions latines (NAL) 106. Ownership is established by the verses of Katherine Killigrew on p. 152 and by E. Gordon-Duff of the Athenaeum, Liverpool, included in an attached provenance note with the volume. As MacFarlane rightly notes, a later pencil marking on the front of the volume suggests the date of 1575, although as the text includes an epitaph on the death on Sir Nicholas Bacon, who died in 1579, this is obviously incorrect. I. MacFarlane, *Buchanan* (1981), p. 303.

230 See chapter 6 below.

231 Ballard, p. 207.

232 MacFarlane, *Buchanan*, p. 303.

233 BN, NAL 106, pp. 57–58, 121. See chapter 6 for Buchanan's verse on Mildred.

234 *Ibid.*, pp. 40–2, 80–1, 89, 95–6, 111.

235 See, for example, BN, NAL 106, pp. 88–90.

236 See, for example, BN, NAL 106, p. 12.

237 CP 298/1–5, fos 1r–47v. For the eclogues, see L. Berry, 'Five Latin poems by Giles Fletcher, the elder', *Anglia*, 79 (1962), 338–77; L. Pièpho, 'The ecclesiastical eclogues of Giles Fletcher the elder', in A. Moss *et al.* (eds), *Acta Conventus Neo-Latini Hafniensis* (Binghamton, 1994), pp. 817–29.

238 LPL 648, fo. 309r: n.d. Wyborn is also known as Wiburn.

239 BL, Lansdowne MS 82, fo. 186r: 14/08/1596.

240 For more on Harrington and Elizabeth Russell, see J. Scott-Warren, *Sir John Harrington and the Book as Gift* (Oxford, 2001), pp. 56–80.

241 Other sixteenth-century women humanists were known to have kept commonplace books, such as Thomas More's daughters and Princess Mary. See Brayman Hackel, *Reading Material*, p. 144.

Chapter 2

'Quod licuit feci':
the power of the word

> Madame, according to your request I have perused your studious labour of transla-
> tion, profitably imploied in a right commendable work ... And now to thende bothe
> to acknowledge my good approbation, and to spread the benefit more largely, where
> you[r] Ladishippe hathe sent me your boke writen, I have with most hearty thankes
> returned it to you (as you see) printed.[1]

Thus wrote Matthew Parker, archbishop of Canterbury, in a letter to 'the
right honorable learned and vertuous Ladie A.B.'. The 'Ladie' in question
is Lady Anne Bacon and the letter was appended to her translation of John
Jewel's *Apologia Ecclesiae Anglicanae*, published in 1564. At first sight, Parker's
dedicatory epistle portrays the translation as a semi-private manuscript work
by a woman, which only accidentally found its way into print. Anne's agency
as a writer seeking a public forum is therefore denied. Such an interpretation
would accord with past scholarship on female religious translations, and the
genre has often been considered as evidence of the silencing of women in
early modern literary culture. Anne's sister Elizabeth would seem to share
this view of the repression of women's opportunities with the written word.
In separate commemorative verses, she returns three times to the same line:
'Quod licuit feci, vellum mihi plura licere' (I have done what was allowed, I
wish more were allowed of me).[2]

Undoubtedly the words of both Elizabeth and Matthew Parker reveal much
about the limitations upon women's writing in this period. However this
chapter argues that, in spite of these limitations, the Cooke sisters' classical
learning allowed them opportunities with the written word, particularly
in their activities as translators and poets. Recent work on other sixteenth-
century female translators, such as Anne Locke and Mary Sidney Herbert, has
revealed their political engagement through the act of translation.[3] Through
their many religious translations, the Cooke sisters likewise sought to influence diverse audiences, never more so than with Anne's translation of the

Apologia. Whilst it was produced by a woman within a domestic setting, Anne had always envisaged a wider readership and was addressing concerns far beyond her own household in the work. Their classical language skills also allowed the sisters to advance their own priorities through verse. For Elizabeth, in particular, neo-Latin and Greek commemorative verse allowed her to express opinions she was unable to communicate through other means. The authority gained from her classical education empowered even her dramatic writing in English, a more contested form of writing for women in this period. Thus, while Elizabeth may have wished to achieve more through her writing, through close analysis of their texts it is possible to realise how much these learned sisters did in fact accomplish with the written word.

THE SISTERS AND TRANSLATION

An Apologie or answere in defence of the Churche of Englande was one of two published translation projects by Anne; the other was the translation from Italian into English of nineteen sermons by the Italian reformer, Bernardino Ochino, published in four different volumes between 1548 and 1570.[4] Her sisters Mildred and Elizabeth likewise drew on their classical language skills to translate religious texts. Mildred undertook at least two translations. One was her translation from Greek into English of St Basil's homily on Deuteronomy xv.9, 'Take hede to thy Selfe'.[5] The other, hitherto unknown, was a sermon on Isaiah.[6] She may also have translated 'a Peece of Chrisostome, out of Greeke into Englishe', and Pauline Croft has suggested that she was involved in the translation of the 1572 revision of the Bishops' Bible.[7] Elizabeth published a translation of John Ponet's *Diallacticon* in 1605.[8]

Religious translation has long been perceived as the most acceptable way in which early modern Englishwomen could engage with print culture; Richard Greaves has shown that before 1650 most religious works published by women were in the form of translations.[9] It has been suggested that translation was seen as an appropriate task for women in this period because it was thought of as a 'defective' and 'degraded' activity, involving only 'the "simple" transmission of the words and thoughts of others – usually men – from language to language in such a way that the direct agency of the translator was thought to be minimal'.[10] As an activity, therefore, translation has been characterised as a primary stage in women's progression towards more independent and sophisticated literary expression.[11] Previous critical considerations of Anne's translation of the *Apologia*, focusing primarily on Parker's epistle appended to the tract, have therefore viewed it as another example of the silencing of women's voices within a patriarchal society. Mary Ellen Lamb characterised it as only a work of 'transliteration' of the original male author, concluding that 'Jewel's

Apologie for the Church of England ... carried too much official weight to allow tampering'.[12] Alan Stewart has declared that Anne Bacon had no independent voice in her translations, only a doubled voice with 'whatever man she was translating'.[13] The other translations by the sisters have received little critical attention at all.[14]

Of the sisters, Anne alone established a reputation for herself as a translator before her marriage. In the late 1540s she translated a wide selection of the sermons of Bernardino Ochino, the Italian evangelical preacher exiled in England since 1547. Anne's translation of five of Ochino's sermons appeared anonymously in London in 1548, around the same time as Princess Elizabeth was also translating another of his sermons; Ochino, only recently arrived in England, was attracting considerable attention.[15] In the same year, Richard Argentine's translation of another six sermons of the Italian reformer was published by Anthony Scholoker in Ipswich.[16] The comparative fortunes of Richard Argentine and Anne illustrate the latter's emerging status as a godly female translator. Later in 1548, Anthony Scholoker moved to London and went into partnership with William Seres. It may have been through Seres that Argentine's translation came to the attention of the publisher John Day, who was a frequent partner of Seres. In 1551, John Day published two editions of Ochino's sermons. One was an anonymous amalgamation of both Anne and Argentine's earlier published translations which also included fourteen newly translated sermons by Anne.[17] To this edition was appended the prefatory epistle which had preceded Argentine's earlier Ipswich translation of six of Ochino's sermons. Argentine's epistle was altered in only one way between 1548 and 1551. To the latter was added the line 'I have translated vi of hys Sermons out of hys toung in to Englysh. Intending to translate the rest very shortely if these shalbe thankefully received."[18] At some point Argentine's earlier letter had been altered, to state explicitly that he was offering six translated sermons, presumably in preparation for a new London printing. Yet what was actually offered in that edition was twenty-five sermons, the six by Argentine and nineteen by Anne Cooke, comprising both her earlier five printed sermons and fourteen newly translated sermons. The suggestion is surely that Anne's translations came to the attention of Day after the prefatory epistle by Argentine had been typeset.

It is striking that in the same year Day also separately published Anne's fourteen new sermons, which dealt with the more explicitly Calvinist elements of Ochino's theology.[19] This time they were published under Anne's own name, with a prefatory epistle by 'G.B.' pleading its special position as a female-authored translation and a dedicatory epistle by Anne to her mother.[20] We can speculate as to why Anne's fourteen translated sermons appeared first anonymously and then under her own name. It may be that the second group of sermons translated by Anne had initially circulated in manuscript and then had been printed in the anonymous 1551 edition without her knowledge; however, that would seem unlikely, given that Day was a close associate of William Cecil, Anne's brother-in-law, and that he later also collaborated with her brother, William Cooke, on the Michael Wood press in 1553–54.[21] It is more plausible that Anne's authorship was stressed in the second 1551 edition to highlight support for Ochino within influential circles at the Edwardian court, including William Cecil, which pushed for further religious reform.[22] This interpretation is borne out by the subject matter of the two sets of sermons. The difference between the sermons translated by Anne and published in 1548 and the next fourteen sermons, published in 1551, is a more explicit engagement with the Calvinist theology of predestination. Anne's five 1548 sermons were translated from the first book of Ochino's published Italian sermons, his *Prediche*, and they contained a few references to election and reprobation.[23] The pastoral ramifications of the Calvinist doctrine were, however, at the heart of Anne's next set of translations, drawn from the later sermons in the second book of the *Prediche*.[24] Day published a later edition of Ochino's sermons in 1570, appending the same dedicatory material highlighting Anne's authorship, but this edition also anonymously included Richard Argentine's original six sermons.[25] Richard Argentine's anonymity in 1570 would certainly have been influenced by his characterisation in the 1570 edition of Foxe's *Actes and Monuments* as a previous evangelical turned enthusiastic conformist and persecutor of his former brethren under Mary.[26]

When Anne's authorship was so clearly appended to the later 1551 version of the sermons, she was as yet unmarried to Nicholas Bacon, although her sister's husband, William Cecil, may have been an influential patron in the advancement of her translations. The prefatory epistle by 'G.B.' to the 1551 edition of Anne's fourteen sermons certainly highlighted concerns about translation by an unmarried woman, revealing the contemporary prejudices against women's writing in this form. G.B. writes that 'pretty pryckemydautes shal happen to spy amote in thys godly labour ... seynge it is meeter for Docters of divinitye to meddle wyth such matters then Meydens'.[27] All the sisters' other extant translations date from the years after their marriages; adopting wifely roles did not act as a brake on their scholarly activities. Admittedly, Elizabeth published her translation, *A Way of Reconciliation*, in 1605, far into her second widowhood. It is likely, however, that the work actually dated from the early Elizabethan period, placing it closer to Anne's publication of the *Apologie* in 1564. Elizabeth herself suggested that the translation was written at an earlier date, for her dedicatory epistle stated that if she did not seek publication herself, the manuscript copy already in circulation would be printed after her death, to the 'wrong of the dead'.[28] It is the identity of 'the dead', the deceased author of the original tract, that is central to the earlier dating of the piece, for Elizabeth added that the author 'in his life approved my Translation with his owne allowance'.[29] Her understanding of the author of the piece was based on previous editions of the tract, in Latin and then in French, which she mentioned in her preface. The author of the Latin original was John Ponet, who wrote the treatise as a Marian exile on the Continent.[30] It is likely, however, that Elizabeth did not believe Ponet to be the author; instead she thought her father had produced the work whilst in Strasbourg. Anthony Cooke bought Ponet's library from his widow in 1557 and thus he acquired the text on the Eucharist.[31] The Latin tract was then edited by Cooke and printed in Strasbourg.[32] The piece was published anonymously as the work of a 'viri boni et literati' (a good and learned man), possibly because Ponet's *Short Treatise of Politic Power*, published the year before in Strasbourg, was the first book by an English reformer advocating regicide.[33] It is suggestive that a French version was published in 1566, the same year that Elizabeth was in Paris with her ambassador husband, Thomas Hoby, which also attributed the work to Anthony Cooke.[34] Elizabeth's belief that her father was the author of the original tract is also demonstrated by a letter she sent in 1605, accompanying the copy of her translation, to her nephew Robert Cecil, recently elevated to the earldom of Salisbury: 'And in token yowr grandfather and moother's father doth thank your Lordship for so muche Honoring his Cooke's Blood. He hath sent yow by me his Daughter, your Lordship's owld Awnt, a Booke of his owne making in Germany, in the tyme of his pilgrimage.'[35] Thus, if Elizabeth believed that her father wrote the treatise, then her statement that the author had 'in his life approved my Translation with his owne allowance' means that the translation must have been completed between the publication of the Latin tract in 1557, most likely after Anthony Cooke's return to England in 1558, and his death in 1576.[36] It seems likely that Elizabeth completed the translation either during her first or second marriage, or perhaps during her first period of widowhood. Marriage therefore did not put an end to the sisters' scholarly pursuits. In fact, their extant translations reveal the opportunities offered to the sisters and their husbands through their acts of religious translation.

For Mildred, her translation of St Basil's homily on Deuteronomy was on one level the act of a suitor, attempting to repay her patron. In dedicating the work to Anne Seymour, the duchess of Somerset, Mildred describes herself as a 'humble servant & dettor', offering 'these fewe leaves thus by me translatyd to move your goodnes ether to take them as some small parte of my service I owe, or insted of some meane frend to intreat for my dett'. The gift was copied out by Mildred herself, in a careful italic hand on finely ruled lines. The early translations of the sisters' contemporary, Princess Elizabeth, were likewise produced for presentation purposes, in her case as New Year's gifts.[37]

Primarily, however, the act of translation was for the sisters a means of strengthening the reformed faith, a way of contributing to 'the chirche of the living god', as Mildred translated Basil's words in his sermon on Deuteronomy xv.9.[38] In her prefatory letter to her first printed translation of Ochino's sermons, Anne wrote that she had undertaken this activity 'for the enformacion of all that desyre to know the truth for they truely conteyne moch to the defacyng of al papistrie, and hipocrysie, and to the advancement of the glorye of God, and the beneftyes of Christ Jesus'.[39] Such aims were only magnified by the more Calvinist content of the second set of Ochino's sermons translated by Anne. Elizabeth chose to translate John Ponet's tract, *Diallacticon*, which had aimed to mediate in the conflict within the Protestant Churches over the nature of Christ's presence in the Eucharist. The work was an endorsement of the Calvinist and Zwinglian position.[40] The subject matter of *A Way of Reconciliation* thus supports the earlier dating of Elizabeth's translation to the period between 1558 and 1576, close to Anne's completion of her *Apologie* and probably closer to 1558, when such topics were still widely debated. Anne's translation of the *Apologie* had admitted that there was dissension between the Lutheran and Zwinglian conceptions of the Eucharist: 'They vary not betwixt themselves upon the principles and foundacions of oure religion ... upon one onely question, whiche is neither weightie nor great: neither mistrust we or make doubte at all, but they will shortely be agreed.'[41] Elizabeth's translation thus attempted to answer the one moot point admitted in Jewel's defence of the Church of England; from its conception, Elizabeth seems to have seen her work as a companion piece to her sister's translation of the *Apologia*.

It is the purpose of Anne's translation of the *Apologia* that appears most opaque at first sight. Matthew Parker's prefatory letter to the translation makes many claims about Anne's intentions for her work that have too long been accepted without questioning. Firstly, Parker suggests that Anne's act of translation was essentially conceived as a semi-private act, that she intended her translation for only a very limited readership. He writes of receiving Anne's manuscript translation, saying that 'Whereof for that it liked you to make me a Judge, and for that the thinge it selfe hath singularly pleased my judgement, and delighted my mind in reading it, I have right heartely to thanke your Ladieship, both for youre owne well thinking of me, and for the comforte that it hathe wrought me.'[42] He then tells Anne that he has also sent the manuscript to the 'chiefe author of the Latine work', John Jewel, the bishop of Salisbury, for perusal.[43] Parker's narrative finishes by suggesting that he has had this manuscript version of Anne's translation published, without her knowledge, stating that such action was necessary 'to prevent suche excuses as your modestie woulde have made in staye of publishinge it'.[44]

There are many elements of this narrative that do not ring true. Firstly, it fails to acknowledge that Anne would have been fully aware of female scribal publication of translations in this period; even in manuscript form, Anne would have intended her translation to find a wide readership. Past research has tended to draw too sharp a distinction between private and public writing, aligning manuscript with the former, whilst print is seen as a public medium.[45] Anne would have drawn no such distinction. Her sister Mildred had already completed her manuscript translation of St Basil's homily on Deuteronomy xv.9 around 1550 and through its dedication to Anne Stanhope Seymour it was likely to have then been circulated through the duchess's courtly circle, in a manner similar to Katherine Parr's manuscript of *The Lamentation of a Sinner* around three years earlier.[46]

Even admitting that Anne would have been aware of scribal circulation of her translation, the argument that she did not seek publication of her work has to be regarded as a trope of modesty, rather than an accurate statement of intent. The editor of Anne's second set of translated sermons similarly suggested that the act of publication was against her will, arguing that as a 'vertuouse meyden ... her shamfastnes would rather have supprest theym, had I to whose handes they were commytted, halfe agaynst her wyll, put them fourth'.[47] This is manifestly untrue, given that in Anne's earlier version of Ochino's sermons from 1548 her prefatory epistle stated that she intended to translate more of Ochino's sermons thereafter.[48]

It therefore is extremely unlikely that Anne's work on the translation was simply a happy coincidence later utilised by Parker. This underestimates both Anne's personal awareness of the initial intentions for the Latin *Apologia* and the significance of a vernacular translation. The original production of the Latin *Apologia* had been overseen from its genesis by members of Anne's circle. Faced with the forthcoming papal Council of Trent, the initial idea for the *Apologia* was conceived at a meeting attended by both Anne's husband, Nicholas Bacon, and her brother-in-law William Cecil.[49] It was Cecil who then commissioned John Jewel, the bishop of Salisbury, to write two defences of the Church of England.[50] The first was an anonymous letter to be published on the Continent and designed to appear as if written by a lay Englishman; the second was the *Apologia*.[51] Published in 1562 for a foreign, scholarly audience, the *Apologia* justified the secession from Catholicism using scriptural and patristic sources.

The national significance of the text was immediately perceived, with an anonymous English translation also being published in 1562.[52] Parker's dedicatory letter makes no specific reference to this earlier translation, although he does allude to the unwillingness of both Jewel and himself to have this important work 'not truly and wel translated'; he similarly applauds Anne's 'cleare translation', as it frees the original *Apologia* from the 'perrils of ambiguous and doubtful constructions'.[53] The suggestion is that the 1562 English translation was flawed, and this explanation is still accepted by scholars.[54] The conclusion is, however, unsubstantiated by analysis of the text. The 1562 version is a largely literal translation. So why, then, did Anne decide to do another translation and why was it presented as a largely serendipitous act by Matthew Parker? I would agree with Alan Stewart that the presentation of Anne and her act of translation in the dedicatory letter is a deliberate framing device, designed to obscure any suggestion that this translation fulfilled official needs.[55] But I would also suggest that it is important to go further and to ask what exactly were these needs, unfulfilled by the earlier translation and designed to be met by Anne's work? By returning to her actual translation, it becomes apparent that it is far from being simply a private, domestic act of translation. Instead it was intended to provide a creed for the Church of England, written for a wide readership in plain English.

Comparison between an original work and its translation is illuminating, as sixteenth-century translators carefully considered their methods of translation. In his *Interpretatio linguarum* (1559), Laurence Humphrey suggests that the least desirable type of translation is the purely literal, word-for-word method, followed by translations which are too loose, which he believes are too self-indulgent. He argues that the most desirable type of translation is one which falls between the two extremes, considering both the words in question and the spirit of the passage.[56] Charting the choices made by the sisters in their translations allows an insight into their priorities for the works and, in particular, reveals Anne's intentions with her *Apologie*.

The vast majority of the sisters' translations are close renderings, either word-for-word or phrase-for-phrase. Mildred appended a statement regarding her own method of translation to her version of St Basil's sermon on Deuteronomy xv.9:

> I have somwhat superstitiously observid the nature of the greke phrase, not omittyng the congruety of english speche but rather the use, that the treatye of so good an Author shold not in so moch serving the english tonge lese his owne efficacies & value. thynkyng it lesse faute that thautor sholde speake grekish english and save his owne sence, than english greke and confound it with a doubtfull. in this sheweng the propertie of the tonge, in the other the veritie of the matter.[57]

Mildred argues that the translator should prefer scrupulous accuracy of translation to fluency in the English language. Mildred's translation of St Basil's homily therefore remains close to the original text at all times and only very rarely uses words which reflect contemporary practices, such as translating references to the state as the 'commonwealth'.[58]

Elizabeth too remained close to the original text with her translation of Ponet's *Diallacticon*. She used *A Way of Reconciliation* as a platform for her own biblical translation, but her aim was to experiment with the closest translation of the Latin version of Scripture, not to offer a looser translation. For example, she tries different translations of John vi.63 in her text, which Ponet had quoted in Latin.[59] She variously translates 'vivificat', stating once that 'It is the Spirit that giveth life', followed by 'It is the Spirit that quickeneth'.[60] All of the published Bible translations that Elizabeth would have had available to her translate 'vivificat' as 'quickeneth', thus Elizabeth was here suggesting her own contribution to the accuracy of scriptural translation.[61] Her translation of John vi.56 follows a similar pattern. All the vernacular Bible translations of Elizabeth's day offer 'He that eateth my flesh, and drinketh my blood, dwelleth in me, and I in him'.[62] Elizabeth, however, rejected 'dwelleth' as a translation of 'manet', instead suggesting the more classically accurate 'remaineth in mee' and 'abideth in me'.[63] Her aim was continually to explore the accuracy and clarity of the scriptural translation, testing which words were most effective in conveying meaning to her audience.[64]

Elizabeth's translations reveal that she was aware of the wider intellectual debate regarding the accuracy of translation, particularly biblical translation. More's attack on Tyndale's New Testament centred on the latter's use of non-traditional terms, one of which was the translation of 'ecclesia' as 'congregation', whereas More felt that 'church' was the correct term.[65] Elizabeth offers different translations of the Latin 'ecclesia', using both 'congregation' and 'church' with an awareness of their different implications. Elizabeth interprets Ponet's discussion of St Augustine as 'there is a great difference betweene the mysterie of the body and blood of Christ which is now received of the faithfull in the Congregation, and that body which was borne of the Virgin Mary', whereas two pages earlier she concludes the discussion of St Ambrose's writings stating that 'he applieth it to the mysterie which is now ministered in the Church'.[66]

The only clear addition of her own text to the work is the insertion of a comment on Clement of Alexandria: 'To this purpose maketh also that which Clemens Alexandrinus, schoolemaster to Origen, teacheth in his booke, entitled Paedagogus, when he saith διττον ἐστὶ τὸ αἶμα τοῦ Χριστοῦ· τὸ μὲν σαρκικὸν, δἰ οὗ ἐλυτράθημεν· τὸ δὲ πνεθματικὸν, ᾧ κεχρίσμεθα. The blood of Christ is two maner of ways: the one fleshie whereby we are washed, the other spirtuall wherewith we have bene anointed.'[67] Elizabeth's contribution amplified Ponet's existing explication of the patristic understanding of Christ's physical and spiritual presence. Whilst this was an addition to Ponet's original, it fitted with the text so well that its presence has not been noted until now.

Anne's translation of Ochino's sermons also remains close to the original text. This must primarily be explained by the fact that the original was a contemporary work. Therefore, the desire to embellish the original text, so prevalent in sixteenth-century translators, is unnecessary.[68] Ochino's highly adjectival style is rendered accurately by Anne. For example, his original line, 'imo per il peccato d'Adamo, siamo maculati, infetti, infermi, fragilli, ciechi, maligni, pieni di veneno, a Dio contrarii, inimici et rebelli' is translated as 'By the sinne of Adam we were all defyled, infected, infirme, frayle, blynde, malignaunte, full of venum, contrary to god, enemies and rebels.'[69] Colloquial phrases used by Anne originated in Ochino's work, for example his 'un batter d'occhio' is rendered as a 'twinke of an eye'.[70] The only variations are the addition of the odd doublet or nod towards English circumstances.

Yet, if all the sisters' other translations are close renderings of the original texts, including Anne's translations of Ochino, how then do we explain the fame of her language in her translation of the *Apologia*? C.S. Lewis, in his volume on sixteenth-century literature, only briefly discusses Anne's work, yet he comes to the following conclusion: 'Anne Lady Bacon deserves more praise than I have space to give her ... Again and again she finds the phrase which, once she has found it, we feel to be inevitable ... If quality without bulk were enough, Lady Bacon might be put forward as the best of all sixteenth-century translators.'[71] Lewis highlights several of Anne's phrases for particular praise, such as translating 'quidam ex asseclis et parasitis' as 'one of his soothing pages and clawebackes' and 'magnum silentium' as 'all mum, not a word'.[72] I would suggest that Lewis is quite right in praising Anne's use of language in her translation: it is extraordinarily vivid. Yet I argue that such vividness is consciously sought for and employed in her translation; that far from using 'inevitable' phrases, as Lewis terms them, they are in fact actively selected to advance Anne's own priorities through the act of translation. In order to demonstrate this, I have compared the translation with the original text, seeking to analyse the language Anne used and any deviations from the original Latin work; this task is made easier due to the existence of the other contemporary translation into English of the *Apologia*, completed two years before Anne's work in 1562, although finding a much more limited distribution.

In the *Apologia*, Anne abandons the close translation of her earlier works and indeed those of her sisters. This accords with the approach of another learned female contemporary. Princess Elizabeth's usual method of translation was, in her words, 'to translate it word for word', yet on occasion she would modify the sense of the original, in order to make it accord more fully with her own beliefs: religious, political or social.[73] This, too, is the practice Anne exploits in her translation of the *Apologia*.

TRANSLATING THE *APOLOGIA*

Anne's first departure from Jewel's original occurs on the title-page and makes clear her didactic intentions for the translation. Jewel's title, *Apologia Ecclesiae Anglicanae*, is expanded to read *An Apologie or answere in defence of the Churche of Englande, with a briefe and plaine declaration of the true Religion professed and used in the same.* Whether Anne herself entitled the printed edition is unclear, but the additional second clause accurately sums up the intent of her following translation: this work will offer 'a briefe and plaine declaration' of the tenets of the Church of England.

This objective is made clear by Anne's only other addition of an extra line of her own text to the translation. From Jewel's original 'Credimus ergo unam quandam naturam esse & vim Divinam, quam appellamus Deum', translated in the 1562 version as 'We beleve therfore that ther is one divine nature & power, which we do cal GOD', Anne interpolates two lines:[74]

This therefore is oure Belieffe.
We beleeve that there is one certaine nature and divine Power, whiche wee call God.[75]

Anne's extra line is inserted to signal the end of the introductory section of the *Apologie* and emphasises what for her is the most important section of the work: the creed of the Church of England.

Jewel had already suggested the credal nature of the second section of his Latin tract, by beginning the first four paragraphs of this part with the verb 'Credimus'.[76] While this echoes, in the plural, the first word of the Apostles' and Nicene creeds, it should be remembered that Jewel's tract was aimed at a hostile Continental audience. The *Apologia Eccelesiae Anglicanae* was designed to respond to Catholic accusations that Protestantism caused division and faction. The *Apologia* was therefore written to prove to a Continental audience that the clergy of the Church of England was united in belief and in loyalty to the Queen; it was a strong declaration of doctrinal unity.[77] 'Credimus' therefore has a very different significance within the Latin work. Moreover, while Jewel does initially highlight the role of this section of his *Apologia* by his unusual word order, he then returns to usual Latinate structure, where such verbs are incorporated into the sentence or omitted from the doctrinal discussions. Anne, translating for a native audience, instead continually uses this structure, prefacing sentences with affirmative statements, even when Jewel's original does not include such verbs.

A comparison of the 1562 translation on the conception of the sacraments, which is largely a literal translation of Jewel's original, with Anne's version, will reveal the latter's insistence on affirmative group statements. The earlier version places its emphasis on the subject, the sacraments, in direct translation of the original Latin, beginning 'Of the sacraments which are proprely to be reckened under that name, we do acknowledge twoe'.[78] Anne's line not only begins with a group assertion, but also includes an additional affirmation of belief: 'Besides wee acknowledge there be two sacraments, which *wee judge* properly ought to be called by this name'.[79] Jewel's text and the 1562 translation then discuss the sacrament of baptism without even prefacing it as a collective statement.[80] Anne's version instead continually reiterates the group belief, stating '*We saye* that Babtisme is a sacrament for the remission of sinnes, and of that washing which *we have* in the blood of Christ'.[81] Anne's approach in this passage, including almost double the number of repetitions of group belief as compared with Jewel's treatise and the 1562 translation, is adopted throughout the credal section of her translation.

The credal emphasis in Anne's translation reveals her grasp of issues far beyond the domestic setting in which she produced her text. It reflects the major challenge faced by the nascent Church of England during that period:

the task of ensuring the preaching of the new Church's message to the laity. During the 1560s and 1570s the provision of religious instruction in England became particularly pressing. There was a dearth of preachers in the Elizabethan Church that was not filled until the early Stuart period.[82] The evangelical preacher Edward Dering described the effects of the preaching dearth at this time, arguing that 'Scarce one of a great many can give an accompt of their faith'.[83] The English translation of the *Apologia* offered by Anne could therefore be used to fulfil this lack of preaching, to provide a creed for the Church of England. The centrality Anne affords the credal element in her translation is in keeping with episcopal thinking at the time. By 1563, the year before Anne's translation was published, there were calls from within the Church of England for the *Apologia* to be disseminated for a native audience. In preparation for the Convocation of 1563, Edmund Grindal, the bishop of London, suggested that articles of doctrine should be drawn out of the *Apologia* by royal authority. Matthew Parker further thought that the *Apologia* should be appended to the Articles of Religion, the two in one book, 'by common assent to be authorised, as containing the true doctrine'.[84] But their intentions for the *Apologia* were not officially met and the Thirty-Nine Articles, as the Convocation's confession of faith, did not fulfil the same role; they did not adopt a credal structure and, moreover, were not available in the vernacular until they were endorsed by Parliament in 1571.

It is also possible that Anne's credal guidance was inspired by a Continental model. The opening of Bullinger's *Decades* was an existing example of an expositional text anchored in the creeds.[85] Anne's father, Anthony Cooke, was a close friend of Bullinger whilst in exile and the men corresponded after Cooke's return to England.[86] Cooke praised Bullinger for his continuing advice concerning the fledging Church of England, which he treated 'like a nurse who cherishes her children ... anxious that no evil should hurt us', and it may be that Anne was introduced to Bullinger's credal model through her father.[87] Whatever the inspiration, it is clear that Anne intended her translation to compensate for the laity's lack of spiritual direction in this period, by expounding the creed of the Church of England.

The credal function that Anne envisaged for her translation is also demonstrated by her extremely close translation of the theological terms of the tract, as well as the text's awareness of a potential oral dissemination. The tropes of early modern preachers are repeatedly used within her translation. Thus the 1562 version closely follows Jewel in beginning the third section of work with 'These be those heresies for the which a good parte of the world is condemned at this daye, unheard'.[88] Anne, however, begins this section of the translation with the following words: 'Beholde these are the horrible heresies for the whiche a good parte of the world is at this day condemned by the Byshop of Rome, and yet were never hearde to pleade their cause'.[89] Anne not only develops the entire secondary clause out of Jewel's original word 'inaudita', but she also uses the verbal trait, 'Beholde', absent in Jewel's work and the 1562 version. The 1562 version similarly offers a literal translation of Jewel's line, 'This is the power of darkenes'; Anne instead again incorporates verbal traits in her version, writing 'This, lo ye, is the power of the darkenes'.[90] The potential oral dissemination of the work is also reflected in the absence of marginal translations, which in Anne's version are incorporated into the text, in contrast to the 1562 translation. This was a common technique for spoken tracts; Jewel used the same method within his 'Challenge Sermon', his oral rehearsal of the *Apologia*.[91] Thus Anne's language suggests that she intended her translation from the outset to have an oral quality, borrowing the persuasive tropes of sixteenth-century preachers and employing language not normally used by women in a household setting.

Anne also engages with contemporary theories of translation in order to make her text more convincing to a wider readership, again highlighted by her extended title. There she states that the work will be a 'plaine declaration', revealing her awareness of the national and largely masculine debate about the purity of the English tongue. Many of Anne's contemporaries felt that English was a poor language in comparison with the classical tongues, or even the current romance languages. Thomas Haward in the preface to his translation of Eutropius, also published in 1564, compared the 'puritye of the Greke and Latine toungues' with the 'barbarousnesse' of English.[92] The main criticism was of the limited vocabulary which English offered translators. One response to this was to appropriate terms from other languages, as demonstrated by Thomas Elyot's *The boke named The Governour*.[93] Yet some also condemned such techniques for needlessly diluting a perfectly adequate vernacular; Thomas Wilson deemed such appropriations 'ynkehorne termes'.[94]

Anne reveals her own allegiance in this debate by using Old and Middle English words, as well as colloquialisms, to give an authentically 'English' feel to her translation. Parker's dedicatory letter reveals a contemporary recognition of Anne's stance, by stating that her translation has 'defended the good fame and estimation of your owne native tongue, shewing it so able to contend with a worke originally written in the most praised speache'.[95] Anne thus turns to words with Old English origins when addressing her readership as 'folk', with the beliefs of the Roman Catholic Church referred to as 'tales'.[96] C.S. Lewis praised Anne's translation of 'parasiti' as 'clawebackes', but her use of this word is again dictated by its Old English origins. Similarly, the Middle English 'huckermucker' is offered as her translation of Jewel's 'dissumulanter', rather than the Middle French choice of 'colorably' in the 1562 version.[97]

The use of this lexicography is calculated to give her translation a native feel, as is her reliance on colloquialisms. Whereas the 1562 version translates one of Jewel's lines as 'Sworde and Fyer they have had alwayes at hande: but of olde Councels and Fathers no worde at all', Anne instead turned to more informal language, writing that as 'for the olde Councels and the fathers, al mum, not a word'; this was another phrase noted by C.S. Lewis for particular praise.[98] Similarly, Anne translates that 'God will not suffer him selfe to be mad a mocking stock' by the Roman Catholic Church, again turning to language in contemporary parlance to push home her message more forceably.[99]

One of the most significant contemporary advocates of 'plain English' was John Cheke. His programme for the English language was that 'our own tung shold be written cleane and pure and unmangeled with the borrowing of other tunges'.[100] Cheke's translation of the gospel of Matthew was thus marked by conscious Anglicisations, such as 'hundreder' instead of centurion.[101] Anne would have had first-hand contact with this theory at many points. Her father, Sir Anthony Cooke, was a tutor to Edward VI alongside Cheke, and a 1541 translation of St Cyprian by Cooke reveals that at this early date he was already eschewing eloquence in favour of simple language, suggesting a later nexus of opinion with Cheke. In the dedication to his translation, Cooke argued for the superiority of Cyprian's linguistic style, for he 'attended not so moche to the perswadyng wordes of manys wysedom', in comparison with Chrysostom, who is 'moche in the apparell of wordes'.[102] Anne's husband and two of her brothers-in-law, Thomas Hoby and William Cecil, were part of Cheke's circle at Cambridge and Cheke appended his statement on 'plain English' to Thomas Hoby's 1561 translation of *The courtyer*.

This is not the only technique Anne uses to make her translation more persuasive, for the classical rhetoric which formed part of her childhood education is also revealed as an influence upon her work. The use of verbal ornamentation was advised by rhetorical manuals to amplify the emotional persuasion of a text. Anne thus adds force, for example, to her argument through the use of doublets, the repetition of nouns. The 1562 version offered the literal translation of the phrase, 'without lawe, without example', yet it is amplified in Anne's text to 'without any exaumple, & utterly without lawe or righte'.[103] Anne's humanist training meant that she would have fully under-stood the power of verbal tropes. Yet even her use of rhetoric in her translation has a particularly English interpretation. Alliterative repetition was seen as a stylistic vice by classical and Continental Renaissance rhetoricians; Susen-brotus called the practice 'ludicrous'.[104] Many English rhetoricians, however, felt that alliteration suited their native language. George Puttenham thus praised the sparing use of alliteration, as did Henry Peacham, who argued that it made 'the sentence more ready for the tongue and more pleasing for the ear'.[105] Thus, translating for an English audience, Anne frequently turns to alliteration to make her message more persuasive. The Pope therefore tells 'fonde fables' in Anne's translation, whilst his abbots are his 'deere darlinges' and the canonists are the 'Pope's parasites', all phrases designed to appeal to an English audience far beyond Anne's own household.[106]

There is, however, a final way in which Anne imposes her personal agency on the translation. The importance of the character of 'Ladie A.B.' to the *Apologie* is established through the dedicatory epistle from Parker. There he makes clear 'the honour ye have done to the kinde of women and to the degree of Ladies', recommending Anne for commendation by the Queen and as an example to all womankind; Jewel, on the other hand, is not named on the title-page and only alluded to by Parker as the 'chiefe author of the Latine worke'.[107] In the later editions of Anne's translation, from 1600 and 1635, the title is appended to read *Published by the most reverend Father in God, John Juell, Bishop of Sarisbury* and these versions are not prefaced by the epistle to Anne.[108]

Anne, therefore, is an important figure in framing the 1564 translation and she builds upon this identification to establish an authorial presence within the work, not in Jewel's original text. The initial use of the first person pronoun 'I' comes swiftly in the second sentence of Anne's work and is inserted by her, in contrast to Jewel's abstract question:

> It hath been an olde complaint ... that the Truth wandereth here and there as a straunger in the world, & doth redily fynde enemies and slaunderers amongst those that knowe her not. Albeit perchaunce this may seeme unto some a thinge harde to bee beleeved, *I meane* to suche as have scante well and narowly taken heed thereunto.[109]

From the very beginning of her translation, Anne emphasises the role of the author, highlighting the personal nature of this defence of the Church of England and its condemnation of the papacy. Anne repeatedly establishes an authorial presence, for example incorporating individual questions and pleas into the text. Literally translating Jewel's text, the 1562 translation asks this question of the Roman Catholic Church: 'But of so many and so grosse errors, what error have these menne purged at any time?'[110] Anne's version instead makes the phrase into a direct question: 'But yet *tell me*, of so manye and grosse errours, what one have these men at anye time refourmed?'[111] Where the 1562 version, again literally translating Jewel, asks the papacy for written proof of its arguments, saying 'For wher did Zvinkfelde ever write them?', Anne instead adds in a personal appeal: 'For *tell me* where hath Zwenkfeldius ever written them?'[112] The persona of the 'Ladie A.B.' may be designed to distract attention from the wider aims of this translation, but it is a persona that Anne exploits to its fullest within her text.

Anne's achievement with her translation of the *Apologia* is remarkable, especially considering the readership reached by her words. In the years after the publication of this translation, John Jewel and the Catholic Thomas Harding engaged in a bitter debate, both using Anne's text as the basis of their arguments; it was therefore printed again as the core text in Jewel's 1567 *The Defence of the Apologie of the Church of England*. Throughout the 1570s there were moves from within the episcopate to make the *Defence* a requisite item in all parishes.[113] In 1609 the *Works* of Jewel were published in one volume, so that every parish church should have a copy, again including Anne's translation within the *Defence*.[114] Furthermore, Catholic polemists were clear on the public importance of Anne's act of translation. Richard Verstegan acknowledged Anne's role as translator in his 1592 *A Declaration of True Causes*, perceiving it as part of William Cecil and Nicholas Bacon's Machiavellian 'plot and fortification of this newe erected synagog'.[115] Yet Anne's success in engaging with and responding to national issues through her rendering of the *Apologia* should not entirely overshadow her earlier translations of Ochino's sermons, nor the translations of her sisters. For all the sisters, translation was a genre through which, in varying ways, they could use their classical language skills to strengthen 'the chirche of the living god', never more so than with Anne's *Apologie*.[116]

VERSE AND CLASSICAL COMMEMORATION

If their classical education allowed the sisters to engage with issues of contemporary importance through the genre of translation, it also enabled them to exploit the potential of poetry written in Latin and Greek. The presentation of verse within a patronage society, such as that of early modern England, was a potent act by a client or intermediary. The sisters' knowledge of Latin and Greek imbued their verse with an additional level of distinction and persuasive power in a society in which classical languages denoted additional authority. As we will see, all the sisters wrote Latin and Greek verses in support of the Italian physician Bartholo Sylva in 1572, yet Katherine and, in particular, Elizabeth, also used neo-classical verse to advance their individual priorities.[117] Although little now survives of Katherine Cooke Killigrew's activities, there is evidence that she exchanged verses with the neo-Latin poet George Buchanan. These verses have, however, received no scholarly attention until now, yet they shed light on the opportunities offered to her by the creation of Latin verse. In one she describes Buchanan as the 'Delitiae alterius mi Buchanane mei'(my dear Buchanan, the delight of my other half).[118] The other has a similar theme: 'Qui Buchanane meo te dicit nomine salvum/ Illum mox iubeas rite valere precor' (I pray that you may duly bid farewell to the man who greets you, Buchanan, by my name).[119] The verses testify to the close relationship between the Killigrews and Buchanan, yet there is more to them. Katherine's husband, Henry Killigrew, and Buchanan may have met upon the latter's visit to England, around 1563–64, but they certainly became friends upon Killigrew's embassy to Scotland between 1572 and 1575.[120] Killigrew's task with his embassy was to seek peace between the regency government in Scotland and the supporters of Mary Stewart. Buchanan was an influential figure in the regency party and the friendship with the Scottish humanist would have been important for Killigrew's mission. In that light, Katherine's verses are not only evidence of a literary relationship between her and the Scottish poet, but also evidence that she attempted to bolster her husband's political networks through her poetical abilities. Katherine was able to draw on the educational background that she shared with Buchanan in order to imbue her verse with particular persuasive power. As we will see, Katherine likewise turned to neo-Latin verse when attempting to influence her sister Mildred to intervene with her husband, William Cecil, to prevent Henry Killigrew being sent on another diplomatic mission.[121]

Neo-Latin and Greek verse was a particularly potent form of communication for Katherine's sister Elizabeth. She celebrated the elevation of her nephew Robert Cecil to the chancellorship of the duchy of Lancaster on 8 October 1597 through verse. The position conferred considerable influence as a patron.[122] On 22 October she sent Robert the following stanza:

> Quid voveat dulci nutricula magis alumno
> Quam sapere et fari posse quae sentiat et cui;
> Gratia fama valetudo contingat abunde
> Et mundus victus non deficiente crumena.
> Gloria Patri Filio et Spiritui Sancto.[123]
>
> (What more may a nurse wish for her sweet nursling
> Than to be wise and be able to say what he feels and to whom;
> May grace, fame, and health abundantly take hold
> And fine living, without lack of money.
> Glory be to the Father, to the Son and to the Holy Ghost.)

Bar the final line, the verse is drawn from Horace's *Epistles* (I.4.8–11). Through Horace's words, Elizabeth emphasises, perhaps with some elaboration, her role as a teacher and guide to her nephew in his youth, which implicitly places Robert in a position of debt to his aunt. The verse is unequivocal in demonstrating Elizabeth's good wishes for her nephew. However, in wishing Cecil 'fine living, without lack of money', she is emphasising her own role as a suitor. On many occasions in her letters to her nephew from this period of her widowhood, Elizabeth highlights her own lack of money.[124] Cecil's new position as chancellor of the duchy of Lancaster placed him in a position to alleviate some of Elizabeth's financial difficulties and the verse works to highlight his indebtedness to his aunt.

On first sight, another Latin verse written by Elizabeth for her nephew, in this instance eight months earlier, in February 1597, had a very different intention. Cecil had lost his wife, Elizabeth Brooke Cecil, the month before and was in deep mourning. His aunt Elizabeth thus sent Robert Cecil an original verse of commemoration:

> Chara mihi multos Coniunx dilecta per annos
> Ah mihi praesidium Mens Horior atque Decus
> Corpore sublato tantum Divina supersunt
> Hac mihi Coecilo parte perennis ades

Gratus odor Christi Mors Mens tua verba Dolores
    Non peritura Die stant Monumenta tui.[125]

(Dear Wife, whom I have loved for many years,
    Alas, my protection, my mind, my honour and my glory,
Now the body has been taken away, only that which is sacred remains.
    But with this part, you are ever present to me, Cecil.
The pleasing fragrance of Christ, your death, mind, your words, griefs,
    These remain as your monuments that will never perish by day.)

Certainly Elizabeth intends her verse to console her nephew, but a letter she wrote to Robert four months later, in June, suggests a different purpose to the piece. In her letter Elizabeth urges Cecil to abandon his excessive grief and return to his vocation as a councillor.[126] There is the suggestion therefore in the poem that Elizabeth wishes to console her nephew precisely so that he can return to his work and to his position as one of her chief patrons.[127]

Yet Elizabeth's verse on Elizabeth Brooke Cecil remains one of consolation, which she ended with the line, 'Quod Licuit feci vellem mihi plura Licere' (I have done what was allowed, I wish more were allowed of me).[128] As already noted, the same line also appears amongst the neo-classical verses Elizabeth wrote to adorn the tombs of her two husbands: that of Thomas Hoby and his half-brother, Philip, at All Saints' Church in Bisham, and John Russell's monument at Westminster Abbey. Rather than perceiving it as representative of the restrictions on her literary expression, Elizabeth's line has previously been seen as expressing the Protestant belief in the moderation of grief and the limitations placed upon mourning.[129] I suggest, however, that Elizabeth's classical learning provided her with a method of circumventing these restrictions. Her commemorative verse is full of allusions to the rites of death and burial in classical literature. For example, she describes John Russell's death in both Latin and Greek verse in terms of dust.[130] The sprinkling of dust on a corpse was held to constitute burial in ancient Greece, especially in cases where it was not possible to dig a grave. Elizabeth could have learnt about this ritual in Sophocles' *Antigone*, where a covering of 'thirsty dust' is all the burial Antigone could perform for Polyneices.[131] Moreover, her epitaph for her deceased children, Elizabeth and Anne Hoby, describes them as being buried together in a tomb as the product of 'Una ... utero' (one womb), suggesting that Elizabeth was recalling Antigone's statement that her brothers deserved equal honour in burial as the products of one womb.[132] Most significantly for Elizabeth, neo-classical writing permits the expression of elaborate female mourning. Extravagant weeping and the chanting of dirges by women were important features in ancient burials. In line with these classical rituals, which portrayed ancient women as almost maddened by grief, Elizabeth represents herself and her daughters in the epitaphs for her second husband, John Russell, as inflicting mutilation upon themselves. 'Mens mea crudeli laniatur saucia morsu' (My wounded mind is torn by death's pitiless feeding), she writes, with her language incorporating violent verbs of wounding and tearing, recalling the lacerations classical women inflicted upon themselves at the graveside. Similarly, her verse on the Hoby monument evokes images of the self-sacrifice of ancient Greek widows upon the death of their husbands, for Elizabeth writes 'Sic, o sic junctos melius nos busta tenebunt,/ Quem meas me solum tristia texta tenent' (Thus, O better thus the tomb will hold us joined/ Than my sad house will hold me now alone). Elizabeth had already used such ideas of self-sacrifice in a manuscript verse written in 1566, just after the death of Thomas Hoby, where she states that she would have followed him to death, 'odiosum caeteris, gratum mihi' (hateful to all others, pleasant to me); she underlines the feminine nature of her mourning by recalling Catullus's poem IV on the death of Lesbia's sparrow.[33] The verse even acknowledges that reference to classical practice permits Elizabeth a greater freedom to mourn, for she writes 'Ego te in perenni, quod licet, luctu memor/ Decorabo moerens eiulatu et lacrimis' (I shall recall you in unceasing grief, as I am permitted to do, and shall honour you in my mourning with groans and tears).[34] The humanist learning that Elizabeth shared with her elite, male contemporaries worked to help legitimise her acts of female mourning.

For Elizabeth, writing Latin and Greek funerary verse not only allowed her greater scope as a grieving woman to commemorate the dead, but also provided her with an opportunity to comment on the concerns of the living. Nigel Llewellyn has suggested that early modern epitaphs attempted to enact what he has characterised as a 'continuity of ritual'. He argues the function of early modern memorials as being to 'replace the individual in order to repair the damage to the social fabric caused by the loss of the deceased'.[35] The aim of verse upon monuments was thus to reinforce the role of the writer within early modern society, as much as to commemorate the dead. For Elizabeth, then, funerary verse was a means of self-representation as much as commemoration, as shown by the inscription on her father's tomb in Romford, Essex. Elizabeth had already used the first line of her poem on Elizabeth Brooke Cecil to commemorate her mother on a memorial near her father's tomb and it is likely that she, perhaps together with her other sisters, wrote the verses on the tomb in memory of their father.[36] Within Sir Anthony Cooke's epitaph there are descriptions of the sisters, highlighting their influential marriages and particularly their learning:

> Cur te, Roma, facit Cornelia docta superbam?
> Quam multas tales, et mage, Cocus habet?
> Quinque sciunt natae conjungere Graeca Latinis,
> Insignes claris moribus atque piis.[37]

> (Why, O Rome, does the learned Cornelia make you proud
> Since Cooke has many such and more?

Figure 1 The Cooke sisters represented on the tomb of their father, Sir Anthony Cooke,
St Edward the Confessor Church, Romford

Five daughters know how to combine Greek with Latin
Distinguished for their illustrious character and piety.)

The inclusion of a personal description within the verse, close to a visual representation of the sisters on the monument (Figure 1), highlights how Elizabeth's epitaphs often went beyond simple commemoration and celebration of the deceased. The sisters' claim to learning came through their late father and thus, through Latin verse, Elizabeth is able to reinforce the sisters' reputation for scholarship, stating their fame as separate and ongoing after their father's death.

Elizabeth's epitaph for the tomb of her sister Katherine likewise praises not only the latter's learned qualities, but also highlights Elizabeth's claim to these same attributes.[138] In Greek verse, Katherine is described as only by death 'διχοτμηθεῖσα ἀδελφῆς' (cut off from her sister); the implication is therefore that whilst in life Katherine was 'Εὐσεβίης διδαχῆς κομψείας σεμνὸν ἄγαλμα' (The holy image of piety, learning, elegance), her sister still holds these characteristics. In a Latin epitaph, Elizabeth continues the same theme:

Mens tua labe carens, pietas, doctrina, modesta
Vita, lepos suavis digna fuere Deo.
Ut junxit Sanguis, nos jungat in aethere Christus.[139]

(Your unstained mind, your pious, learned, modest
Life and sweet grace have made you worthy of God.
As kinship has joined us, in heaven may Christ unite us.)[140]

Katherine's possession of piety, modesty, learning and grace was shared by her sister through kinship; whilst Katherine has died, Elizabeth remains by association a living embodiment of these virtues.

This process of enacting continuity and self-representation through epitaphs finds fullest expression in the verses that Elizabeth wrote to adorn the tombs of her two husbands. A Latin verse written not by Elizabeth but by Walter Haddon in 1558 foreshadows the nature of the epitaphs Elizabeth would write upon the death of her first husband, eight years later. Haddon's verse was written to commemorate the marriage of Elizabeth Cooke to Thomas Hoby, and also to mark the marriage of her sister Margaret Cooke to Ralph Rowlett on the same day, 27 June 1558:

Margaritam Roulete tuam faec mente recondas,
Gemma sit ut tuto tam pretiosa loco.
Sit frater fratri similis, sit filia patri,
Sic vir erit dignus conjuge, sponsa viro.[141]

(Make sure that you keep Margaret Rowlett safe in your heart,
So that this precious jewel may rest in a safe place.
May brother resemble brother, may daughter resemble father,
Thus husband will be worthy of wife, and wife of husband.)

Figure 2 Tomb of Philip and Thomas Hoby, All Saints' Church, Bisham

The marriage of Margaret and Ralph Rowlett was celebrated as an equal and complete union by Haddon, with the characters of both spouses lauded. However, the Hoby marriage is portrayed as essentially aspirational in character. Elizabeth is shown as desirous of her father's public, learned status, whilst Thomas Hoby is portrayed as notable only for his brother's fame, gained through the latter's diplomatic service. When Elizabeth came to write the verses to adorn the monument to Thomas and Philip Hoby at Bisham (Figure 2), her choice to write in Latin and Greek reveals her desire to ensure her learned reputation. Yet she is also concerned with ensuring the status brought to the Hoby family through their diplomatic service, again a theme identified by Haddon's earlier verse. The shared occupation of Thomas Hoby and his elder half-brother, Philip, is therefore a key element in Elizabeth's verse for their Bisham monument. For, as Walter Haddon had emphasised, Philip was the more prestigious and established diplomat of the two brothers, a fact recognised by Elizabeth in verse:

> Tuque tuae stirpis non gloria parva Philippe,
> Cujus erat virtus maxima nota soris.
> Itala quem tellus norat, Germania norat,
> Qui patriae tuleras commoda magna tuae.[42]

> (No little glory have you and your family, Philip,
> Whose virtue was especially known abroad.
> Whom the land of Italy and Germany both knew,
> Who for your homeland did important service.)[43]

In line with her description of her brother-in-law's diplomatic service, she presents her late husband, Thomas, as aspiring to a similar position: 'Dum patriae servis, dum publica commoda tractas,/ Occidis, ignota triste cadaver humo' (While you serve your country, public affairs in hand,/ You have died, a sad corpse in an unknown land).[44] Beyond the linkage between the status of Philip and Thomas, Elizabeth explicitly positions herself as part of the diplomatic service of the family.[45] In verse, she describes her own role along-side her husband, as a diplomatic wife: 'Anglia faelices, faelices Gallia vidit,/ Per mare, per terras noster abivit amor' (England saw us happy, France saw us happy,/ Through sea and lands our love has passed).[46] She then describes the circumstances of her husband's death as the English resident ambassador in Paris in 1566, with his passing leaving his pregnant wife and children stranded in the French capital. As part of her duties as a diplomat's wife, Elizabeth herself fulfils her husband's embassy and returns, with his body, to England, again immortalising her efforts through her verse:

> Exeo funestis terris, hic rapta cadaver
> Conjugis, hinc prolis languida membra traho.

Sic uterum gestans, redeo terraque Marique
In patriam luctu perdita, mortis amans.[147]

(Plundered as here I've been, I leave these funereal lands,
I take my husband's corpse and my children's feeble limbs.
And so with filling womb I return by land and sea
To our homeland, lost in sorrow, lost in death.)[148]

The description of the diplomatic service of all three family members works to suggest that both Thomas and, through him, his widow, Elizabeth, should partake of Philip Hoby's public status. Elizabeth underlines this conclusion in her verse by emphasising that she has designed one tomb for both brothers: 'Mortua nunc capiet corpora funus idem./ Et soror et conjux vobis commune sepulchrum,/ Et michi composui' (And now the same burial will receive your bodies./ Both sister and wife, I have planned one tomb for you,/ In common).[149] Yet the tomb will hold more 'in common' than just the Hoby brothers. Elizabeth states in verse her desire to join the brothers in the tomb: 'Non ero vobiscum, donec mea fata vocabunt,/ Tunc cineres vestros consociabo meis' (I shall not be with you until my fates call,/ Then I'll join your ashes with my own).[150]

Why, though, would Elizabeth use the medium of neo-classical commemorative verse to mark the diplomatic status of the Hoby family, highlighting herself as the living heir to that tradition? I would suggest that the verses need to be placed within the context of early modern diplomatic culture. The diets and extraordinary expenses were not sufficient enticement for an early modern diplomat, 'rather they served for the potential reward', namely the reward that would come from the Crown after the completion of a diplomatic mission.[151] The Hobys had been forced to spend a great deal on the Parisian embassy in 1566, yet Thomas's early death had prevented them from recouping that loss through later rewards and more lucrative service for the Queen.[152] Elizabeth wrote to the Queen detailing her travel expenses upon returning to England, but she clearly felt that the letter she received in reply from the Queen, praising both her late husband and her own conduct in arranging the end of the embassy, was not sufficient reward for the diplomatic service of the family.[153] In neo-classical verse, she had a medium through which to keep the memory of that diplomatic service alive and a language in which she could express her extravagent grief; it would remind learned visitors to Bisham, including her brothers-in-law, but particularly royal visitors, of her entitlement to compensation by the Crown. This goes far beyond the purely domestic nature of her self-characterisation perceived in past research. Patricia Phillippy has seen the verse cycle on the Hoby memorial as an attempt by Elizabeth to guarantee 'her right to wield domestic power' and 'undertake her husband's domestic privileges'.[154] I argue instead that Elizabeth's focus in the verse is not upon domestic privilege, but instead upon privilege from the Crown. The Queen and the earl of Leicester agreed to act as godparents for Thomas Posthumous Hoby, born, as his name suggests, after his father's death in France, which may have reflected a sense of royal obligation to the widowed Elizabeth.[55]

With the series of verse she wrote for the tomb of her second husband, Lord John Russell, Elizabeth had a different priority. John Russell's death on 23 July 1584 was unexpected; heir to the earldom of Bedford, he died before his father and so Elizabeth did not become the countess of Bedford as she had desired. Elizabeth never entirely accepted this loss of status. The verses which Elizabeth wrote for the tomb of her second husband, in Westminster Abbey, are therefore overtly concerned with reiterating his claim to noble status. The idea of nobility and honour through virtue, rather than birth, is a claim that Elizabeth had already made in the verses commemorating her first husband, Thomas Hoby.[56] Yet ultimately it is John Russell's claim to aristocratic nobility through birth that dominates the Westminster cycle of verse. While he never inherited the earldom, he was a 'flower' set to grow into his nobility: 'Vere novo haeres Comitis tu floris ad instar' (Indeed so lately heir of an earl, like a flower always).[57] As with the Hoby verses, Elizabeth again restates her own identity as a noblewoman through association with the deceased, enacting a 'ritual of continuity' that counteracts the damage of John Russell's premature death.[58] She includes verses on the tomb for her deceased son and heir to the Bedford line, Francis Russell, which highlight that through her dead son she shares his claim to the earldom: 'En solamen avi, patris pergrata voluptas,/ Ipsa medulla mihi' (O comfort of a grandfather, a father's happiest desire,/ The very marrow of me).[59] Her son had been recognised as an heir by his still-living grandfather, Francis Russell, and so through him, her 'marrow', Elizabeth argues she shares in his title.

Yet again, it must be asked why Elizabeth is so concerned with using her epitaph on John Russell to restate her claim to noble and honourable status. For Elizabeth, as she repeatedly told Robert Cecil, 'Honowre [is] Derer to me then my life'.[60] However, her claim to the Russell earldom was a weak one. Her repeated attempts in later years to stop her daughters from selling Russell House testify to the fragility of her claim.[61] Commemorative verse was a medium through which Elizabeth could present her late husband, and so her family, as the Russell heirs without fear of derision.[62] Moreover, she presented John Russell's nobility on his tomb to bolster her claim that her daughters should be recognised as his heirs. A year after John Russell's passing, his father died and Elizabeth discovered that her daughters' claim to the Bedford estate was contested; the wording of her father-in-law's will had not been amended after the early death of his heir, John Russell.[63] An extended legal battle ensued between Elizabeth and her relatives, the surviving children of Francis Russell, over the inheritance for her daughters, Bess and Anne.[64] Elizabeth therefore used the Westminster tomb of her late husband to legitimate her daughters' claim to the Bedford inheritance, writing of them on the tomb 'Haeredi Comitis quin vos succrescite, tali/ Ortu qui nituit sed bonitate magis' (Heirs of an earl, grow up indeed – from such a springing/ Start you have thrived – but grow mainly in goodness).[165] Elizabeth's knowledge of classical burial practice supported the presence of her daughters on the tomb. The sisters had walked in the funeral procession for their father. This was unusual in early modern England, yet such practice was common in ancient Greece, where women played a key role in burial rites, including the *ekphora*, the funeral procession, where they would walk behind the men.[166] Following their role in the funeral procession, the Russell daughters are thus visually represented on the tomb, holding a triumphal arch, above their recumbent father.[167] The classical heritage behind their acts of female mourning enables Elizabeth to legitimate the inclusion of two verses on John Russell's tomb 'in superstites filias' (on her surviving daughters).[168] In Latin and Greek verses, Elizabeth's instructions for her grieving daughters are presented in classical terms: 'Plangite nunc natae, nunc flebile fundite carmen,/ Occidit heu vestrae gloria sola domus' (Weep now, daughters, now chant out a mourning poem,/ Alas he has died, the only glory of our home).[169] She repeatedly describes her daughters as the 'shorn ones', implying they have cut their hair in line with ancient Greek mourning tradition.[170] Thus classical imagery works to legitimate the prominence of the two sisters on the tomb, which in turn highlights their claim to nobility, and inheritance, through their father.

Ultimately, Elizabeth was unsuccessful in her battle to win her daughters' inheritance.[171] Yet her neo-classical commemorative verse ensured that their claims were continually presented before visitors at Westminster Abbey, a popular recreational destination for the early modern elite; for example, in December 1600 her daughter-in-law, Margaret Hoby, recorded going 'to the minister to see the monementes'.[172] Elizabeth's decision to include an English verse alongside her Latin and Greek epitaphs on the tomb was no doubt designed to make her message accessible to all. Yet the decision to write English verse was a rare one for Elizabeth.[173] It was Latin and Greek verse which allowed her opportunities to appeal to classical modes of feminine mourning, facilitating her claims to the status of her deceased husbands. Through her composition of neo-classical commemorative verse, Elizabeth could, moreover, put forth her self-image as a learned woman and ensure her fame in her own lifetime. John Harrington wrote in his 1591 translation of Ludovico Ariosto's *Orlando Furioso* that she deserved as much praise as Vittoria Colonna for the verses she wrote upon the deaths of her husbands.[174] In 1600 William Camden published the text of Elizabeth's verses on the Russell tomb at Westminster.[175] A German visitor to England in 1598, Paul Hentzner, even recorded her Latin and Greek verses on John Russell's tomb and included them in the 1612 account of his travels, published in Nuremberg.[176]

Figure 3 Elizabeth Cooke Hoby Russell represented on her tomb,
All Saints' Church, Bisham

However, as Elizabeth herself acknowledged in her commemorative verse, there were limits to the power of the word in this form. The visual imagery on the Russell tomb, including its pictorial representations of the two Russell sisters, indicates the boundaries of Elizabeth Russell's literary opportunities and reveals how she used images to reinforce the message of her words. On the Hoby tomb, the recumbent, armoured pose of the two brothers signifies their honourable status.[77] John Russell is shown dressed in his baron's robes on the Russell tomb, with his dead son and heir depicted at his feet.[78] For her own tomb, perhaps surprisingly, Elizabeth chose the visual medium over the literary.[79] Her memorial in All Saints' Church, Bisham, visually represents her claim to nobility, showing her still in mourning dress for the loss of John Russell, but also wearing a countess's coronet, with the dead body of the Russell heir, Francis, lying before her (Figure 3). Ever the learned, godly woman, her eyes rest upon the Scripture in Latin in front of her and Job's promise of eternal life.[80]

DRAMA AND THE LEARNED WOMAN

The presence of Latin Scripture in Elizabeth's memorial provides an insight more widely into the power of her classical learning to legitimate her presentation. Even in her own memorial, Elizabeth's learning empowers her self-image. Her excursions into drama provide further evidence of how her classical learning gave authority even to her vernacular writing. Drama was a more contested form of writing for women in this period, compared to religious translation or the composition of verse. Women did not write publically performed stage plays until the latter half of the seventeenth century, although there were opportunities for women to undertake dramatic writing before the 1660s. Translation was one way in which sixteenth-century women could engage with drama; for example, Elizabeth's contemporary Lady Jane Lumley translated Euripides' *Iphigenia in Aulis* from Greek into English in the early 1550s.[81] Although not using her classical language skills to translate drama, Elizabeth still drew legitimation from her high levels of education when writing household drama. In 1592 the Queen visited Bisham Abbey and Elizabeth Russell presented her with an entertainment, as 'the Lady of the farme'.[82] Nine years later, she staged a masque, again for the Queen, to mark the marriage of her daughter Anne Russell to Henry Somerset, Lord Herbert, the eldest son of the earl of Worcester. It is extremely likely that Elizabeth Russell was the author of both these entertainments, or, at least, closely dictated their themes.[83] While the text of only the Bisham entertainment is still extant, it is clear that Elizabeth reflected upon her educational status in writing both dramatic interludes. The 1601 masque begins with the entrance of eight ladies, including Bess Russell, the bride's sister, who in a 'fine Speach' tell the Queen that they are eight of the nine classical muses, seeking their lost sister.[184] The learned Queen is presented as the ninth Muse, and so Elizabeth's plot is therefore not only chosen to 'honor and praise' the Queen, but also to draw attention to her own educational status.[185] The theme of female education receives closer attention in the 1592 Bisham drama. The Queen's learning is again highlighted for praise in the entertainment, for she is described as one 'In whom nature hath imprinted beauty, not art paynted it; in whome wit hath bred learning, but not without labour; labour brought forth wisdom, but not without wonder.'[186] As a similarly learned woman, Elizabeth Russell understood the efforts which the Queen had made in gaining her education. Whereas nature is responsible for her beauty, her learning and, consequentially, her wisdom, have been wrought through hard work. It is within this context that Elizabeth Russell presents her two daughters, Bess and Anne, who are central characters within the entertainment.

After an opening speech by a wild man, at the top of the hill at Bisham, the action moves to the middle of the hill and Pan's attempted seduction of 'two Virgins keeping Sheepe, and sowing in their Samplers', namely the two Russell girls, here named Isabel and Sybil.[187] It has already been noted that this was the first occasion on which English noblewomen had speaking roles within a quasi-dramatic performance.[188] Yet women's voices are more significant within the piece than has previously been acknowledged, for they highlight its theme of female education. This is first suggested when Pan proposes that the girls should be writing, rather than sewing: 'How does you burne time, & drowne beauty, in pricking of clouts, when you should bee penning of Sonnets? You are more simple than the sheepe you keepe, but not so gentle.'[189] The Russell sisters have two retorts, firstly that women can communicate through their needlework; in this case, the girls embroider classical scenes showing virgins rewarded for chastity by becoming goddesses, and gods who were made into beasts for their lusts.[190] Their second retort, however, reveals the power of their eloquence:

> *Syb*: Alas poore Pan, looke how he looketh Sister, fitter to drawe in a Harvest wayne, then talke of love to chaste Virgins, would you have us both?
> *Pan*: I, for oft I have hearde, that two Pigeons may bee caught with one beane.
> *Isab*: And two Woodcocks with one sprindge.
> *Syb*: And many Dotterels with one dance.
> *Isab*: And all fooles with one faire worde.[191]

The virgin sisters can defeat Pan's enticements through the power of their words, evidence of their education in the art of rhetoric. In the above extract, the sisters mock Pan's attempt to persuade through the use of a commonplace, by suggesting alternative sayings, apparently appearing to agree with him, until Isabel's final suggestion reveals that they have seen through his words. The entertainment thus underlines the distinction between the words of educated men and women. Man, according to Isabel, has two hearts, one poisoned by lust and the other 'dissembling', 'wherewith his tongue is tipped'. Education for men therefore has a very different end in this entertainment, than that for women: 'Men must have as manie loves, as they have hart-strings, and studie to make an Alphabet of mistresses, from A. to Y. which maketh them in the end crie, Ay. Against this, experience hath provided us a remedy, to laugh at them when they know not what to saie, and when they speake, not to beleeve them.'[192] For men, rhetorical education is practised as a means for pursuing women. Yet the sisters' education has provided them with the confidence to laugh at male lapses in eloquence, as much as at their rhetorical tropes; like the Queen, these learned virgins are protected by their education.

Saved from the contagion of lust, women's words are presented in the entertainment as honest and reliable: 'weomen's tongues are made of the same flesh that their harts are, and speake as they thinke'.[193] This is the setting for the introduction of Elizabeth Russell's words, as the sisters report their mother's speech to the audience. When Pan asks who is coming their way, Jupiter or Juno, Sybil replies by telling Pan 'What our mother hath often tolde us', namely of the majesty of the Queen. Thus the description of the Queen's virtuous government, supporting Protestant forces in France and the Netherlands, is in fact the words of Elizabeth Russell: 'By her it is (Pan) that all our Carttes that thou seest, are laden with Corne, when in other countries they are filled with Harneys ... One hande she stretcheth to Fraunce, to weaken Rebels, the other to Flaunders, to strengthen Religion.'[194]

The product of her learned status, Elizabeth Russell's trustworthy words remain important in the third and final scene. Ceres, the goddess of fertility and fruitfulness, welcomes the Queen to the farm, surrounded by her nymphs. Yet the Queen's childless status means that Ceres cannot be celebrated as the pre-eminent goddess 'in this Ile', instead 'Cynthia shalbe Ceres' Mistres'; the moon goddess here rules to 'receive Ceres' crowne'.[195] The comparison of the Queen with Cynthia was not an unusual technique; Ralegh's 'The Ocean to Scinthia' was probably written near to this date.[196] The yielding of Ceres to Cynthia may, however, also represent the yielding of one classically educated woman, Elizabeth Russell, the 'Ladie of the farme', to another, the Queen. Ceres is a goddess associated with motherhood and, through the inclusion of her daughters, Elizabeth Russell highlights her maternal status within the entertainment; similarly, she is presented as the 'Ladie of the farme', associated with the fertility of the countryside, which she suggests bolsters the Queen's government. Despite the fact that Ceres yields sovereignty to Cynthia, Elizabeth Russell remains empowered to speak in this drama, due to her educated status; only Ceres' words are heard in the entertainment, not Cynthia's. Elizabeth Russell even ends the entertainment with her own words: 'And this muche dare we promise for the Lady of the farme, that your presence hath added many daies to her life, by the infinite joies she conceyves in her heart, who presents your highnesse with this toye and this short praier, poured from her hart, that your daies may increase in happines, your happines have no end till there be no more daies."[97]

Education therefore provides both the themes and legitimation for Elizabeth's dramatic writing. There are limits, however, to how much Elizabeth can speak through drama. Both masques admittedly are not explicit as to Elizabeth's authorship. This is not unusual for the period, but uncertainty over Elizabeth's involvement with the authorship of the dramatic interludes, particularly the printed 1592 Bisham entertainment, is most likely a deliberate ambiguity.[98] Undoubtedly the entertainments do, however, reveal how Elizabeth's humanist learning provided a basis from which she could mould her self-presentation and reveal how drama was another medium through which she could set forth her priorities.

CONCLUSION

Elizabeth Russell was thus entirely correct to perceive limits to the opportunities for women's literary engagement. The composition of translation and verse, particularly commemorative verse, was an accepted activity for sixteenth-century women writers; however, drama was a more contested genre. Yet their classical learning offered the sisters opportunities in all these genres of writing. Rather than simply being evidence of female silencing, the act of translation offered the Cooke sisters the chance not only to bolster their political networks, but also to contribute to strengthening their national church. Close engagement with Anne's translation of the *Apologia* moreover reveals her remarkable involvement with issues of national importance to the reformed faith. She asserted a form and created a lexicography for her translation which was vital to the recognition the text received, whilst establishing her own role within this widely disseminated translation. Elizabeth too used her humanist education to advance her own priorities. Like her sister Katherine, Latin verse allowed her to increase her agency within patronage networks. It was a particular opportunity for Elizabeth in the form of neo-classical commemorative verse. Through writing Latin and Greek funerary verse, she could advance her self-image as a learned woman, seek reward for her first husband's diplomatic service or strengthen the claim of her family to the earldom of Bedford after her second husband's early death. Moreover, the use of Latin and Greek allowed her to utilise classical ideas of female mourning. Therefore, when reading Elizabeth Russell's line, 'Quod licuit feci, vellum mihi plura licere' (I have done what was allowed, I wish more were allowed of me), while it is important to heed the limits inherent in the second clause, the opportunities expressed in the first half of the line should not go unnoticed.

NOTES

1 M. Parker, 'Epistle to Lady A.B.', in J. Jewel, *An Apologie or answere in defence of the Churche of Englande*, trans. Anne Bacon (1564) (*Apologie*), 1st unpaginated leaf, r. The manuscript of Anne's translation has not survived.

2 The line occurs on the Bisham monument for Thomas and Philip Hoby and on the Westminster Abbey tomb for John Russell. For the line's inclusion in both sets of inscriptions, see E. Ashmole, *The Antiquities of Berkshire* (3 vols, 1719), II, p. 468 and W. Camden, *Reges, reginae, nobiles, & alii* (1606), sig. G2r. The line also occurs under a poem written by Elizabeth Russell for her nephew Robert Cecil. See BL, Lansdowne MS 140, fo. 82r.

3 See, for example, D. Clarke, 'The politics of translation and gender in the Countess of Pembroke's *Antonie*', *Translation and Literature*, 6 (1997), 149–66; M. White, 'Renaissance Englishwomen and religious translations: the case of Anne Lock's *Of the Markes of the Children of God* (1590)', *English Literary Renaissance*, 29 (1999), 375–400; B. Hosington, 'Translation in the service of politics and religion: a family tradition for Thomas More, Margaret Roper and Mary Clarke Basset', in J. de Landstheer and H. Nellen (eds), *Between Scylla and Charybdis: Learned Letter Writers Navigating the Reefs of Religious and Political Controversy in Early Modern Europe* (Leiden, 2010), pp. 93–108. Brenda Hosington's forthcoming book promises to shed much light on the wider activity of English women translators.

4 B. Ochino, *Sermons of Barnadine Ochine of Sena godlye, frutefull, and very necessarye for all true Christians*, trans. anon (1548); B. Ochino, *Certayne Sermons of the ryghte famous and excellente Clerk Master Barnadine Ochine*, trans. anon (1551); B. Ochino, *Fouretene sermons of Barnadine Ochyne, concernyng the predestinacion and eleccion of god*, trans. A[nne] C[ooke] (?1551); B. Ochino, *Sermons of Barnadine Ochyne (to the number of 25) concerning the predestinacion and eleccion of god*, trans. A[nne] C[ooke] (1570).

5 BL, Royal MS 17 B.XVIII.

6 This previously unknown translation was mentioned in a sale of manuscripts in 1890 in Boston, USA: 'Sermon Isaiae primo and prayer, very neatly written autograph manuscript, ruled with red ink throughout, and containing the writer's autograph in full, and a MS pedigree of her family. Small 4° vellum, with silk ribbons. About 1550'. See *Catalogue of the Library: Manuscripts, Autograph Letters, Maps and Prints, forming the collection of G.E. Hart* (Boston, 1890), p. 152. I have been unable to discover the current location of the translation.

7 The reference to her translation of Chrysostom originated with the 'Anonymous Life' of Burghley and the author may have confused it with her translation of St Basil, as there is no other evidence of its existence. See F. Peck, *Desiderata curiosa* (2 vols, 1732–75), I, p. 7. P. Croft, 'Mildred, Lady Burghley: the matriarch', in P. Croft (ed.), *Patronage, Culture and Power: The Early Cecils* (2002), pp. 290–1.

8 *Reconciliation.*

9 R. Greaves, 'The role of women in early English nonconformity', *Church History*, 52 (1983), 305. See also E. Beilin, 'Current bibliography of English women writers, 1500–1640', in A.M. Haselkorn and B.S. Travitsky (eds), *The Renaissance Englishwoman in Print* (Amherst, Mass., 1990), pp. 347–60.

10 M.E. Lamb, 'The Cooke sisters: attitudes toward learned women in the Renaissance', in M. Hannay (ed.), *Silent But for the Word* (Kent, Ohio, 1985), p. 116; K. Morin-Parsons,

'Introduction', in K. Morin-Parsons (ed.), *A Meditation of a Penitent Sinner: Anne Locke's Sonnet Sequence* (Waterloo, 1997), p. 26. See also P. Parker, *Shakespeare from the Margins: Language, Culture, Context* (1996), pp. 139–40.

11 L. Schleiner, *Tudor and Stuart Women Writers* (Bloomington, Ind., 1994), p. 51; D. Bornstein, 'The style of the Countess of Pembroke's translation of Philippe de Mornay's *Discours de la vie et de la mort*', in M. Hannay (ed.), *Silent But for the Word* (Kent, Ohio, 1985), p. 134.

12 Lamb, 'The Cooke sisters', p. 124.

13 A. Stewart, 'The voices of Anne Cooke, Lady Anne and Lady Bacon', in D. and E. Clarke (eds), *This Double Voice: Gendered Writing in Early Modern England* (Basingstoke, 2000), p. 89.

14 Schleiner, *Tudor and Stuart Women Writers*, pp. 34–9; E. Beilin, 'Introductory note', in E. Beilin (ed.), *Protestant Translators: Anne Lock Prowse and Elizabeth Russell*, The Early Modern Englishwoman (Aldershot, 1998), pp. xi–xii; P. Demers, *Women's Writing in English: Early Modern England* (Toronto, 2005), pp. 84, 87–8.

15 The dating of Princess Elizabeth's translation of Ochino's 'Che Cosa è Christo' to 1547–8 relies upon the argument of Mueller and Scodel. See *Elizabeth I: Translations, 1544–1589*, ed. J. Mueller and J. Scodel (Chicago, 2009), pp. 292–3.

16 B. Ochino, *Sermons of the ryght famous and excellent clerke Master Bernardine Ochine*, trans. R. Argentine (Ipswich, 1548).

17 *Certayne sermons*, trans. anon.

18 *Ibid.*, sig. A3r.

19 *Fourtene sermons*, trans. A[nne] C[ooke].

20 Anne Overell suggests that G.B. may stand for 'Gulielmus Baldwinus', namely William Baldwin. See M.A. Overell, *Italian Reform and English Reformations, c. 1535–1585* (Aldershot, 2008), p. 55.

21 See J.N. King, 'John Day: master printer of the English Reformation', in P. Marshall and A. Ryrie (eds), *The Beginnings of English Protestantism* (Cambridge, 2002), pp. 180–208; E. Evenden, *Patents, Pictures and Patronage: John Day and the Tudor Book Trade* (Aldershot, 2008), pp. 31–35.

22 Overell, *Italian Reform and English Reformations*, p. 54.

23 Similarly, Princess Elizabeth's translation of Ochino's sermon makes some limited engagement with the doctrine of predestination. See *Elizabeth I: Translations, 1544–1589*, pp. 312–13, 314–15, 318–19, 320–1.

24 In contrast, Argentine drew his six sermons from the earlier sermons in the second book of the *Prediche*. See *Sermons*, trans. Argentine and B. Ochino, *Prediche* (5 vols, Basel, 1562), II, sermons 1, 2, 3, 5, 6, 7.

25 *Sermons of Barnardine Ochyne*, trans. A[nne] C[ooke].

26 J. Foxe, *The Acts and Monuments of John Foxe*, ed. S.R. Cattley (8 vols, 1837–41), VIII, pp. 219–25.

27 'To the Christen Reader', in B. Ochino, *Fourtene sermons*, sig. A2r.

28 *Reconciliation*, sig. A2v.

29 *Ibid.*

30 W.S. Hudson, *John Ponet, 1516?–1556* (Chicago, 1942), p. 79.

31 M.K. McIntosh, 'Sir Anthony Cooke: Tudor humanist, educator, and religious reformer', *PAPS*, 119 (1975), 244.

32 Hudson, *Ponet*, p. 80.

33 *Diallacticon viri boni et literati, de veritate, natura atque substantia corporis & sanguinis Christi in Eucharistia* (Strasbourg, 1557).

34 A. Cooke, *Diallacticon, c'est-à-dire réconciliatoire d'un bon et sainct personage ... (par A. Cooke)* (Paris, 1566). A 1576 printing of the Latin tract also raised the question of authorship in its preface, asking whether the responsibility lay with the bishop of Winchester or Anthony Cooke, including the partial answer that the author was exiled to Strasbourg for his religion under Mary I. *Diallacticon de veritate, natura atque substantia corporis & sanguinis Christi in eucharistia* (Unknown, 1576), sig. A1v.

35 CP 197, fo. 53r: c.05/1605.

36 *Reconciliation*, sig. A2v.

37 *Elizabeth I: Translations, 1544–1589*, pp. 2–3.

38 BL, Royal MS 17 B.XVIII, fo. 11r. For a similar sentiment expressed by Anne Locke, see J. Taffin, *Of the markes of the children of God, and of their comforts in afflictions*, trans. A. Locke (1590), sig. A2r.

39 *Sermons of Barnardine Ochine*, trans. anon, sig. A4r.

40 Hudson, *Ponet*, p. 79.

41 *Apologie*, sig. E7v.

42 Parker, 'Epistle', 1st unpaginated leaf, r.

43 *Ibid.*, 1st unpaginated leaf, v.

44 *Ibid.*, 2nd unpaginated leaf, v.

45 See, for example, M. Ezell, *The Patriarch's Wife: Literary Evidence and the History of the Family* (Chapel Hill, 1987), pp. 62–100; M. Ezell, *Writing Women's Literary History* (Baltimore, 1992); M. Ezell, *Social Authorship and the Advent of Print* (Baltimore, 1999); J. Stevenson, 'Women, writing and scribal publication', *English Manuscript Studies 1100–1700*, 9 (2000), 1–32.

46 J.N. King, 'Patronage and piety: the influence of Catherine Parr', in M. Hannay (ed.), *Silent But for the Word* (Kent, Ohio, 1985), p. 50.

47 *Fourtene sermons*, sig. A2r.

48 *Sermons of Barnardine Ochine*, sig. A4r.

49 *CSP Spain, 1558–1567*, p. 201: 05/05/1561.

50 J.E. Booty, *John Jewel as Apologist of the Church of England* (1963), pp. 42–5.

51 *Epistola cuiusdam Angli* (Paris?, 1561).

52 J. Jewel, *An Apologie, or aunswer in defence of the Church of England*, trans. anon (1562).

53 Parker, 'Epistle', 2nd unpaginated leaf, v.

54 Booty, *John Jewel*, p. 56.

55 Stewart, 'The voices of Anne Cooke', p. 94.

56 For discussion of L. Humphrey, *Interpretatio linguarum* (Basel, 1559), see J.W. Binns, *Intellectual Culture in Elizabethan and Jacobean England* (Leeds, 1990), p. 210.

57 BL, Royal MS 17 B.XVIII, fo. 2v.

58 I disagree with Patricia Demers that Mildred's use of the term 'galtrope', a type of trap which snares the feet, particularly exemplifies her utilisation of 'the idiom of Tudor English': 'thou goest in the middest of snares, thine enemye hathe prevey galtropes layde for the on everi side'. The etymology of the word developed from Latin, Old English, Old French and Middle English roots and so whilst a commonplace word in Tudor England, it was not particularly evocative of the contemporary idiom. See BL, Royal MS 17 B.XVIII, fos 7v, 13v, 16r; Demers, *Women's Writing*, p. 84.

59 *Diallacticon*, sigs C1r, C3v.

60 *Reconciliation*, sigs D2v, D4v.

61 *The Byble in Englyshe* (1539), fo. 39v; *The Bible and Holy Scriptures* (Geneva, 1560), sig. MM2r; *The holie Bible, conteynyng the olde Testament and the newe* (3 parts, 1568), III, sig. H2v.

62 *Ibid.*

63 *Reconciliation*, sigs C1r–v.

64 Elizabeth's scriptural translation lends support to Pauline Croft's suggestion that her sister Mildred participated in the 1572 revision of the Bishops' Bible. See Croft, 'Mildred, Lady Burghley', pp. 290–1.

65 T. More, *The workes of Sir Thomas More Knyght* (1557), pp. 220–1.

66 *Reconciliation*, sigs I2v, I1v.

67 *Ibid.*, sig. D3r.

68 For embellishment in Tudor translation, see M. Morini, *Tudor Translation in Theory and Practice* (Aldershot, 2006), pp. 85–6, 92–4.

69 Ochino, *Prediche*, II, sig. PP3r; *Certayne sermons*, sig. G5r.

70 Ochino, *Prediche*, II, sig. QQ1r; *Certayne sermons*, sig. G8v.

71 C.S. Lewis, *English Literature in the Sixteenth Century* (Oxford, 1954), p. 307.

72 *Ibid.*

73 'Princess Elizabeth to Queen Katherine', in Elizabeth I, *Collected Works*, ed. L.S. Marcus, J. Mueller and M.B. Rose (2000), p. 12; *Elizabeth I: Translations, 1544–1589*, p. 5. See also A.L. Prescott, 'The pearl of the Valois and Elizabeth I: Marguerite de Navarre's *Miroir* and Tudor England', in M. Hannay (ed.), *Silent But for the Word* (Kent, Ohio, 1985), pp. 61–76.

74 J. Jewel, *Apologia Ecclesiae Anglicanae* (1562), sig. C8v; *An Apologie*, trans. anon, sig. C1v.

75 *Apologie*, sig. B7v.

76 Jewel, *Apologia*, sigs A8v–B1r.

77 Booty, *John Jewel*, p. 45.

78 *An Apologie*, trans. anon, sig. D2r.

79 My italics. *Apologie*, sig. C8r.

80 Jewel, *Apologia*, sig. B4v; *An Apologie*, trans. anon, sig. D2r.

81 My italics. *Apologie*, sig. C8r.

82 C. Haigh, *English Reformations: Religion, Politics and Society under the Tudors* (Oxford, 1993), pp. 268–76; F. Heal, *Reformation in Britain and Ireland* (Oxford, 2003), pp. 290, 433–34.

83 E. Dering, 'To the Christian Reader', in E. Dering, *A Briefe and Necessary Instruction* (1572), sig. A4v.

84 J. Strype, *Annals of the Reformation* (4 vols, Oxford, 1820–40), I, i, p. 474.

85 H. Bullinger, *The Decades of Henry Bullinger*, trans. H.I., ed. T. Harding (5 vols in 4, Parker Society, Cambridge, 1849–52), I, pp. 12–35.

86 *The Zurich Letters*, ed. H. Robinson (2 vols, Parker Society, Cambridge, 1842), II, pp. 1–2, 13–14, 76; *Original Letters*, ed. H. Robinson (2 vols, Parker Society, Cambridge, 1846–47), I, pp. 139–40.

87 *Zurich Letters*, II, p. 1.

88 *An Apologie*, trans. anon, sig. E2r.

89 *Apologie*, sigs D8r–v.

90 Jewel, *Apologia*, sig. A4v; *An Apologie*, trans. anon, sig. B1r; *Apologie*, sig. A7r.

91 J. Jewel, *The copie of a Sermon pronounced by the Bisshop of Salisburie at Paules Crosse* (1560). It is very possible Anne would have heard the sermon, either at court or at Paul's Cross; her experience of Paul's Cross is demonstrated in a later letter to Burghley in 1585, where she writes of her experience 'hearing odd sermons at Powle well nigh 20 yere together'. See BL, Lansdowne MS 43, fo. 119r.

92 Eutropius, *A briefe chronicle, where in are described shortlye the originall, and the successive estate of the Romaine weale publique*, trans. T. Haward (1564), sig. B2v.

93 T. Elyot, *The boke named The Governour* (1531).

94 T. Wilson, *Arte of Rhetorique*, ed. G.H. Mair (Oxford, 1909), p. 162.

95 Parker, 'Epistle', 3rd unpaginated leaf, r.

96 See, for example, *Apologie*, sigs A6r–v.

97 *Apologie*, sig. N1r; Jewel, *Apologia*, sig. E6v; *An Apologie*, trans. anon, sig. D2r.

98 *An Apologie*, trans. anon, sig. L2r; *Apologie*, sig. K3v.

99 *Apologie*, sig. Q6v. For use of the word 'mockingstock', see also sigs A4v and N5r.

100 J. Cheke, 'A Letter of Syr J. Cheekes', in B. Castiglione, *The courtyer of Count Baldessar Castilio*, trans. T. Hoby (1561), unpaginated appendix.

101 J. Cheke, *The Gospel according to St Matthew*, ed. J. Goodwin (1843), p. 41.

102 NA, SP 6/12, fo. 16r.

103 *An Apologie*, trans. anon, sig. B3r; *Apologie*, sig. B3r.

104 Susenbrotus, cited in P. Mack, *Elizabethan Rhetoric* (Cambridge, 2002), p. 97.

105 *Ibid.*, pp. 97–8.

106 *Apologie*, sigs K6v, N2r, P4v.

107 Parker, 'Epistle', 2nd unpaginated leaf, v.

108 J. Jewel, *The Apologie of the Church of England*, trans. A. Bacon (1600); J. Jewel, *The Apologie of the Church of England*, trans. A. Bacon (1635).

109 My italics. *Apologie*, sig. A1r.

110 *An Apologie*, trans. anon, sig. K1r.

111 My italics. *Apologie*, sig. I2v.

112 My italics. *An Apologie*, trans. anon, sig. K2v; *Apologie*, sig. I5v.

113 J. Bruce and T.T. Perowne (eds), *The Correspondence of Matthew Parker* (Parker Society, Cambridge, 1853), pp. 416–17; W. Kennedy, *Elizabethan Episcopal Administration* (3 vols, 1924), II, p. 79.

114 Booty, *John Jewel*, p. 7.

115 Verstegan confuses the writer of the dedicatory epistle in *An apologie*, reading M.C. for Mildred Cecil rather than Matthei Cantauriensis (Matthew Parker). See R. Verstegan, *A Declaration of the True Causes of the Great Troubles* (Antwerp, 1592), p. 12.

116 BL, Royal MS 17 B.XVIII, fo. 11r.

117 See chapter 5.

118 BN, NAL 106, p. 152.

119 *Ibid.*

120 I.D. MacFarlane, *Buchanan* (1981), p. 236; L. MacMahon, 'Henry Killigrew', A.R. Matthew (ed.), *The Oxford Dictionary of National Biography* (Oxford, 2004) (*ODNB*).

121 See chapter 4.

122 P. Croft, 'Robert Cecil', *ODNB*.

123 CP 175, fo. 118r: 22/10/1597.

124 See, for example, NA, SP 12/255, fo. 37r: c.12/1595; CP 49, fo. 92r: 03/1599; CP 82, fo. 50r: 08/12/1600.

125 CP 140, fo. 82r: 02/1597.

126 CP 175, fo. 92r: 06/1597. See chapter 3 for a fuller exploration of this letter.

127 A similar motive may have inspired her Latin verse for the Lord Keeper, Thomas Egerton, on the death of his son in 1599. For the verse, see S. May, *Elizabethan Courtier Poets: The Poems and Their Contexts* (Columbia, 1991), p. 365. For Elizabeth's letters to Thomas Egerton, see Mertoun House, Roxburghshire, Ellesmere MS EL 45: 28/06/1597; EL 46: c. 1600; EL 47: c. 1600.

128 CP 140, fo. 82r.

129 P. Phillippy, *Women, Death and Literature in Post-Reformation England* (Cambridge, 2002), p. 183.

130 Schleiner, *Tudor and Stuart Women Writers*, p. 48. For the Russell cycle of verse and accompanying translations used in the following discussion, see *ibid.*, pp. 47–50.

131 See Sophocles, *Antigone*, trans. H. Lloyd-Jones (1994), pp. 26–7 [245–7].

132 Schleiner, *Tudor and Stuart Women Writers*, p. 209. See Sophocles, *Antigone*, trans. Lloyd-Jones, pp. 48–9 [511]. For the Hoby epitaphs and accompanying translations used in the following discussion, see *ibid.*, pp. 205–10.

133 BN, Dupuy 951, fo. 122v. The line, 'Iter per illud te secuta iam forem', recalls Catullus's poem IV, 'Lament for a sparrow'.

134 *Ibid.*

135 N. Llewellyn, 'Honour in life, death and the memory: funeral monuments in early modern England', *Transactions of the Royal Historical Society* (*TRHS*), 6th series, 6 (1996), 180, 192.

136 The memorial for Anne Fitzwilliam Cooke is no longer extant. For the text, see Strype, *Annals*, II, ii, p. 606.

137 *Ibid.*, p. 605.

138 Katherine was buried in the chancel of St Thomas the Apostle in the City of London and a monument was erected in her memory. The church was destroyed during the Fire of London and the inscription on Katherine's monument is now known through the record in John Stowe, *The Survey of London* (1633), pp. 259–60.

139 *Ibid.*

140 The translation is from Schleiner, *Tudor and Stuart Women Writers*, p. 210.

141 W. Haddon, *Poematum Gualteri Haddoni, Legum Doctoris, sparsim collectorum* (1576), sig. H2r.

142 Schleiner, *Tudor and Stuart Women Writers*, p. 207.

143 *Ibid.*, p. 208.

144 *Ibid.*, pp. 206–7.

145 For more on Elizabeth's actual role as a resident diplomat's wife, see chapter 4.

146 Schleiner, *Tudor and Stuart Women Writers*, pp. 206–7.

147 *Ibid.*, p. 206.

148 *Ibid.*, p. 207.

149 *Ibid.*, pp. 207–8.

150 *Ibid.*

151 G.M. Bell, 'Tudor–Stuart diplomatic history and the Henrician experience', in C. Carlton *et al.* (eds), *State, Sovereigns and Society in Early Modern England* (Stroud, 1998), p. 36. See also G.M. Bell, 'Elizabethan diplomacy: the subtle revolution', in M. Thorp and A. Slavin (eds), *Politics, Religion and Diplomacy in Early Modern Europe* (Kirksville, 1994), p. 270.

152 Only seven weeks into his new post in 1566, Thomas Hoby was complaining to Cecil that his expenses 'be overgreat'. See NA, SP 70/84, fo. 172r: 11/06/1566.

153 BL, Additional MS 18764, fos 1r–2v; NA, SP 70/85, fo. 78r: 07/1566

154 Phillippy, *Women, Death and Literature*, pp. 187, 189.

155 E. Farber, 'The Letters of Lady Elizabeth Russell (1540–1609)' (PhD thesis, Columbia University, 1977), p. 32.

156 Thomas Hoby was commemorated by Elizabeth as one 'Cujus erat rectum, et nobile quicquid erat' (In whom was right and noble all that was). See Schleiner, *Tudor and Stuart Women Writers*, pp. 206–7. High standards of behaviour defined honourable people in Elizabeth's eyes. When she thought Henry Brooke, Lord Cobham, had reneged on a promise to rent Dacre's House from her, she wrote to him saying that 'Nether will it be eny Honowre to your Lordship thus to have broken promiss'. See NA, SP 12/255, fo. 36r: 09/1599.

157 Schleiner, *Tudor and Stuart Women Writers*, p. 48.

158 Llewellyn, 'Honour in life, death and the memory', 180.

159 Schleiner, *Tudor and Stuart Women Writers*, p. 49.

160 NA, SP 14/69, fo. 26r: after 06/05/1608. See also CP 90, fo. 152r: 1601.

161 Elizabeth opposed the sale of Russell House in 1599 on the grounds that it would destroy the claim of her and her children to the noble family. See CP 74, fo. 1r: 09/1599. See also CP 73, fo. 115r: 09/1599. She also attempted to bolster her noble status by reference to the nobility of her sister Mildred and her family in her later correspondence. See, for example, CP 88, fo. 120r: 12/10/1601; CP 90, fo. 152r: 1601; CP 197, fo. 53r: c. 05/1605; NA, SP 14/69, fo. 26r: c. 1608–9.

162 For an example of Elizabeth's claim to nobility being met with scorn, see the discussion of her 1606 Star Chamber suit against the earl of Nottingham in chapter 6.

163 Farber, 'The Letters of Lady Elizabeth Russell', pp. 115–16.

164 For this legal battle, see CP 170, fo. 54r; CP 1949; NA, SP 12/245, fo. 36r.

165 Schleiner, *Tudor and Stuart Women Writers*, pp. 48–9.

166 K. Stears, 'Death becomes her: gender and Athenian death ritual', in S. Blundell and M. Williamson (eds), *The Sacred and the Feminine in Ancient Greece* (1998), p. 116.

167 For the identification of the female figures as the Russell daughters, see H. Gladstone, 'Building an Identity: Two Noblewomen in England, 1566–1666' (PhD thesis, Open University, UK, 1989), p. 272.

168 Schleiner, *Tudor and Stuart Women Writers*, p. 48.

169 *Ibid.*

170 *Ibid.* Elizabeth describes herself and her daughters as 'shorn' in a Greek verse for John Russell omitted in Schleiner. For the missing verse, see Camden, *Reges, reginæ, nobiles*, sigs G1v–G2r. For ancient Greek mourning rituals, see M. Alexiou, D. Yatromanolakis and P. Roilos, *The Ritual Lament in Greek Tradition* (Oxford, 2002), pp. 8, 27. Elizabeth could have learnt of these rituals through her reading of classical tragedies, such as *Antigone*, or even through the Greek Church Fathers, who condemned the excesses of pagan Greek female mourners. For the Church Fathers, see *ibid.*, p. 28.

171 NA, SP 12/245, fo. 36r: 05/1593.

172 M. Hoby, *The Diary of Lady Margaret Hoby, 1599–1605*, ed. J. Moody (Stroud, 1998), p. 127.

173 There is also English verse on the tomb for her father; however, it strikes a very different note from the neo-classical verse. It is offered as 'rude unlearned verse' and does not discuss the accomplishments of his scholarly daughters, only referencing his care in seeing that he did 'well bestow/ His children all before their prime was past'. See Strype, *Annals*, II, ii, pp. 606–7. The vernacular poem on the Hoby tomb has been shown to be the work of Thomas Sackville. See J. Malay, 'Thomas Sackville's elegy to Thomas and Philip Hoby: the discovery of a draft manuscript', *Notes and Queries*, 56 (2009), 513–15.

174 Harrington wrote 'that honorable Ladie (widow of Lord John Russell) deserveth no lesse commendation [than Colonna], having done as much for two husbands'. See J. Harrington, *Ludovico Ariosto's 'Orlando Furioso'*, ed. R. McNulty (Oxford, 1972), p. 434. Harrington later sought Elizabeth Russell's patronage for his *Metamorphosis of Ajax* (1596), so his remarks should be seen within that context. For more on Harrington and Russell, see chapter 1.

175 Camden, *Reges, reginæ, nobiles*, sig. G2r.

176 P. Hentzner, *Itinerarium Germaniae, Galliae, Angliae, Italiae* (Nuremberg, 1612), p. 125.

177 Llewellyn, 'Honour in life, death and the memory', 197. For more on Elizabeth Russell's

introduction of French forms of funereal sculpture into the memorial, see Gladstone, 'Building an Identity', p. 52.

178 Gladstone, 'Building an Identity', p. 204. See also Phillippy's discussion of the memorial to Elizabeth (Bess) Russell: Phillippy, *Women, Death and Literature*, pp. 202–4.

179 It has been suggested that Elizabeth left the blank panels at the back of the monument to be inscribed with verses written by her children upon her death; if that was the case, her wishes were not fulfilled. See Phillippy, *Women, Death and Literature*, p. 210 and Gladstone, 'Building an Identity', pp. 29–30.

180 The passage depicted is Job xix. 25–7.

181 For a printed text, see H. Child and W. Greg (eds), *Iphigenia at Aulis, Translated by Lady Lumley* (1909).

182 J. Barnes, *Speeches delivered to Her Majestie this last progresse* (Oxford, 1592), sigs A2r–A4v.

183 Davidson and Stevenson make the important point that if Russell was not the sole author of the Bisham piece, she at least was its 'deviser'. See P. Davidson and J. Stevenson, 'Elizabeth I's reception at Bisham (1592): elite women as writers and devisers', in J.E. Archer, E. Goldring and S. Knight (eds), *The Progresses, Pageants and Entertainments of Queen Elizabeth I* (Oxford, 2007), pp. 208–9. See also A.F. Johnston, 'The "Lady of the farme": the context of Lady Russell's entertainment of Elizabeth at Bisham, 1592', *Early Theatre*, 5 (2002), 71–85.

184 A. Collins, *Letters and Memorials of State* (2 vols, 1746), II, p. 201.

185 *Ibid.*

186 Barnes, *Speeches*, sig. A3v.

187 *Ibid.*, A2v.

188 Davidson and Stevenson, 'Elizabeth I's reception', pp. 208, 216.

189 Barnes, *Speeches*, sig. A2v.

190 *Ibid.*, sig. A3r.

191 *Ibid.*, sigs A2v–A3r.

192 *Ibid.*, sig. A3r.

193 *Ibid.*

194 *Ibid.*, sig. A3v. Queen Elizabeth had sent troops to France to support the then Huguenot Henry of Navarre's claim to the throne in 1591 in the war of succession against the Catholic League; she had already sent troops to the Netherlands to support the Dutch Revolt against their Catholic Spanish overlords in 1585.

195 *Ibid.*, sig. A4v.

196 M. Payne and J. Hunter (eds), *Renaissance Literature* (Oxford, 2003), p. 481.

197 Barnes, *Speeches*, sig. A4v.

198 A masque written by Mary Sidney Herbert for Queen Elizabeth's visit to Wilton, probably in 1599, entitled 'A Dialogue betweene two shepheards', was only decisively attributed to her at a later printing in 1602. See M. Sidney, *The Collected Works of Mary Sidney, The Countess of Pembroke*, ed. M. Hannay, N. Kinnamon and M. Brennan (Oxford, 1998), p. 82.

Chapter 3

———◆———

'Haud inane est quod dico': female counsellors

This good Mistris K. you knowe, but yet this I also put yow in mind of; for though God have blessed you, yet you are but a weake woman, and have need (in the common frailty of man's nature) to bee stirred up with exhortation.[1]

Edward Dering, the godly preacher, thus counselled Katherine Cooke Killigrew in a letter of February 1575. Katherine was one of Dering's many female correspondents and his letters have been read to show a strong male religious counsellor offering guidance to a weak female beneficiary, plagued by religious doubt.[2] Lacking Katherine's own letters to Dering or indeed those of any of his female correspondents, the narrative is therefore of female dependency upon male epistolary counsel.[3] The letters of Katherine's sisters, however, allow for a more detailed investigation of the possibilities for women's expression through their correspondence. The previous chapter has shown how the sisters' classical education allowed them to use the written word to speak on behalf of their own priorities, particularly in the genres of translation and verse. This chapter looks more closely at whether their humanist education offered the sisters further opportunities to put forth their own opinions through their correspondence.

Humanist thinkers taught that the provision of counsel was a primary duty for early modern men, with Sir Thomas Elyot concluding that the 'end of all doctrine and study is good counsel'.[4] A humanist education was thus designed to equip men with the appropriate expertise to counsel. Study of classical and scriptural texts would provide male students with the moral, political and rhetorical skills necessary to become authoritative public servants. In its most ambitious formulation, this education thus aimed to equip men to advise their monarch to 'govern with the better advice', although educated men had a duty to counsel more widely, advising in their capacities as local magistrates and judges, as preachers and even in the context of the household.[5] Letters were perceived as one of the spaces in which men could and should offer counsel to other men; Erasmus argued that letters of advice had a 'twofold purpose', to point out the fault that needed correction and also to provide a course of action 'to one that does not know what should be done, as if he did know'.[6] He suggested that letters of counsel were as necessary for a 'schoolmaster or would-be courtier' as 'a good doctor, prince, or bishop, general, soldier, or good politician'.[7]

Counsel was, however, not a 'neutral concept' in early modern England; humanist authority was only one way of legitimating advice-giving, and debate raged over the basis from which counsel was offered.[8] Yet if counsel was not 'neutral' for men, it was even more of a contested activity for women. There was little encouragement of female counsel of men in sixteenth-century England, in the form of letters, print or even speech. The prescriptive material is unequivocal in its rejection of women adopting the role of counsellor or teacher over their adult male counterparts in any form. Thomas Elyot denounced female teaching of men after the age of seven in *The boke named the Governour* (1531), and eight years earlier Juan Luis Vives had been more explicit, writing 'a woman should not teach, lest she hath taken a false opinion and belief of any thing, she spread it unto the hearers'.[9] Vives drew on St Paul's injunctions as justification for such views: 'But I permit not a woman to teache, nether to usurpe authoritie over the man, but to be in silence.'[10] There are suggestions, however, of a more complex reality, even in the prescriptive material. For both Elyot and Vives, motherhood placed specific demands upon women. Elyot dedicated his *The education or bringinge up of children* (1532) to his sister, so that she would be 'marvaylously instructed ... in ordrynge and instructynge your children, circumspectely and discretly'.[11] Vives wrote that mothers should aspire to be good teachers unto their 'little children'.[12] Widowhood only intensified women's educative responsibility to their children, with Erasmus writing in his *De vidua christiana* (1529) that whilst all mothers should educate their children as 'an act of piety', the raising of fatherless children by a widow was 'an act of compassion more pleasing to God than any sacrifice'.[13] The Pauline epistles also offered a complex model for early modern women; St Paul's epistle to Titus suggests that women could teach doctrine to younger girls, and his writings on edification state that the task was of such importance that both men and women should contribute.[14] Even St Paul's restrictive precepts could be interpreted more loosely. Anne Askew argued that St Paul's strictures only restricted women from speaking to a public congregation, rather than from private teaching.[15]

Moreover, there is evidence of some sixteenth-century women adopting counselling roles in their letters.[16] Anne Knevet and Margery Cooke provided religious counsel to the Marian martyrs in their letters, although Henry Bull and John Foxe erased their advice in their printed editions.[17] The Elizabethan letters of Joan Thynne similarly suggest that she was comfortable counselling her husband over political matters.[18] The correspondence of the Cooke sisters allows a more detailed exploration of the counselling roles adopted by one group of sixteenth-century women. In their extant letters, the sisters are most often found counselling male family members; there is evidence that Mildred advised her cousin William Fitzwilliam, and Elizabeth frequently counselled her nephew Robert Cecil by letter. The greatest numbers of surviving letters of advice are those written by Anne to her son Anthony; presumably she wrote to her other son, Francis, as he acknowledged receiving her words of counsel, but only one letter is still extant.[19] Yet the sisters did advise men outside of the family; Elizabeth's letter of advice to Peregrine Bertie, Lord Willoughby, survives, whilst Anne counselled members of the Essex circle by letter, ranging from an army captain to the earl of Essex himself.

Following the divisions of classical oratory, Renaissance rhetoricians argued that letters of counsel belonged to the deliberative or persuasive genre.[20] Women seeking to advise through their letters thus needed to use persuasive strategies in their correspondence if they were to be accepted as counsellors to men, in doing so adopting the role of teacher. Yet, whilst attention has focused on the strategies women used in another type of persuasive letter, the petitionary letter, there has been little consideration of the construction of female letters of counsel.[21] Previous research has suggested that letters of advice between family members, particularly those between mothers and sons, had little need of conscious crafting.[22] A letter written by Elizabeth to her youngest son, Thomas Posthumous Hoby, certainly appears to be written with little recourse to her rhetorical training. Elizabeth counselled her son over his marital suit for Margaret Dakins, the late widow of Walter Devereux, in 1591, writing 'Now, chyld, it standeth yow aper for your owne creditt's sake to trye your frends. My Lady Perrott the wisest, surest, and fittest to your good ... [she] may, on some tyme of the gentlewoman's comming to visitt my Lady Dorothie, let you understand of the tyme when yowrself may mete her there.'[23] Elizabeth's language is terse and she gives little account of the reasoning behind her advice; her superior knowledge is established with her reference to her twenty-five-year-old son as 'chyld'. Elizabeth, however, had little fear as to its reception. Thomas had already approached Lady Dorothy Perrot, Margaret's sister-in-law, for information and Dorothy had shown herself keen to please Elizabeth Russell through acting as an intermediary.[24]

With the majority of the letters of counsel written to men by Elizabeth and her sisters, a positive reception to their advice was far from assured, even though much of it was written to family members. Anne certainly often worried that her advice was mocked and, worse, ignored by her sons, writing, for example, in the summer of 1595 'Read not my lettre after scoffingly or carelesly which hath ben used to much ... For I humbly thank god I know what I write & cownsell.'[25] There is evidence that Elizabeth too worried her advice was not acted upon. She questioned whether Robert Cecil had received one of her letters of counsel, for she never had a response.[26] The sisters echoed the prescriptive literature in highlighting that their counsel derived from the responsibilities of motherhood. Advice-giving was a duty Anne associated with her role as mother: 'I cannot cease to warn as long as I am a mother that loveth yow in the lorde most deerly.'[27] 'As your good mother I thus certefie,' she similarly appended to her admonition to Anthony in April 1595, 'Think of it.'[28] Elizabeth too offered maternal guidance, even to those other than her natural children. Her nephew Robert Cecil was described as her 'sweet nursling', revealing a maternal context to her advice; when Elizabeth counselled Lord Willoughby on his marital disagreements with his wife and his subsequent absence from court, she did so within the context of Lady Willoughby being seen as a 'dawghter' to her.[29] There were, however, limits to how far the claims of motherhood legitimated advice-giving. Anne's letters in particular show that a claim to a mother's wisdom was insufficient to guarantee a good reception for her advice by her sons. She noted in May 1592 'but my sonnes hast not to harken to their mother's goode cownsell in time to prevent'.[30] The failure of maternal authority to ensure a positive reception must have stemmed from the age of Anne's adult sons. Even the prescriptive texts that encouraged mothers and widows to teach their children envisaged the exchange as between adult mother and infant child. Yet the boundaries of adulthood in sixteenth-century England were contested; if marriage was taken to be a marker of adulthood, then both of Anne's sons failed to reach adulthood during her widowhood.[31] Anne's letter from 3 February 1592 is revealing as to why she sought to offer maternal counsel. 'Remember yow have no father,' she writes to her son Anthony, 'And yow have litle inowgh, yf not too litle, Regarded your kind & no symple mother's holsome advyse from time to time.'[32] As a widow of father-less sons, Anne is explicit that she is 'no symple' mother. She, unlike many early modern women, has a particular platform from which to present her counsel: her unusually accomplished education.

This chapter argues that the sisters were able to turn to their humanist education to provide them with strategies for bolstering their advice, particu-larly over issues of politics and religion, the most contentious areas for female counsel. The relationship between the Cookes' counselling of men and their exceptional educational background has been questioned in previous analyses of their letters; in her sensitive treatment of the contexts for Anne Bacon's epistolary exchanges, Lynne Magnusson has argued that the use of classical learning in Anne's correspondence could have 'little effect' on the reception of her advice.[33] Yet I would suggest that the demonstration of various types of learning was used to strategic effect by the sisters in their letters in order to bolster their political and religious agency.

CONCEALING FEMALE COUNSEL

One of the most practical effects for the sisters of a humanist education was that it provided a measure of epistolary privacy. Contentious information was often excluded from early modern letters, as correspondence could be read by prying eyes.[34] The sisters were aware of the insecure nature of their letters. Anne repeatedly included injunctions to burn her letters after reading, as did her sister Elizabeth. 'I pray burn my lettre,' Anne wrote to her son Anthony in December 1594, 'your men & your Brothers prye in every matter & lysten. I pray send back or burn this letter.'[35] Elizabeth told Sir Thomas Egerton in a letter 'send this back that I may burne it'.[36] A letter by Mildred Cooke Cecil to her cousin William Fitzwilliam advised him 'to keep close your friends' letters ... Some about you may be corrupted to show them.'[37] Elizabeth even refused to replicate on paper the libels she had heard circulating regarding their nephew Robert Cecil in 1599, instead stating that she would inform him of them at their next meeting.[38]

To hide such information, particularly from the bearer of the letter, it was necessary to adopt some form of code. Knowledge of Greek was still rare, even among the elite, at the end of the sixteenth century, due to a lack of competent teachers and the dominance of Latin in the curriculum.[39] Mildred was close friends with the Edwardian diplomat Richard Morison, who turned to transliteration, using Greek letters in place of Roman characters, to encode names in his official letters, in case of interception.[40] Mildred's husband, William Cecil, used the same method to disguise the valuable objects in his household inventory.[41] Thus there was precedent for Anne's decision similarly to turn to her knowledge of the Greek alphabet to conceal political counsel in her correspondence, as exemplified in a letter to Anthony from April 1595:

> Beware in eny wyse of the lord H. Όυαρδε (Howard), he is a dangerous intelligen-cyng man. no dowt a subtile papist inwardly & lieth in wayte. Peradventure he hath some close working with Στανδεν (Standen) & the Σπανιαρδε (Spaniard) ... he wyll bewray yow to diverse & to your Αυντε Ρυσσελ (Aunt Russell) among. The duke had ben alyve but by his practising & styll soliciting hym to the Duke's undoing & the Εαρλε Αρυνδελ (Earl Arundel).[42]

This was not a foolproof system, but it did give some level of protection from prying eyes. Her classical education not only provided Anne with the opportunity of transliteration, it also allowed her to conceal whole sentences of her own political counsel within her correspondence. On his return from the Continent in 1592, Anne warned Anthony of the danger from the archbishop of Canterbury, John Whitgift; however, she chose to conceal what was an unsurprisingly damning indictment. Thus she wrote in Greek, stating in that language that since Whitgift had been made councillor, he was proving the destruction of the church, 'φιλεῖ γὰρ τὴν ἑαυτοῦ δόξαν πλέον τῆς δόξης τοῦ χρίστου' (for he loves his own glory more than the glory of Christ).[43] Similarly, when she heard rumours that the earl of Essex had embarked upon an affair with one of the Queen's maids of honour in April 1595, she appended a Greek postscript to a letter to Anthony, strongly advising the cessation of such a dangerous course.[44] Her letter of 5 August 1595 warns Anthony of the duplicitous nature of the countess of Warwick, a gentlewoman of the Privy Chamber and one of the Queen's closest intimates during this period. Here Anne turns instead to her Latin, writing that Anne Dudley was one 'quae nec sentias aulica perferre ad reginam, et patrissat in illa re nimis' (whom you would not notice performing court duties for the queen, and in this matter she takes too little after her father).[45] Anne Dudley's father, Francis Russell, the earl of Bedford, was the father-in-law of Anne Bacon's sister Elizabeth.

Anne's letters firstly provide an insight into the sort of political and religious material which sixteenth-century women were uncomfortable committing to paper and, secondly, reveal that a humanist education offered one method of seeking epistolary privacy. Without such learning, other early modern women offering counsel needed alternative codes to hide their advice. Anne Percy, the countess of Northumberland, for example, used ciphers in her correspondence from exile in 1576; in the seventeenth century Brilliana Harley used four-letter codes and prearranged sheets of paper with cut-outs when conveying messages to her son Edward during the Civil War.[46] The comparable advantage of Anne's method was that it did not need to be prearranged, relying only on the shared educational background between her and her male recipient.

THE RHETORICAL VALUE OF EXPERIENCE

The sisters' education was of greater import to their epistolary counsel than simply providing a method of concealment. Classical rhetoricians taught that it was not enough to possess wisdom and to offer valuable advice; the counsellor instead needed to master the rhetorical strategies necessary to put their message across effectively and persuasively. The Roman rhetorician Quintilian argued that in offering counsel 'what really carries weight ... is the authority of the speaker'.[47] In his letter-writing manual, *De conscribendis epistolis* (1522), Erasmus echoed this classical guidance, suggesting that the writer of epistolary advice should establish some form of 'authority' over his correspondent, drawing on their 'advantage in years, in which we far outstrip him, or breadth of experience, in which he cannot yet be our equal by reason of age, or long study, in which we have been engaged over many years, while he is only entering upon it'.[48]

Such advice was directed at male counsellors, but the lessons had also been learnt by the Cooke sisters, for they highlighted their experience for strategic effect in their epistolary counsel.[49] Only one letter of political counsel composed by Mildred survives, written to her cousin William Fitzwilliam. Fitzwilliam's position as Lord Deputy of Ireland was vulnerable in October 1573, yet Mildred advises that he should remain at his post until a time when he can be replaced without danger to his standing at the English court.[50] The letter is striking for the bold tone of Mildred's personal guidance. 'And therfor I think it best,' she instructs her cousin, 'this storme were over blowen, and after some sarvis done, a better time may be found to seke your departure.'[51] Mildred emphasises that this counsel is born of hard-earned political knowledge: 'It is not you that suffer alone; this greffe is common to all those that deall in princes' affaryes, which I wish my frendes had less cause to know by experience.'[52] Elizabeth, too, makes recourse to her political experience in her letters, drawing on the lessons she learnt having long been, in her words, 'a Coortier and a parlament woman'.[53] Her appeal to her knowledge as a 'parlament woman', a play on the contemporary phrase 'parliament man', may have particularly resonated with the recipient of those words, Robert Cecil, who would have known of his aunt's past interest in parliamentary activity; she had previously tried to influence her nephew in a bill touching the hue and cry of the hundred of Beynhurst in Berkshire and he would have likewise known of the parliamentary interests of his other aunt, Anne Bacon.[54] Yet Elizabeth's unusual identification as a 'parlament woman' would have been striking in this period and she more often emphasised in her letters the authority she gained as an experienced 'Coortier'. For example, when petitioning Robert Cecil to support William Day in his refusal of the bishopric of Worcester, she counsels him to be 'no doer for feare of afterclapps by her majestie's indignation'.[55] In advising Peregrine Bertie, Lord Willoughby, to put aside his marital disagreements with his wife and to return to court, she again highlights her political experience as legitimising her advice; in particular, she notes her knowledge of the Queen's long-standing regard for his wife, Lady Willoughby.[56]

Anne, however, makes the greatest reference to her experience in her letters to her son Anthony. As the widow of a Privy Councillor and the Lord Keeper of the Great Seal, Anne was explicit with her sons that she had valuable experience of the political arena: 'I think for my long attending in coorte & A cheeff cowsellar's wyffe few praeclarae feminae meae sortis (distinguished women of my sort) are able or be Alyve to speak & judg of such proceedings & worldly doings of men.'[57] Her advice to Anthony repeatedly stems from her long-term experience of and dealings with members of the court. In August 1595 she turned to past knowledge when warning Anthony against involvement with the countess of Warwick: 'upon advise & some Experience, I wold ernestly cownsell yow to be ware & circumspect & not be to open in wyshing to prolong speche with the cowntess of Warwicke. She after her Father's fashion wyll search & sownd & lay upp wth diligent marking.'[58] Anne's counsel is based not only on her long acquaintance with Anne Dudley, the countess of Warwick, but also on her knowledge of her father, Francis Russell, the earl of Bedford. Anne's advice to Anthony to avoid Lord Henry Howard, already discussed above, is again based on her knowledge and experience. She informs Anthony that she has 'long known him & observed him'; Howard's suspected Catholic sympathies had led to his being placed under house arrest at the Bacons' Suffolk house in July 1585. Her conclusion was that Howard was a 'very instrument of the Spanish papists' who would 'pretendyng curtesy worke micheff Devilyshly'.[59]

Her particular concern was that, in contrast to her own familiarity with the English political arena, her son Anthony was far less experienced, returning to England in 1592 after a twelve-year absence in Europe. Anthony's lack of knowledge is thus highlighted in his mother's letters, in comparison with her understanding. 'Yow have ben long absent,' Anne tells him, '& by your sickliness cannot be your own Agent & so wanting right Judgment of our state may be much deceaved.'[60] After a prolonged stay in a Catholic country, she informs him he must be sure to mark himself from the outset as a godly Protestant. 'This one cheffest cownsell your christian & naturall mother doth geve yow even before the lorde,' she tells Anthony, 'that Above all worldly respects yow carie yourselff ever at your first comming as one that doth unfeinedly profess the tru Religion of Christ.'[61] This advice, however, is not purely that of a godly mother, for it is based on past experience of the political sphere: 'For the propertie of our world is to sownd owt at first comming & after to contemn ... Yow wylbe observed at first now.'[62] Anne was particularly concerned that without a detailed knowledge of past political affairs, Anthony would be a poor judge of his new acquaintances. 'Beleve not every one that speakes Fayre to yow at your Fyrst comming,' his mother tells him, 'It is to serve their turn.'[63] She worried that Anthony was moving in a world 'full of false semblance' and that he would prove an easy target for the unscrupulous, both in the political arena and in the management of his country estates.[64] Anne considered that her greater experience continued to legitimate her counsel long after Anthony's return to England, as his ill-health prolonged his lack of familiarity with English political culture. Regarding his dealings with his cousin Robert Cecil, after the latter's elevation to the secretaryship in July 1596, she tells Anthony, 'yow are sayd to be wyse & to my comfort I willing thynk so, but surely sonne on thother syde for want of home experience by Action & your teadious unaqwaintance for your own cowntry by continuall chamber & bedkeeping, yow must nede myss of considerate judgement in your verball onely travayling.'[65] Therefore she advises Anthony, from her own greater experience, that 'yow had more nede now to be circumspect & advised in yor troblelong discoorsinges & doinges & dealinges'.[66]

LATIN LETTERS OF COUNSEL AND THE USE OF *SENTENTIAE*

In *De conscribendis epistolis,* Erasmus offered further advice to the writer of epistolary counsel, arguing that they should 'point out in dignified language what should be done and how'.[67] Erasmus's concern was with the quality of the correspondent's Latin, rather than the choice to turn to classical languages at all. For the Cooke sisters, however, the decision to write in classical languages was one which highlighted the intellectual training behind their advice to their recipient. Mildred thus turned to Latin to counsel her sister Anne over her marital prospects, at some point between late 1552 and mid-1553, writing 'Mea soror, Cantabrigis fui, tuum vidi Haddonum, quem amabis, si sapis, et plane tuum esse statues. Nihil illi praeter fortunam deest, nec haec quidem diu abesse potest in tanto reliquorum concursu vel ornamentorum, vel oppor-tunitatum.'[68] (My sister, I have been in Cambridge, I saw your Haddon whom you will love, if you have sense, and clearly make him yours. He lacks nothing save fortune and this indeed cannot long be wanting where there is so great a combination of other distinctions and advantages.) Mildred's choice to write in Latin underscores the educational background she shares with her sister Anne. Their scholarly upbringing is significant to a letter concerned with the importance of humanist education in sixteenth-century society. Mildred counsels Anne to accept Walter Haddon, for, as a highly educated man, he will achieve great things in the future; she cites the examples of her husband's father-in-law from his first marriage, John Cheke, and Thomas Smith, who, both possessing 'eruditionis et ingenii' (learning and talent), have acquired fame, and so, she suggests, Haddon will similarly establish himself. Their father, Anthony Cooke, is described as opposed to the match, yet Mildred suggests that Anne should not yield entirely to his opinion. Mildred's decision to write in Latin is designed to highlight to her sister that she has the learning and wisdom to offer valuable advice, rivalling that extolled by their father.

Anne's own use of Latin in her letters of advice makes such concerns more explicit. Underpinning her usage of classical language to emphasise key points in her advice is the perception that her humanist education qualifies her, unusually for a woman, to extend counsel, particularly regarding political matters. Thus, when she defends the value of her epistolary advice against what she perceives as indifference from her sons, she turns to her Latin, stating angrily 'matris monita nihil estimantur' (The counsels of your mother are estimated as nothing).[69] Even more plainly, she again breaks into Latin to declare to Anthony 'crede mihi fili' (believe me, son) and 'haud inane est quod dico' (what I say is not foolish).[70] The link between Anne's unusual degree of learning and her right to offer political counsel is even made explicit in a letter to Anthony. Anne unequivocally depicts herself and the small circle of classically educated women, 'praeclarae feminae meae sortis', as successful participants in the humanist tradition of learning, as we have seen, enabled thus to 'speak & judg of such proceedings & worldly doings of men'.[71] Instead of viewing their educational potential as marginalised and silenced, Anne considers that her humanist education provides a training equivalent to that of her male contemporaries.

Similar considerations lie behind the sisters' use of *sententiae* in their epistolary counsel. Humanist training in this period encouraged the collection of pithy moral axioms or *sententiae* from classical and biblical works, which could then be recorded in commonplace books. The sisters' humanist education under their father would have equipped them for the collection of *sententiae* and, although no commonplace books belonging to the sisters are still extant, we know that their learned female contemporaries did collect *sententiae*. As we have seen, Lady Mary Fitzalan presented her father, the earl of Arundel, with three small volumes of *sententiae* as successive New-Year gifts.[72] Similarly, the extant marginalia in the sisters' books suggest that they highlighted the thematic content of their reading, possibly for recording in a commonplace book.[73] As already discussed, the sisters' letters therefore reveal *sententiae* drawn from a wide variety of texts.[74] Their male contemporaries were taught the political utility of such *sententiae*. These moral axioms were intended to provide the basis for future debates. Erasmus noted that such phrases provided 'extremely useful ammunition for the future speaker'.[75] Henry Peacham wrote that such quotations 'declareth by an apte brevity, what in this our lyfe ought to be done, or not done'.[76] Erasmus's suggestion in *De conscribendis epistolis* was reflective of the prevailing wisdom regarding the use of Latin phrases in epistolary counsel, for he suggested the use of 'many sayings and examples from the approved authors, particularly those who hold the most authority for the person we are advising'.[77]

The strategic possibilities of *sententiae* for the sisters can be seen in the letter of counsel written by Mildred to William Fitzwilliam in October 1573. Whilst it is filled with personal counsel, as already discussed, Mildred chose to end her letter with a *sententia* from Ovid's *Fasti*, quoting 'Conscia mens recti famae mendacia ridet' (A mind conscious of integrity laughs at gossip's lies).[78] The abiding impression of Mildred's letter is therefore not of her personal advice, but rather of the congruence of her own counsel with that of an established, classical authority. In March 1594 Anne, similarly, turns to the knowledge of Terence's *Eunuchus* that she shared with her son Anthony, when highlighting the ancient truth of her advice that he should keep his servants in good order: 'yow learned in terence long ago, *sic luxuriantur Famuli cum absunt Domini*' (in this way the servants grow indulgent when the masters are absent).[79] She uses Seneca's wisdom in *Epistulae morales* to bolster her unwelcome advice to Anthony regarding his ungodly choice of friends, echoing a *sententia* which was painted upon the walls of their Gorhambury house in Anthony's youth:

'as Seneck by philophy [*sic*] onely cowlde say ... *mallem successu[m]* ... *quam fidem deesse*' (I should prefer to lack success rather than to lack faith).[80]

Anne's younger sister, Elizabeth, relied even more heavily on classical citation in her letters. A letter written in October 1599 to her nephew Robert Cecil, then secretary of state, warns him that vicious libels were circulating regarding his role in the earl of Essex's recent arrest. She presents her counsel, however, through quotations from Horace's *Epistles* and Virgil's *Aeneid*. Cecil must 'take heede' of his aunt's counsel to protect his reputation, 'lest as the poet sayeth, *Ille Dies primus, Lethi, primusque malorum: Causa fuit*' (That day the first of death, that first of calamity was cause).[81] Elizabeth then goes on to advise Cecil of the threat from Essex's popularity, citing again from Virgil's *Aeneid*:

> I do but put yow in mynde of what may follow by former example. Ac veluti magno in populo cum saepe coorta est seditio, saevitque animis ignobile vulgus iamque Faces et Saxa Volant Furor arma ministrat.[82]
> (And as, when often in a great nation tumult has risen, the base rabble rage angrily, and now brands and stones fly, madness lending arms.)[83]

In both instances, Elizabeth makes it explicit that her advice is drawn from classical authorities. She thus emphasises that her counsel is based on established wisdom, rather than purely personal opinion; although Elizabeth is offering political insight, it is Virgil who speaks for her.

The Cooke sisters do not use *sententiae* merely to appropriate the wisdom of classical authors. Their utilisation of moral axioms is also calculated to persuade their correspondents of the legitimacy of the claim by these educated women to offer counsel to men. Mary Ellen Lamb has argued that the significance of Elizabeth's quotation from Virgil, above, is that it describes the ocean before it is calmed by Neptune in the *Aeneid*, signalling the possibility of Robert Cecil's future success in regaining his reputation.[84] However, there is a greater significance to Elizabeth's use of this quotation. The success of the *sententia* relies upon her confidence in Cecil's knowledge of the exact context of the original extract. The lines are drawn from a simile which compares Neptune's calming of the sea with the effect of a great orator upon the people, 'ille regit dictis animos et pectora mulcet' (with speech, he sways their passion and soothes their breasts).[85] Thus, by using the extract to put Cecil 'in mynde' of Virgil's narrative, Elizabeth is not only explicitly warning of the power of the rabble, but implicitly offering Cecil the solution: to turn to his powers as an orator.[86]

Elizabeth had already used this technique when writing to Robert Cecil after the death of his wife in January 1597. Lady Elizabeth Brooke Cecil had miscarried and died during her third pregnancy and her husband grieved deeply for his loss. Elizabeth sent a verse of her own composition as consolation, as already discussed in the previous chapter.[87] In June, she sent her nephew a letter which counselled Cecil to be strong and return to his political vocation. This was precisely the same advice Walter Ralegh had given Cecil earlier that year, with Ralegh writing 'yow should not overshado your wisedome with passion, butt looke aright into things as the[y] are ... Sir, beleve it, that sorrows ar dangerus companions, converting badd into evill and evill in worss & do no other service then multeply harms.'[88] Ralegh's advice is without rhetorical embellishment, written simply and plainly. In contrast, Elizabeth again uses the persuasive strategies provided by her education. She turns to Scripture, quoting Solomon's words from Ecclesiastes in the Old Testament. She tells Cecil that 'according to Salomon yow may study nothing more then *Letari et bene facere*' (to rejoyce, and to do good).[89] This is another example where Elizabeth's advice is amplified by recognition of the original context of the *sententia*. It comes from the third chapter of Ecclesiastes, which begins 'To all things there is an appointed time, and a time to everie purpose under the heaven. A time to be borne, & a time to dye'.[90] Elizabeth's quotation comes from the point in the chapter which underlines that, in spite of life's tribulations, every man should 'seeth the commoditie of all his labour, this is the gift of God'; by the wider context of her citation, Elizabeth is suggesting that Cecil's extended grief is an insult to God.[91] She then includes an unacknowledged quotation from Cicero's *De officiis*:

> yow may ... think no thinge better then to walk in yowr vocation, in yowr place a wise eloquent Orator; thogh *parum vehemens Dulcis tamen ut patris discipulum possis agnosci*.[92]
> (not impetuous enough yet charming, so that you are able to be recognised as your father's disciple)

The power of her counsel again comes from the wider context of the *sententia*. Cicero's quotation describes Demetrius of Phalerum, who he suggests may be the only Greek to combine the skills of oratory with calm philosophy. This is precisely the same advice that Elizabeth is presenting to Cecil throughout her letter: to leave his grief, and once again become the composed, philosophical orator. Again, it is left to Cecil to recognise the context of the *sententia* and to understand its value. Elizabeth therefore uses classical citations to stress the shared humanist education of female counsellor and male reader, qualifying her to offer political advice.

The advantage that *sententiae* offered the sisters can be seen most fully in Anne's letters of counsel to her son from August 1595. Anthony had decided to move from his house in Bishopsgate Street into the earl of Essex's house on the Strand. His mother was opposed to the move from its inception. She wrote to Anthony on 15 August, saying that, from experience, it would only lead to 'some encrease of suspicion & disagreement which may hurt yow privetly if not publikly or both by all lykelihodes'; her vehemence is highlighted by her recourse to Latin, for she laments 'crede mihi fili' (believe me, son).[93] Yet the letter had little effect. She wrote again on 20 August 1595, saying that she could not 'put some feare owt of my mynd yet'. However, this time she presented her counsel to Anthony in the form of *sententiae*: 'verses have come to my rememorance thynking of your purpose. long forgotten but now fresh. the one rather A proverbial cownsell then A verse, which is as I have sene it by fyrst syllable onely sett down thus. *Ni= Fa= pa= con=*.'[94] The proverb to which Anne is here alluding is *Nimia familiaritas parit contemptum* (Too much familiarity breeds contempt) from the writings of Publilius Syrus and so, from the outset, she is highlighting that her counsel corresponds with that of classical, male writers.[95] Her letter then goes on to reinforce the truth of this maxim by reference to a line from Horace's *Epistles*, 'Dulcis inexperto cultura potentis amici' (Those who have never tried think it pleasant to court a friend in power).[96] Significantly, however, Anne does not finish the *sententia*, trusting in her son's learning to supply the crux of the maxim, 'expertus metuit' (The one who has tried it, fears it). In both cases, it is left to Anthony to 'fill in the blanks' from his own classical education, to recognise the actual proverb cited and complete the *sententia* in order to understand his mother's message. Anne's use of classical citations therefore works to highlight the congruence of her counsel with classical, male wisdom and stress the shared humanist education of female counsellor and male reader, legitimating her right to offer her son the fruits of her learning. Once that context has been established, Anne then offers Anthony more explicit advice in the vernacular, telling him 'every thing yow do shalbe spoken & noted abroad & yourself browght as it were into A kind of Bondag where now yet free. many, many wylbe the unqwait & Hurtfull molesatations.'[97]

Anne and Elizabeth also turn to *sententiae* in order to access more authoritative forms of language in their correspondence. Elizabeth's letters reveal that, whereas strong admonitions would have alienated their male recipients, such commands were more acceptable if mediated through citation. When advising Robert Cecil to appoint Henry Grey, earl of Kent, to the Lord Lieutenancy of Essex, Elizabeth writes, 'I beseche yow, *Quod facis Fac cito*' (That thou doest, do quickely).[98] By quoting the Gospel of John in Latin, she allows the extract to issue her imperative to Cecil, whilst her own words remain deferential.[99] Elizabeth uses the same technique when she urges Cecil to be wary of the danger to his political position from extended grief after his wife's death. Citing Horace's *Satires*, she baldly commands him to 'Tu, Romane, caveto' (You, Roman, beware).[100] Elizabeth ends this letter by dismissing her own counsel, yet here her use of biblical citation complicates the significance of her words. She writes of her advice, 'It may do good, if not Burne it for telling yow so foolish a tale, as *ex abundantia Cordis os Loquitur*' (For of the abundance of the heart, the mouth speaketh).[101] By quoting Christ's words from the gospels of both Matthew and Luke in Latin, Elizabeth creates a paradox within the sentence.[102] Ostensibly, she is allowing Cecil to dismiss her words as 'foolish', yet she is also negating such a course of action, through the biblical resonance of her language. As the gospels go on to state that 'A good man out of the good treasure of the heart bringeth forthe good things: & an evil man out of an evil treasure bringeth forthe evil things', the context again undercuts Elizabeth's overt dismissal of her words by highlighting the scriptural wisdom of her counsel.[103]

BIBLICAL *SENTENTIAE* AND RELIGIOUS COUNSEL

In comparison to her sister, Anne relied even more heavily on biblical citation in her letters. Three out of the four extant letters from Anne to the earl of Essex contain spiritual advice and, unlike in many of those directed at her sons, Anne had taken great care in the composition of those letters.[104] In one letter of religious exhortation to the earl, Anne writes that, after hearing a sermon in London, she encountered a friend who informed her that Essex was 'A terrible swearer', which 'me thowght stroke my hart'.[105] Anne then provides Essex with five biblical injunctions against swearing. 'For I protest to your Honour,' she writes, 'that those words (A terrible swearer) did so terrefye me in your Behalff ... my mynde cowlde not be well qwieted, till I had committed thus in scribling to your Honour, my Deere Lorde, & licence me, I pray yow withall, to add these Few textes For your Remembrance, being diverse wayes drawn to Forgett.' Anne then offers scriptural citations from both the Old and the New Testaments:

> The Fyrst is the charge the lorde him selff Joyneth with his own commandment that he wyll not hold him gyltless that takes his name in vain.[106] our Saviour christ also Biddeth, sweare not at all. math. 5.[107] The Apostle James teacheth sayeng, Above all things my Brethren sweare not. 5.[108] The prophet Hoseas, soare accusing that people in his time that by many horrible vices they brake owt, at the Fyrst Front nameth by swearing cap. 3.[109] to conclude with the profecte Ieremye cap. 23. he complayneth saying to that people, the Jewes, the lande, sayth he, is full of Adulterers, & by reason of Oathes the lande morneth.[110]

These biblical citations are set against repeated statements of Anne's deference to the earl. Yet, in spite of her humble stance, the biblical *sententiae* allow her to speak authoritatively and effectively to the nobleman.

The origins of the scriptural extracts used in this letter, deriving from both testaments of the Bible, are an unusual choice for Anne. The greatest proportion of biblical quotations in her correspondence was, instead, drawn from the New Testament epistles. The scriptural epistles were an obvious source for Anne, as they are concerned with offering epistolary religious counsel. She therefore characteristically turned to this source when again writing to the earl of Essex with spiritual advice, this time exhorting him to forsake his extramarital affairs. Anne had heard a rumour about Essex's involvement with her great-niece and Burghley's grand-daughter Elizabeth, Lady Derby, and thus she wrote to counsel him to relinquish his affair in December 1596:

> But yow my good Lord have not so learned Christe and hearde his holie worde in the 3d.4.5. verses of the 4 chapter to the first Thessulonians. that is written this is the will of god that yea should be holie & abstaine from fornication and everie one know how to keepe his owne vessell, in hollines and honor, and not in the luste of concupiscence, as doe the gentiles which knowe not god: and more yf it please yow to reade and marke well, yt is a heavie thret that fornicators and Adulterors god will judge and that the[y] shalbe shut out, for such things saith the Apostle commonlie commeth the wrothe of god uppon us.[111]

Anne not only explicitly cites verses from St Paul's first letter to the Thessalonians, she also quotes from his letter to the Colossians.[112] Anne then goes on to embed unacknowledged citations from the New Testament epistles throughout the letter. She ends, for example, by urging Essex against his reputed adulterous liaisons: '*be stronge in the Lord*[113] your and our good patient god, feare him and *walke upritelie in his truths*[114] and for *his promise in Christe*[115] he will assist yow and looke favorably uppon yow and yours'.[116] Anne includes two unacknowledged references from Paul's letter to the Ephesians and one from his letter to the Galatians. This technique of embedded scriptural citation was also employed by Anne's male contemporaries. The evangelical preacher Edward Dering repeatedly used such citation in his letters of religious counsel to Anne's younger sister Katherine.[117] However, this is a strategy which has particular utility for a female counsellor. The origins of the citations work to emphasise the congruence of Anne's advice with accepted scriptural wisdom, working to persuade Essex of the truth of her counsel. Moreover, the quotations allow Anne to write in the imperative, apparently offering bold counsel to the earl, whilst her own words in the letters maintain a deferential stance.

In all her spiritual epistolary counsel, Anne carefully avoids any detailed discussion or exegesis of her biblical quotations. We can, however, discover the significance of her scriptural citation, beyond that of simply advising her correspondents of godly standards. This is clearly revealed in a letter written to her son Anthony, where she provides advice to be passed on to his brother, Francis Bacon. Here Anne explicitly criticises Francis's worldly focus in his practice of law, writing:

> his profession is not or owght not to be of vayn devises & unprofitable. Be ye holy as I am holy sayth god by his prophett.[118] let him reade the 5 to the Ephesians towching unclean speache & thowghte.[119] Trust in the lord with all this hart sayth the wysedom of god & not in thin own. read the 3rd of the proverbs.[120] The Apostle sayth or rather the holy gost, yf eny man think [him] selff, let him be A Foole in this world that he may be wyse.[121] ... the sownde preaching wheroff consisteth not all in the wordes [of] men's wysdom but in the power & evidence of the spirit.[122] which god graunt.[123]

In this passage, Anne cites widely from various books in the Bible, with all her quotations centred on the necessity of rejecting profane knowledge for spiritual wisdom. Her final citation from St Paul's first letter to the Corinthians is particularly significant. Anne paraphrases that the 'sownde preaching ... consisteth not all in the wordes [of] men's wysdom but in the power & evidence of the spirit'. On one level this can be read to advise her son that the power of his words, his legal oratory, should be inspired by piety, rather than his rhetorical skill. Yet, following Anne's wider employment of scriptural citations, I would suggest that her use of this verse also reflects her understanding of reformed doctrines of Scripture and their significance to Elizabethan preaching. Scripture was perceived as more than a record of Christ's sayings and actions; rather, it was a revelation of what Edward Dering termed 'God's Spirit speaking through his Prophets'.[124] That Anne shares this assumption is made explicit in another of her biblical citations in this letter, where she writes that it is 'the holy gost' who spoke through Paul when he said 'yf eny man think [him] selff, let him be A Foole in this world that he may be wyse'.[125] Anne believed that the Holy Spirit was operative in Scripture and thus, when she cites Paul on the 'power and evidence of the spirit', she also reveals the belief that her correspondents will receive the grace to be edified by her scriptural citation, through the power of the Holy Spirit. Anne makes explicit her confidence in the value of her scriptural advice in her letter to Essex counselling him against swearing. She tells the earl that 'by expownding well the law & commandments of god, sinn is layde open & disclosed to the hearers & worketh in them by god his spirit, more hatred of evell & checketh our proneness naturall, to all synn'.[126]

For Anne, therefore, scriptural exhortation must be valued for its edifying exposure to the Holy Spirit, regardless of the gender of its progenitor. As she tells Essex, when mitigating her boldness as a woman offering spiritual exhortation to a man, 'it may be the lorde god wolde have yow know the matter thowgh by such A poore weake meanes as this'.[127] She is here referencing the biblical prescription, again in Paul's first letter to the Corinthians, that God, through the Holy Spirit, may use the weak to chastise the strong.[128] This verse was often cited in their defence by women circumventing their lowly role in the ecclesiastical hierarchy and, by paraphrasing the verse, Anne is again emphasising the power of the Holy Spirit to legitimate her own act of religious counsel.[129]

Anne's frequent recourse to the Pauline Epistles has another significance for her epistolary religious counsel. The Pauline Epistles are striking for their extensive use of intercessory prayer.[130] The use of written prayers within letters was not unusual in the period; Edward Dering, for example, often begins his letters of counsel with written prayers.[131] The value of intercessory prayer for Anne, as a female counsellor, is that she can offer bold and authoritative godly advice through what is a religiously sanctioned act. Anne repeatedly uses intercessory prayers in her epistolary counsel to her sons. When counselling Anthony and Francis to forsake their Catholic friend, Antonio Pérez, 'A prowde prophane costly fellow, whose being abowt him I verely feare the lord god doth mislyke', Anne concludes her advice with an intercessory prayer: 'The lord in mercy remove them from him & evell from yow both & geve yow A sownde judgment & understanding to order your selffs in all things to plese god in tru knowledg & in his tru feare unfeyned & to harken to his word which onely maketh wyse in dede.'[132] The prayer form allows Anne to express her counsel to her sons, setting out what she believes should be their religious priorities, but as the prayer is directed to the Lord, her otherwise stark imperatives are mitigated. This technique is more noticeable in Anne's letters of religious counsel to men in her wider social networks. Her letter to Francis Goad, an army captain and member of the Essex circle, in April 1596 begins with an extended written prayer for the earl of Essex, which she concludes with an 'Amen', explicitly echoing the Pauline Epistles. After providing Goad with biblical injunctions against swearing, which Anne has heard to be rife amongst Essex's soldiers, she closes her letter with an encapsulation of her religious counsel in the form of an intercessory prayer for the earl: 'I write this hartely, thowgh Bowldely, & pray the lorde to gwyde that worthy Earle, your grawnd worthy, & to prosper him & to preserve him From all treacheries & From all maner evell & be his continuall cownsellor & comfort.'[133]

Anne's utilisation of the New Testament epistles is significant for her conception of the relationship between widowhood and religious counsel. Widowhood was an important status for Anne and she chose to sign herself as 'ABacon Χηρα' in eight of her letters, 'Χηρα' being the Greek for widow.[134] The role of godly widows is discussed in the epistles of St Paul, in his first letter to Timothy. The biblical passage discusses how poor widows will be maintained and suggests that a special group of widows 'be taken into the nomber': 'Let not a widowe be taken into the nomber under thre score yere olde, that hathe bene the wife of one housband, And wel reported of for good workes: if she have nourished her children, if she have lodged the strangers, if she have washed the Saintes' fete, if she have ministred unto them which were in adversitie, if she were continually given unto everie good worke.'[135] The standard reading of the passage is that widows without any other means of family support will receive assistance from the church. Lynne Magnusson, however, has argued that Anne must have read this passage instead to suggest that, as a godly widow, she was admitted into a special class of the ministry, which imbued her religious advice with particular authority. She reveals that Théodore de Bèze, Thomas Cartwright and Lambert Danaeus all conceived of a formal order of widows taking on an official role in church government.[136] Magnusson thus suggests that Anne chose to sign herself as 'Χηρα' 'in her letters to powerful figures', which she takes to indicate a 'positive sign of authority'.[137] However, of the eight times that Anne signs herself as 'Χηρα', only two of the letters are directed to an influential figure, both times the earl of Essex; of the remaining letters, five are sent to her son Anthony, and one is written to her stepson Nicholas Bacon. One of the two letters to Essex signed with 'Χηρα' does not contain religious counsel, instead it is a petitionary letter written on behalf of William Dike, one of Anne's godly preachers; the other two extant letters by Anne to the earl, clearly including religious counsel, are not signed in this way. Letters to Edward Stanhope, Lord Burghley and his son, Robert Cecil, all are signed without reference to Anne's status as a widow. So what, then, do the letters signed 'Χηρα' have in common? The significance of these letters is that they all include some form of intercessory prayer on behalf of the recipient; the letters to Anthony and Nicholas are familial correspondence, covering diverse matters, but all include at least a short intercession.

This is not to argue that Anne did not draw her conception of the role of a 'Χηρα' from St Paul's first letter to Timothy; however, I suggest that Anne's concern was not with the formal recognition of an order of widows, nor with 'arrogating in her discourse a ministerial role unimagined for women in the Elizabethan Church of England'.[138] The difficulty of the discussion of widowhood in Timothy is whether godly widows were to perform specific tasks in return for assistance and, if so, how those tasks were to be defined. Magnusson suggests that they would be 'usually imagined as charitable activities'.[139] While there is no definitive answer in the passage, the suggestion is that the primary duty of a godly widow is that she 'trusteth in God, & continueth in supplications and prayers night and day', which also characterises the duties of Anna, another godly widow of the New Testament, this time in the Gospel of Luke.[140] This is where I would argue that Anne's identification with the role of the godly widow lies: in the daily religious duties of a widow, particularly centred on prayer. Her letters reveal the importance of prayer as a primary duty of her widowhood. She wrote to Burghley in 1585, telling him that she understood she must attend 'publyck exercysees, as A cheff duty commanded by god to weedoes'.[141] Burghley indeed responded in a similar way to Anne eight years later, making reference to her religious activities, imploring God to keep her in his favour 'by your meditacons, and that I as your olde frende, maie be the partaker of your good wishes and prayers'.[142] In October 1593 Anne grieved over the passing of her estate manager because he had enabled her, as a widow, to have 'very much qwiett of mynde & leasure to spende my tyme in godly exercises, both publick & private'.[143] Prayer therefore served a variety of functions in Anne's epistolary counsel. It allowed her to reiterate her advice to her sons, setting out what she believed should be their religious priorities. It was both a form of gift for the recipient and a biblically sanctioned act for the godly widow. Ultimately, it was yet another strategy for Anne to use when offering religious counsel.

RECEPTION

The question remains, however, as to whether the sisters' strategies were effective. Extant letters of response are most fulsome regarding Anne's episto- lary counsel, but the evidence is also often seemingly contradictory. Anthony's replies sometimes reveal anger at his mother's endless counsel. In response to her advice for him to forsake his ungodly friends in June 1594, he rebukes her, suggesting that she is possessed by 'a Soveraigne desire to overrule your Sones in all thinges, how litle soever yow understande eyther the grounde or circumstances of their proceedings'.[144] However, on other occasions her sons appear to value her counsel. Anthony responded to his mother in March 1594, telling her that he did 'humblie thanke your Ladyship for your lettres and will not faile to remember and endeavour to followe your wise and kinde advise'.[145] Lynne Magnusson has highlighted that the relationship between Anne and her sons was affected by diverse issues, particularly concerning the financial standing of Anthony and Francis; Anthony's appreciation of his mother's counsel was often accompanied by requests for money and household goods from the Gorhambury estate.[146]

However, I would question the suggestion that Anne had nothing to gain from 'writing better texts or striving for greater learning'.[147] The language that Anne's male correspondents used in response to her epistolary counsel suggests that they recognised and responded to the learned construction of her advice. Anthony thanks his mother for a letter warning him of the danger from Robert Cecil and praying to the Lord that he would harken to her counsel, in terms which acknowledge the construction of her epistolary advice. Recog- nising her prayer of guidance, Anthony adds that his own scriptural study has strengthened his patience in these matters: 'For mine owne part the reding and Christian meditation of the 36 & 37 psalmes shall with god's grace serve me for trew preservatives to keep me from emulating any worldly prosper- etie or greattnes or fearing the effects of human power & malice.'[148] Beyond her sons, there was again recognition of the construction of Anne's epistolary counsel. Only one copy of a letter survives from the earl of Essex in response to Anne's religious admonitions, in reply to her counsel for him to forsake his extramarital affairs. Essex is gracious in accepting Anne's advice, stating 'I take it as great argument of god's favour in sendinge so good an angell to admonishe me'.[149] He protests his innocence of the charges laid against him, the result, he claims, of rumour and conspiracy, and cites his response to such accusations, writing 'Plutarch taught me longe since to make profit of my enemies, but god teacheth it me muche better nowe'. Essex's reply is significant because he has not only noted the learned construction of Anne's religious counsel, but has also felt it necessary to reply in kind, citing the example of both his classical and scriptural reading.

The success of Anne's epistolary counsel can also be considered through the continued willingness of her son Anthony to disseminate political news to his mother. Partly this is again a gift for his mother in return for her support, both financially and with goods from Gorhambury, but it also aided her future advice-giving to her sons. Anthony sent a letter to his mother on 5 February 1594 to 'advertise yow that which a frende of mine hath particularly written unto me by the Earle of Essex appointment, prencipally concerninge my Brother'.[50] He tells his mother that in what follows 'I alter not one worde thinkinge it best to set it downe as it hath bene delivered from my Lord'. He then provides his mother with a detailed description of the earl's efforts in his campaign on Francis's behalf for the office of attorney-general, particularly concerning Robert Cecil's opposition to Francis's appointment. Similarly, on the 12th of that month Anthony again wrote to his mother, enclosing a letter written to him by Henry Gosnold, a young laywer at Gray's Inn, concerning Francis's reputation.[51] Anne's response to Anthony's news was again to provide Francis with advice; although Anne's letter to Francis is no longer extant, he acknowledged her 'good Counsell everie waie' on 14 February, adding 'And I hope by god's assistance to followe the same'.[52] As Anne's counsel was grounded in a detailed knowledge of the contemporary political and religious situation, Anthony's dissemination of news reveals his acceptance of her advice-giving. The relationship between news dissemination and female counsel is significant. Recent work on women's involvement in intelligence networks has importantly delineated the scope of female interest in this area, but Anne's letters further demonstrate that sixteenth-century women processed and transformed their access to news.[53] Anne's news-gathering was key to her continuing efforts to provide counsel to her sons. Her networks stretched beyond her family, for example incorporating Dorothy Stafford, a gentlewoman of the privy chamber.[54] News-gathering for Anne was not merely a pastime, but was instead integral to her role as a female counsellor.

In many ways, however, too close a focus on the reception of the sisters' counsel is unhelpful. In order to overcome the inequalities created by gender, the sisters turned to precisely the same strategies as did their male contemporaries, when seeking to persuade either those of a higher social status or those who would simply not welcome their counsel. Nicholas Bacon, Anne's husband, for example, turned to a quotation from Seneca when trying to persuade Francis Walsingham of the value of his advice against military intervention in the Netherlands in 1578. Understanding that such counsel would be unpopular with Walsingham, Bacon cited Seneca, saying 'And I had rather you should see myne error in Judgemente then in friendshippe. Seneca saythe Mallem in amico consilium quam fidem deesse' (In warning a friend, I would rather lack success than faith).[55] Over fifteen years later, his wife turned to exactly the same quotation when trying to persuade their son Anthony of the value of some unwanted advice, in this case to forsake his ungodly compan-ions.[156] The techniques discussed in this chapter did not guarantee a positive reception of advice, for sixteenth-century men or women; rather, they helped to improve the odds.

CONCLUSION

This chapter has engaged specifically with the construction of the sisters' letters of counsel. They also used these techniques in other types of persuasive letters, particularly petitionary letters.[157] Whilst they strove in such letters for deference, rather than authority, experience was a significant trait to empha-sise. For example, Elizabeth cited her long experience of the respective suitor both when supporting William Day's decision to decline the bishopric of Worcester in 1596 and when recommending Matthew Dale for the Master of Requests in the same year.[158] *Sententiae* also offered the sisters opportunities in petitionary correspondence. Elizabeth cited one of the Ten Commandments when petitioning Robert Cecil not to steal away her footman in August 1601.[159] Similarly, Elizabeth closed a letter written in 1608, during her second widow-hood, to her nephew Robert Cecil with the following: 'Helpe, swete Lord, Help, god will Helpe yow and your Cuntry with prolonging yowr Dayes et totus populus Dicat Amen' (and all the people say Amen).[160] This Latin *sententia* is drawn from Deuteronomy, where it is written 'Cursed be he that hindreth the right of the stranger, the fatherles, & the widowe: And all the people shal say: So be it.'[161] Elizabeth was therefore turning to the biblical prescription to protect the widow, in order to bolster her request to her nephew.

Scriptural conceptions of widowhood thus provided ways in which both Elizabeth and Anne could advance their own priorities. Widowhood, moreover, has a wider significance for the sisters' counselling activities. We have seen examples of Mildred adopting counselling roles during her marriage, yet the evidence of this chapter is drawn primarily from the widowhoods of Anne and Elizabeth. Whilst in some ways this reflects the nature of the extant evidence, the state of widowhood did provide the sisters with not only the opportunities to counsel, but also the perceived necessity to counsel, as seen in Anne's belief that she must advise her adult, yet fatherless, sons.

This chapter's treatment of the sisters' letters of counsel may seem to elide the different social status of their male correspondents. However, the letters written to family members of varying status are in fact remarkably undiffer-entiated in their tone. Early modern letter-writing manuals grouped letters of advice, according to classical rhetorical categories, within the persuasive or deliberative genre and separate from judicial, demonstrative and familial correspondence.[162] Yet the sisters' advice more often formed sub-sections of their familial letters. The letters written by Anne to the earl of Essex are more formally structured; two of them adopt, unlike the majority of her correspondence, the formal rhetorical structure of early modern letters.[163] In terms of content, however, the strategies discussed in this chapter were used by the sisters to persuade male correspondents, both within the family unit and in their wider social networks.

The epistolary counsel of Mildred, Anne and Elizabeth therefore demonstrates that a humanist education did have a political and religious utility for women, although the outlets were admittedly restricted in scope compared to those offered to their male contemporaries. Their education provided guidance for writing effective letters of counsel. The Cooke sisters used their humanist learning in their letters to conceal, emphasise and legitimate their counsel to men. Ultimately, the sisters' letters of counsel show that skilful use of female learning allowed them a means of offering advice, letting them speak as unusually authoritative women in a patriarchal society.

NOTES

1 E. Dering, *Certaine godly and comfortable Letters* (1614), sig. C3v.

2 P. Collinson, 'Godly Master Dering', in P. Collinson (ed.), *Godly People* (1983), p. 317.

3 Katherine's only extant letter is one of thanks for a suit granted, and thus the dominant theme is again her humility to a male patron, her brother-in-law, Lord Burghley. NA, SP 12/155, fo. 178r: 18/11/1582.

4 T. Elyot, *The Book Named The Governor*, ed. S.E. Lehmberg (1962), p. 238.

5 *Ibid.*, p. 13.

6 D. Erasmus, *De conscribendis epistolis*, ed. J.K. Sowards, *Collected Works of Erasmus*, 25 (Toronto, 1985), p. 189.

7 *Ibid.*, p. 190.

8 J. Guy, 'The rhetoric of counsel in early modern England', in D. Hoak (ed.), *Tudor Political Culture* (Cambridge, 1995), p. 293.

9 Vives, p. 56.

10 1 Timothy ii.12. See also I Corinthians xiiii.34–35 and Ephesians v.22–33.

11 T. Elyot, *The Education or bringinge up of children, translated oute of Plutarche* (1532), sigs A2r–v.

12 Vives, pp. 123–4.

13 D. Erasmus, *Spiritualia*, ed. J. O'Malley, *Collected Works of Erasmus*, 66 (Toronto, 1988), p. 202.

14 S. Wabuda, 'The woman and the rock: the controversy on women and Bible reading', in S. Wabuda and C. Litzenberger (eds), *Belief and Practice in Reformation England* (Aldershot, 1998), p. 41.

15 A. Askew, *The Examinations of Anne Askew*, ed. E. Beilin (Oxford, 1996), p. 30.

16 For seventeenth-century women offering religious advice, see M. Morrissey and G.

Wright, 'Piety and sociability in early modern women's letters', *Women's Writing*, 13 (2006), 38–50.

17 T. Freeman, '"The good ministrye of godlye and vertuouse women": the Elizabethan martyrologists and the female supporters of the Marian martyrs', *Journal of British Studies*, 39 (2000), 8–33.

18 A. Wall, 'Elizabethan precept and feminine practice: the Thynne family of Longleat', *History*, 75 (1990), 31.

19 LPL 650, fo. 255r.

20 See Erasmus, *De conscribendis epistolis*, pp. 71, 189–90.

21 See, for example, J. Daybell, 'Scripting a female voice: women's epistolary rhetoric in sixteenth-century letters of petition', *Women's Writing*, 13 (2006), 3–20; J. Daybell, *Women Letter-Writers in Tudor England* (Oxford, 2006), pp. 250–64. See also L. Magnusson, 'A rhetoric of requests: genre and linguistic scripts in Elizabethan women's suitors' letters', in J. Daybell (ed.), *Women and Politics in Early Modern England, 1450–1700* (Aldershot: 2004), pp. 51–66.

22 R. Anselment, 'Katherine Paston and Brilliana Harley: maternal letters and the genre of mother's advice', *Studies in Philology*, 101 (2004), 432; Daybell, *Women Letter-Writers*, p. 179.

23 The original letter was destroyed in a nineteenth-century fire, but a copy exists in S.R. Gardiner (ed.), *The Fortescue Papers* (CS, new series, 1, 1871), pp. x–xi.

24 *Ibid.*, pp. ix–x.

25 LPL 653, fo. 330r: n.d.

26 CP 52, fo. 52r: 24/06/1597.

27 LPL 650, fo. 331r: 07/09/1594.

28 LPL 651, fo. 89r: 08/04/1595.

29 CP 175, fo. 118r: 22/10/1597; Lincolnshire Record Office, 10ANC/333: n.d. [after 1584].

30 LPL 648, fo. 172r: 24/05/1592.

31 See I.K. Ben-Amos, *Adolescence and Youth in Early Modern England* (New Haven, 1994), p. 11; E. Foyster, *Manhood in Early Modern England: Honour, Sex and Marriage* (Harlow, 1999), p. 46.

32 LPL 653, fo. 343r: 03/02/1592. Anne had long worried about the lack of paternal influence on Anthony, as shown, for example, in her 1581 letter to Theodore de Bèze. See *Correspondance de Théodore de Bèze*, ed. H. Aubert *et al.* (38 vols, Geneva, 1970), XXII, p. 108.

33 L. Magnusson, 'Widowhood and linguistic capital: the rhetoric and reception of Anne Bacon's epistolary advice', *English Literary Renaissance*, 31 (2001), 6.

34 Daybell, *Women Letter-Writers*, pp. 128–33.

35 LPL 650, fo. 333r: 05/12/1594.

36 Mertoun House, Roxburghshire, Ellesmere MS EL 46: c. 1600.

37 Bodl., Carte MS LVI, fo. 475r: 26/10/1573.

38 CP 179, fo. 92r: 10/1599.

39 J.W. Binns, *Intellectual Culture in Elizabethan and Jacobean England* (Leeds, 1990), p. 218; K. Milne, 'The forgotten Greek books of Elizabethan England', *Literature Compass*, 4 (2007), 679.

40 See, for example, NA, SP 68/6, fo. 213r: 28/04/1551.

41 BL, Lansdowne MS 118, fo. 83v.

42 LPL 651, fo. 108r: 01/04/1595.

43 LPL 653, fo. 343r: 03/02/1592. Translation from Spedding, p. 112.

44 LPL 651, fo. 108r: 01/04/1595.

45 LPL 651, fo. 328r. Anne also turned to Latin to conceal a warning to Anthony regarding the election of MPs in St Albans: LPL 649, fo. 23r: 25/01/1593.

46 Daybell, *Women Letter-Writers*, pp. 140–1.

47 Quintilian, *Institutio Oratoria*, trans. H.E. Butler (4 vols, 1920–22), I, p. 485 [III.viii.12–13].

48 Erasmus, *De conscribendis epistolis*, p. 190.

49 Mildred, at least, owned a copy of Erasmus's *De conscribendis epistolis*. See chapter 1.

50 For a more on Fitzwilliam's situation, see chapter 4.

51 Bodl., Carte MS LVI, fo. 475r: 26/10/1573.

52 *Ibid.*

53 CP 90, fo. 151r: c.12/1601.

54 CP 49, fo. 13r: 01/1598. For sixteenth-century use of the phrase 'parliament man', see the *Oxford English Dictionary*. The parliamentary activity of Elizabeth's sister Anne is discussed below in chapter 5. For the sporadic evidence of sixteenth and early seventeenth-century women's involvement in parliamentary elections, see H. Smith, 'Women as sextons and electors: King's Bench and precedents for women's citizenship', in H. Smith (ed.), *Women Writers and the Early Modern British Political Tradition* (Cambridge, 1998), pp. 324–42. There is fuller evidence of the parliamentary activity of Leveller women in the mid-seventeenth century. See, for example, E. McArthur, 'Women petitioners and the Long Parliament', *English Historical Review*, 24 (1909), 698–709; P. Higgins, 'The reactions of women, with special reference to women petitioners', in B. Manning (ed.), *Politics, Religion and the English Civil War* (1973), pp. 177–222; A. McEntee, '"The [un]civill-sisterhood of oranges and lemons": female petitioners and demonstrators, 1642–53', in J. Holstun (ed.), *Pamphlet Wars: Prose in the English Revolution* (1992), pp. 92–111; A. Hughes, 'Gender and politics in Leveller literature', in S. Amussen and M. Kishlansky (eds), *Political Culture and Cultural Politics in Early Modern Europe* (1995), pp. 162–88.

55 CP 25, fo. 51r: 24/02/1596.

56 Lincolnshire Archives, 10 ANC/333.

57 LPL 651, fo. 156r: 12/05/1595.

58 LPL 651, fo. 328r.

59 LPL 651, fo. 108r: 01/04/1595.

60 LPL 648, fo. 196r: 24/07/1592.

61 LPL 653, fo. 343r: 03/02/1592.

62 *Ibid.*

63 LPL 648, fo. 12r: 02/03/1592.

64 LPL 653, fo. 317r: 03/07/1593.

65 LPL 658, fo. 28r: 10/07/1596.

66 *Ibid.*

67 Erasmus, *De conscribendis epistolis*, p. 190.

68 BL, Lansdowne MS 104, fo. 156r: n.d. There are questions over the authenticity of the letter. It is written in Walter Haddon's hand, so may possibly have been composed by him; more probably, however, Haddon was shown and then made a copy of Mildred's letter of advice.

69 LPL 651, fo. 95r: 12/05/1595.

70 LPL 651, fo. 330r: 15/08/1595. LPL 651, fo. 225r: n.d.

71 LPL 651, fo. 156r.

72 BL, Royal MS 12 A.I–IV.

73 See chapter 1.

74 See chapter 1.

75 D. Erasmus, *The Right Way of Speaking Latin and Greek*, trans. M. Pope, *Collected Works of Erasmus*, 26 (Toronto, 1985), p. 402.

76 H. Peacham, *The Garden of Eloquence* (1577), sig. U3r.

77 Erasmus, *De conscribendis epistolis*, p. 190.

78 Bodl., Carte MS LVI, fo. 475r; Ovid, *Fasti*, IV.311.

79 My italics. LPL 650, fo. 130r: 25/03/1594. Terence, *Eunuchus*, III.v.600.

80 My italics. LPL 650, fo. 331r: 07/09/1594. Seneca, *Epistulae morales ad Lucilium*, XXV.2.

81 My italics. CP 179, fo. 92r: 10/1599; Virgil, *Aeneid*, trans. H.R. Fairclough (1999), pp. 432–3 [IV.169–70].

82 My italics. CP 179, fo. 92r.

83 Virgil, *Aeneid*, trans. Fairclough, pp. 272–3 [I.148–50].

84 M.E. Lamb, 'The Cooke sisters: attitudes toward learned women in the Renaissance', in M.P. Hannay (ed.), *Silent But for the Word* (Kent, Ohio, 1985), p. 121.

85 Virgil, *Aeneid*, trans. Fairclough, pp. 272–3 [I.153].

86 CP 179, fo. 92r.

87 See chapter 2.

88 CP 37/92_2r: 24/01/1597.

89 My italics. CP 175, fo. 92r: 06/1597.

90 Ecclesiastes iii.1–2.

91 Ecclesiastes iii.12.

92 My italics. CP 175, fo. 92r. Cicero describes Demetrius of Phalerum as 'a rather spiritless orator, yet he is charming, so that you can recognize in him the disciple of Theophrastus' ('orator parum vehemens, dulcis tamen ut Theophrasti discipulum possis agnosci'). Cicero, *De officiis*, trans. W. Miller (1968), pp. 4–5 [I.i.3].

93 LPL 653, fo. 330r: 15/08/1595.

94 My italics. LPL 653, fo. 326r: 20/08/1595.

95 Anne's nephew Robert Cecil used the same *sententia* in a letter to Christopher Hatton in September 1591. See I. Archer *et al.* (eds), *Religion, Politics, and Society in Sixteenth-Century England* (CS, 5th series, 22, 2003), p. 252.

96 Horace, *Epistles*, I.xviii.86.

97 LPL 653, fo. 326r.

98 My italics. CP 30, fo. 26r: 27/01/1597.

99 John xiii.27.

100 CP 175, fo. 92r; Horace, *Satires*, I.iv.85.

101 My italics. CP 175, fo. 92r.

102 Matthew xii.34; Luke vi.45.

103 Matthew xii.35; Luke vi.45.

104 Anne sent her son Anthony a copy of one of the letters, which testifies to her care in its composition. See LPL 660, fo. 151r: n.d.

105 CP 128, fo. 68r: 23/12/n.y.

106 Exodus xx.7, Leviticus xix.12 and Deuteronomy v.11.

107 Matthew v.34.

108 James v.34.

109 Hosea iv.2.

110 Jeremiah xxiii.10.

111 LPL 660, fo. 149r: 01/12/1596.

112 The line 'saith the Apostle commonlie commeth the wrothe of god uppon us' draws on Colossians iii.6.

113 My italics. Ephesians vi.10.

114 My italics. Galatians ii.14.

115 My italics. Ephesians iii.6.

116 LPL 660, fo. 151r.

117 See, for example, embedded citations from Psalms xxxiii.11, 2 Timothy ii.19 and Matthew xvi.18 in Dering's letter to Katherine on 14 August 1575: Dering, *Certaine godly ... Letters*, sig. C5r.

118 Leviticus xi.44; 1 Peter i.16.

119 Ephesians v.4.

120 Proverbs iii.5.

121 1 Corinthians iii.18.

122 1 Corinthians ii.13.

123 LPL 653, fo. 330r: n.d.

124 M. Morrissey, 'Scripture, style and persuasion in seventeenth-century English theories of preaching', *JEH*, 53 (2002), 689–90.

125 LPL 653, fo. 330r.

126 CP 128, fo. 68r.

127 *Ibid.*

128 1 Corinthians i.27.

129 Morrissey and Wright, 'Piety and sociability', 52.

130 For the significance of intercessory prayer in the Epistles, see G. Wiles, *Paul's Interces-sory Prayers* (Cambridge, 1974).

131 For example, see Dering, *Certaine godly ... Letters*, sig. C4v.

132 LPL 653, fo. 318r: 17/04/1593.

133 LPL 656, fo. 319r: 27/04/1596.

134 See LPL 648, fo. 177r; 650, fos 84r, 329r, 333r; 653, fo. 303r; 655, fo. 215r; 660, fo. 149r; D. MacCulloch (ed.), *Letters from Redgrave Hall: The Bacon Family, 1340–1744* (Suffolk Record Society, 50; Woodbridge, 50; Woodbridge, 2007), p. 75.

135 1 Timothy v.9–10.

136 Magnusson, 'Widowhood', 28–32.

137 *Ibid.*, 28.

138 *Ibid.*, 28.

139 *Ibid.*, 32.

140 1 Timothy v.5; Luke ii.36–37.

141 BL, Lansdowne MS 43, fo. 119r: 26/02/1585.

142 LPL 649, fo. 180r: 29/08/1593.

143 LPL 649, fo. 340r: 18/10/1593.

144 LPL 650, fo. 228r: 12/06/1594.

145 LPL 649, fo. 89r: 25/03/1593.

146 Magnusson, 'Widowhood', 12–13.

147 *Ibid.*, 6.

148 LPL 658, fo. 6r: 13/07/1596.

149 LPL 660, fo. 281r: 01/12/1596.

150 LPL 649, fo. 49r.

151 LPL 649, fo. 50r. See LPL 653, fo. 187r for Gosnold's letter.

152 LPL 649, fo. 60r.

153 J. Daybell, '"Suche news as on Quenes hye wayes we have met": the news and intel-ligence networks of Elizabeth Talbot, countess of Shrewsbury (c. 1527–1608)', in J. Daybell (ed.), *Women and Politics in Early Modern England, 1450–1700* (Aldershot, 2004), pp. 114–31; Daybell, *Women Letter-Writers*, pp. 152–7; N. Mears, *Queenship and Political Discourse in the Elizabethan Realms* (Cambridge, 2005), pp. 104–82.

154 LPL 652, fo. 86r: 21/10/1595.

155 Huntington Library, HM 1340, fo. 94r: 24/07/1578.

156 LPL 650, fo. 331r: 07/09/1594.

157 Their male correspondents also used similar techniques in their letters to the sisters. For example, Nicholas Trott turned to Latin when excusing himself to Anne for selling a horse she had given him, citing Tertullian and Scripture in his effort to persuade. See BL, Harleian MS 871, fos 80r–v: 03/09/1594.

158 CP 25, fo. 51r: 24/02/1596; CP 41, fo. 74r: 15/06/1596.

159 CP 87, fo. 85r: 10/08/1601.

160 CP 197, fo. 54r: c.1608, before May.

161 Deuteronomy, xxvii.19.

162 See, for example, Erasmus, *De conscribendis epistolis*, p. 71.

163 CP 128, fo. 68r; LPL 660, fo. 149r. The formal rhetorical structure of early modern letters consisted of an *exordium* (introduction), *propositio* (declaration of the substance of the letter), *confirmatio* (amplification), *confutatio* (countering of objections) and a *peroratio* (conclusion). For more on this structure, see J. Gibson, 'Letters', in M. Hattaway (ed.), *A Companion to English Renaissance Literature and Culture* (Oxford, 2000), pp. 615–19; Daybell, *Women Letter-Writers*, pp. 240–3.

Chapter 4

'Cecil's wife tells me': political networks

In July 1553 William Cecil's career, and perhaps his life, hung in the balance.[1] A reluctant witness to the King's instrument to alter the succession, he began to prepare for flight as support swung behind Mary Tudor. However, when the Privy Council turned allegiance and declared in favour of Mary, Cecil was sent as their representative to the new Queen at Ipswich. It could have been a very difficult meeting, yet Cecil was forewarned. His secretary, Roger Alford, had been sent ahead of his master and, once in Ipswich, he met with Cecil's sister-in-law, Anne Bacon. She had already ridden to join Mary at Kenninghall and had pledged her support to the new Queen. Thus, on Alford's arrival, she informed him that the Queen now 'thought verye well of her brother Cicell and sayde you were a verie honest man'.[2] Anne had been acting as an intermediary, passing on political information; not only was she supplying Cecil with news about his likely reception from Mary, but she had also been central in providing the information on which the new Queen judged the actions of both Cecil and her own husband, Nicholas Bacon. Mary Tudor was staying in Robert Wingfield's house at Kenninghall and the latter recorded that 'Bacon's wife, who had once been a waiting woman of Queen Mary's, was their chief aid in beseeching pardon for them'.[3] In many ways, Anne's actions in 1553 were fortuitous and contingent on circumstance, for Kenninghall was but a few miles from where the Bacons were then living at Redgrave.[4] Yet they can also be seen as more widely reflective of female roles within early modern political networks. Anne was acting as an intermediary or 'broker' between patron and client and her influence proved a vital link in this network. Her gender was no restriction to her fulfilment of this role and, in fact, was in many ways an advantage. Her very lack of office and her overtly domestic role within the new Queen's household meant that she could supply political information without appearing threatening, whilst still operating as a powerful intermediary for Mary's clients, her brother-in-law and husband.[5]

Barbara Harris's seminal essay on women and politics in early Tudor England reconceptualised female involvement in an area which had traditionally been seen as male.[6] By moving away from a conception of politics based on male institutions, Harris highlighted the political roles held by women within a patronage society. Recent work has emphasised the interests of the family as lying behind women's involvement in such political networks; as Harris has argued for the early Tudor period, their 'interest in politics centred on the pursuit of patronage for themselves, their kin, and their clients'.[7] Despite our increased awareness of the political activities of aristocratic and gentry women in the early modern period, important questions still remain unanswered concerning both the scope and the nature of elite female political agency. The difficulty in fully delineating female political agency in the early modern period arises because female political influence was informal and achieved through 'sociability patterns'.[8] It therefore has to be reconstructed through a variety of sources; women's letters, both those they wrote and those they received, are a particularly fruitful source. The previous chapter revealed the political counsel within the Cooke sisters' correspondence. This chapter looks more widely at the political agency demonstrated in their letters. Unlike those of many of their female contemporaries, the sisters' surviving letters are unusually diverse and allow for a detailed picture to be drawn of their activities within their political networks. It demonstrates that they were most commonly found operating as intermediaries within such networks, often as brokers of information between clients and patrons.[9] This chapter explores that process in more depth, seeking to consider the types of information brokered by these female intermediaries.

By focusing particularly on the activities of Mildred and Elizabeth, the chapter demonstrates female detailed understanding of and contribution to issues central to Elizabethan politics. In doing so, it explicitly seeks to highlight women's contribution to mainstream narratives of politics in this period, marking a break with Harris's work on the early Tudor period, which distanced itself from 'traditional political history'.[10] The contribution of the Cooke sisters provides another perspective on the key issues of Elizabethan diplomacy, the Queen's marriage and the political divisions of the 1590s. This chapter therefore builds on previous work emphasising the role of the family as a motivating factor for women's political activities, although its focus on 'high politics' suggests that the range of female political activities considered as being motivated by kin advancement has often been perceived too narrowly. Furthermore, this chapter also questions whether there was a particular appeal in a female intermediary, beyond her closeness to male patrons and based on the unofficial nature of her position. Implicitly throughout the chapter, and specifically in its final section, the language used by the sisters to those in their political networks is analysed, reflecting on whether a high

degree of education was an advantage for the Cooke sisters in their activities
as intermediaries.

LADY MILDRED CECIL AND DIPLOMACY

Elite women in the Elizabethan period have been represented as being
isolated from the world of diplomacy.[11] Natalie Mears has recently questioned
this argument, looking in particular at the involvement of Lady Mary Sidney
and Katherine Ashley in two key episodes in Elizabeth I's marital negotiations,
although she admits that wider evidence of female involvement in diplomatic
matters is 'fragmentary and scattered'.[12] Mildred Cecil's activities throughout
the Elizabethan period instead reveal her sustained and lifelong interest in
diplomacy. She undoubtedly had particularly fruitful opportunities for this
sort of political involvement, due to her marriage. William Cecil's role first
as Principal Secretary and then as Lord Treasurer made Mildred an attractive intermediary for clients wishing to influence her husband, and her diplomatic activities were dependent on his power and influence. While always
supportive of her husband's political aims, her involvement in this area went
far beyond the scope of those female activities which previous research has
considered as motivated by family advancement. In particular, Mildred's activities reveal her understanding of the foreign policy objectives of her husband
and, moreover, that she worked to further his priorities. William Cecil has
been delineated as a councillor with a vision of England as the hub of a Protestant British Isles, ranged against a Continental Catholic threat.[13] Cecil has been
shown as an integral figure in a web of intelligence-gathering that stretched
to Scotland and Ireland, as well as into Europe.[14] While far less rich evidence
survives concerning Mildred's diplomatic activities as compared with those
of her husband, it is apparent that Mildred acted as an intermediary in these
information-gathering networks and that her primary focus on correspondence with Scotland and Ireland reflects her husband's political concerns.

For William Cecil, the survival of a Protestant England at the start of Elizabeth's reign depended on Scotland and support of the rebellion of the Lords
of the Congregation.[15] Mildred's letters reveal that her primary interest at this
time was likewise north of the border. William Maitland, the Scottish diplomat
and key member of the Lords of the Congregation, noted her pre-existing
concern for Scottish affairs on 18 April 1560, when, excusing his delay in
writing, he wrote 'I know what Care you have alwayes for our Maters'.[16] In
another letter, from July that year, Maitland again noted Mildred's concern for
her co-religionists in Scotland, stating 'having found so moche favour at yowr
Handes, if I shuld ever forget it, I myght most worthely be estemed unworthy
to be reputed ane honest Man'.[17] One basis for this close relationship was their
personal acquaintance with each other, for Maitland revealed 'I wold not yow

shold conceave any evill Opinion of me, or esteme me so unthankfull, that the Memory of yowr gentleness did no longer continew with me then yowr Presence'. Mildred had most likely met Maitland on his previous diplomatic journeys to London, for his relationship with her husband was forged on his visit to the English capital in March 1559, ostensibly as an agent for Mary of Guise; it was surely consolidated during Maitland's embassy to England between December 1559 and February 1560, when William Cecil worked alongside Maitland in seeking to convince the Queen of the necessity of armed support for the Scots.[18]

Maitland's letters to Mildred from April 1560 focused, however, on one particular issue: the strength of the Lords' campaign. Maitland's first letter to Mildred, on the 18th of that month, was optimistic about the possibility of winning over the neutral Scottish lords, following their appeal to them the previous month to stand as true Scotsmen against the French: 'If we wer ones clere ryd off all Termes of Treaty, I se no lykelyhode but off good Succes. Saving that we stand in doute, that the Quene's Majestie may be entreated to fall into a Communication, I se nothing yet to be mislyked.'[19] To that end, he informed Mildred that the Lords of the Congregation had resolved to send James Sandilands, Lord St John of Torpichen, 'direct' to the Queen; Lord St John would also bring news from Scotland for Mildred and her husband, for Maitland added that he would send with the envoy 'Ample Advertissement of all Things'. Maitland was also swift to reassure Mildred against the rumours that the Lords' campaign was floundering, increasing the threat of French domination in Scotland.[20] 'Praying you to putt all mistrust out of your Mynd,' he wrote, 'and so to juge off all of us that, rather then we shall at any tyme become ingrate, or unmyndfull off hir Majestis Goodness towards ws, we shall hassard Lyves, Lands and all: Let the malecious Report off ws what they list, thus it shall prove in dede.' On 28 April Maitland wrote again to Mildred, with more positive news regarding their affairs, stating 'We ar already in a good forewardnes: Now quhen all Communication is dissolved, owr Newtrals begyn to cum in a paas.'[21]

Such information was highly politically sensitive, as Mildred's husband was to travel to Scotland with Dr Nicholas Wotton at the end of May 1560 with the aim of brokering a settlement between the Lords of the Congregation, the French and the English. Mildred was kept appraised of her husband's progress by figures at the English court. Cecil's letters to Sir William Petre, acting as secretary in his absence, and Sir Thomas Parry, Controller of the Household, repeatedly requested that they send word of his health to Mildred; Petre wrote to her in early June with news, as did Sir Thomas Parry.[22] Conyers Read was mocking of Cecil's continual requests to remember Mildred in his biography, as if they were quaintly unnecessary, but they justify further consideration.[23] By asking Petre and Parry to write to Mildred, Cecil was keeping his wife tied to key figures at court in his absence. Moreover, Mildred herself acted to maintain these connections. She invited her brother-in-law Nicholas Bacon to dine during her husband's absence, and later went to court to celebrate the Treaty of Edinburgh.[24]

Maitland's letter to Mildred on 19 July mentioned the signing of the Treaty of Edinburgh earlier that month and her husband's role in the negotiations: 'Now by Mr Secretaryis Wisdome ar we come to a good End of our Troubles, if promiss be kept.'[25] Maitland then highlighted to Mildred a particular ramification of the Treaty, stating 'Mary, now we shall begynne to have more nede off yowr help, in the Mater quharonto, yow know, I most ernestly prease. I beleve Tyme is not able so to overcome yow, that you will waxe cold in it.'[26] Maitland was here referencing the proposed marriage of the earl of Arran to Queen Elizabeth. Cecil had raised the possible match in March that year, through the English ambassador to Scotland, Thomas Randolph.[27] Robert Melville also wrote to Mildred on 21 September 1560 expressing Scottish hopes for the match. Melville had accompanied Maitland on his envoy to London between December 1559 and February 1560, so may have become acquainted with Mildred then; he was certainly known to her by July 1560, for he is mentioned in Maitland's letter. In his own letter from September 1560, Melville informed Mildred that the earls of Morton and Glencairn, along with William Maitland, were now planning an envoy to England to convey officially the proposed match with Arran; the Lord St John, whom Melville had hoped to accompany to England, had instead been sent to the Scottish queen in France. Regarding the proposed marriage, Melville told Mildred 'the Estaits hes agreit indifferently weill at this Parliament, and the spiritual Papists with the Newtrals hes consentit to seik that Thyng, yat may be gretest Comfort to zoure first Friend. Theire is no instant truble nor Seditione among ws. For sum for fear of zoure Frendis comfort, and sum luif to haif it, makis ane quietnes and ane rest.'[28] Melville's language is that of friendship, emphasising the social nature of their correspondence, yet he is also passing on to Mildred detailed information, in return for her acting as a broker with Cecil.

The earl of Arran himself even wrote to Mildred on 28 September 1560; Maitland's letter from 19 July had suggested that Arran was in regular correspondence with Mildred.[29] Arran had stayed with the Cecils in Westminster upon his flight from France in August 1559, so was very probably already acquainted with Mildred, for Maitland noted that Arran would 'not forget how far he is bound to yow'.[30] Arran's letter was again not explicit, trusting his message to the bearer of his letter. Yet he did make clear that he sought Mildred's help in the marriage proposal, writing that 'the hale Cuntrie sutis for at the Quenis Majesteis Handis'.[31] For himself, he added that 'I beseke you this of my awin Mouthe, testifeit with my awin Hand, that God lede that worthy Hart of hiris quhome I serve, to quhat Effect he Plesis, the end of my Lyfe and Will to serve hir Majestie, fall baith rest in one.' Individually, these letters offer only hints about Mildred's interests during this period; collectively, however, they suggest a strong interest in the potential match with the earl of Arran, at least until late 1560, when the extant correspondence ceases.[32] The vagueness of the letters should not, however, be seen as evidence of Mildred's marginality in these affairs. Her correspondents repeatedly highlight the insecurity of their letters, citing it in apology for the lack of detailed news from Scotland. For example, in his letter from July 1560 Maitland made explicit the difficulties of ensuring that letters reached Mildred without interference: 'The cause of my Silence wes, that all my Letters past my Lord of Norfolk's Hands, and wer by him opened; and I know it was not yowr Mynd, that any Letters direct to yow, shold come in any Manis Hand.'[33] Maitland repeatedly protested, therefore, that certain individuals, such as Mildred's brother-in-law Henry Killigrew, or the Lord St John, would provide Mildred with more specific details from Scotland in person.[34] The earl of Arran similarly trusted important information to the bearer of the letter, rather than to paper.[35] Melville had hoped to visit Mildred in person and deliver his news; instead, he sent his cousin Walter Melville, whom he described as an 'honest Persone'. Melville also detailed writing two other letters to Mildred, which he sent along with those intended for her brother-in-law Henry Killigrew; no trace of these letters remains and Melville himself questioned whether Mildred 'resaivit them, or not'.[36] A letter from Henry Percy, the earl of Northumberland, written to Cecil on 30 April 1560 whilst he was participating in the Scottish campaign, also recorded writing two letters to Mildred and questioned her husband as to whether she had received them: 'I did write unto my Lady two severall lettres and unto you one sence my comminge into Scotland.'[37]

The letters that have survived testify to Mildred's involvement in further diplomatic networks. Maitland, for example, acted as an intermediary between Mildred and other Scottish figures. In July 1566 he passed on the commendations of Lord James Stewart, writing that the latter thought himself 'never able to recompense the good Mynd yow have borne to the furtherance of this common Cause'.[38] Stewart understood the importance of cultivating Mildred as an intermediary, for he sent her a token via Maitland, who then entrusted it to Thomas Windebank.[39] This was a relationship which clearly developed, for at the end of Stewart's delegation to his half-sister in France in 1561, Nicholas Throckmorton, the English ambassador in Paris, reported that he was forwarding letters from Stewart not only to William Cecil, but also to Mildred herself.[40] Melville similarly introduced Lord St John to Mildred, writing 'my Lord is desirus to offer his Service unto zoure Ladyship and to be acquentit, that he may be the moire able to rander zow Thankis for the gret Courtasye his Freindis hes resavit at zoure Handis'. Lord St John would also be useful to Mildred, suggested Melville, for he could 'let zoure Ladyship knaw moire of the Estait of this Countrey thane I can wret'.[41]

At this time, Mildred was largely in correspondence with those Scottish moderates inclined to bow to English will in their negotiations. In this sense, William Maitland was particularly praised by Mildred's husband for his determination 'to work all myndes of the nobilite to allow any thyng' to the English; Mildred's other correspondents, such as Lord James Stewart and the earl of Arran, were also pragmatic in their approach to the English.[42] As will be discussed in the next chapter, Mildred has often been represented as uncompromisingly godly. However, her Scottish correspondents were not drawn from those nobles for whom religion was the overriding and primary concern; like her husband, she was in contact with the more moderate elements in the Congregation. There is evidence too that Mildred's interest in Scottish affairs continued throughout the 1560s. After the abortive Chase-about Raid by James Stewart, the earl of Moray, in the summer of 1565, he was exiled to Newcastle. A letter written to William Cecil in November of that year thanked Ceil for his advice and his support; it also specifically commended Mildred and the efforts she had made on his behalf as a 'banyst man'.[43] With Mildred's knowledge of Scottish affairs, it is perhaps not surprising that she was chosen by the Queen in February 1567 to take the news of Darnley's death to his mother, the countess of Lennox, accompanied by Lady Katherine Howard.[44]

Mildred's concern with Anglo-Scottish relations was therefore considerable, yet she was also involved with the other half of the 'British dimension' in Elizabethan policy, as there is evidence of her sustained interest in Irish affairs during the 1560s and 1570s. She was perceived as an intermediary to her husband by many Irish figures. James Wingfield, master of the ordinance and constable of Dublin Castle, wrote to Mildred in September 1562 from the Irish capital, entreating her to advance his case to her husband and sending her a goshawk.[45] Sir Henry Sidney, Lord Deputy of Ireland, remembered Mildred and her sister Anne in a letter from January 1566.[46] Her correspondence with Sidney increased in 1569, after the latter had proposed the marriage of Anne Cecil to his son, Philip Sidney.[47] The Lord Deputy wrote to Mildred from Dublin Castle in October 1569, sending his letter in the hands of one Johan Tassel. Tassel had been sent at Mildred's request to teach French to Anne, suggesting the prior communication between the correspondents.[48] In many ways, these were friendship connections, yet such contacts were important in her promotion of her cousin and Sidney's brother-in-law, William Fitzwilliam, who had been involved in Irish governance since 1554.

In the autumn of 1567 Fitzwilliam was appointed Lord Justice in Ireland while Sidney was absent in England. Mildred was clearly in regular contact with him, as Fitzwilliam's extant letters reference lost correspondence sent by Lady Cecil.[49] By January 1568 Fitzwilliam was facing strong critique from the Queen; a force of up to seven hundred MacDonald Scots had landed in Antrim in November 1567.[50] Lord Deputy Sidney, then in London, did little to defend Fitzwilliam from the charges of failing to prevent and expel the Scots landing.[51] Mildred, however, petitioned for her cousin, as he acknowledged in a letter to her on 20 January 1568, praising 'your ernestnes as by mr secretaire's letter I fynde to have spokene with some in my behaulf of who in ther doinges carry not so frindly partes towarde me as reason wolde they shoulde'.[52] Fitzwilliam wrote to William Cecil two days later, again acknowledging Mildred's 'fryndly and naturall care' of him.[53] Mildred was similarly advising Fitzwilliam in the summer of 1568, at the time when more Scots were planning on sailing for Ulster; Fitzwilliam had led an unsuccessful expedition to Carrickfergus in Antrim in the spring and had been forced to return to Dublin by May. After thanking Mildred for her 'fryndly and deer counsell', Fitzwilliam once again offered a justification for his failure to overcome the Scottish threat.[54] These letters offer more than just a defence, however, for Fitzwilliam provided Mildred with information, presumably to be relayed to her husband, on the state of the Scots in Ireland. For example, he told Mildred in his letter of 20 January 1568 that he was unaware of the new alliances between the Ulster lords and of the Scots landing until after the event, adding that he felt that the Scots could not be successfully expelled at that time of year.[55]

Despite these tribulations, Fitzwilliam was appointed to the Lord Deputyship of Ireland in January 1572. When more criticism was levied upon the Lord Deputy in October 1573, it is no surprise that Fitzwilliam and his wife turned again to Mildred, as well as her husband. Sidney had started a campaign against Fitzwilliam, criticising several aspects of his brother-in-law's administration. Moreover, Fitzwilliam had quarrelled with Edward Fitton in June over the Lord Deputy's handling of the murder of one of Fitton's servants; the resulting dispute split the Irish Privy Council and led to Fitton's imprisonment for contempt. Fitzwilliam had written to his cousin Mildred, detailing the controversy in the months that followed. She responded in October 1573, writing 'I am hartely sory for the great & contynuall Injuris you have, which I well understode, before the receypt of my Ladis' & your lettres'.[56] Mildred reveals that her knowledge of Irish affairs was based on information not only from Fitzwilliam, but also from his wife, Anne, sister to Sir Henry Sidney, previous Lord Deputy of Ireland. Fitzwilliam and his wife must have thoroughly appraised Mildred of his dislike for his position and of the financial encumbrance he had shouldered during his service of the Crown in Ireland, for Mildred wrote 'I would be most glad, you were well delyverd from that burdenos sarvis'. Although her knowledge of Irish affairs was therefore considerable, she noted the limits to her information. Writing from experience of the English political scene, rather than the Irish, she advised Fitzwilliam to 'Kepe close your frends' lettres', adding 'nor that I know eny thing before god, but because I know the lyke practiss used with some here'.

The letter makes it explicit that Mildred was acting as a broker between her husband and her cousin: 'my lord, I know, both hathe & dothe contynew your defendor here, what soever he writith to you there, to the uttermost of his powar; & onely he alone, I must nedes say, is dryven to Answer in your behalf.' Burghley's role as Principal Secretary meant that he was in contact with both sides during the controversy, yet his wife assured her cousin of both his and her partiality. Her counsel that Fitzwilliam should remain in his post was based on her knowledge of the Queen's position in the matter. The Queen was known to favour Fitton rather than Fitzwilliam in the controversy, so Mildred had reasoned that to resign the lord deputyship during this period would only lead to disgrace for her cousin on his return to England and, perhaps more importantly, would mean there was little chance of restitution of all the money Fitzwilliam had advanced on behalf of the Crown.

Mildred's personal protection of Fitzwilliam was recognised by other members of the Irish political elite. Sir Nicholas White, Master of the Rolls from 1572, defended Sir Edward Fitton in his controversy with the Lord Deputy.[57] His letter to Burghley on 4 November 1573, however, described his attempts to reconcile Fitzwilliam and Fitton, stating explicitly that Mildred should not think him opposed to her cousin: 'And I protest it is one of my greatest feares ... that my Lady Burghely shuld susspect me of any unfrend-lynes towards so dear a kynsman. Wherin I wilbe tyed by Mr chefe Baron, one of her daly bondmen here and I wish of god that he had a wife of my ladie's disposition to peas and concord.'[58] The Lord Chief Baron of the Exchequer referred to by White was Sir Lucas Dillon, a moderate force on the Irish Privy Council. Dillon was in regular correspondence with William Cecil during this period and, by White's reference to his actions as one of Mildred's 'daly bondmen', it is clear that Dillon also corresponded regularly with her; there is also evidence that Dillon had conveyed letters from Mildred in England to her cousin William Fitzwilliam in 1568.[59]

Like those of her husband, Mildred's diplomatic activities also stretched beyond 'British' interests. Resident ambassadors in England understood that Mildred was an influential conduit to her husband, as demonstrated by a letter she received from the Portuguese ambassador on 23 May 1562. John Pereira Dantas wrote in Latin to Mildred that he was about to leave England and that he wanted to leave the furtherance of Portuguese interests in England in the hands of her husband, the Principal Secretary. If William Cecil would accept this role, then Dantas said he would receive a pension of 2000 gold pieces a year, writing that he had briefly outlined the offer to Mildred's husband, but wished to discuss the matter at length with Mildred herself.[60] He was clear as to why he chose to approach Mildred with this proposition rather than her husband, stating that he would ensure that the first payment was available before his departure, so that it could be used for Anne Cecil's dowry: 'Cuius collocandae cura cum ad te aeque atque ad illum pertineat malui tibi quam illi munus hoc offerre, quae minus es occupata.' (Since the responsibility of finding her a husband is yours as much as your husband's, I have preferred to offer this gift to you rather than to him, as you are less busy.)[61] Mildred was perceived as another, less congested channel by which to approach William Cecil concerning Portuguese interests and Dantas used all his knowledge of the familial concerns of the Cecils to advance his suit. Dantas was certain, however, that Mildred had sway over her husband: 'Iam vero peto a te, mea Domina, agas id ut boni ipse consulat, Regis enim liberalitati injuriam faceret nisi libenter acciperet quod illi Majestas sua libentissime largitur.' (Now indeed, my Lady, I beg you to act in such a way that he takes it in good part, for it would do injury to the King's generosity if he failed to accept freely what his Majesty is most freely bestowing upon him.)[62] Dantas's aim at this time was to gain a further restriction on English trading in Portuguese-controlled ports in Ethiopia; in this venture, his suit to William Cecil, placed in Mildred's hands, was unsuccessful, for Cecil reported that he was loath to commit to any assurance which would prejudice English trade.[63]

Four years later, in 1566, Guzman de Silva, the Spanish ambassador, went to Mildred for information regarding the matrimonial suit of the Archduke Charles. 'Cecil's wife tells me', he reported back to the Emperor, 'that the French Ambassador says that if the Archduke comes hither he will cause discord in the country, as he will endeavour to uphold his religion, and will have many to follow him. She thinks that the Queen will never marry Lord Robert, or, indeed, anyone else, unless it be the Archduke, which is the match Cecil desires,' adding 'Certainly if anybody has information on the matter it is Cecil's wife, and she is clever and greatly influences him.'[64] Not only was Mildred in contact with the French ambassador, de Foix, and aware of his opinions of the potential match, she was also acting as an intermediary between Cecil and the Spanish diplomat. De Silva returned to Mildred as a source of information in September 1566, reporting that 'Cecil seems to desire this business so greatly that he does not speak about the religious point, but this may be deceit, as his wife is of a contrary opinion, and thinks that great trouble may be caused to the peace of the country through it. She has great influence with her husband, and no doubt discusses the matter with him, but she appears a much more furious heretic than he is.'[65] By this point, Mildred was recognised as holding contrary opinions to those of Cecil and, once again, de Silva acknowledged her influence over her husband, although he was uncertain as to its extent. The question of whether Mildred had the opportunity to act as an intermediary with the Queen herself in these matters is tantalising. A letter from William Cecil to Lord Cobham suggests that Mildred single-handedly entertained the Queen and her ladies on at least one occasion during this period. 'My lady Clynton,' he wrote in May 1567 to Lord Cobham, 'hath underhand procured my wiff to mak hir a supper to morrow, wher she sayth a gretar person will be covertly, as she is wont: I meane not to take knolledg, but shall be glad to se hir content with [my] poverty'.[66] Cecil might ostensibly state that he wished to take no 'knolledg' of the proceedings, but Mildred would certainly have been prepared either to pass on relevant information to the Queen or report back to Cecil any 'knolledg' gained under the guise of sociability.

Mildred's diplomatic activities continued until the last decade of her life. In 1585 her nephew Anthony Bacon was resident in the Huguenot town of Montauban, collecting information from Henry of Navarre's court to report back to England. On 19 March he sent Francis Walsingham 'two late discourses which for as much as by reason of the bearer's hast I had no leysure to copy out fayre, I have given order to my brother Francis to see that done there with all speede possible'.[67] There is little information given about the nature of the discourses, although Anthony stated that while Walsingham might have heard of one of the discourses, the other was 'of so freshe a date that I am assured that hath never passed the sea'. Anthony had in fact already caused copies to be made of the tracts; Francis Bacon's role was to disseminate them more widely. 'I have sent you two discourses twice doubled, the copies written in gilt paper', wrote Anthony, on the same day, 'I have promised by letter to my Lady Burghley requesting you to cause the lyke copies to be made there out of hand to present to my Lord of Bedford and Mr Secretary Walsingham'.[68] Mildred was clearly in correspondence with her nephew in exile and was aware of his intelligence-gathering activities. The implication is that the discourses were sent to England at her request and were forwarded to Francis Russell, the earl of Bedford, and Walsingham at her instigation, showing Mildred's own role in this informal network of intelligence acquisition.

Beyond her actual activities, European figures thought that Mildred had an even greater potential in diplomatic circles. Johann Sturm, the Strasbourg theologian and humanist, thought she would be of considerable advantage in diplomatic negotiations with the German princes.[69] Between 1577 and 1578, Robert Beale was acting as a special ambassador to the German courts, trying to arrange a united response to what Sturm termed the 'great conspiracy, or rather sworn league, of monarchs – the Pope, the King of France, the King of Spain'.[70] In December 1577 Beale was planning to visit Augustus I, the Elector of Saxony. According to Sturm's letter to Walsingham, the difficulty was to know how correctly to approach the Elector. Sturm argued for the importance of sociability gestures in this process and suggested that wives could be useful in instilling trust between rulers: 'In my sleep I wished that the Lord Treasurer was in Denmark with his wife, or someone else of the same rank, whose wife could talk Latin; and that such person should bring from our Queen presents to the King of Denmark's wife, and messages to himself, as good neighbours should.'[71] He argued that there was a special role for women in the diplomatic process, suggesting that Mildred should act as an intermediary between Elizabeth I and Sophie of Mecklenburg-Güstrow, the Queen of Denmark; as in Mildred's exchange with the Portuguese ambassador, Latin would act as their language of communication, so Sturm admits that Mildred's place could possibly be filled by another high-profile Englishwoman, if she were also skilled in Latin. Sturm then envisaged that Mildred would join the delegation to Saxony. The role of wives would help to foster the social aspect of the delegations, which Sturm feared would be Beale's undoing. Yet he admitted the unlikelihood of Mildred's travelling to Saxony, suggesting that even in the absence of a female deputation in the diplomatic efforts, gifts should be exchanged between the wives of the men involved. 'If it cannot be done through wives, it may be done by suitable men,' he wrote to Walsingham, 'and presents may be sent, and the mutual goodwill of the queens may be established, with the approval of gods and men, and to the grief of enemies.'[72] Sturm repeated his argument in a letter to Burghley, written on the same day. Augustus would prove, he feared, a difficult figure to convince: 'I fear that tree will not fall with one blow. You will have to try again; the chop must be repeated, the cut renewed. There is no better hand than that of a wife.'[73] He advised going through the mediation of Augustus's wife, Anna of Denmark, as they were a couple 'vehemently in love'. Again, he suggested that Mildred could aid this process or, failing that, he provides another suggestion as to a high-profile substitute, arguing that her daughter, Anne Cecil de Vere, wife of the earl of Oxford, could take her place, 'for I believe his lady speaks Latin also'; the Latin language skills of these women would be key to their success in these diplomatic affairs. Sturm dismissed the idea to Burghley as 'dreams and senile meditations', yet his suggestion was not altogether unusual.[74] Visits between courts by other elite women in this period were also perceived to be politically motivated. For example, Cecilia, the sister of Eric XIV of Sweden, visited the English court in 1565. Guzman de Silva, the Spanish ambassador, noted that 'It is suspected that she is coming to try again to bring about the marriage of her brother with the Queen.'[75]

It would, therefore, be wrong to dismiss Mildred's involvement in diplomatic affairs as an aberration. She was in some ways a unique figure. Her political activities were facilitated by her marriage to such a high-ranking statesman, and the marriage was widely perceived to be an unusually close one. Katherine, the duchess of Suffolk, suggested that it was common knowledge that Mildred assisted with and read her husband's correspondence. On 4 March 1559 she described a previous letter sent by Cecil: 'the hand with in the letter semethe to be my lade your wyffe, the subscrypsion ser wyllem onlly, but hows so evere it be, it is al one'.[76] Yet, like Mildred, other elite women were also involved in diplomatic affairs, particularly concerning Elizabeth I's marital politics. Lady Mary Sidney was involved with negotiations for the Archduke Charles match in 1559, and three years later Katherine Ashley was an intermediary in Eric XIV of Sweden's suit.[77] Lady Elizabeth Parr, first marchioness of Northampton, was similarly involved in the negotiations surrounding the Swedish match.[78] De Quadra, the then Spanish ambassador, noted in 1561 that she was being courted as a potential intermediary: 'I do know that the marchioness of Northampton, who is in a better position to judge than anyone else, is very intimate with the Swedish ambassador, and has received valuable presents from him.'[79] Three years later, Guzman de Silva also recognised the power of the marchioness as an intermediary to the Queen: 'the marchioness of Northampton is a great favourite of the Queen, and I am gaining the goodwill of her intimates, so as to gain more influence over her mistress'.[80] Promising to pass information on to de Silva, the marchioness arranged for him to visit her at her Westminster house on 15 September 1564. When he arrived, the Queen herself was there, which the women 'laughed greatly at', before launching into conversation until the evening: 'What passed were mostly tales told by the Queen and ordinary conversation, into which she was constantly slipping some slight allusions to marriage. I told her she was wrong to keep the world in suspense and ought to decide.' The Queen then promised to tell de Silva more about 'the business', but after walking with him for while on her way to St James's Palace, she passed on no more information.[81] It is important not to underestimate either the perception of Elizabeth Parr as a potential intermediary, or the extent to which both she and the Queen were consciously playing with de Silva's expectations of information. Here Elizabeth Parr's gender seems to be an advantage, allowing her to mix serious diplomacy with light conversation. As with Mildred Cecil, the role of women as mediators of information was based on their informal status and the power of female sociability to mask their involvement in 'high politics'.

ELIZABETHAN AMBASSADORIAL WIVES

Two of Mildred's sisters, Elizabeth and Katherine, were also involved as intermediaries in diplomatic affairs, and again marriage facilitated their activities, for both were the wives of ambassadors. While Katherine remained in England, Elizabeth Hoby accompanied her husband abroad. The diplomatic wife accompanying her husband's embassy was a new Tudor figure. The Henrician development of singly accredited, resident embassies resulted for the first time in the inclusion of wives within diplomatic households. The significance for female political agency of this development in diplomatic culture has largely gone unmarked by historians. Katie Hickman's extensive study of diplomatic wives begins only much later, with the countess of Winchelsea's journey to Constantinople in 1661. Hickman even comments that, while she believes there may have been other women who accompanied their husbands on embassies before that date, 'any records are almost impossible to find'.[82] While difficult to uncover, it is possible to find evidence of diplomatic wives travelling with their husbands in the Tudor period. Elizabeth Wallop, Bridget Morison and Anne Throckmorton had all accompanied their husbands on embassies before Elizabeth Hoby's 1566 migration to France, while Eleanor Bowes followed her example during the later Elizabethan period.[83] The evidence in most cases is fragmentary, perhaps the odd reference to ambassorial wives in diplomatic correspondence, even more rarely a letter from the women themselves. Unusually, however, more detailed evidence does exist for Elizabeth Hoby's residence in France in 1566. This exceptional survival is largely due to Elizabeth's personal circumstances. Her brother-in-law William Cecil received the bulk of her husband's diplomatic correspondence as Principal Secretary. Information regarding his wife in Thomas Hoby's letters was most likely purposely included for the consumption of her brother-in-law, and particularly Elizabeth's sister Mildred, who, as has been shown above, was already widely assumed to read her husband's letters.

The first reference to Thomas Hoby's proposed appointment as French ambassador introduces a theme which unites those diplomatic wives who travelled abroad with those who stayed at home. Both are most commonly discovered in this period acting as intermediaries, exerting resistance against the forced migration of an ambassadorial appointment. In 1560, six years before the family's actual departure to the Continent, Nicholas Throckmorton wrote to William Cecil regarding his successor. 'But that yowr sister willbe angry,' he remarked, 'I could remembre yowr brother Mr Thomas Hobby.'[84] Elizabeth and her husband were still objecting to the latter's proposed appointment in 1566 and only grudgingly agreed to the proposition when the earl of Leicester was sent to let them 'understand peremptorily hir Majestie's pleasur'.[85] Resistance against the enforced move was probably the reason for certain heated words which Elizabeth's correspondence reveals 'passed unawars' from her mouth at her departure from her brother-in-law. She sent word from Dover, apologising for any offence caused to Cecil, but argued that she had been unable to leave her 'husband's minde and arrand undon for which cause he sent me'.[86] Here, too, Elizabeth was acting as an informal broker of information from her husband and her excuse that such words 'passed unawars' from her mouth should not obscure her role.

Her sister Katherine also acted as an intermediary for her diplomat husband. She attempted to utilise Mildred's influence over her husband, and so over the Queen, to prevent Henry Killigrew from being sent on another diplomatic mission, through sending her sister a Latin verse:

Si mihi quem cupio cures Mildreda remitti,
Tu bona, tu melior, tu mihi sola soror:
Sin male cessando retines, vel trans mare mittis,

Tu mala, tu peior, tu mihi nulla soror.
Is si Cornubiam, tibi pax sit et omnia laeta,
Sin mare, Ciciliae nuncio bella. Vale.[87]

(If Myldred thowe procure, my Joyes retorne to be,
Thow shalt be good and better to, a sister dere to me,
But tryflynge yf he staye, or passe the seas he shall,
thow shalt be yll, and wors then yll no sister then at all.
To Cornwall yf he come, in peace then shalt thow dwell,
but yf to Sea, to Cycyll then, I warre proclaym, farewell.)[88]

It is difficult to date the poem accurately; however, it must have been written between November 1565, when Katherine married Killigrew, and late 1570; Mildred became Lady Burghley in February 1571, so would no longer be referred to as Lady Cecil.[89] Killigrew was almost continually away from home on diplomatic missions from February 1569. The lack of a precise dating for the poem makes it impossible to judge the success of Katherine's intercession, yet she has turned to the most persuasive language possible in her request, emphasising the sisters' shared childhood education.

The sisters' outspokenness was, of course, partly conditioned by their personal circumstances. Yet these protests have resonance in the broader context of appeals against Tudor diplomatic appointments. Philippa Smith always remained in England; however, her petitioning for the return of her ambassador husband, Thomas, was perceived as so significant that Thomas Hoby was told to name her as a supplicant for Smith's revocation in 1566, when explaining the change of personnel to the French King.[90] Five years earlier, Anne Throckmorton was similarly a key figure in appealing for her husband's recall from France. Anne had accompanied her husband on his embassy, and a letter written to William Cecil in August 1561 makes clear that she had long been at the forefront of those who have been 'suters' for her husband's revocation.[91] She pleaded with Cecil 'to thynke that nothyng can be more greves unto me then to retayne my husbond here longer to hys and my undoyng'.[92] The impassioned letter, however, is not written in Anne's own hand, but in that of her husband, Nicholas Throckmorton. Later correspondence suggests that Anne was able to write, yet here her husband was acting as scribe.[93] Nicholas Throckmorton thus had a key role in the composition of the letter and he perceived that such a plea would be most convincing scripted in the voice of his wife. In another letter to William Cecil later in the year, Nicholas Throckmorton even stated that his wife would be forced to turn to Cecil's own wife, Mildred, for assistance in ensuring her husband's swift replacement by Thomas Dannett, Mildred's relative.[94] There is thus a particular significance to female brokerage in this area. Appeals against diplomatic appointments were by their nature lengthy, emotional processes, with Thomas Smith even going so far as to term it disdainfully as 'brawlynge'.[95] Wives in this situation

were able to employ a cultural script, evoking images of the divisive and potentially ruinous nature of early modern diplomatic appointments for the family
unit, which perhaps were perceived to be more successful in influencing the
Queen. This was a script, written in what Anne Throckmorton termed the
'words of a passtyonnte wyffe', that women were more able to capitalise upon
than their husbands when resisting diplomatic appointments.[96]

In spite of Elizabeth Hoby's attempts to broker her husband's stay in
England, the decision was taken for the whole family to move to Paris in April
1566. Yet, once arrived in the French capital, Elizabeth proved a valuable asset
for her husband's embassy. Thomas Hoby's responsibilities as English ambassador in Paris were complex. He was charged with maintaining good relations
with the French royal family, whilst attempting to navigate the religiously
charged world of French politics. English policy during this period was to try
to minimise the Catholic Guise influence which could potentially be exerted
on behalf of Mary Queen of Scots at the French court, whilst not becoming
embroiled with the Huguenot faction.[97] In accompanying her diplomat
husband, Elizabeth had to understand and move within this sensitive political
arena. Her brother Edward Cooke joined the embassy and recorded Elizabeth's experiences at the French court. 'Mownsr Gowinor ...,' reported Edward
Cooke, 'never as yet shewed any manner of cowntenance to my Lord nor to my
sister, when they were at the Court, whereby I gather that he is alltogether of
the Guyze faction.'[98] From the outset of the embassy, sociability was politicised
for both husband and wife.

News-gathering was the primary responsibility of Tudor diplomats;
complex negotiation was a secondary task, often entrusted to special envoys.[99]
Intelligence could be bought, as is revealed by the bill for Thomas Hoby's
embassy.[100] The other method of acquiring news was through the development of friendship networks which allowed access to intelligence.[101] Elizabeth
clearly understood both the centrality of these networks to early modern diplomatic culture and her own agency to foster such relationships. Thomas Hoby
reported that it was his wife who first made acquaintance in Paris with the
duchesse d'Étampes, erstwhile mistress to Francis I, whom he described as
'one of the staies of the refourmed religion in fraunce'; in this instance, their
Protestant faith may have initially facilitated the friendship between the two
women.[102] Thomas Hoby only later became acquainted with the duchess and
reported that she was eager to offer her services to the English, a product of the
friendship developed by his wife, Elizabeth.[103]

Elizabeth's friendships in Paris with Madame Bochetel and Marie Bourdin
further demonstrate both the breadth of her personal networks and their
centrality to the success of her husband's embassy. Madame Bochetel was the
wife of Jacques Bochetel, French Ambassador to England in 1566, while Marie
Bourdin was married to Jacques Bourdin, French Secretary of State. On one visit

to Elizabeth, the Parisian ladies brought with them the renowned humanist, Jacques Amyot, together with 'others of good credit'; Amyot's presence may have been the result of Elizabeth Hoby's European reputation for learning.[104] Thomas Hoby's report of the visit reveals the politicised nature of these friendship networks and their potential as sites of information brokering. A prolonged discussion took place regarding the nature of worship within both France and the Church of England. Thomas Hoby's description of the event makes clear that diplomatic wives participated in these politicised debates; Madame Bochetel joined the critique of the Church of England, commenting during the dispute that if ambassadors' houses in England were not privileged to hear the Mass, then it would prove very difficult 'to have over manie masses'.[105]

Elizabeth's role as an intermediary in French intelligence networks, implicit in her earlier friendships, is revealed more clearly upon Thomas Hoby's death on 13 July 1566 from the plague sweeping Paris at the time. Courtesy to Elizabeth, as a representative of England, was politicised, as was especially highlighted in the sending of Protestant representatives from the French court to express condolences to the young widow. Edward Cooke reported that the French King stated 'that yf there were any thinge in his realme that might stand her in steed, she might as well command that as yf she were in England'. The Queen Mother went further in expressing her sympathy, sending one of her Ladies in Waiting to Elizabeth, with her chief physician, 'a very earnest Protestant'. The Queen of Navarre also sent her chief minister to comfort the young widow, with 'godly Cowncell'. Elizabeth Hoby was visited by the Venetian, Scottish and Florentine ambassadors, along with Paul de Foix, erstwhile French ambassador to England.[106] When James Stewart, Protestant half-brother of Mary Queen of Scots, visited Elizabeth on behalf of the Huguenot leader, Admiral Coligny, he reported that when Coligny first heard of Hoby's death he said 'all his purpose was dashed'.[107] Yet Stewart was commanded to tell Elizabeth that within a month Coligny believed they would be 'together by the eares'.[108] 'Together by the ears' was an expression for animals fighting, thus it seems that Coligny was warning the English of future violence by the Huguenots; this was increasingly likely in the summer of 1566, as Protestant agitation in the Netherlands was coming to a peak, leading to a wave of iconoclastic violence in August, just weeks after Coligny's warning. The imprecise nature of the warning reveals in itself Elizabeth's personal understanding of the political arena in which she was moving. Furthermore, she was playing a distinct role in the complex dissemination of diplomatic news back to England; the message from Coligny was passed through three intermediaries before it reached the English court via Edward Cooke's letter to Cecil.[109]

Elizabeth was not the only diplomatic wife in this period actively involved in the movement of intelligence from outside of England. For example, Eleanor Bowes, wife of the English ambassador in Scotland, received repeated correspondence regarding political developments.[110] In a letter from July 1596 she told James Hudson, the resident agent of James VI in London, with a clear understanding of the relations between the two countries, that she could not write of any good news 'in these present causes now in handling'. Eleanor added, however, that she had hopes for a reconcilement that 'will very shortly be knowne unto yow ... as plainely as with us'.[111] Eleanor Bowes, like Elizabeth and Mildred, was thus recognised as a political figure in diplomatic circles and, moreover, passed on information which could be used in the formulation of English foreign policy. Elizabeth's role as an intermediary in France was even recognised by the Queen, who wrote to her after Thomas's death saying that they had received 'good reports' of Elizabeth's activities in France and praising her for her 'sobre, wise and discret behaviours in that Court and Contry'.[112]

THE FEMALE INTERMEDIARY AND FAMILY NETWORKS

Beyond the realm of diplomacy, the sisters adopted further roles as intermediaries. Here too the role of the family in their patronage networks was important, although often in more complex ways than acknowledged by previous research. Mildred's marriage to William Cecil was again central to their political agency, as it made her and her sisters influential brokers for potential clients to target. Laurence Cockson petitioned Lord Burghley for support of his oil-making scheme in July 1579, after Walsingham had raised local objections to the arrangement.[113] Cockson wrote a long response to the various complaints, but, instead of sending it directly to Burghley, he enclosed it with a letter to Mildred. Her family connections were here of particular importance. It appears that Cockson was an old acquaintance of her father and he emphasised his past obligation to Lady Burghley.[114] Yet why go through Mildred, rather than approach Burghley directly? Cockson believed that it was more effective to use Mildred as a means of ensuring that her husband gave due attention to the long list of articles; he admitted the articles were 'very tedious', but emphasised how important it was for Burghley to 'rede the hole'.[115] Mildred was asked to read the articles before passing on the information to her husband. She clearly fulfilled his request, as Burghley has annotated his wife's letter, highlighting elements of Cockson's proposal.[116]

Mildred's reputation for learning may have been the reason why she was often approached by literary figures, seeking her intercession with her husband.[117] This reputation meant that she was even contacted by Catholic petitioners, who must have calculated that her love of the written word would overcome their religious differences. Mildred was still acting as an intermediary for John Heywood, the Catholic playwright, in 1578. 'I understand of Late,' he wrote to Burghley, from exile on 18 April, 'what a good earnest sewtor it hath pleased my good honorable Ladie, your good wiffe, to be for me, now in my poore old Age, when my frendes are in a maner all dead. And manie of them utterlie forsaken me.'[118] Similarly, another Catholic, Dominic Lampson, who had been Cardinal Pole's secretary, also requested Mildred to act as an intermediary in 1583. He wrote from Liege in October of that year, asking her to intercede with her husband on behalf of Henry Dethick, the Latin poet.[119]

The other sisters' closeness to Burghley was also known to potential suitors and utilised to similar ends. Lady Mary Sidney turned to Elizabeth in April 1573 to inform Burghley of her suit, presumably to lessen the financial difficulties she and her husband were suffering.[120] Fearing to trouble Burghley further with her own 'rude and tedius Letters', she first asked Elizabeth to 'move it to your Lordshipe knowinge no better meane nor more Lykely to opteyn my most neadefull and ernest request off your Lordshipe then by her Ladyshipe, whose vertus and Noble mynde, besydes the nearnes of allyanse betwene your Lordshipe and her, I kno hath bin allwayes dearly exsteamied off you'.[121] Repeated petitions to Burghley, in the case of both Sidney and Cockson, would be ineffective, whilst the additional pressure from a close, female family member could make all the difference. After having acted as an intermediary for Mary Sidney's suit, Elizabeth had written to her, informing her of Burghley's favour. Assured of a favourable reception, Mary had then felt able to write again to the Lord Treasurer on her own behalf. Sir Henry Cocke, the Deputy Lieutenant of Hertfordshire, also felt that the influence of his neighbour Anne Bacon would aid his repeated petitions to Burghley.[122] Writing to Robert Cecil in January 1597, he praised Anne's actions as an intermediary with both Burghley and Robert Cecil and recorded receiving the latter's letters by her means.[123]

Whether the sisters chose to utilise their family connections for suitors was not, however, always straightforward. The competition for valuable wardships, for example, was an area in which Mildred, Anne and Elizabeth all acted as intermediaries. Mildred was clearly best placed to appeal informally to her husband as Master of the Wards. Sir Thomas Cecil wrote to his father in September 1578 regarding the wardship of Lord Sheffield. Cecil had wished to purchase the wardship, but his father had warned him that the earl of Leicester was also interested. Mildred was here acting as a broker of information, for through the secondary intermediary of Sir Roger Manners, Thomas Cecil had heard from his stepmother that the wardship would be valued at £2000.[124] Evidence also exists demonstrating that Mildred did not act simply for friends and family, rather her intervention could be purchased by outsiders. Thomas Fermor, of Somerton in Oxfordshire, left a son and heir on his death in 1580 and the wardship was purchased by George Shirley.[125] Shirley's accounts reveal the sums expended in order to obtain the wardship. Burghley's secretaries were paid £6. Ten shillings went to Sir Christopher Hatton's man for writing to Burghley. The greatest expenditure, however, went on obtaining Mildred's help in the matter. Richard Bradshaw, her chamberlain, was rewarded with

£10 for 'first moving' Mildred to deal with the case and was given an additional £3 for giving 'speed' to Mildred's intervention; twelve pence was also spent on writing two letters to Mildred. Far in excess of these amounts, however, was the £250 'Given to my Lady Burghley for obtaining the wardship'. The official price paid to the Queen for this wardship was £233 6s 8d, so Mildred had exceeded that by £16 13s 4d.[126]

The case of Robert Bacon also reveals Anne and Elizabeth acting as inter-mediaries in another wardship case, although in markedly different ways. Robert Bacon had been given the wardship of his niece's son, Mr Tyrel, according to his testimony through Elizabeth Russell's 'most honnorable good meanes'.[127] The problem lay with the interest in the lands that accompa-nied this wardship, which had been contested by the ward's mother. Robert Bacon again approached Elizabeth Russell for help in his suit. He sent his letter to Elizabeth firstly to his cousin Anthony Bacon for his opinion.[128] In his letter, Robert asked Elizabeth to tell Burghley of his 'resonableness' regarding the contested interest and also to write 'iii or iiii lynes' to the Lord Keeper Egerton in his favour.[129] Anthony must have approved of the letter, for he made additions to only its last few lines. Robert Bacon had concluded by asking for Elizabeth's intercession with the Lord Keeper and providing suggestions for what such a note might include. Anthony deleted Robert's final comment, removing the proviso for Elizabeth to write what she should 'think mete'.[130] Instead, he included a more humble subscription to the letter, calculated to appeal to Elizabeth's sense of importance, adding 'And so I most humblie take my leave besechinge god longe to preserve your Ladyship in all health and happines, Your Ladyship's most humblie to comande'.[131]

The careful drafting of the letter did not, however, guarantee a favourable reception from Elizabeth. She responded angrily on 22 September 1596. 'Mr Robert Bakon yow shall pardon me,' she wrote, 'I will neather speak to the Lord Thresurer nor send to the Lordkeper in your behalf, for that I think this so unresonable an Alottment as that the widdowe that was your Nece hath just cawse to think yow no way to have loved her, who trusted yow above eny other, to acquyte her so very ill and unconscionably.'[132] The wardship and lease of a third of the lands to Robert Bacon would leave the ward's mother unable to meet her debts of £1400 and would grant only a £250 annuity, unthink-able in Elizabeth's eyes for a 'gentlewoman of that worth and reputacyon', adding 'God Bless my Dawghter from such a kinsman as shall love hers and suffer her self to want.' Elizabeth's long dispute with the countess of Warwick over the settlement made to her daughters upon her second husband's death may have coloured her views here and outweighed her obligation to more distant kin.[133] Her views on such matters were unchanged in 1608, when she protested to Robert Cecil regarding another inheritance case, which through so 'wicked a Cosinage' had left a daughter dowerless.[134]

Robert Bacon responded to Elizabeth by defending the settlement made at the Court of Wards.[135] He continued to ask for Elizabeth's support in furthering his suit, but surely with little hope of success. Anthony then attempted to assuage the effects of Elizabeth's stance, by appealing to the earl of Essex. He accused his aunt of a 'most violent, passionate partialitie & dishonorable inconstancy'.[136] He sent Essex letters written by Robert Bacon and by his aunt Elizabeth, urging him to peruse them and, if he agreed, to write to Thomas Egerton, the Lord Keeper, on his cousin's behalf. Essex replied on 26 September, determining that Anthony had made a 'trew judgment' in siding with his cousin.[137] It appears that the case was still disputed the following March, and so Anthony Bacon asked his mother for her 'meadiation' in writing to the Lord Treasurer on Robert Bacon's behalf.[138] Anne obliged, telling Burghley that this was the first matter in which Robert had ever asked for her intercession, and she argued that his actions proceeded from familial affection.[139] The case of Robert Bacon demonstrates the desirability of female intermediaries and reveals that clients did not limit their approaches to single family members. It also shows that female kin were not necessarily obligated to intervene on behalf of family members, emphasising their own personal agency over the decision to act as an intermediary.

Beyond the realm of wardships, close family similarly relied on the sisters' agency as intermediaries in their suits. Here too the results were not always positive. The earl of Oxford noted Elizabeth's role in the negotiations for the allowance of his daughter, Elizabeth's great-niece, following her marriage to the earl of Derby in January 1595. In moving Robert Cecil to appeal to his father to support the allowance of £1000 per annum, Oxford revealed that it was Elizabeth 'fyrst that moved this allowance' with the earl of Derby. By April, however, she had 'altred her mynde upon sume conceyt' and 'my Ladie Russell, for sume offence conceyved of my doughter, hathe lat[e]ly written to my Lord Thresorer to discorage and diswade him to urge the Earle of Darby'.[140]

After the death of their father in 1579, Anthony and Francis Bacon were in need of the assistance of their uncle, Burghley, with their career advancement. Anne had attempted to intervene with her brother-in-law on her sons' behalf in August 1593. She had obviously cited her sons' learning and virtue, for Burghley's reply noted that if they had health, 'they wanted nothinge'. He then promised to do what he could to advance his nephews: 'for my goodwill to them, thoughe I am of lesse power to doe my frends good than the worlde thinketh, yet they shall not want the intention to doe them good'.[141] Anne again attempted to act as intermediary between the Cecils and her sons in January 1595, by visiting her nephew Robert Cecil. She reported her conversation to her son Anthony by letter, but strikingly set her epistle in the form of a dialogue. Thus, upon visiting her nephew and after having discussed Anthony's sickness, she immediately turned to the subject of her visit, namely her son Francis: 'well inquam (I say) the Eldest of my but two in all sonns is visited by god, & the other me thinks is but strangely used by man's Dealing, god knowes who & why. I think he is the very Fyrst yownge gentleman of some accompt made so long such a common spech of – this time placed & then owt of dowt – & yet nothing done.'[42] Anne seems to have prepared her case in advance, for Robert is forced into an extempore reply, arguing that his father would be glad to see his nephew settled. Anne had seemingly expected such an answer, for she retorted 'or this I hope to my selff inquam. but some think yf my lorde had ben earnest it had ben don'. Robert responded by offering proof of his father's attempted advancement of his nephew, stating that, only the Tuesday before, his father had suggested to the Queen that she needed to appoint a Solicitor General. According to Robert Cecil, the Queen herself was unmoved by Burghley's appeal. Anne then tried another line of accusation, stating that 'him selff was secretary in place but not nominate'. Her nephew's response offered his own circumstances as proof of the limits of his father's advancement: 'as For that, sayth he, I deale nor speake no more of it. but as long as none is placed I wayt still, thowgh I may think my selff as hardly used as my cosin.' Robert then broke away from the line of questioning initiated by Anne, to offer advice to his cousin not to be discouraged: 'it may be sayde her Majestie was to much preased at the First which she lyketh not & at last come of her selff'. This advice fitted so closely with Anne's own opinion that 'her Majestie's nature is not to Resolve but to delay' that it appears she was satisfied with Robert's answers. She told her son that 'truly his spech was all kindly owtward & dyd desyre to have me think so of him'.[43]

Francis had already approached both Burghley and Mildred in seeking support for his advancement. His letter to Burghley on 16 September 1580 detailed a prior conversation with the Lord Treasurer, in which Francis had sought his help with obtaining an honorary legal post from the Queen, which would enable him to pursue his studies without pecuniary worries.[44] Burghley had given his nephew a 'good hearing as so fourthe as to promise to tender it unto hir majestie'. Francis wrote to his uncle to reiterate his hope that Burghley would act as his patron, emphasising his need to advance in the common law, unusually for a man of his class, due to his financial situation. He regretfully admitted that his need to appeal to Burghley was 'rare and unaccustomed', implying his greater need due to the recent death of his father.[45] On the same day, however, he also wrote to his aunt Mildred. His letter to her took a different approach. Whereas with Burghley his entire letter discussed his suit, with his aunt he initially wrote of more general matters, pursuing a line of sociability. He regretted not visiting her whilst she was briefly at court, but he felt he could not, as he had no 'earnest errande'. He admitted his naivety in relation to courtly etiquette, however, he argued that Mildred, who was 'wise, and of good nature to discerne from what mynde everie action procedeth', would make no account of such 'Common disguising'. He styled the letter as a simple act of courtesy to his aunt, only adding at the end a few lines asking whether she would 'vouchsafe the mencion and Recommendacion of my sute' in a letter to her husband, 'wherin your ladyship shall bynd me more unto yow then I can looke ever to be able sufficientlie to acknowledg'.[146] There is no mention of such an appeal to his aunt being 'rare and unacustomed', suggesting that such approaches to Mildred may have been more common, as would accord with his reference to the 'earnest errande' accompanying his past visits.[147]

Elizabeth Russell more obviously tried to intervene for her nephews' advancement, particularly that of Anthony Bacon. She passed information, for example, from the court to her nephew. In October 1593 he had been unable to travel to court to present himself to the Queen, as kidney stones obliged him to stop at Eton. He had sent notification of his ill-health to the Queen via the earl of Essex, who had informed him that her majesty had 'very gratwaslie accopted thereof'.[148] He also received word of his standing at court from his aunt Russell, who told him 'that her majesty about a seven night agoe openly in the parcke befoere divers vouchsaffed of her self with out any other occasion to make mencion of me and to moane muche my infirmity protestinge ... that yf I had but half as muche health as honestie and other sufficientcie shee knowe not throughout her Realme where to finde a better servant and more to her lykinge'.[149]

Elizabeth most regularly acted as an intermediary in the 1590s between the Cecils and the Essex circle, the latter including her own nephew Anthony Bacon. Her brother-in-law had won an 'unprecedented share of power and influence' by the start of this decade, particularly following the deaths of other key councillors, such as Leicester, Walsingham and Hatton.[150] Burghley's solicitude for the advancement of his son, Robert Cecil, as his successor clashed with the earl of Essex's rising influence and quest to become the chief English statesman after Burghley's death. Antagonisms developed between Essex and his perceived rivals, particularly the Cecils. Figures sympathetic to both sides adopted the role of mediator between the Cecils and the Essexians during this period, such as Thomas Heneage and Henry Carey, Lord Hunsdon.[151] The attempts at mediation by Elizabeth Russell have previously received little attention.[152] Close engagement with her activities during this period firstly demonstrates in more detail her precise role within these circles and, secondly, reveals that her intention on occasion may have been less straightforward than outright conciliation.

In March 1595, together with Sir Walter Ralegh, Elizabeth had attempted to broker reconciliation between the earl of Essex and the Cecils.[153] She was again employed by Burghley in an attempt at reconciliation with Anthony Bacon in September 1596, which is discussed in more detail in the final section of the chapter. At the end of September 1596 Elizabeth Russell once again positioned herself as a mediator, this time between Burghley and Essex over the question of the division of spoils from the Cadiz expedition. According to his own testimony, Burghley had disagreed with the Queen, who thought Essex should not have profit of the prisoners taken and that such spoils should come to the Crown. Burghley had not only angered the Queen by his stance in favour of Essex, but also annoyed Essex himself by his interference: 'I am farder laden withe reporte of your displeasure also whereof my Lady Russell hath advertised me larglie by her lettre.' Burghley's letter is full of self-pity. He thought himself to be more unfortunate than Aeneas, citing Virgil's description that 'incidit in Scyllam qui vult vitare Charibdim' (wanting to avoid Charybdis, he runs into Scylla).[54] His letter was taken to Essex by Elizabeth Russell, and the earl replied the next day. He thanked the Lord Treasurer for his gracious letter, but questioned his tone, thinking it 'so strange a style'. The fault on this occasion, he argued, lay with Elizabeth: 'yet the occasion of writing in so strange a stile, *lesse then I thinke my Lady herselfe that heard me did apprehend.* Your Lordship applyeth to me the phrase of displeasure and to your selfe of being kept downe, when both the matter and manner of my speach was full of reverence to your Lordship.'[55] Essex continued to assert his humility to Burghley, although he did allude in passing to ill treatment at Burghley's hands: 'Whither I did receave prejudice by your Lordship's speach or noe, I will make your selfe judge.' Burghley replied with a letter also seeking conciliation, again sent through Elizabeth. 'The prejudice,' Burghley wrote, 'which your Lordship noteth to have received by my speeches, I knowe not, but shalbe content I hope to satisfie yow, or otherwyse, yf I can, to make amends.'[56] Throughout this exchange, Elizabeth appeared not to attempt to clarify the nature of Essex's displeasure with Burghley; Essex's letter stated that Burghley had only had notice from Elizabeth that Essex felt some 'sense of some unkindness' from him. It is possible that both men were seeking to distance themselves from Elizabeth's mediation; however, it seems more likely that Elizabeth's vague messages were consciously constructed, her aim having been only to alert Burghley to Essex's displeasure. Her gender here was a distinct advantage, as once the information had been passed to Burghley, Essex was able to disassociate himself from her message, arguing that Elizabeth was mistaken in her understanding of him. Such an impression was reinforced by Essex himself, who noted to Anthony Bacon, two days after Burghley's last letter, that Elizabeth Russell had been 'very kind to me, and desirous to negot[iate] for me, as I will acquaint yow when I see yow'.[57] Certainly Essex was not deterred from meeting with Elizabeth; he was making time, in what he acknowledged to be a fraught schedule, to visit her only weeks later.[58]

Elizabeth was similarly undeterred from attempting to mediate between factions, and in March 1597 she was involved in another effort. Walter Ralegh again had been acting as a 'Mediator of a Peace' between Essex and Robert Cecil in the hope of mutual benefits for all three men.[159] Elizabeth similarly appealed to Essex for a resolution and on the 4th of that month the earl spent two hours in conversation with her at her Blackfriars house. Rowland Whyte questioned whether her nephew Robert Cecil would welcome Elizabeth's intervention, but added that Essex was willing to listen to her and other intermediaries, since the earl, 'wearied with not knowing how to please, is not unwilling to harken to those motions, made unto him for the Publiq Good'.[160] Her information networks allowed Elizabeth to attempt again to adopt the role of mediator in January 1599. She had heard of disagreement between Robert Cecil, Sir William Knollys and the earls of Nottingham and Essex.[161] It is likely that this was the dispute over Essex's preparations for Ireland, which had become so tense that Essex had even challenged Nottingham, the Lord Admiral, to a duel.[162] Elizabeth offered to come to court to do whatever she could for her nephew.[163] Cecil's response is not extant, but it seems unlikely that he would have taken his aunt up on her suggestion in this instance. Her offer does, however, reveal her continued role in political intelligence networks.[164] Even at nearly sixty years old, Elizabeth was still apprised of recent events at court.

In this case, as with many of the above examples, too singular concern with the outcomes of the sisters' actions as intermediaries is in many ways unhelpful; Elizabeth's efforts must be placed alongside those of her male contemporaries, such as Ralegh, who also acted as an intermediary between the Cecils and Essex. More generally, clients often worked through a variety of intermediaries in this period, as in the case of Robert Bacon, so it is almost impossible to ascertain whether success or failure can be ascribed to particular individuals.[165] The documentary evidence of the Cooke sisters instead reveals the widespread acceptance of such female political agency and warns against the simple equation that such activities were the unthinking product of kin advancement.

EDUCATED AS INTERMEDIARIES?

Throughout this chapter, there has been evidence that the sisters' education was an asset in their political careers. Their letter-writing skills facilitated their brokerage of political information. Language skills were also central to their activities as intermediaries. The Portuguese ambassador could therefore write to Mildred in 1561 in Latin.[166] While the ambassador could have had this letter translated, Mildred's classical education allowed her to be fully involved in the world of diplomacy. Language skills also helped other elite women to act as diplomatic intermediaries. Mary Sidney, for example, was able to speak in Italian directly to the Spanish ambassador during the negotiations for the Archduke Charles match in 1559.[167] Beyond language skills, there is evidence that their education aided the sisters' political agency in more diverse ways.

Anne, for example, reported her questioning of Robert Cecil in January 1595 to her son in the form of a classical dialogue. The particular interaction between Elizabeth and her nephew Anthony Bacon in September 1596, noted above, is worth analysing closely for what it reveals regarding the types of opportunities created for learned women to engage in political activities on similar terms to educated men. The whole incident has previously been dismissed as a 'fiasco' and Elizabeth has been criticised for her 'indignant tone', yet the role of her humanist education in dictating the form of the exchange deserves further attention.[168] Elizabeth was essentially concerned with attempting to heal the mistrust which had developed between the two sides of the family, the Bacons and the Cecils, since Robert Cecil's elevation to the secretaryship in July. At that time her sister Anne had advised her own son Anthony Bacon that he should be more wary of his uncle, Burghley, and particularly his cousin: '[Cecil] now hath great Avantage & strength to intercept, prevent & to toy ... yow know what termes he standeth in toward your self & wold nede [not] have me tell yow so'.[169]

To assuage this mistrust, and in line with her other efforts as an inter-mediary, Elizabeth visited her brother-in-law, Burghley, on 8 September 1596 to discover whether he held any ill will towards his nephew Anthony Bacon. Burghley suggested to Elizabeth that he was worried about Anthony's religious persuasion, particularly after his nephew's long Continental sojourn, and given his companionship with Anthony Standen, an English Catholic, and Thomas Wright, a seminary priest. He was also concerned regarding his nephew's reported involvement in spy networks, and particularly his contacts with Scotland. Finally, Burghley told Elizabeth that he believed his nephew did him 'ill offices', together with the earl of Essex, both in England and abroad.[170] Elizabeth then went directly and without warning to her nephew at Essex House. Anthony relayed the nature of her visit to the earl of Essex by letter, stating that he had recorded his conversation with his aunt 'so nere as I can remember, without affectation or meditation'.[171] In some ways, his letter must be treated with caution. It took Anthony four days to write and he also begins the epistle by wishing he had greater narrative abilities, stating 'I wishe from my harte that I could conjoure either my Lord Harrie or Signor Perez his genies to assist me withe the facillitie and grace they have in relatinge their own actions'.[172] Yet his description of his conversation with his aunt aligns so very closely with the points raised in Elizabeth's later letters on this subject that it seems Anthony provides a relatively accurate report.

From the outset of her visit, Elizabeth turned to her childhood training in rhetoric to put Burghley's accusations to her nephew. As all the accusa-tions stemmed from Anthony's past behaviour, she turned to her knowledge of forensic or judicial oratory in order to set out, in Anthony's words, 'the particulers of my Lord Tresurer's charge'; the Aristotelian definition, followed by later rhetoricians, was that judicial orations were those concerned with past actions.[73] Upon reading Anthony's account of her conversation, Essex also perceived it as an act of judicial oratory, referring to the exchange between Elizabeth and Anthony as 'the charg of my Lord Treasurer and the particular aunswers'.[74]

Elizabeth's judicial oratory moreover reveals the five stages of composition in classical and Renaissance rhetorical theory: *inventio* ('invention', the selection of argumentative strategies), *dispositio* ('disposition', the ordering of the argument), *elocutio* ('elocution', the style and language of the argument), *memoria* ('memory', committing the argument to memory) and *pronuntiatio* ('pronunciation', the performance of the argument).[75] For the invention of her argument (*inventio*), it is made explicit that Elizabeth is acting as an intermediary, delivering Burghley's own argument. Elizabeth states to Anthony that the accusations concern 'the indisposition or alteration of your minde, which is said to be growne corrupted in religion, factious and busie, undutyfull and unnaturall, and all this I tell yow from my Lord Treasurer'. According to classical and Renaissance rhetoricians, certain types of argument were especially persuasive. Aristotle divides these arguments into 'inartificial' and 'artificial' proofs. Inartificial proofs are not dependent on rhetoric for their success, rather they are, in Quintilian's formulation, 'from outside the art of speaking'.[76] Aristotle and Quintilian argue that such inartificial proofs are central in judicial oratory, comprising of factual information or the judgements of earlier courts.[77] In contrast, there are three types of artificial proofs which act to influence the audience through rhetorical skill: *ethos*, persuading the listeners through setting out the trustworthy personal character of the speaker, *pathos*, convincing the audience by putting them in an emotionally receptive state of mind, and *logos*, which persuades by the words chosen, for example, through the use of commonplaces. Both Elizabeth and Anthony reveal their understanding of the proofs of oratory in this exchange. After Elizabeth has set out her accusation to Anthony, he replies thus:

> Madame, said I, here are verie heavie propositions, and a protestation of greate price. for the first my hope and comforte is, that their *proofes* wilbe as light for my Lord's protestation as it is comfortable to me ... so when I call to minde the contrarie effectes I have felt, I apprehende the facillitie of his Lordship's so great an adventure. for that Nephewe, saith she, let my Lord looke to it, and bethinke your selfe how to answer my *proofes*.[78]

Whereas the vast majority of their argument will deal in inartificial proofs, as befits the type of oratory, Elizabeth underscores her argument at the outset with an appeal to *ethos*. Rather, however, than citing her own personality as central to the persuasive effect of the argument, it is Burghley's character which is lauded, Elizabeth saying 'all this I tell yow from my Lord Treasurer who protesteth uppon his salvation that he hath alwaies loved yow as a seconde father, and never not so much as in thought wronged yow'.[79]

For *dispositio*, the ordering of her argument, Elizabeth is explicit as to Burghley's accusations and the need for an answer to each. In setting out Burghley's points, she relies upon the skills of *memoria*, taught by her early education, to recall accurately the Lord Treasurer's accusations. The accuracy of Elizabeth's memory is borne out by subsequent letters she sent to Anthony on this subject, discussed below, which reiterate Burghley's points of concern.

In terms of the final two elements of classical oratory, *elocutio* and *pronun-tiatio*, she tries two different approaches, again linked to her knowledge of artificial rhetorical proofs. In order to persuade Anthony to heed the information she has received from her brother-in-law, Elizabeth turns to *pathos*: 'Good Nephewe are not yow much bounde to your Aunte that will make such a postinge Journie, onlie withe one gentlewooman, first in Coatch to Parris garden, and then in a wherrie over here to yow, to visite yow, and to performe a verie kinde office.'[180] Elizabeth uses the language and gestures of feminine weakness to put forth her case, 'lookinge wistelie' upon Anthony, which he understands as 'belike to see whether I was dismaide'. However, such appeals had the opposite effect upon him, for 'those wordes served rather as a Trompet to chere up and muster my spirits, and gave me occasion to replie'. From then on Elizabeth changes her manner of *elocutio*, saying 'Well Nephewe, seinge yow sowe armed, I will not flatter yow a white', before launching into her main argument. Anthony recognises this adoption of a more masculine style of speech, for he informs Essex that 'the particulers of my Lord Tresurer's charge [were] delivered most advantageouslie in sublimi genere dicendi' (the sublime style of oratory). To make her account more persuasive Elizabeth has turned to the 'sublimi genere dicendi', the highest style of oratory as defined by Cicero, reserved only for the best orators and capable of the 'greatest power' over the audience.[181] According to his account, Anthony's lack of preparation places him at a disadvantage, for he delivers a 'plaine trewe extemporall answer', bolstered only by his honesty.[182]

Anthony then responded to the accusations, informing his aunt of the basis of his defence, which should be passed on to Burghley. He begins by protesting his firmness in religion, providing what he termed a 'confession of my faith', but which actually consists of a variety of inartificial proofs of his orthodoxy.[183] He argues firstly that his uncle demonstrated his faith in his religious belief by entrusting him with making acquaintance in France with the Catholic conspirator William Parry; according to Anthony, his uncle defended him to the earl of Leicester, saying that 'parrie could never shake neither my religion nor honestie'. He cites the dedication of works by both Théodore de Bèze and Lambert Danaeus as further evidence of his Protestant zeal.[184] In Bordeaux, Anthony argues that he was even charged by an English papist and two Jesuits with aiding the Huguenots.[185] He says that he escaped the rack only through the protection of Jacques de Goyon, comte de Matignon,

151

the lieutenant-general of Henri III. Anthony then discusses how favourably he had initially been received at the court of Henri de Navarre in Montauban, stating 'theire be witnesses enoughe howe confidentlie the King's then cheef Councellors ... did use me, vouchsaffinge to sit divers times in Councell in my Chamber'.[186] He was here on stronger ground, protesting the quality of his proof, suggesting that his uncle already knew this information from the first-hand testimony of the Navarrian counsellors and that Burghley himself had confirmed this knowledge to Anthony in his correspondence.

Anthony argues that his difficulty came in 1584, when he made an enemy of Charlotte Arbaleste, the wife of Philippe du Plessis-Mornay, the Huguenot leader. According to Anthony, Madame du Plessis-Mornay had turned against him, due to his failure to marry her daughter, her reluctance for Anthony to be repaid a debt by her husband, and for his siding with the minister of the Montauban church, Michael Bérault, who was intent on enforcing the sumptuary rules against the ornate headwear she favoured.[187] Anthony then argues that he was forced to develop a relationship with the bishop of Cahors in order to sustain himself; he had agreed to write to Burghley on behalf of two Welsh Jesuits, only because he thought it would safeguard the passage of his servant, Thomas Lawson, who was to 'deliver saffelie to my Lord Treasurer's handes cortaine advertisements verie important for her Majestie's service, and dangerous for my self'. Burghley subsequently saw Lawson imprisoned for ten months and Anthony blames his uncle for 'givinge waie (without anie resistance by his grave aucthoritie and wisdome) to my Mother's passionate importuintie, grounded uppon false suggestions and surmyses aucthorised by de Plessi and his wyfe; and out of mere envie against the said Lawson's merite and credite withe me'.[188] Anthony is here attacking Burghley, speaking through his aunt, for his reliance in a judicial case on artificial proofs, the *pathos* of his mother, whilst again questioning the *ethos* of the Lord Treasurer, giving in to 'mere envie'.

Anthony then turns to the accusation that he was 'busie ... with matters above your reach, as forraine intelligences, and intertainment of spies'.[189] He admits that he has made acquaintance with many French and Scottish figures, but he protests that his actions were the result of official promotion. Again, he produces inartificial proof of his honesty, showing his aunt a letter written to him thirteen years earlier by the late Francis Walsingham on behalf of the Queen, 'conteyninge her gratious acceptance of my poore indeavours and asseurance of her princelie favour and good opinion'.[190]

Elizabeth's reaction to the strength of this proof is, according to Anthony, vehement: 'god's bodie Nephewe, said she, thou arte mightelie wronged, for here is not onlie warrant but incoragment'. His response was to build upon his proof, now by resorting to *pathos*, telling his aunt that, had only Walsingham been still alive, his position would have been more assured: 'Is it not a verie hard case, Madame, that an honest loyall subjecte, sonne of so faithfull a servant and trewe patriate, havinge so manie yeares sowne obedyence, care and expenses, should reap no other fruites then jealosies, suspitiones, and misimputations."[191] He finally turns to the issue of his friendship with the Catholic Anthony Standen. Anthony Bacon argues that on his return to England, Burghley offered him nothing but 'faire wordes which make fooles faine, and yet even in those no offer, or hopefull asseurance of reall kindenes'.[192] He therefore made contact with the earl of Essex, not least because of his standing with the Queen and his relationship with his brother, Francis. Anthony then argues that he was driven to seek the earl's kindness again in 1593, when Standen was purposely abandoned in Calais by Burghley, without means of returning to England. Here though, Anthony relies upon the artificial proof of *logos*, turning to a commonplace, and he tells his aunt that 'Verbum enim sapienti' (A word is indeed enough to the wise).[193] In a judicial setting, commonplaces were less persuasive and Elizabeth's answer is to express indignation, 'yf thy tale be trewe'; the 'yf' in her statement perhaps suggests that she senses the weakness in his argument here. Anthony then moves on to Thomas Wright, the seminary priest, where he has stronger evidence. As two 'interrogatories' by the Lord Treasurer failed to condemn Wright, regardless of his religion and profession, Anthony states that he had only followed the Queen in extending support to the priest. He discusses a letter that he had sent to the dean of Westminster, Gabriel Goodman, in whose house Wright had been imprisoned for supposed remarks against the English church; Anthony produces the letter as inartificial proof that he in fact did not write anything 'presumptuous or irreligious'.

He ends with another attack on his aunt's proofs: the standing or *ethos* of her brother-in-law, Burghley. Anthony has attacked Burghley for duplicity throughout his defence, but now he produces proof of the Lord Treasurer's lack of care for his nephews. According to Anthony, even the Queen has marvelled 'what should make him so loth, yea, so backward to advance his Nephews'. He then states that his cousin Robert Cecil had admitted to Anthony's mother, Anne, that he held a 'deadlie fude' with Anthony, seeing him as a 'mortall enemie, and would make me feele it when he could'; Anthony did not know whether this was with Burghley's knowledge. He closes his argument with a rhetorical flourish, turning to humour to win over his aunt:

> whether it be trewe or no, Madame, I referre to my Mother, who marveyled when she tould me of it, that I did but laughe at it, alleging and expoundinge to her Ladyship a gascon proverb, which was brame l'asne ne monte pas al ciel (The braying of donkeys does not reach heaven). by god, said myne Aunte, but he is no Asse. let him goe for a Mule then, Madame, said I, the most mischevous beast that is. whereat she laughed hartelie and seemed to be verie glad to understand such a monsterous insolencie which brought her into a verie good temper, and altered her stile quite from censures and reproches to praise of my extemporall Apologie.

Classical and Elizabethan rhetoricians were united in the belief that laughter was a powerful weapon against an adversary.[194] The limits of Elizabeth's adoption of the role of prosecutor are here uncovered, for she is happy to enjoy the mockery of her nephew Robert Cecil. Elizabeth is adamant that Anthony should commit this defence to writing, which she would then convey to her brother-in-law. Yet Anthony resists such a move, arguing that his aunt's greater command of oratory would enable her to deliver the answer more effectively; she 'would smoothe the harshnes and shadowe the blemishes of this my free yet dutyfull and trewe discource in defence of innocencie'.[195]

He admitted later to Essex that he had no thought to write to his uncle, most probably fearing such evidence would be refuted by Burghley or used against him, although after his aunt had left, Anthony wrote to her, thanking her for her kind visit. He acknowledges the intellectual construction of their conversation, characterising Elizabeth as a 'judicious' listener, adding that he hoped his extempore defence had met with her satisfaction, 'howsoever I mought have erred in forme of uttering the same in such choice termes'. He argues that he is comforted by the thought that he was justified by the truth and so would not trouble Elizabeth with putting his account into writing. He then applauds her skill in *memoria*, saying that he hopes she will store his defence in her memory 'till your kinde love & judgement see fitt time & occasions to commaunde their apparance & plea in the behalfe of your absent, sicklie, & innocent nephew'.[196]

Elizabeth, in fact, had already taken what she had heard from her nephew to the Lord Treasurer. She wrote to Anthony, with the result of her conversation with his uncle, later that day, 8 September 1596.[197] Elizabeth's actions again reveal clear evidence of her education. Now acting as the defence for Anthony, she had prepared her argument carefully, in the form of a written letter to her brother-in-law. Burghley both read this personally and asked her 'to rede it agayne to him'; her defence of her nephew, like Anthony's own epistolary report to Essex, is therefore likely to have been carefully composed.[198] Both that letter and her subsequent one to her nephew also reveal the powers of her *memoria*. She reports all of Anthony's defence to her brother-in-law, point by point. Burghley's response is to affirm his nephew's defence of his religion, in contrast to Elizabeth's earlier report that the Lord Treasurer had accused his nephew of being 'corrupted in religion, factious and busie'.[199] Elizabeth also reports that Burghley is 'gladd' of Anthony's friendship with Essex, although he admits that he thought Anthony should bring his intelligences to him, rather than the earl, after his past 'kyndness' to his nephew.[200]

Elizabeth is alert to the quality of proofs offered by each of the men. She gives Burghley notice of Anthony's mistrust of his cousin Robert Cecil. Burghley defends his son, saying that he never heard any complaint from his son regarding Anthony, until the latter was reported to have 'rayled on him every wher'. Elizabeth offers Anthony's proof that such reports came via his mother; Burghley's answer is to vow, drawing on the persuasive appeal of *ethos*, that 'till now never to have understood eny thing to have passed betwene yow, eather to your moother or otherwise'.[201] When Burghley responds that he still dislikes Anthony's friendship with Standen and Wright, he reveals that the former 'being at the first directed to the Lord Thresurer, yow cawsed *as he sayth* to Coome to the Erle, after yow had procured him to come to your self first'.[202] With the addition of 'as he sayth', Elizabeth emphasises the unresolved nature of this issue: neither side can provide strong inartificial proof of their assertions. Burghley himself alludes to several inartificial proofs to rebut Anthony's claims. He states that he took offence at Anthony's 'falling owt with Plessy' on the word of the Huguenot, 'who Complayned of it Here'. He argues that he had written to Anthony regarding his fraternisation with the bishop of Cahors and 'other bad fellowes' in Montauban. He also adds that Anthony was made aware of his disapproval of Thomas Lawson when he detained and imprisoned him on his trip to England, but that, notwithstanding that knowledge, Anthony 'sent for him agayne'. He ends by asking whether Anthony could provide a justification or proof of any of those points: 'if yow have more then a warrant for theys and other dealings he is gladd with all his hart, but he hath great cawse to dowbt the Contrary'.[203]

According to Elizabeth's report, Burghley finally demanded proof of Anthony's accusations of his unkindness to him: 'He prayeth yow to sett downe wherin justly in eny one thing yow can charge him self with the leste unkyndness.'[204] Elizabeth has told Burghley that her nephew wanted 'reall assurance, for that yow ment yow woold beleve no more woords'. Here Burghley's interpretation of his nephew's meaning differs from Elizabeth's: 'He tooke it that yow ment yow woold beleve no more his woords, saying that he woold not wryte nor bestow his woords but upon those that woold beleve them. *I awnsered that I thought not that to be your meaning*, for that yow had letters from his Lordshipp all redy but rather somme reall assurance from her majesty by somme deede to yowr good.'[205] Elizabeth smoothes and mediates Anthony's meaning, as he himself had suggested she would, whilst attempting to procure royal favour for her nephew. Rather than simply working as an intermediary, Elizabeth is now acting for the defence, putting the case across to the best of her training.

Her letter also reports details from her original conversation with Anthony, not recorded in his description for Essex. Burghley apparently pitied his nephew's sickness and financial situation when it was reported by Elizabeth. This was perhaps elaboration by his aunt, drawing on the power of *pathos*.[206] Certainly, Anthony removed the more unflattering details of his discussion with his aunt from his written version. According to her letter, Elizabeth passed on to Burghley his nephew's accusation that he had called him 'a good trencher man'. Anthony, understandably, did not pass such details on to Essex, yet Elizabeth's power of *memoria* apparently recalled all the points from her earlier conversation.[207]

After reporting her meeting with Burghley, Elizabeth therefore demands that Anthony write a letter either to Burghley or to her, which she would take to her brother-in-law, 'to his satisfaction in theis poynts'; this is clearly a discursive exercise for her, which she believes can be resolved through argument and the exchange of proofs. Despite her adoption respectively of the role of prosecutor and then defence, she does reveal a partiality in this letter for Anthony, rather than for Robert Cecil, although acknowledging that both be 'my sisters' soones'. Burghley had returned her letter to her, so she assures Anthony it will not fall into Robert's hands. She also admits that while she was comforted as to Burghley's affection for his nephew, justified by the power of his *ethos*, she was less sure of Robert Cecil's stance, writing that he will receive 'as his desart shall requyre', ending 'you know who'.[208]

Anthony was pleased to hear his aunt's 'comfortable message', as he wrote to his mother on the same day.[209] His words in this letter closely echo those he wrote earlier the same day to his aunt. He references that he was called to make his defence without preparation, stating in both that it was done without 'meditation or affectation'. Similarly, in both he makes reference to the defence he finds in his 'truth and innocincy'.[210] However, in his letter to his mother he reveals the limits of his trust in his uncle, writing that he accepted the news of Burghley's goodwill 'with more thankfullness then I meane to rely uppon with confidence'; he was glad at least that it had 'drued upp the torrent of my Lord Tresurer's mightie indignation at the least by show and his owne profession and so autenticall a testemony as my Lady Russell's'.[211] Anthony's last reference to his aunt's testimony is telling, for two reasons. Firstly, his reference to her 'autenticall' testimony seems to indicate his trust in his aunt's *memoria*. Secondly, it suggests the public nature of his aunt's actions as an intermediary: at the very least, her testimony will be put abroad as 'autenticall'.

Anthony answered his aunt again the next day, expressing the depth of his obligation to her. His response to Burghley's points was less gracious, as suggested by his earlier letter to his mother:

> perceivinge therebie rather the depthe of my Lord Tresurer's conceite and his Lordship's doubtfull acceptance of my trewe and simple apologie then anie stamp of his Lordship's likinge and credit thereof, I hope his Lordship will neither finde it strange nor amis in me yf, withall reverent and dutyful regarde to his Lordship's greatnes, I continewe my former honest course in givinge no just cause of his Lordship's displeasure, the heavines whereof, yf it be my ill hap to have unjustlie cast uppon me by misinterpretacons, misreports, and sinister impressions, without mine owne deserte, I maie esteeme my self unfortunate, but by god's grace I shall never be proved guilty.[212]

Anthony sent a copy of this letter to Essex, who judged it to be a 'good and wise lettre', yet Elizabeth was surprised by this response, which was far from her 'expectation'.[213] Her explanation of such an answer from her nephew was that he must have misunderstood her: 'yow mistake me and my letter to your self if yow interprett otherwise'. Switching back to the case for the prosecution, she once again reiterates the four main points of Burghley's response: firstly, he wanted him to set down any unkindness he had shown to his nephew; secondly, he disapproved of his relationship with Standen; next, he desired clarification of the words 'reall assurance'; and lastly, he pitied Anthony's health and poverty, which he attributed to his living with 'bad people'. Elizabeth urges him to reply; Burghley only 'requyred to be satisfied in the poynts above'. She ends by suggesting that Anthony is obliged to reply in order to answer the proofs offered by Philippe du Plessis-Mornay regarding his stay in Montauban ('For plessy Complayned here of yow').[214]

Here the evidence of Elizabeth's role as an intermediary between Burghley and Anthony Bacon ceases, suggesting that the exchange of letters dried up. Fuelled by confidence in her rhetorical skills, Elizabeth felt that a verdict could be reached and a mediation be sought between warring branches of the family tree, through an exercise of judicial oration and an exchange of proofs. Burghley was happy to oblige his sister-in-law, as he was to later use her as intermediary between himself and Essex. Elizabeth's letters reveal Burghley's accusations to be unchanging and set out point by point. Anthony, however, was less keen to engage with this trial by letter. He provided proofs as to his innocence in his first conversation with his aunt, but then refused to respond to her plan. Despite the eventual breakdown of this particular attempt at mediation, it is apparent that Elizabeth's education created a role for her in brokering information. Moreover, it allowed her accurately to memorise and recall the various accusations and refutations offered by both sides. Her abandonment of more feminine techniques, the 'kinde enchauntments' she initially used with Anthony, for more masculine forms of judicial oratory and writing reveals a limit to wider female involvement in such information networks, yet this should not obscure the congruence of Elizabeth's actions with the types of agency discussed in this chapter and her wider efforts as an intermediary between the Cecils and the Essex circle in the late 1590s. Whilst she could draw on masculine forms of language, it was the very informality of Elizabeth's status as an aunt and sister-in-law which allowed her to explore the grievances of male family members, seeking the information on which reconciliation could be based.

CONCLUSION

This study of the sisters' roles as intermediaries and brokers has demonstrated female involvement in a wider range of political networks than acknowledged by existing scholarship, particularly their concern with the issues of 'high politics'. Their agency within diplomatic circles shows not only female handling and understanding of information with a national significance, but also the geographical spread and recognition of their influence as information brokers. Yet there are differences between the sisters' activities as intermediaries. Although there is evidence of Mildred's communication with her nephew Anthony Bacon over Huguenot affairs as late as 1585, only four years before her death, there is fuller extant material on her activities in the pursuit of 'British' security in the 1560s and 1570s. The absence of the majority of Mildred's correspondence means that only a partial picture of her political role can be reconstructed; however, it is clear that she was still recognised as an influential intermediary in the late 1570s and 1580s. Her contact with both her Bacon nephews in the last decade of her life means that it is attractive to speculate that, had she not died in 1589, she would have occupied an important role as an intermediary between her husband and son and the Essex circle in the next decade. Her death meant that her widowed sister Elizabeth had a greater opportunity to act as an intermediary between warring family members in the 1590s, while the attention of Anne was focused on religious matters, as we shall see in the next chapter. Elizabeth's role as an intermediary between the Cecils and the Essex circle may have been ultimately unsuccessful, yet her continued use as mediator, particularly by Burghley, reveals contemporary recognition of the value of her activities.

For the Cooke sisters, the family remained the basic political unit. Marriage, particularly Mildred's marriage to William Cecil, facilitated much of the sisters' political activity, with Elizabeth continuing to use these political networks far into her second widowhood, yet their example reminds us that kin relationships did not always guarantee that women would work on behalf of potential suitors. Moreover, whilst it was their relationships with powerful men, particularly Lord Burghley, which made them desirable intermediaries, this chapter highlights that the sisters themselves held significant and influential roles in political and patronage networks, offering a corrective to 'bottom-up' views of patronage which characterise women primarily as suitors to male brokers and patrons. Finally, education did have an impact on female involvement in these information networks. At the most basic level, it allowed women to be written to and to write letters of confidential political information themselves. At the highest level, as with the Cooke sisters, it allowed them to communicate with foreign ambassadors and to memorise and understand complex political material. Yet the sisters' unofficial political status allowed them to conceal the import of their actions behind a veneer of family and sociability, thereby exploiting patriarchal restrictions within sixteenth-century society to their advantage.

NOTES

1 Cecil had written a letter to Mildred, advising her in the case of his execution, which he entrusted to his brother-in-law, Nicholas Bacon. See BL, Lansdowne MS 104, fos 3r–4v. It is not in Cecil's hand, but appears to be a copy made by his secretary, Michael Hickes.

2 BL, Cotton MS Titus B.II, fos 377r–v.

3 D. MacCulloch, 'The *Vita Mariae Angliae Reginae* of Robert Wingfield of Brantham' (*Camden Miscellany* 28, CS, 4th series, 29, 1984), p. 270.

4 R. Tittler, *Nicholas Bacon: The Making of a Tudor Statesman* (1976), p. 53.

5 For female sociability in a European setting, see O. Hufton, 'Reflections on the role of women in the early modern court', *The Court Historian*, 5 (2000), 1–13.

6 B. Harris, 'Women and politics in early Tudor England', *HJ*, 33 (1990), 259–81.

7 B. Harris, *English Aristocratic Women, 1450–1550: Marriage and Family, Property and Careers* (Oxford, 2002), p. 237. See also H. Payne, 'Aristocratic women, power, patronage and family networks at the Jacobean court, 1603–1625', in J. Daybell (ed.), *Women and Politics in Early Modern England, 1450–1650* (Aldershot, 2004), pp. 164–80; H. Payne, 'The Cecil women at court', in P. Croft (ed.), *Patronage, Culture and Power: The Early Cecils, 1558–1612* (2002), pp. 265–82.

8 Hufton, 'Reflections', 1.

9 Brokerage is a term developed by social scientists, although it is helpful in describing the role of the intermediary in early modern patronage networks. See J. Boissevain, *Friends of Friends: Networks, Manipulators and Coalitions* (Oxford, 1974), pp. 147–69.

10 B. Harris, 'The view from my lady's chamber: new perspectives on the early Tudor monarchy', *Huntington Library Quarterly*, 60 (1997), 243.

11 Pam Wright suggested that Elizabeth's Privy Chamber women were deprived of any 'independent initiative' in matters of diplomacy. See P. Wright, 'A change in direction: the ramifications of a female household, 1558–1603', in D. Starkey (ed.), *The English Court from the Wars of the Roses to the Civil War* (1987), pp. 147–72 (p. 168). Joan Greenbaum Goldsmith and Charlotte Merton likewise found little sustained evidence of Privy Chamber women being involved in diplomatic relations. See J.B. Greenbaum Goldsmith, 'All the Queen's Women: The Changing Place and Perception of Aristocratic Women in Elizabethan England, 1558–1620' (PhD thesis, Northwestern University, Illinois, 1987), pp. 135–6, 139–41; C. Merton, 'The Women Who Served Queen Mary and Queen Elizabeth: Ladies, Gentlewomen and Maids of the Privy Chamber, 1553–1603' (PhD thesis, Cambridge University, 1992), pp. 165–70.

12 N. Mears, 'Politics in the Elizabethan Privy Chamber: Lady Mary Sidney and Kat Ashley', in J. Daybell (ed.), *Women and Politics in Early Modern England, 1450–1700* (Aldershot, 2004), pp. 67–82 (p. 72). See also N. Mears, *Queenship and Political Discourse in the Elizabethan Realms* (Cambridge, 2005), pp. 54–5.

13 J. Dawson, 'William Cecil and the British dimension of early Elizabethan foreign policy',

History, 74 (1989), 196–216; S. Alford, *The Early Elizabethan Polity: William Cecil and the British Succession Crisis, 1558–1569* (Cambridge, 1998).

14 Alford, *Early Elizabethan Polity.*

15 *Ibid.*, pp. 42–96.

16 S. Haynes, *A Collection of State Papers ... left by William Cecil, Lord Burghley* (1740) (Haynes), p. 293: 18/04/1560.

17 *Ibid.*, p. 359: 19/07/1560.

18 See Alford, *Early Elizabethan Polity*, pp. 64–5.

19 Haynes, p. 293.

20 For the rumours, see NA, SP 12/12, fos 50r–51v and Alford, *Early Elizabeth Polity*, pp. 79–80.

21 Haynes, p. 301: 28/04/1560.

22 Haynes, pp. 320: 02/06/1560; *ibid.*, p. 323: 04/06/1560; *ibid.*, p. 333: 23/06/1560; NA SP 12/12, fos 86r, 88r: 06/06/1560.

23 C. Read, *Mr. Secretary Cecil and Queen Elizabeth* (1955), p. 179.

24 NA SP 52/4, fo. 25r: 17/06/1560; NA SP 52/4, fo. 179r: 15/07/1560.

25 Haynes, p. 359.

26 *Ibid.*

27 S. Doran, *Monarchy and Matrimony: The Courtships of Elizabeth I* (1996), pp. 36–7, n. 127.

28 Haynes, p. 362: 21/09/1560.

29 *Ibid.*, p. 359.

30 For Arran at Cecil House, see R.K. Hannay, 'The earl of Arran and Queen Mary', *Scottish Historical Review*, 18 (1920–21), 265.

31 Haynes, p. 363: 28/09/1560.

32 Cecil's own interest in the match had lessened by the end of 1560, when he began to doubt the political benefits of the marriage. See Doran, *Monarchy and Matrimony*, p. 37.

33 Haynes, p. 359.

34 *Ibid.*, pp. 293, 301.

35 *Ibid.*, p. 363.

36 *Ibid.*, p. 362.

37 NA, SP 52/3, fo. 145v: 30/04/1560.

38 Haynes, p. 359.

39 Windebank had accompanied William Cecil on his trip to Scotland in May 1560, acting as a secretary. See R.C. Barnett, *Place, Profit and Power: A Study of the Servants of William Cecil, Elizabethan Statesman* (Chapel Hill, 1969), pp. 147–8.

40 NA, SP 70/26, fo. 9r: 01/05/1561.

41 *Ibid.*, p. 362.

42 Alford, *Early Elizabethan Polity*, p. 81.

43 NA, SP 52/11, fo. 204v: 24/11/1565. William Cecil was forwarding his letters to Moray

through Melville. Given Mildred's pre-existing correspondence with the latter, it is possible that she was also forwarding letters to Moray in this way.

44 *Scrinia Ceciliana, Mysteries of State & Government in Letters of the Late Famous Lord Burghley* (1663), p. 140: 20/02/1567.

45 NA, SP 63/7, fos 1r–v: 01/09/1562.

46 NA, SP 63/16, fo. 19v: 09/01/1566.

47 For letters to William Cecil regarding the match, see *Calendar of State Papers, Ireland, 1509–1573*, ed. H.C. Hamilton (1860), pp. 401, 421, 422, 464.

48 CP 157, fo. 15r: 26/10/1569.

49 See, for example, Bodl., Carte MS LVIII, fo. 664r: 29/08/1568.

50 NA, SP 63/22, fo. 62r: 24/11/1567; SP 63/23, fos 44r–v: 22/01/1568.

51 SP 63/23, fo. 48v: 22/01/1568.

52 Bodl., Carte MS LVIII, fo. 218r: 20/01/1568.

53 NA, SP 63/23, fo. 49r.

54 Bodl., Carte MS LVIII, fo. 664r: 29/08/1568.

55 *Ibid.*, fo. 218r. For the alliances between the Ulster lords, see C. Brady, *The Chief Governors: The Rise and Fall of Reform Government in Tudor Ireland, 1536–1588* (Cambridge, 1994), pp. 128–9.

56 Bodl., Carte MS LVI, fo. 475r: 26/10/1573.

57 J.G. Crawford, 'Sir Nicholas White', *ODNB*.

58 NA, SP 63/42, fo. 149r: 04/11/1573. White was acquainted with Mildred from at least 1571, as shown by his references to her in letters to her husband. See NA, SP 63/32, fo. 30v: 09/04/1571; NA, SP 63/40, fo. 77v: 10/05/1573.

59 Bodl., Carte MS LVIII, fo. 664r: 29/08/1568.

60 BL, Cotton MS Nero B.I, fo. 98b: 23/05/1562.

61 *Ibid.*

62 *Ibid.*

63 NA, SP 70/38, fos 75r–v: 08/06/1562.

64 *CSP, Spain, 1558–1567*, p. 544: 22/04/1566.

65 *CSP, Spain, 1558–1567*, p. 580: 14/09/1566.

66 CP 155, fo. 53r: 27/05/1567.

67 NA, SP 78/13, fo. 161v: 19/03/1585.

68 Edinburgh University Library, Laing MS III.193, fos 143v–144r: 19/03/1585.

69 For Sturm, see chapter 1 and *Ascham Letters*, p. 300.

70 *Calendar of State Papers, Foreign Series, of the reign of Elizabeth I, 1558–1603*, ed. J. Stevenson (23 vols, 1863–1950) (*CSP, Foreign*), *1577–78*, p. 349. Latin original NA, SP 81/1, fos 117r–119Av: 04/12/1577.

71 *CSP, Foreign, 1577–78*, p. 349.

72 *Ibid.*, p. 350.

73 *Ibid.*

74 *Ibid.*

75 *CSP, Spain, 1558–1567*, p. 445: 02/07/1565.

76 NA, SP 12/3, fo. 28r: 04/03/1559.

77 Mears, 'Elizabethan Privy Chamber'.

78 *CSP, Spain, 1558–1567*, p. 36: 13/09/1561.

79 *Ibid.*, p. 214. See also Mears, 'Elizabethan Privy Chamber', p. 72.

80 *CSP, Spain, 1558–1567*, p. 382: 23/09/1564.

81 *Ibid.*

82 K. Hickman, *Daughters of Britannia: The Lives and Times of Diplomatic Wives* (1999), p. xxiii.

83 For Elizabeth Wallop, see NA, SP 3/8, fo. 49v. For Bridget Morison, see NA, SP 68/6, fo. 28v; 68/8, fo. 113r; 68/10, fo. 128r. For Anne Throckmorton and Eleanor Bowes, see below.

84 NA, SP 70/14, fo. 62v: 10/05/1560.

85 BL, Lansdowne MS 102, fo. 122v.

86 NA, SP 15/13, fo. 14r: 07/04/1566.

87 CUL, Ff.5.14, fo. 107r. This version of the verse was recorded in the commonplace book of a W. Kytton.

88 *Ibid.* Kytton also provided this English translation of the verse.

89 L. Schleiner, *Tudor and Stuart Women Writers* (Bloomington, 1994), p. 45.

90 NA, SP 70/83, fo. 31r: 15/03/1566.

91 BL, Additional MS 35830, fo. 195r: 30/08/1561.

92 *Ibid.*, fo. 195v.

93 BL, Egerton MS 1671, fo. 140r; 2713, fos 144r–145r.

94 NA, SP 70/32, fo. 59r: 26/11/1561.

95 NA, SP 70/83, fo. 231r: 28/04/1566.

96 BL, Additional MS 35830, fo. 195r.

97 S. Doran, *England and Europe 1485–1603* (1996), p. 78.

98 NA, SP 70/84, fo. 213r: 21/06/1566.

99 M.S. Anderson, *The Rise of Modern Diplomacy, 1450–1919* (1993), pp. 12–13.

100 BL, Additional MS 18764, fo. 1v.

101 G. Mattingly, *Renaissance Diplomacy* (1955), pp. 198–9.

102 NA, SP 70/84, fo. 211v: 21/06/1566.

103 *Ibid.*

104 *Ibid.*, fo. 203r: 19/06/1566. For Elizabeth's reputation, see chapter 6 below.

105 *Ibid.*

106 NA, SP 70/85, fo. 41r: 17/07/1566.

107 *Ibid.*

108 *Ibid.*

109 In August, the count of Montgomery told Edward Cooke that the French Protestants were determined to aid their co-religionists in the Netherlands. NA, SP 70/85, fo. 113r: 18/08/1566.

110 LPL 658, fo. 60r: 07/1596.

111 *Ibid.*

112 NA, SP 70/85, fo. 78r: 07/1566.

113 BL, Lansdowne MS 28, fo. 54r: 22/07/1579.

114 Mildred's father, Anthony Cooke, leased Cocks Quay in London six years earlier, in 1573, to Cockson. See B. Dietz (ed.), *The Port and Trade of Early Elizabethan London: Documents* (London Records Society, 8; Leicester, 1972), p. 163. Daybell notes that Cockson demonstrated his deference to Mildred by placing his signature in the bottom far left of his letter. Daybell, *Women Letter-Writers*, p. 50.

115 BL, Lansdowne MS 28, fo. 54r.

116 *Ibid.*, fo. 52r.

117 For more on Mildred's reputation, see chapter 6.

118 NA, SP 15/24, fo. 45r: 18/04/1578.

119 BL, Lansdowne MS 38/57, fos 149r–v: 06/10/1583.

120 NA, SP 12/91, fos 29r–30v: 04/04/1573. For the Sidneys' financial difficulties, see NA, SP 12/86, fos 159r–160v: 02/05/1572.

121 NA, SP 12/91, fo. 29r.

122 See, for example, BL, Lansdowne MS 51/28, fo. 74r: 16/11/1587; NA, SP 12/218, fo. 61r: 25/11/1588.

123 CP 37, fo. 96r: 23/01/1597.

124 CP 161, fo. 52r: 11/09/1578.

125 J. Hurstfield, *The Queen's Wards: Wardship and Marriage under Elizabeth I* (1958), p. 265.

126 *Ibid.*, p. 266.

127 LPL 659, fo. 41r: 23/09/1596.

128 LPL 659, fo. 42r: 29/09/1596.

129 LPL 659, fo. 41r.

130 *Ibid.*

131 *Ibid.*

132 LPL 659, fo. 148r: 22/09/1596. See also a copy, LPL 659, fo. 87r.

133 See chapter 3 for more on this dispute.

134 CP 197, fo. 54r: 1608.

135 LPL 659, fo. 43r: n.d.

136 LPL 659, fo. 1r: 26/09/1596.

137 LPL 659, fo. 140r: 26/09/1596.

138 LPL 656, fo. 5r: 09/03/1597.

139 LPL 656, fo. 95r: 09/03/1597.

140 CP 31, fo. 106r: 24/05/1595.

141 LPL 649, fo. 276r: 29/08/1593.

142 LPL 650, fo. 33r: 23/01/1595.

143 *Ibid.*

144 L. Jardine and A. Stewart, *Hostage to Fortune: The Troubled Life of Francis Bacon, 1561–1626* (1998), p. 80.

145 BL, Lansdowne MS 31, fo. 29r: 16/09/1580.

146 BL, Lansdowne MS 31, fo. 28r: 16/09/1580.

147 Jardine and Stewart elide the differences between the two letters by suggesting 'To both he admitted that his request was "rare and unaccustomed"': Jardine and Stewart, *Francis Bacon*, p. 80. Francis used such a term and an approach in his letter to his uncle, but made no such reference to his approach to his aunt as being unusual.

148 LPL 649, fo. 337r: 19/10/1593.

149 *Ibid.*

150 P. Hammer, 'Patronage at court, faction and the earl of Essex', in J. Guy (ed.), *The Reign of Elizabeth I: Court and Culture in the Last Decade* (Cambridge, 1995), p. 73.

151 *Ibid.*, p. 82.

152 For passing references to Elizabeth's mediation, see, for example, *ibid.*, p. 83; P. Hammer, '"The bright shininge sparke": The Political Career of Robert Devereux, 2nd Earl of Essex, c.1585–c.1597' (PhD thesis, Cambridge University, 1991), pp. 310–12; P. Hammer, *The Polarisation of Elizabethan Politics: The Political Career of Robert Devereux, Second Earl of Essex, 1585–1597* (Cambridge, 1999), p. 376.

153 A. Collins, *Letters and Memorials of State* (2 vols, 1746), II, pp. 24–5: 04/03/1595.

154 LPL 659, fo. 201r: 22/09/1596.

155 My italics. LPL 659, fo. 196r: 09/1596.

156 LPL 659, fo. 133r: 24/09/1596.

157 LPL 659, fo. 140r: 26/09/1596.

158 LPL 659, fo. 342r: 13/10/1596.

159 Collins, *Letters and Memorials of State*, II, p. 24: 04/03/1597. See also N. Mears, 'Regnum Cecilianum? A Cecilian perspective of the court', in J. Guy (ed.), *The Reign of Elizabeth I: Court and Culture in the Last Decade* (Cambridge, 1995), p. 56.

160 Collins, *Letters and Memorials of State*, II, p. 24.

161 CP 176, fo. 88r: 01/1599.

162 See *CSP, Spain, 1587–1603*, pp. 649–50.

163 CP 176, fo. 88r.

164 Elizabeth Farber has previously suggested that Elizabeth's information was out of date by a month, explaining her nephew's unwillingness to accept her mediation. This assertion is, however, based on confused dating. Elizabeth Russell's letter is endorsed

by Cecil's secretary as 'January, 1598' in Old Style dating; thus, if the year is taken to start on 1 January rather than 25 March, the letter dates from January 1599. E. Farber, 'The Letters of Lady Elizabeth Russell (1540–1609)' (PhD thesis, Columbia University, 1977), pp. 215–19.

165 See Daybell, *Women Letter-Writers*, p. 230.

166 BL, Cotton MS Nero B.I, fo. 98b.

167 Mears, 'Elizabethan Privy Chamber', p. 70.

168 Hammer, 'Patronage at court', p. 83, n. 72; Hammer, *Polarisation of Elizabethan Politics*, p. 376.

169 LPL 658, fo. 28r: 10/06/1596.

170 The following account of Elizabeth's actions that day is drawn from LPL 659, fos 23r–26r: 12/09/1596.

171 LPL 659, fo. 26v.

172 *Ibid.*, fo. 23r.

173 Aristotle, *The Art of Rhetoric*, I.iii.4; Q. Skinner, *Reason and Rhetoric in the Philosophy of Hobbes* (Cambridge, 1996), p. 41.

174 LPL 659, fo. 142r: 12/09/1596.

175 See, for example, Skinner, *Reason and Rhetoric*, pp. 45–7.

176 Quintilian, *Institutio Oratoria*, trans. H.E. Butler (4 vols, 1920–22), II, p. 156 [V.i.1].

177 *Ibid.* Aristotle, *Rhetoric*, I.ii.2.

178 My italics. LPL 659, fo. 23v.

179 *Ibid.*

180 *Ibid.*, fo. 23r.

181 Cicero, *Orator*, trans. H.M. Hubbell (1939), p. 377 [xxviii.97]. See also Quintilian, *Institutio Oratoria*, XII.x.61.

182 LPL 659, fo. 23r.

183 *Ibid.*, fo. 25r.

184 *Ibid.*, fo. 24r. As discussed in chapter 1, Bèze dedicated his meditations on the Penitential Psalms to Anne Bacon; Anthony argues in this letter that it was done 'for my sake'.

185 *Ibid.*

186 *Ibid.*, fo. 24v.

187 For more on this dispute see *A Huguenot Family in the XVI Century: The Memoirs of Philippe de Mornay Sieur du Plessis Marly Written by his Wife*, trans. L. Crump (1926), pp. 71, 198–217; D. du Maurier, *Golden Lads: Anthony Bacon, Francis and their Friends* (1976), pp. 61–2; Jardine and Stewart, *Francis Bacon*, p. 102.

188 LPL 659, fos 24v–25r.

189 *Ibid.*, fo. 23v.

190 *Ibid.*, fo. 25r.

191 *Ibid.*, fo. 25r.

192 *Ibid.*

193 *Ibid.*, 25v.

194 See, for example, Quintilian, *Institutio Oratoria*, VI.iii.1–5; T. Wilson, *Arte of Rhetorique*, ed. G.H. Mair (Oxford, 1909), pp. 134–7.

195 LPL 659, fo. 26r.

196 LPL 659, fo. 199r: 08/09/1596. For a copy, see LPL 659, fo. 187r.

197 LPL 659, fos 104r–105r: 08/09/1596.

198 Her letter to Burghley is, unfortunately, no longer extant and is recorded only in her subsequent report to her nephew. See LPL 659, fo. 104v.

199 LPL 659, fo. 23v.

200 LPL 659, fo. 104r.

201 LPL 659, fo. 104v.

202 My italics. LPL 659, fo. 104r.

203 LPL 659, fo. 104v.

204 LPL 659, fo. 104r.

205 My italics. LPL 659, fo. 104v.

206 LPL 659, fo. 104v. Informing Burghley that the duc du Bouillon, Henri de la Tour d'Auvergne, had been staying with Anthony, shortly before her visit, may have also been an appeal to Anthony's *ethos*: *ibid.*, fo. 105r. For the duc de Bouillon's visit to Anthony, see his letter to his mother on 7 September 1596: LPL 659, fo. 9r. For the duc de Bouillon, see Hammer, *Polarisation of Elizabethan Politics*, p. 96.

207 LPL 659, fo. 105r. 'Trencherman' in this context means 'One who frequents a patron's table; a parasite, dependent, hanger-on' (*Oxford English Dictionary*, 'trencher-man').

208 LPL 659, fo. 104v.

209 LPL 659, fo. 211r: 08/09/1596.

210 *Ibid.*; LPL 659, fo. 199r.

211 LPL 659, fo. 211r.

212 LPL 659, fo. 199v: 09/09/1596.

213 LPL 659, fo. 142r: 08/09/1596; LPL 659, fo. 106r: 09/09/1596.

214 LPL 659, fo. 106r.

Chapter 5

'Building up of the bodie of
the fellowship of Saincts':
religious networks

By meanes whereof it is come to passe, that as you are much beloved at home in
the midst of God's saincts and faithfull servants here, and these not onlie common
professors, but many worthie ministers ... so you are made truely famous abroad in
forraine Churches and countries, & highly reverenced of many worthie men there,
indued doubtles with singular graces for God's glory, and the building up of the
bodie of the fellowship of Saincts.[1]

Thomas Wilcox thus described the religious networks of the widowed
Anne Bacon in 1589. One of the authors of the 1572 Presbyterian
manifesto, *An Admonition to the Parliament*, Wilcox corresponded with Anne
from 1577 and also served as a curate at Bovingdon in Hertfordshire, close
to Anne at Gorhambury manor.[2] In this passage, Wilcox detailed the contribution of Anne's godly religious networks to 'the building up of the bodie
of the fellowship of Saincts'. Following Wilcox's characterisation, Anne and
her sisters have long been recognised as staunch Puritans.[3] The work of
Patrick Collinson and Peter Lake on the godly has, however, emphasised that
such beliefs encompassed a wide spectrum of opinion.[4] This chapter therefore looks more closely at the religious identity of the Cooke sisters through
exploring their religious networks, taking into account the development of
the sisters' individual spiritual views and the differences between the piety
of the four women. Firstly, it develops the theme of female brokerage of
patronage within a religious context, explored in relation to political issues in
the previous chapter. The distinction between political and religious networks
may appear anachronistic, yet in many ways the distinction is justified by
the activities of the sisters. The breadth of Anne's agency as an intermediary
for religious patronage contrasts with her seeming unwillingness to act as
a broker within more secular and political networks; Anne's intervention in
such matters was infrequent, limited to cases involving close family or those
of a godly persuasion in their political life, such as the Deputy Lieutenant

167

of Hertfordshire, Sir Henry Cocke. The distinction is also reflective of the lifecycles of the sisters. Although there is confirmation of the sisters acting as intermediaries for godly figures during their husbands' lifetimes, the greatest evidence comes from the widowhoods of Elizabeth and Anne. Partly this may be due to the nature of the extant material, which reflects relationships conducted on paper rather than in person, yet for Mildred and Anne public intervention on behalf of godly figures would have impacted upon their privy councillor husbands. During the lives of their husbands, it is also often difficult to distinguish the actions of the sisters from those of their spouses. For example, it is impossible to attribute the employment of two godly chaplains, Thomas Fowle and Robert Johnson, within the Bacon household directly to Anne's influence during the life of Nicholas Bacon, yet her later activities suggest that she would have approved of the appointments.[5] Despite these evidential difficulties, family networks are shown to continue to play an important role in the sisters' religious activities, highlighting the continuities between their brokerage in both the political and religious spheres. In the latter, there is further evidence of the complexity of family networks, with the sisters working both together and in opposition to their husbands as religious intermediaries.

The second half of the chapter turns its attention to the sisters as religious patrons in their own right. Widowhood is again important, for during their widowhoods Elizabeth and Anne held their own ecclesiastical patronage. The household has long been perceived as an important space for early modern female piety, yet this chapter goes beyond household walls to explore the continuities with lay female religious patronage in a parish setting.[6] As a widow, Anne's selection of godly chaplains for her household was mirrored by her patronage of preachers in the benefices under her control in Hertfordshire. The sisters also exercised religious patronage in their London parishes, in Oxford, in Cambridge and in Europe. This chapter thus delineates the spatial breadth of the sisters' religious networks, including the Cooke sisters' use of traditional political spaces, such as the court and Parliament, to advance their religious priorities. Finally, this chapter explores the question of the impact of the sisters' learned status on their religious networks. We have already seen how the act of religious translation allowed the sisters to contribute to strengthening their national church.[7] Building on the earlier discussion of Anne's credal translation of the *Apologia*, this chapter ultimately offers a new identification of Anne as the patron of Field and Wilcox's Presbyterian creed for the Church of England and in doing so highlights the differences between the four sisters' religious networks.

FEMALE RELIGIOUS BROKERAGE AND FAMILY NETWORKS

Contemporaries recognised that Mildred and Anne's marriages to privy councillors brought them considerable potential influence as brokers of ecclesiastical patronage. As Lord Keeper, Nicholas Bacon exercised patronage for the Crown, and personal influence was often key in the bestowal of these livings.[8] Anne's role in allocating the presentations under her husband's care is often difficult to discern, although the Lord Keeper's favour to Percival Wyborn was continued by Anne during her widowhood.[9] There is also evidence that Anne was approached regarding the allocation of ecclesiastical patronage. In February 1568 Matthew Parker, the archbishop of Canterbury, wrote to Anne appealing for her to use her influence over her husband. He told Anne of his disagreement with Nicholas Bacon over Parker's dismissal of two unlicensed prebendaries whom the Lord Keeper had installed in Norwich cathedral. Nicholas Bacon refused to allow Thomas Smyth, his prebendary, to follow Parker's advice to resign his living due to a lack of scriptural knowledge and instead offer his place to John Walker, desired by the 'whole city ... for his gift of preaching'.[10] Parker stated in his letter that he had not discussed such matters with his own wife, yet he recognised that Anne could and would bring pressure to bear upon Nicholas Bacon over the provision of preaching.[11] Although her initial response to Parker's request is unknown, there is evidence that Anne's views triumphed over her husband's in this instance. Walker was presented to a prebendal stall in the cathedral by the Lord Keeper on 25 January 1570.[12]

There is also evidence that Mildred sought to broker clerical presentations. In May 1594 Richard Webster wrote to Robert Cecil petitioning for the advowson of a prebend in Windsor. In his letter he lamented the death of Robert's mother, Mildred, arguing that he now had few friends to advance his cause, describing Mildred as 'the staff of poore Chapleynes in her Ladyship's lief time, whos want since that time I my self am privie of diverse that bewayle'.[13] It may therefore have been through Mildred's influence that in November 1586 Burghley had decided that Webster should be appointed to a prebendal stall at Westminster Abbey.[14]

Their married status could, however, make it difficult for the sisters to support controversial godly figures. Such concerns are highlighted by the different types of support all four sisters gave to an Italian manuscript treatise associated with Edward Dering, the godly preacher, in 1572. Dering's religious views had increasingly brought him into conflict with the authorities since Thomas Cartwright's lectures in the spring of 1570. Dering had launched a personal crusade in that year to reform the preaching ministry in the Church of England, attacking both William Cecil and Matthew Parker by letter, and the Queen in her Lenten sermon.[15] Dering remained ostracised from royal and governmental favour in 1572, when he contributed dedicatory verses to the Italian manuscript treatise entitled the *Giardino Cosmografico*.[16] The work was a collection of scientific thought compiled by Bartholo Sylva, a physician from Turin. The prefatory materials reveal Sylva to have been a Protestant convert seeking favour at the English court through the medium of the earl of Leicester, to whom the book was dedicated.[17] The text is prefaced by a series of dedicatory verses, including pieces from each of the Cooke sisters. Previous research has underestimated the significance of the sisters' verses, both by failing to place them in an exact chronology and by downplaying the differences between the sisters' poems.[18] An awareness of the more complex chronology surrounding the Sylva manuscript reveals the precise nature of the sisters' support for Edward Dering.

The manuscript's significance for the Cooke sisters lies in the separation of pages in the work: one includes the Greek poems by Dering, Mildred and Elizabeth, while the other contains dedicatory pieces in Latin by Anne and Katherine, as well as by Dering's wife, Anne Locke. Schleiner treated the poems as of equal importance, yet the page containing the Greek poems is highlighted through its strikingly different presentation from the rest of the work.[19] The entire manuscript was autographed as being the work of a scribe named D.M. Pettrucho, a Florentine.[20] Pettrucho possessed a fine italic script, and capitals throughout the text were painted in gold, within florid purple boxes. The earlier page containing the poems of Dering, Mildred and Elizabeth was, however, written in an entirely different, far rougher hand, without any adornment, and this cannot simply be the result of the poems being composed in Greek: the titles of all the poems are in Latin. The key is that the date following Bartholo Sylva's dedicatory epistle has been altered, from what was February 1571 to 24 May 1572.[21] It therefore seems likely that the page of verses by Dering, Mildred and Elizabeth was contributed to the volume at a later stage, after the rest of the work had been completed by Pettrucho. The verses were either unfinished or uncommissioned when the work was copied together by Pettrucho, so they were inserted on a blank page between Sylva's declaration to his readers and the first anonymous verse, 'Carmen incerti Auctoris Lectori benevolo' (A poem of an undetermined author to a friendly reader). Therefore the context in which Anne and Katherine had previously offered support to a member of the Italian Stranger Church seeking patronage was radically changed when Elizabeth and Mildred contributed their verses, alongside those of Dering, in an additional page in the volume.

The changed date highlights the significance of these additional poems. By May 1572 Dering had attempted to counteract the disfavour he had brought upon himself in 1570. He had written to Burghley on 24 March 1572, appealing to the latter to encourage Thomas Cartwright's return from Geneva. He had, however, used the letter to question Burghley's lack of true religion.[22] Burghley had responded on 3 April 1572 against these 'diverse ejaculations' with rage.[23]

Two days later, he was answered, somewhat apologetically, by Dering.[24] Only a month after this exchange, Mildred contributed her poem to the volume and by doing so she was signalling her support of Dering against the position of her husband and in favour of the earl of Leicester as an alternative patron for the preacher.[25]

Dering's two Greek verses set the agenda for the new page. His first poem is an extended play on the closeness between the Latin word *silva*, meaning 'wood' or 'forest', and Bartholo's surname, Sylva. Dering's second verse, however, declared itself an autobiographical piece, entitled τοῦ αὐτοῦ (On himself). The verse stated that ῞Ος ταύτην σκοτοδασυπυκνόκλαδον ἡμῖν ἅ νοιγεν᾽ λόχμην λοχμαῖου οὐκ ἀνέωξε χάριν᾽ (He who has opened for us the shaded, bushy, dense, leafy/ And wooded thicket has not opened up favouring grace).[26] Dering was thus presenting himself as the preacher who converted the 'wooded thicket', namely the new Protestant, Bartholo Sylva. Mildred then followed his lead on this inserted page, suggesting that 'νῦν κ᾽ ἐφύτευσε καλὸν σόφος ὡς ἐκ νηρίτου ὕλης᾽ (Now a wise man has made from a vast forest a lovely garden).[27] Elizabeth's verse also consciously focused on Dering's role in the conversion, asking the reader, 'Τίς πόθεν ἢ ἀνερῶν ὁ χαρακτηρίσας ὁ Σύλβας᾽ τοῦδε πέδον κήπου τοῦ σάφα οἶδε φίλε.᾽ (Who, from where among men, has designated for Sylva/ The place of this garden, which he clearly knows, O friend?)[28] These poems are differentiated from the Latin verses contributed at an earlier date by Anne and Katherine. Although Anne noted the 'artificem ... manum' (hand of the creator) which made a forest into a garden, it seems likely that this was a reference to Sylva's eternal creator. Like Katherine's piece, Anne's primarily focused on Sylva, describing only his personal conversion from sylvan wood to garden; Anne Locke's poem does not mention Sylva's conversion at all.[29] It thus appears that Mildred and Elizabeth were responding to the increased hostility towards Dering in May 1572, and the defence they provided was that he was too valuable a preacher to be silenced.

Dering was subject to a series of judicial processes over the next year, both in and out of the Star Chamber. Field and Wilcox had published their *An Admonition to the Parliament* in 1572 and Dering had subsequently visited them in Newgate. In April 1573 Burghley, probably acting on the Queen's encouragement, therefore asked Bishop Sandys about Dering's opinion of Cartwright's *Replie* to Whitgift's *Answere to the admonition*, which had been circulated a few days before; the bishop replied that Dering was in favour of the work, along with two of the Bacon chaplains, Percival Wyborn and Robert Johnson.[30] The three men were then brought before the Council of the Star Chamber on 29 May 1573.[31] A striking aspect of this process was the reluctance of Burghley personally to be seen as prosecuting Dering.[32] Collinson argues that it was Dering's emphasis on the primacy of temporal authority over church government that explained 'Burghley's reluctance to see him silenced', but I suggest that it is also possible to see the Sylva manuscript as evidence for how far Mildred was prepared to influence her husband to support Dering.[33] Yet whereas Burghley distanced himself from this process, Nicholas Bacon was the primary examiner of the preacher in Star Chamber; during the 1570s, Bacon placed the prosecution of governmental policy before his personal godly beliefs.[34] As the Sylva manuscript had latterly become a vehicle for support of Edward Dering, Anne was now placed in a difficult position, and hence her name was partially erased from the manuscript, with only her initials remaining and the spaces for the name which once would have read 'Anna Baconia'.[35] The sisters' support of Edward Dering caused familial conflict which was resolved in divergent ways; Mildred's support of Dering was reflected in her husband's disassociation from the preacher's prosecution, whereas Nicholas Bacon's commitment to Dering's silencing also led to the silencing of his wife's contribution to the Sylva manuscript.

Widowhood placed the sisters in a more independent position to challenge governmental policy with their support of godly figures. Edmund Rockray was one of Cartwright's supporters and was a signatory to two letters sent to Cecil on his behalf during 1570. Rockray expounded his godly opposition to the statutes of Cambridge University in a sermon in November 1570, which brought him into conflict with John Whitgift, the vice-chancellor.[36] Elizabeth wrote to her brother-in-law on Rockray's behalf on 31 January 1571, revealing her knowledge of the 'truble' in which Rockray was held, 'for certaine words spoken by him, for the defence of certain liberties, which arr construed, to farr other meaning, then he thought'. Elizabeth's defence of Rockray was again based around his ability as a preacher, for she assured Burghley 'that what fond words soever passed him, perhaps in some heate, they proceded not from a minde desirows of sedition'. Elizabeth argued that Rockray's abilities in providing spiritual guidance were too valuable to the Church of England for him to be silenced and she begged that Burghley would 'pardon this his first folly'.[37]

Anne's activities as an intermediary for the godly are also more apparent after the death of her husband in 1579 and particularly after the elevation of John Whitgift to the archbishopric of Canterbury. Whitgift set out to remove godly ministers through the imposition of the 'Three Articles', which required either full subscription or the forfeiting of the right to preach; the second article, declaring there was nothing in either the Book of Common Prayer or the episcopal church hierarchy contrary to the word of God, led to the suspension of many godly clergy. Nicholas Faunt celebrated Anne's response to the 'Three Articles' in March 1584, saying 'The Lord rayse upp many such holly Matrones for the Comfort of his poore afflicted Churche'. Faunt described Anne's activities at court on behalf of the suspended preachers, writing to her son Anthony 'that I have bene a wittenes of her earnest Care and travaile for the restoring of some of them to their places by resorting often unto this place to sollicite those causes'. He then added 'otherwise I have not often seene [Lady Bacon] in Cort and am throughly perswaded therein not to take any Comfort or delight except to see her Majestie and other her Ladyship's good frendes'.[38]

The godly used their connections with powerful patrons at court to secure a two-day conference on the articles at Lambeth in December 1584; Burghley and Leicester supported the proposed debate and Walter Travers was selected as one of the spokesmen. There is evidence of Anne's support of Travers at this time; however, the most powerful suggestion for Anne's involvement in the organisation of the Lambeth Conference is a letter she sent to her brother-in-law, Lord Burghley, on 25 February 1585, after the abortive conference had given way to a petition against the articles.[39] Anne was 'extraordinarly admitted' through Burghley's favour into the House of Commons when Whitgift gave his response to the petition.[40] This was a particularly heated session, for Whitgift dismissed every point of the petition. Anne feared to linger too long in such an inflammatory atmosphere and to discuss the matter fully with her brother-in-law; therefore she wrote to Burghley 'to enlarge the same more playnly & to what ende I did mean'.[41]

The letter reveals the disappointment felt by Anne and her 'learned' friends at their treatment at the Lambeth Conference: 'yf it may like your goode lord, the report of the late conference at lambath hath ben so handled to the discrediting of those learned that labour For right Reformation in the ministery of the gospell that it is no small greef of mynde to the Faythfull preachers, because the matter is thus by the othersyde caried away as thowgh their cawse cowlde not sufficiently be warranted by the worde of god.'[42] The Lambeth Conference had been hastily convened at the request of the earl of Leicester. Due to lack of time, discussion was kept to limited issues; their objections to the Prayer Book were not treated at all and Travers evaded an attempt by Whitgift to discuss their more radical objections to the government of the Church.[43] Anne instead suggested to Burghley an alternative to the conference of the previous year. She wrote that the godly clergy,

> humbly crave ... that they might obtein qwiett & convenient Audience ether before her Majestie her selff, whose hart is in god his hand to towch & to turne, or before your honours of the cownsell whose wysdome they greatly Reverence; & yf they can not strongly prove before yow owt of the worde of god that Reformation which they so long have called & cryed For to be according to christ his own ordinance, then to lett them be rejected with shame owt of the church for ever.[44]

Yet Anne also proffered some caveats to Burghley. The godly ministers sought other judges than the bishops 'who are parties partiall in their own defence because they seek more worldly Ambition then the glory of christ Jesus'.[45] They also needed time to 'assemble & to consult together purposely', which up to this point they had not done, for fear of being accused of holding conventicles. If Burghley would grant them an audience, they would cause no dissension, argued Anne, but would prove their case clearly from the Scripture, 'the infallible towchstone of the worde, the substantiall & Mayn grownde of their cause'.[46]

There is no evidence as to any positive outcome from her appeal to Burghley, but it did not serve to deter the widowed Anne and her sister, Elizabeth, from intervention on behalf of the godly. Thomas Cartwright was imprisoned in the Fleet in 1590 and he appealed to both Anne and Elizabeth as potential intermediaries. Anne and her son Anthony regularly visited him in the Fleet for counsel and the act of providing spritual advice was used by Cartwright as a means of prolonging his association with such well-connected figures.[47] In a letter written from the Fleet on 23 May 1591 he offered his counsel to Anthony with thanks 'for keeping open the Door of your acquaintance unto to me still, & to Mr Francis [Bacon] for so ready an opening of it unto his'.[48] The political importance of Anne's goodwill was also not forgotten, for although he chastised Anne to 'more sparingly use her Authority' over her son, he was also keen that Anthony would write to his mother and testify to the 'religious and wise Discourse' that had passed on his last visit to the imprisoned preacher.[49] Cartwright was also regularly writing to Elizabeth Russell during his imprisonment.[50] In a letter from 13 August 1591 he accepted Elizabeth's offer to help his plight: 'whom that it pleased to become (after a sort) a suter unto me that your Ladyship might doe me good'.[51] He was moved to accept her offer of assistance, due to his poor condition and his lack of access to other patrons; Elizabeth's connection to key councillors is noted by the preacher. 'Then I lay hold of the fruites of your favour,' he wrote, 'as far forth as the same may be convenient for your estate in your honorable mediation towards such as yow shall thinck good, especially toward my singuler good Lord, the Lord Treasurer'.[52] Cartwright explained that he was at a loss to know what suit he wished to put before Elizabeth's brother-in-law. He understood that Burghley knew their case and their innocence; although he was astonished that they were not given audience with the Queen, he suggested that he would like to know of the Lord Treasurer 'what they were likely to be granted'. In using Elizabeth as a suitor to Burghley, he accepted her personal judgement, writing 'I will make an end, leaving all to your honorable consideracion, what to keepe to your self and what to communicate to his Lordship, what to ask or what to leave unasked'. Elizabeth's response was to send the entire letter to her brother-in-law, with the endorsement 'Good my Lord, rede this thorow and do what good yow can to the poore man'.[53] The immediate effect of Elizabeth's letter alone is hard to determine, yet the prisoners continued to try to influence Burghley, sending him a petition for bail on 4 December of that year, before Cartwright was eventually released to house arrest in May 1592.[54]

According to Whitgift, his proceeding against Cartwright was the motivation for the actions of James Morrice, a godly relative who also called upon

Elizabeth Russell for assistance in 1593.[55] Morrice, an attorney of the Court of Wards, had instituted an attack in Parliament earlier that year against Whitgift's use of the *ex officio* oath in the High Commission when questioning clergy on his expanded twenty-four articles. Morrice had described the oath as 'an ungodly and intolerable inquisition'; the articles which Whitgift had imposed on the clergy were termed by Morrice as 'a lawless subscription'.[56] As an antidote to what he believed was an attempt 'to maintain a Romish hierachy', Morrice proposed two bills to the House of Commons.[57] As a result, he was summoned before the Privy Council for his outburst, confined for eight weeks and stripped of his lucrative position as attorney for the Court of Wards. Upon his release, Morrice visited Elizabeth and asked her to intercede on his behalf for a new position. She applied to her nephew Robert Cecil, suggesting that Morrice be made a councillor and master of the rolls, although she seemed aware of the unlikelihood of her request being granted. She acknowledged her fear that England would not be so happy as to enjoy Morrice as a councillor, since 'god in his providence' had 'diposed to plage us for our unthankfullnes and wickedness'.[58] The letter reveals the complex motivations for Elizabeth's act of intercession, beyond religious sympathy. Morrice had provided Elizabeth with legal advice on his visit, regarding her daughters' inheritance case, and so her actions were also the result of gratitude for Morrice's assistance in her 'uncomfortable cawse'.[59]

There is, however, the suggestion of a divergence over the figures on whose account Anne and Elizabeth were prepared to intervene. Unlike Anne, Elizabeth was also willing to act as an intermediary for episcopal figures. William Day, the dean of Windsor, had been offered the see of Durham in October 1594, but, after some clandestine manoeuvres by Robert Cecil and the earl of Essex, the position went to Tobie Matthew. Elizabeth wrote advising her nephew against supporting Matthew's suit, deeming that it would come to be seen as against 'her Majestie's good'.[60] Day, with reluctance, instead accepted the position of bishop of Worcester, but formally withdrew from the position on 5 January 1595. As he explained to Robert Cecil, he had investigated the potential income from Worcester and realised that 'If I should take yt, yt would utterly beggar me'.[61] Elizabeth Russell was moved to write to her nephew excusing Day's *volte face*. 'I trust your Divinytie stretcheth not so farr as to think eny man bownd in Conscience to empayr his owne estate to the good of others and to his owne disgrace by Commandment of her majesty,' she wrote to Robert Cecil on 24 February 1595, 'if he should remove to his owne detriment, for others' benefitts, I wold think it hard for the recompence of his so many yeres' service in being so godly and worthy a Laborer in god's vineyard: and I dare affirme him to have ben as learned and good a precher as eny hath ben of his tyme and more fitt for a Cownseller then eather Burne, Boxall or Whytegift.'[62] Elizabeth's use of the term 'godly' to petition for an elevation to the episcopacy highlights her particular brand of moderate Puritanism. Moreover, in her letter Elizabeth commended Day's anti-papist stance, arguing that had Day been appointed to the see of Durham, rather than Matthew, he would have been more 'for the good of the Queene's Service in the Skottish Bankes', against the threat of Jesuit infiltration. Yet, at that time, Elizabeth was also prepared to act as a broker for Catholic figures, as Mildred is shown to have done in the last chapter.[63] Elizabeth intervened in 1606 to secure the release of Thomas Frears, a well-known physician arrested for his Catholic beliefs, although two years earlier she had criticised Lady Stourton, accused of recusancy, for her 'bad religion'.[64] These mixed reactions to Catholicism contrast with the stark horror with which Anne viewed the papists whom she perceived surrounding her sons, such as Anthony Standen, Antonio Pérez and Lord Henry Howard, believing that they should be cast off for 'such have seducing spirits to snare the godly'.[65]

The evidence highlights the breadth of the sisters' religious networks and the diversity of their actions as intermediaries. Admittedly, on many occasions the practical import of their actions is hard to determine, as is common with many cases of early modern patronage. It is here important to recognise that the sisters continued to be sought by contemporaries as intermediaries, in recognition of their potential influence, despite the difficulty on many occasions of ascertaining the outcome of their brokership. As widows, however, Anne and Elizabeth held real power as lay ecclesiastical patrons.

FEMALE PATRONS AT HOME AND IN THE PARISH

The household was one space in which Anne and Elizabeth could exercise religious patronage as widows. It is not to argue that the chaplains and tutors serving their households during the lives of their husbands were appointed without their consent, nor that Mildred and Katherine had no control over clerical appointments within the household. There is evidence of continuity of service between marriage and widowhood for Anne, as Percival Wyborn was appointed as chaplain to the Bacons in June 1560, returning again to the role when Anne was a widow.[66] Yet it is in their widowhoods that the responsibility for household appointments can be confirmed as lying solely with Anne and Elizabeth. The latter welcomed Edmund Rockray into her house as a chaplain and schoolmaster after her first husband's death, when she had 'no small tryall of him, both for religion, good nature, and disposition to learning'.[67] Geoffrey Fenton wrote in 1571 of Elizabeth's patronage within her Blackfriars household, writing 'your borde ... was seldome without the fellowship of deep Divines and Preachers, to the ende that as your example drew others to seeke God in Sermons abroade, so also your selfe by private conference might be thoroughly resolved in every doubte touching your Christian opinion.'[68]

Anne made reference to the 'comfortable company' at Gorhambury in 1592 of Percival Wyborn and Humphrey Wilblood, both of whom had been deprived of their benefices for their godly views. Although Anne recognised the spiritual benefit she received from the preachers, she lamented that they were prevented from continuing their work to the greater good of their local communities: 'Thei may greatly be Afraide of God his displeasure who worke the woefull disapointing of God his worke in his vineyard by putting such to silence in these bowlde sinning dayes. Haud impune ferent (They will not go forth without punishment) come when it shall.'[69] Wyborn stayed at Gorhambury at various points throughout the early 1590s, assisting the household in its spiritual edification.[70] 'I have been more comfortable this Christtyd by the special favour of God to me and my household,' wrote Anne in 1597 'by Mister Wyborn's fatherly wholesome heavenly instruction beside the public.'[71] Wyborn's presence allowed the increasingly ailing Anne access to spiritual counsel when getting to church was difficult. 'I thank god for Mister Wyborn', Anne wrote in December 1596, when her foot was injured; both riding or 'hobleing on Foote' to church through the ice was near impossible and Anne resolved that she would have to 'crawle to the church'.[72]

In patronising godly clergy within her household, Anne believed they would spread religious edification both within and without the walls of Gorhambury. She organised Bible readings for her household servants, followed by prayers and the Psalms both morning and evening.[73] She ensured that they were 'caterchised' by arranging afternoon sessions in which her 'Folk [were] examined by Mister Wyblud'.[74] She also turned to Humphrey Wilblood to provide edification for her local community. In 1594, Anne visited a sick local man who had previously served in her household. For Anne, the illness was evidence of the correcting hand of God and she went to the man to provide 'godly exhortation', accompanied by Wilblood; Anne was certain that the preacher's counsel, comfort and prayers would revive the man's soul.[75] Likewise, she feared that Anthony was without a godly minister in Chelsea, so she repeatedly tried to send Percival Wyborn to visit her son's household to provide 'private & holsom conference to styrr yow upp to remember the lorde & serve him cheffely with yours'.[76]

For Anne, support of godly clergy within the household was mirrored in her wider ecclesiastical patronage within the parish. She believed that 'true proffiting in matters of faith' could only be 'atteyned unto in a settled vocation and place of a resident Ministery and Congregation'.[77] During her widowhood she held the rights of presentation to two benefices, as Nicholas Bacon bequeathed his wife the rights of two livings in Hertfordshire: St Michael's in St Albans and Redbourn parish.[78] Thomas Wetherhead was already incumbent as vicar when Anne gained the rights of presentation to St Michael's church upon her husband's death in 1579.[79] Although not a graduate, he was able to give an account of his faith in Latin.[80] Wetherhead, however, was not a preacher and his parishioners later lamented that during this time 'we knew not as we ought what did belong to god, what to our prince, to our Rulers, to our neighbours, neyther to our famylies to bringe them up in that obedience and subjection as is mett. Neyther did not know how to kepe them from suche abuses as are common in the world, so as ignoraunce and disorder was uppon us and uppon ours for want of teachinge.'[81] Even Lord Burghley later described Wetherhead as a 'very insufficient, aged, doting man', and he was judged as one of the 'unlearnedler sorte' of clergy in the archdeaconry.[82] By 1585 the situation at St Michael's had changed, with the arrival of William Dike as an assistant curate.[83] The new preacher was outspoken in his condemnation of Wetherhead.[84] According to a later local enemy, Dike subjected the 'readinge' minister to 'plaine Raylinges'.[85] Dike himself protested such a course, instead arguing that when he preached upon Luke i.15, decrying drunkeness, dicing and carding, Wetherhead's own conscience led him to believe he was the subject of attack: 'And this his offensyve life was such above in the eye of the worlde that they could not but saye that he justly fell within the compasse of the censure of god's worde.'[86]

According to the parishioners of St Michael's, it was 'through the godlie endevours of our very good Patronesse the Lady Bacon, at her speciall and almost onlie chardge, we enjoyed one Mr Dyke, a preacher aucthorised'.[87] It was Dike who preached every Sunday at St Michael's church, rather than Wetherhead, who by 1586 was described as ailing.[88] Dike had strong views on the importance of a preaching ministry, which mirrored those of Anne. Through his sermons, Dike endeavoured to show the parishioners 'the necessitie of a learned Ministery, and laboured by doctrine and exertation to stirre them up to that dewtie'.[89] He argued that the preaching of the Gospel rather than reading was appointed by God as a means of converting the people; he added, however, that reading of the holy Scriptures still had efficacy for congregations, 'servinge thoughe not to converte ordynarely yett to confirm faith in the godlye, and to increaseth theire knowledge and comforte'.[90]

Dike's impact upon Hertfordshire spread beyond the parish of St Michael's. He also preached at other churches nearby, including another parish under Anne's patronage, Redbourn, as well as at Shenley, Harpenden and at the town church in St Albans.[91] According to Innocent Read, who accused Dike of causing dissension locally, many people both at St Michael's and from around St Albans had heard and spoken with Dike: 'Many absent them selves from theire owne parishe churches on the sabath daie, yea refuse to heare theire owne ministers beinge preachers, & repaire to dike to heare hym, and many of this gaddinge people came from farre and went home late, both yonge men and yonge women together.'[92] Dike's own response to this charge was that he had exhorted those who had a preaching minister to remain in their own parish and hear the minster speak. However, he argued that those parishioners in Hertfordshire without a preaching ministry should come to hear him, heeding Proverbs xxiv.18, 'where there is no preaching the people perishe'.[93]

Dike was zealous in his attempts to enforce godly standards of behaviour on the people of St Michael's parish and beyond. After a group of men had played football throughout the time of the service and near to the churchyard one sabbath, Dike made them the subject of his evening sermon. Drawing on Psalm cxix.119 and 1 Corinthians iv.13, the preacher labelled such men 'the scume of the earth, the donge of the earthe'.[94] Dike also preached against the Whitsun Ales in Redbourn, which parishioners of St Michael's had also attended, arguing

> theire Whyttson Ales in theire originall beinge badd, and by the marvelous and shamefull abuses in them made farre worse, drawinge the people of other parishes unto them from the exercises of god's words which they might have had at home, and havinge in them pypinge, dauncinge, and Maid Marion comyinge into the Churche in the time of prayer and preachinge to move laughter with kissinge in the churche besides sondrie other abuses, they justly deserve to be called prophane, riotous and dissorderly meetings.[95]

Dike was suspended by Aylmer, the bishop of London, in 1589 after a series of accusations were compiled against him by Innocent Read. The parishioners of St Michael's then petitioned Anne's brother-in-law, Lord Burghley, for Dike's restitution, most probably following Anne's advice. The parishioners argued that under the influence of Dike, provided for the people solely by Lady Bacon, they had been 'broughte from their ignoraunce and evyll wayes to a better lyfe, to be diligent herers of God's worde, willinge to everye servyce of the prynce, readye to distrybute to the poore, havinge our servantes in better order and government then in tymes past'.[96] They were now 'as shepe with[out] a shepherde, exposed and leyde open to manyfolde dangers, even to retorn to our former ignoraunce and cursed vanities'.[97] Burghley wrote to the bishop of London on the parishioners' behalf, yet Aylmer was adamant that he would not reinstate Dike. An inquiry was begun at the next session of the Archdeaconry Court, in which a witness brought against the preacher openly admitted perjury and begged for forgiveness. Dike was duly acquitted.[98] Burghley again wrote to Aylmer, calling for Dike's reinstatement at St Michael's, quoting the Gospel, 'magna est messis, et operaii pauci' (The harvest is great and the labourers are few).[99]

Despite Dike's reinstatement as assistant curate, Wetherhead was still the vicar at St Michael's. In April 1590 Anne made an attempt to replace him. Her candidate, Richard Smith, craved presentation in Lady Bacon's name, but he was unable to produce letters of orders, either testimonial or dismissory, and so his application was denied.[100] Upon Wetherhead's death, Anne presented the vicarage to Erasmus Cooke in June 1591.[101] He was a graduate of

Trinity College, Cambridge, ordained two years previously.[102] Cooke, however, swiftly came under the same ecclesiastical scrutiny as Dike. In December 1593 Anthony was moved by his mother to write to Edward Stanhope regarding Cooke's position at St Michael's.[103] He wrote a certificate, signed by Cooke, together with the churchwardens and sidesmen of St Michael's, which stated that in October 1593 the vicar 'read the Booke of prayer appointed by authority to be [used] with pub[lic] fastinge. And at the same tyme did preache a Sermon in which he exhor[ted] those that werre present unto moderation of dyet for that daye, and charitable Almes for the poore'.[104] Cooke was again accused of holding private fasts in 1596, and then of disobeying the canon in 1604.[105] He was finally declared 'contumacious' in 1607 for not attending the Archdeacon's Court and was replaced by Zephaniah Besouth, although by this time the rights of presentation had passed from Anne to her son Francis.[106]

Anne also held the presentation rights to Redbourn vicarage in Hertfordshire, and her first candidate there was Edward Spendlove, a graduate of Magdalen College, Oxford.[107] Spendlove resigned in 1588 and for a short while the parish was without a vicar; Anne, however, appointed George Phillips in November 1589 as a curate.[108] Little is known about Phillips, although he was a graduate. Shortly after Phillips's appointment, Humphrey Wilblood was instituted as vicar of Redbourn. Wilblood had previously been a preacher in Rutland; however, he had been suspended for nonconformity and his living had been sequestered, sometime before 1586. Wilblood's patron in Rutland was Sir Thomas Cecil, Anne's nephew, who pressured the archbishop to restore Wilblood.[109] Perhaps through the influence of her nephew, Anne presented the vicarage of Redbourn to Wilblood and he was instituted on 25 November 1589.[110] Wilblood was the subject of multiple accusations of nonconformity during his three years as vicar of Redbourn parish. He was accused of refusing to use the sign of the cross in baptism and of refusing to wear the surplice; he also came under pressure for omitting parts of the prayer book and for substituting his own devotions.[111] He was deprived of his benefice in 1592, but remained in Hertfordshire under the household patronage of Anne Bacon. Wilblood was living with Anne and Percival Wyborn at Gorhambury in May of that year, when Anne thanked God for the preachers' 'comfortable company'.[112] At some point during this period, Wilblood was arrested under Aylmer's orders, 'that godles Bishop', as Anne described him to her son Anthony: 'I am at this time greatly greved because Mister Wyblud is committed by that godles Bishop to the gatehowse For refusing to pay unlawfull charge to A wycked Fellow of Redborn that hath had Mister Wylblud's lyving by seqwistration this yere ... Boner I think did not so Far cruelly in such case.'[113] Anne's suggestion that the Catholic bishop Bonner was more lenient than Aylmer reveals her anger at the deprivation of her clerical choice. She was, however, determined to intercede on Wilblood's behalf, with divine help in the 'good cause &

injust ponishing of his most Faythfull servants'.[114] Wilblood was licensed again in 1594 to officiate and teach in the archdeaconry, but was forbidden from preaching or acting as a schoolmaster.[115] Through Anne's intercession, he was eventually instituted to the living of Pinner vicarage in 1601.[116]

Anne replaced Wilblood at Redbourn church with Rudolph Bradley. Although again her choice was not a graduate, Anne had a high estimation of Bradley's influence as a preacher over the people of Redbourn.[117] She described him as 'an honest man & careful by his godlie paines to make the gainsaying & waiward people to become the people of god'.[118] Throughout Bradley's time at Redbourn Anne continued to observe his care of the parishioners. In a letter written to her son Anthony she told him that she had 'hard avowched that Mister Bradley did not preach this day'. She concluded that Bradley must have been deprived of his place once again, for else he was 'two careless of his charge specially Among such A people who lyke eny save A Faythfull & paynfull preacher'. Anne here reveals her belief that if the parishioners are not guided by a preacher, they will fall away from godly living, writing to Anthony that she feared that in the absence of Bradley's scriptural instruction from the pulpit, 'now belyke Robin Hoode & Mayd Marian are to supply with their prophan partes'.[119]

Like Anne's other clerical appointments, Bradley was unpopular with the ecclesiastical authorities and was asked on several occasions to produce letters of orders, which he failed to do.[120] In February 1597 he was required to send a certificate of orders to Edward Stanhope, chancellor to the London diocese, and on the latter's failure to receive them, Bradley was declared excommunicate.[121] A kinsman of Anne, Stanhope had been an ecclesiastical judge and a member of the High Commission since 1584; his opposition to the godly cause had led to his being labelled 'Tarquinius Superbus, Doctor Stanhope', Tarquin the Proud, in the Marprelate Tracts.[122] Anne heard of the excommunication of Bradley when she was in London and her response was to send a vehement letter of reproach to Stanhope. 'Sir I cannot but marvell what ails yow Mister Doctor,' she wrote to Stanhope, 'still to vex the godlie Ministers of Christ, & by your undeserved excommunication to hinder the glorie of god so pittifully'. In her letter Anne reveals that she considered it her duty to defend her candidate. 'I take my selfe bound', she wrote, 'since he was there lawfully placed by me to assist him & to further him in his minstrie to the advauncing therby of god's honor.'[123]

Anne argued to Stanhope that Bradley's case 'being god's cause ought nerelie to touch everie christian hart'. She refuted any suggestion that Bradley might have caused dissension in the parish, although she admitted he was 'not to gentle among such alenolling & bad people'. Instead, Anne wrote, depriving the people of Redbourn of their 'godlie minister' would cause a 'grevous disturbance' in the parish and a 'pernitious disquieting of the hartes of her

[Majesty's] good subjectes, who by the Gospell preached sincere amongst them love, dread and redelie obey her with willing hartes'. Her advice to Stanhope was that he should instead 'incouradge the faithfull & painfull preachers of Jesu Christ that they maie labour comfortablie', for his present actions would serve only to bring God's wrath upon the chancellor:

> by report the enemies of God, of her Majestie & of our Cuntrie are mighty & with cruell & fiery hartes preparing the readie to the pray & spoile of us all, we had need with most humble submission intreat the lord of hostes to be with us & on our side by publick fasting & unfained humilation & that troughout the land, and not presumptuouslie to beat back his faithfull & appointed servants ... and as to torne away his wrath, so greatlie provoked daily by the fearfull contempt of his holie gospell, so hevelie & lamentablie is manifested everie where by our professed wickednes and most carnall securitie.[124]

Anne's advice to Stanhope is a striking example of how conviction in one's godly duty could overcome the expectations of hierarchy and female defer-ence. Anthony Bacon himself later wrote to Stanhope, yet, in spite of reading his mother's letter, he chose a very different register for his own letter.[125] He told Stanhope that he 'thought meete' to represent to him the unfortunate series of events which had caused this situation: 'To wit that Mr Bradelie havinge bene injoyned to sende certeficate unto yow by a certaine daie by yow appointed, thoroughe the negligence of the messenger by whom Mr Bradley sent it, yt was not delivered till the next daie after whereupon he was excom-municated.'[126] He appealed to Stanhope for leniency 'at my mother's request and mine', adding that they 'shall thinke our selves bothe behouldinge unto yow in regarde of the interest we have in the place whereof mr Bradelie hathe the chardge'. Bradley was reinstated and continued at Redbourn until 1602, although Anne refused to see herself as beholden to Stanhope. Anne later told Anthony that, notwithstanding their kinship, she would 'never more write Again' to Stanhope 'but upon great occasion by god's sending'. The unmarried Stanhope was, according to Anne, 'A love man ... A Fylshy Adulterer yf not Fornicatour too according to his profession. Blackwell's wyffe is noted in strete as she goeth & pointed at as his harlot.' Anne's sense of personal godliness meant that she perceived herself as being of a higher rank than Stanhope, despite her lower position in the patronage network. Revealing her concep-tion of the boundaries of godly community, Anne told Anthony that Stanhope could only be a contagion: 'good sonne, write not to him at all in this, nor be beholding to him For eny sute'.[127]

Bradley resigned his orders in 1602 and Anne presented the living of Redbourn to Richard Gawton.[128] He had previously been a minister of Hemel Hempstead parish, which he resigned in 1594.[129] Gawton gave up the living in favour of William Dike, who had previously been installed by Anne as assistant curate of St Michael's. Dike had been living in Hemel Hempstead since 1591, apparently at Gawton's own invitation, as well as at the request of the parishioners.[130] He had been preaching throughout the three years in the town and, from such experience, Gawton suggested that Dike's 'sufficiency and fitness' to be the parish priest in 'every way is thoroughly known'.[131] Dike was appointed to the living of Hemel Hempstead and remained at the parish until 1604. Anne stayed in contact with Dike throughout this period, even lending him her late husband's coach on occasion.[132]

Little is known of Gawton's activities as vicar of Redbourn, although he remained a close acquaintance of Anne's during her final years.[133] Whilst at Redbourn he 'preached here everie Saboth day twice' and celebrated Holy Communion monthly.[134] His view of the role of the ministry is set out in the godly apologia *A Parte of Register*. It describes the 'troubles' Gawton encountered whilst a preacher in Norwich in 1576. He argued to the bishop of Norwich that he did not think himself 'by lawe bound precisely' to every part of the servicebook; he said that he did follow the service appointed and read the chapters set, 'except by reason of preaching I omitted them, or either of them as by law I might, I observed the rest, except in baptism the crosse and vowes, which things I tooke not my selfe precisely bounde to observe'.[135] Despite his nonconformist views, Gawton remained in the living of Redbourn until his death on 7 March 1616.[136]

Anne's support of godly ministers went beyond her gift of benefices. She even supported them with her own ever-decreasing funds, as is shown by the petition from the parishioners of St Michael's in support of William Dike.[137] Her pecuniary support of godly preachers was also testified to by Anthony's servant Edward Spencer, who stayed periodically with Anne at Gorhambury and sent frequent letters to his master in London.[138] On 16 August 1594 Spencer wrote to Anthony regarding conditions at Gorhambury, telling him that his mother does 'falle out withe all and is not in Charitey one Daye in awecke: but withe prests whiche will undoe hur'. Spencer then wrote of the nature of Anne's support of the godly priests: 'Mr Willcockes had a paper withe agrete Delle of gould in it, Willblod had 2 quartares of whete, Dicke had somthinge the other Day, what I know not.'[139] Spencer's testimony again reveals Anne's expansive conception of the boundaries of her religious community. Wilblood remained in St Albans, at Gorhambury, during this period, but Wilcox and Dike were not under Anne's direct patronage, residing to the west of the county, in Bovingdon and Hemel Hempstead respectively. These advowsons were under the patronage of the dean and chapter of St Paul's, yet Anne used her connections to the earl of Essex to gain the livings for the clergymen.[140] Despite this, Anne still perceived the preachers as being under her care and sought to maintain financially their efforts to edify the godly community.

Anne's patronage of the godly in Hertfordshire was supported by members of her wider friendship network. Her sister Mildred provided funds for sermons to be preached quarterly in her Theobalds parish of Cheshunt in Hertfordshire by a fellow of St John's College, Cambridge.[141] Anne praised the countess of Warwick, Anne Dudley, and her sister Margaret Clifford, the countess of Cumberland, as 'both ladies that fear god & love his word in dede. Zealously, specially the yowger syster'.[142] Like Anne, as a widow, the countess of Warwick controlled a benefice in Hertfordshire, appointing to the parish of Northaw after the death of the earl in 1590.[143] Bridget Russell, the widowed countess of Bedford, was another lay female ecclesiastical patron in Hertford-shire and a member of Anne's wider circle. The countess appointed Anthony Watson to the living of Watford parish in 1587. A graduate of Christ's College, Cambridge, Watson was a resident preacher, 'most painfully preching every Sabbothe, ordinarylie forenoone & after', even lecturing in Watford market every Tuesday.[144] His godly views were testified to by his several suspensions for various offences, in both his own parish and beyond in Hertfordshire, including not wearing the surplice, administering to communicants standing and for not using the sign of the cross.[145]

John Clark, the mayor of St Albans, was another member of Anne's circle who supported her godly patronage. 'Mister κλαρκ (klark)', she wrote to Anthony in 1596, 'is An honest man & so hath ben cownted even in your Father's tyme For an oppidanus (townsman)'.[146] Clark supported Anne's choice of clergy for her benefices. When later arraigned before the court of the High Commission he was accused that he 'often times lefte your owne parish church and gone out of your parish to heare one William Dyke ... preach'. Clark prevailed upon the minister of St Albans, Roger Williams, to permit Dike to preach at the church. He repeated this request as mayor, 'notwithstandinge the commandement of the bishop of the Dioces and the order of the officiall aforesaide to the contrarie, in Manifest contempt of the Authorities of the saide Bishoppe & officiall'. Clark was also accused of having 'permitted divers and sundry other ministers not licenced' to preach in the town, including the separatist John Penry.[147]

The case of Thomas Newton again reveals Clark's place within Anne Bacon's godly circle of patrons. Newton was a preacher who was imprisoned numerous times for 'divers contemptes of Ecclesticuall Authoritie'.[148] Anne revealed her knowledge of his case in a letter to Anthony from the mid-1590s:

> my man sayd as he came away Forenone he mett mister kempe coming to yow with one cheined ... had I thowght he had come to yow I wolde have desyred some motion to him For poore Newton prisoned by such as he & others now in place. The lorde pull them owt of ther dwelling in his goode tyme. & their Backyon Bishop.[149]

The extent of Anne's efforts to liberate Newton is unknown, but other members of her circle were working to free the preacher. John Clark negotiated with Newton's keeper for his liberty and employed the preacher as a private employee in the mowing of his grounds. The mayor then gave his consent for the chancellor of the archdeacon and his official to be charged for the false imprisonment of Newton. When Newton was later called to swear an oath of obedience, he called on Clark for assistance. Instead of swearing that he would be 'obedient to her Majestie's Ecclesiasticall Lawes and in particular such her Majestie's Ecclesiaticall Lawes as are exercised by the Archdeacon of St Albans or his officiall', Clark suggested that the words 'such lawes of her Majestie's as are agreable with the worde of god' should be added so that Newton could take the oath.[50]

Compared with this detailed picture of Anne's local religious networks, little is known about the patronage of her sister Elizabeth. After the death of Thomas Hoby she presented the living of her parish church at Bisham in Berkshire to John Bowen in 1571, to George Asburn in 1580, to William Hudson in 1594 and finally to Richard Chamberlain in 1607.[51] Elizabeth's choice of clergy seems to have occasioned little official notice, which may reflect the tenor of their godly zeal, yet it is clear that Elizabeth was highly concerned with their quality. In 1603 she discussed the appointments to her clerical livings to be made after her death with her daughter-in-law Margaret Hoby.[52] Elizabeth's will also provides evidence of her ecclesiastical patronage within her London parish of Blackfriars, as she chose to remember the godly preacher Stephen Egerton. Elizabeth bequeathed him ten pounds a year for the remainder of his life, payable from the tithes of Hampton.[53] Her patronage was based on personal experience of Egerton's preaching, for she regularly attended his sermons at St Anne's, Blackfriars, both with her sister Anne and with her daughter-in-law Lady Margaret Hoby.[54] Elizabeth's patronage in her will also reflected her support of Egerton during her lifetime, demonstrated in a petition to the Privy Council in 1596. James Burbage had bought an old roofed playing-house in St Anne's parish and was intent on transforming it into a new theatre. Elizabeth led a group of parish residents, including Egerton, in petitioning the Council not to permit the conversion to the new playing-house. The reasons not only included the general bad living which the play-goers would encourage in the parish and the threat of sickness, but also the effect it would have on the piety of the people. The playhouse was so near the church of St Anne's that 'the noyse of the Drummes and Trumpetts will greatly disturb and hinder both the Ministers and Parishioners in tyme of Divine service and Sermons'.[55]

The capital is also a location which reveals Anne's patronage of the European Protestant community. Anne repeatedly wrote of the quality of preaching at the French Stranger Church and advised her son Anthony to attend their services whilst in London 'to heare the publick preching of the word of god as it is his ordinance & Armed so with prayer'.[56] Her younger sister Katherine was a more direct supporter of the Church. Together with her husband, she attended communion with the congregation on 2 December 1565 and the couple donated funds to support the Church.[57] The epitaph on Katherine's death by Robert Masson, a minister of the French Church, may have been written in recognition of her support.[58]

Both Anne and Katherine's religious networks stretched beyond the capital. Katherine was in contact with the Scots Presbyterian Andrew Melville, as demonstrated by his epitaph on her death, and Anne's networks stretched into Europe, as shown by her correspondence with Theodore de Bèze in 1581.[59] In the 1580s the Genevan community was undergoing severe hardship and appealed to English sympathisers for assistance. On 5 August 1583 Anne was recorded by the Genevan agent as contributing £20 to the cause.[60] In 1590 Anne was again prevailed upon to donate money to the church. Jean Castol, minister of the French Church in London, wrote to Theodore de Bèze informing him that Anne had given the generous sum of 100 marks to him and Monsieur Lect.[61] Anne had specified that sixty-six ecus and two tiers were to go to needy ministers, whilst the rest was a gift to Bèze himself.[62]

In 1593 Anne was once again prevailed upon to contribute to the Genevan church. According to Percival Wyborn, Bèze often sent his correspondence to England via the French Church and so, in June of that year, Anthony Bacon received a visit from Jean Castol and Jean le Preux, the Genevan printer.[63] They came bearing a recent edition of Theodore de Bèze's meditations on the Penitential Psalms, printed that year in Geneva by le Preux.[64] Bèze had dedicated the French edition of his meditations to Anne in 1581 and the 1593 edition of the work was sent to Anne as a 'remembrance and token from good Mister Bezea'.[65] Castol and le Preux told Anthony to tell his mother that 'yf it please your Ladyship to wright anie thinge [to Bèze] they have promised me to attend heare upon friday next for the same'.[66] Castol and le Preux returned to see Anthony Bacon on 8 June and were surprised to find no response from Anne to Bèze's gift. Once again, they asked Anthony if his mother would 'wright or commande any thinge to Mr Bezea', before underlining their purpose more clearly to Anthony: 'to be plaine with your Ladyship they gave me at their first cominge and now likewise to understande that Mr Bezea expected more then a letter from your Ladyship'.[67] To that end and 'to revive my ancient acquaintance with the good ould father', Anthony himself sent a gift to Bèze. The draft of his letter to his mother, explaining the gift he sent, is revealing through its multiple corrections and editions: 'I was bould to sende him ^in your Ladyship's name^ and myne owne a~~ girdle of gould~~ a present ^not of bare monie^ ~~to the valewe of xx marke~~ but otherwise imploied to the valewe of xx marke accompanied with a letter of myne owne to him self and two more to two other of my espetiall frends at Geneve.'[68] Anthony corrected his original letter to emphasise that he had not only sent a gift to Bèze in his own name, but also that it came in the name of his mother; he was obviously aware that no further donations would be forthcoming from her. It would appear that, by 1593, Anne was less predisposed to donate to the European cause. This could very well have been the result of her strained financial situation. She wrote of her impoverished state to Anthony in April of the same year: 'goodes shall I leave none as mony or plate ... I have ben too ready for yow both till nothing is left'.[169] Anthony, although himself in debt, showed no such caution, sending Bèze 'a present', and although he stated that it was not simply a monetary gift, he did reveal it was a gold girdle worth 20 marks. The comparison between the responses of Anne and her son to Bèze's request reveals the limits to the widow's religious networks. Edward Spencer testified to Anthony only a year later that his mother was 'not in Charitey one Daye in awecke: but withe prests whiche will undoe hur', giving gifts of money and goods to local preachers.[170] In Anne's more strained financial circumstances during the 1590s, it would appear that she needed to prioritise her godly patronage, and her telling decision was to advance edification at home, beyond reformation abroad.

SCHOLARLY NETWORKS AND *THE PARTE OF A REGISTER*

This chapter has shown that the sisters' educated status informed their religious activities in diverse ways, for example in the contribution of verses to the Sylva manuscript alongside those of Edward Dering, or in Anne's composition of the strongly worded letter of reproach to Edward Stanhope. For Anne, it sometimes served to lessen her disdain for episcopal figures. Her evaluation of Aylmer's successor as the bishop of London, Richard Fletcher, was that although he was to be condemned as 'επισκοπαλλ (episcopal)', he was at least 'learned', meaning 'he usd me cautiously & Mister [Erasmus] Cooke & Mister [Humphrey] Wyblud comfortably'.[171] The widowed Anne and Elizabeth both patronised religious education, as Mildred did secretly during her lifetime, though this was revealed to her husband only after her death. Mildred and Elizabeth had a special interest in Westminster School, most probably stemming from their long-term acquaintance with Gabriel Goodman, who became dean of Westminster from 1561. Goodman had been employed by William and Mildred Cecil as a household schoolmaster in late 1554 and had remained with the family for four years.[172] Elizabeth lived with her sister during her father's exile and so would have been well acquainted with Goodman during this period. The sisters' association with Goodman is intriguing. He has been memorably described as being 'as far to the religious right as a conforming Elizabethan churchman could get', and Julia Merritt has highlighted the conservative aspects of Goodman's churchmanship, together with his disapproval of lay godly activism; services at Westminster Abbey under Goodman as dean emphasised ceremonalism and the use of clerical vestments and church music.[73] Despite the difference between the sisters' godly religious outlook and Goodman's more conservative credentials, both Mildred and Elizabeth were supportive of Goodman's educational schemes; long acquiantance must have overcome religious zeal. As dean of Westminster, Goodman became closely involved with the overseeing of the boys' school and he devoted much energy to ensuring the school's future. When Mildred chose to endow anonymously two scholarships from Westminster School to St John's College, Cambridge, the lands to fund the places were purchased secretly, under Goodman's name.[74] The dean also pointed out bright Westminster pupils to Lady Burghley, such as Richard Neile, later archbishop of York. The schoolmaster at Westminster suggested that Neile should be apprenticed to a bookseller in Paul's churchyard, yet Goodman recommended him to Lady Burghley, who educated him at St John's at her own expense. The patronage had a cumulative effect, for when Neile became dean of Westminster he regularly funded places for two scholars who had missed election.[75]

Mildred's choice of supporting Westminster boys in their further education at St John's College, Cambridge, stemmed from her personal knowledge of the institution. It was the alma mater of her husband and son and she herself visited the College with her husband.[76] Mildred Cecil donated her own books both to Westminster School and to St John's College, Cambridge, in order to bolster their religious literature. Mildred's most valuable gift, as we have seen, was Christopher Platin's eight-volume polyglot Bible, which she presented to St John's College in 1580.[77] Her other donations included works on what Burghley described as 'physick, and of other science', but there was a strong emphasis in her donations on 'divinite'.[78]

Elizabeth supported a scheme of Gabriel Goodman's to send boys from Westminster School to Christ Church, Oxford, with a bequest in her will. Thomas Wilson, a former student of Westminster School, had matriculated at Christ Church on 10 June 1608.[79] Writing her will nearly a year later, Elizabeth bequeathed Wilson ten pounds per annum for the space of ten years 'for his better mayntenance in the Universitie of Oxenford'. After the first ten years Wilson's legacy would cease, unless he became a Professor of Divinity, in which case, and if he proved to be 'a good Labourer in God's Vineyeard', he would be granted the annual sum for the rest of his life.[180]

Anne too supported religious education, although not through her own patronage. Nicholas Bacon had overseen the new orders for the refounding of a grammar school in St Albans.[181] He had appointed a Dutch Calvinist, John Thomas, as master of the grammar school. Thomas was a godly man, with a keen interest in his local community; he died on 13 January 1597 and the appointment of his successor was a matter of great local concern.[182] John Clark, the mayor, recommended Thomas Streatley to Anthony Bacon. However, Anne in this instance had very different ideas to those of her godly friend. She wrote to her son on 25 January that there was a 'Report ... that streatly by your means shulde [replace] Mister Thomas. surely sonne, yf it shulde be so, yow wyll sustein much discredit by him'.[183] For Anne, godliness was the foremost quality in a schoolmaster, and it was esteemed above all by her late husband, for she wrote to Anthony 'your Father Rejoysed that God sent him such A man as the late [John Thomas] was & did much encourag him commending him in my hearing & to me persaepe (very often)'. Her advice to Anthony was clear: 'Regard more the great Necessitie & duty of A Religious sufficient Scoolemaster, Furnished with Godliness with his teaching & wyse discretion, then carnall Frendshipp to seek to place one that wanteth all these. [Streatley] hath not been but ill spoken of & reconed inpudicus (unchaste) & effrenis (unruly).'[184] In this case, Clark triumphed and Anne's advice was ignored, for Streatley was admitted as schoolmaster.[185] However, Anne's advice to her son reveals her disdain of the role of 'carnall Frendshipp' in what she deemed to be another opportunity for godly patronage. Anne also supported Walter Travers in his role as provost of the newly founded Trinity College, Dublin. She wrote to Burghley on 22 May 1595, requesting him to grant an audience to Matthias Holmes, a Fellow, who came to plead for greater financial support for 'her Majestie's yowng colleg'.[186]

Anne's past role as a religious translator informed her choice of patronage. She has long been associated with the Puritan apologia *A Parte of a Register*, published in 1593. John Field was responsible for collecting a mass of documents recording the struggle of the godly between 1565 and 1589; some of these documents were printed to form *A Parte of a Register* and the remainder were preserved in manuscript. The aim was to form a Puritan register which would imitate Foxe's *Acts and Monuments*.[187] William Urwick, the Victorian historian of nonconformity, suggested that *A Parte of a Register* was 'probably issued with the sanction and at the expense of Lady Bacon' and this suggestion has been echoed by later scholars.[188] Urwick cited as evidence the inclusion in *A Parte of a Register* of a 'Copie of a Letter with a Confession of Faith, written by two faithful servants of God unto an Honourable, and vertuous Ladie'. The letter was written by Thomas Wilcox (T.W.) and John Field (J.F.) and, although it is undated, it must have been written before 1584, nine years before the volume's eventual publication; Field's relationship with Wilcox broke down at this point and Field died in 1589.[189] In the letter, the authors 'acknowledge our selves very much bounde' to the 'vertuous Ladie' in question.[190] This agrees with Wilcox's later acknowledgement in 1589 of the 'cristian kindness' and 'sundrie favours' he had received from Anne over the years; in dedicating his commentary on the proverbs of Solomon to her, as discussed at the beginning of the chapter, Wilcox wrote of her support of 'many worthie ministers', adding 'for kindness towards whom, and particularlie towards my selfe, I doo humblie here in all our names thanke GOD, and you as his gracious instrument'.[191]

189

In their letter to the 'vertuous Ladie', Wilcox and Field then go on to offer their work in exchange for the patronage they have received at the lady's expense. From Urwick onwards, scholars have read this to mean that they are offering Anne the entirety of *A Parte of Register* as the result of her financial support. Yet the title of their letter would question this assumption, stating as it does that what follows is 'The copie of a Letter, *with a confession of Faith*, written by two faithfull servants of God, unto an Honourable, and vertuous Ladie'.[192] I would suggest that it is the 'confession of faith', which follows immediately after the letter in the *Register*, that the men offered to Anne in exchange for her support.

The letter is, moreover, clear about the purposes of the confession: it is not to offer Anne further instruction, as they are certain that she is already fully instructed in the principles of religion, nor is it a personal defence by the two men. Rather, it is so that 'your honor migh[t] have at all times in a readinesse by you, some short writing of ours, by which you might stoppe the mouths of suche persons, as, without any knowledge of us or our judgements, spare not uppon light credite to lewde reports many times to condemne as wicked men and heretikes'.[193] In the face of such accusations, Wilcox and Field offer the following rebuff:

> we are not (as they say) Puritanes, Anabaptists, Donatists, Libertines, of the Family of love, or anue such like, for wee confesse our selves before God to bee greevous sinners, wee daily pray for, and duetifully reverence Magistrates, as God's word appointeth: we make no separation from the Church of England, acknowledging it, notwithstanding the manifold deformities wherewith it is spotted (all which we earnestly wish, desire, and pray, might be removed) to be the church of God. We like of other men, use their companie, and account them as our brethren, though they agree not with us in the points of sinceritie and reformation.[194]

In this, Wilcox and Field are rejecting accusations against the godly of heresy in terms remarkably similar to those used by John Jewel in his 1562 *Apologia Ecclesiae Anglicanae*, defending members of the Church of England. As we have seen, Jewel's work, translated by Anne in 1564, is concerned with establishing the unity of the nascent Church of England and with rebutting the notion that 'we are all heretiques, and have forsaken the fayth, and have with newe perswasions and wicked learninge utterly dyssolved the concorde of the Churche ... that we sow abroade newe sects, and suche broyles as never yearst weare hearde of'.[195] Like Wilcox and Field's rejection of Elizabethan separatists, Anne's translation of Jewel states that the Church of England had no association with such 'Monstres' as 'the Anabaptistes, Libertines, Menenians, & Zvenkfeldians', asking 'What hath there ever ben written by any of our company, which might plainely beare with the madnes of any of those heretiques?'[196] The 1564 translation underlines that the Church of England taught men 'to obey their Princes and Magistrates', seeking only to leave a

Church 'wherein we could neither have the word of God sincerely taught, nor the sacraments rightly administered' for a church wherein 'all thinges be governed purely and reverently, and, asmuch as we possibly could, very neere to the order used in the olde time'.[197]

This is not the only similarity between the texts. As argued previously, the most important section of Anne's translation of the *Apologia* was the creed for the Church of England, which she begins with the line 'This therefore is oure Belieffe./ We beleeve that there is one certaine nature and divine Power, whiche wee call God.'[198] It seems that Wilcox and Field used the credal section of the *Apologie* as a template for their 'confession'; while it is possible that they may have had a more general credal model in mind, it is significant that the order of the points in the confession they presented to Anne so closely mirrors that in the *Apologia*.[199] They thus begin by following the credal section of the *Apologia*, discussing the nature of the Holy Trinity. The only substantive divergence between the early sections is that the Confession discusses Calvinist election.[200] Both works then discuss Scripture; the difference of doctrine between the two works is that while the *Apologia* states 'that in them be habundantly and fullye comprehended all thinges what soever be nedefull for our salvation', the Confession insists that, concerning Scripture, 'it is not lawfull, for anie creature whatsoever to diminish, neither to adde therto'.[201] Other godly beliefs are then discussed in credal terms in the Confession, including the importance of public prayer without the minister's being constrained to certain forms, fasting and sabbatarianism.

These issues herald the credal treatment of church government in the Confession, which starkly contrasts with the *Apologia*'s defence of episcopacy in its insistence on a Presbyterian organisation of the church. Yet, even at this juncture, the Confession continues to mirror the structure of the *Apologia*. The latter follows its discussion of episcopacy with the assertion that 'yet not withstanding we say that there neither is nor can be any one man, which may have the whole superioritie in this universall state', an attack directed at the pope.[202] The Confession then mirrors and ultimately goes beyond the *Apologia*, stating 'Wee beleeve that all true Pastors in whatsoever place of the world they be, have one and the selfe same authoritie, and bee of equall power under that chiefe and universall Bishop Jesus Christ'.[203] The two texts then both discuss the two sacraments of baptism and the eucharist in credal terms, although the Confession makes explicit that the Eucharist provides only 'a spirituall nourishment'.[204] Both works share too a rejection of papal indulgences, and ultimately both stress their membership of the one Catholic church.

I suggest that the Confession was dedicated to Anne because of her well-known association with the *Apologia*, which provided a model for Wilcox and Field's Confession. The elements of unity between the two works stress the legitimacy of the godly's credal beliefs: they are presented as refinements upon the creed of the Church of England as set forth in Jewel's *Apologia*, rather than as seditious novelties. It is impossible to prove that Anne acted as a patron for the entire *Parte of a Register*, yet the lessons Anne learnt when translating Jewel's *Apologia*, so apparent in the Confession, suggest that she was more likely the patron of this new godly creed for the Church of England. Anne's involvement with the Confession moreover highlights the developments within her own spiritual beliefs, in contrast to past accounts which stress the static nature of her godliness: the translator of the Church of England's *Apologia* later became the patron of the Presbyterian Confession.

CONCLUSION

This chapter reveals the breadth of the sisters' activities as both religious brokers and patrons. As intermediaries for religious patronage, they did not simply follow the lead of their husbands. There is evidence of familial conflict over the sisters' patronage; Mildred's support of Edward Dering reveals that she was capable of working against her husband, whilst the erasure of Anne Bacon's name in the Sylva manuscript reveals an alternative resolution to marital disagreement over godly clients. It was widowhood that allowed Anne and, to a lesser extent, Elizabeth to act as independent ecclesiastical patrons in their own right. Both in their households and in their local communities, widowhood allowed them to wield often uncontested power over religious patronage. The breadth of the sisters' agency must therefore also be understood in spatial terms. Their religious networks extended from the local community to the court and Parliament, even encompassing an awareness of the European Protestant community, contributing to a more diverse picture of the religious activities of early modern women.

Ultimately, this chapter highlights the complexity of the sisters' support for religious reform in later sixteenth-century England and allows a more detailed picture to be drawn of their religious views. Collinson and Lake have shown that Puritanism encompassed a wide spectrum of opinion.[205] It is apparent that the sisters shared the beliefs that unified this diverse and 'hotter' type of Protestantism. The importance of the preaching of the word of God above all other concerns was at the heart of their actions; all four sisters thus worked together to advance the preacher Edward Dering. Yet there are still divergences within their beliefs, which become clear through this detailed and comparative exploration of the sisters' religiosity. It is apparent that Anne held more radical godly views than her sisters, shown, for example, in their differing opinions over the issue of episcopacy. Anne was explicit in her condemnation of episcopal figures, and her involvement with Wilcox and Field at the very least appears to testify to a sympathy for Presbyterian beliefs; Elizabeth, in contrast, supported William Day's advancement to the episcopacy and was friendly with John Thornborough, the bishop of Limerick and dean of York.[206] Both Mildred and Elizabeth were also close to the conservative Gabriel Goodman, the dean of Westminster. All these relationships raise the issue of the role of friendship within the sisters' religious networks and its complex relationship with their religious zeal. Placed alongside the different arenas in which the sisters worked for spiritual reform, the varying ways in which their godly beliefs impacted upon their religious networks emphasise in a different way the breadth of their religious agency.

NOTES

1 T.W. [Thomas Wilcox], *A short, yet sound Commentarie; written on that woorthie worke called; the Proverbes of Salomon* (1589), sigs A3r, 4r–v.

2 For a list of Wilcox's female correspondents, see P. Collinson, 'The role of women in the English Reformation', in P. Collinson (ed.), *Godly People* (1983), p. 275. Bar the published dedicatory letters discussed in this chapter, no more of the correspondence between Wilcox and Anne survives.

3 For recent work highlighting the sisters' godly beliefs, see, for example, P. Croft, 'Mildred, Lady Burghley: the matriarch', in P. Croft (ed.), *Patronage, Culture and Power: The Early Cecils* (2002), pp. 283, 285; J. Stevenson, 'Mildred Cecil, Lady Burleigh: poetry, politics and protestantism', in V. Burke and J. Gibson (eds), *Early Modern Manuscript Writing: Selected Papers from the Trinity/Trent Colloquium* (Aldershot, 2004), p. 53.

4 P. Collinson, *The Elizabethan Puritan Movement* (1967); P. Collinson, *Godly People* (1983); P. Lake, *Moderate Puritanism and the Elizabethan Church* (Cambridge, 1982).

5 For Fowle and Johnson, see R. Tittler, *Nicholas Bacon: The Making of a Tudor Statesman* (1976), p. 61.

6 For another recent exploration of lay female religious patronage in the sixteenth-century parish, see M. Franklin Harkrider, *Women, Reform and Community in Early Modern England: Katherine Willoughby, Duchess of Suffolk and Lincolnshire's Godly Aristocracy, 1519–1580* (Woodbridge, 2008).

7 See chapter 2.

8 R. O'Day, 'The ecclesiastical patronage of the Lord Keeper, 1558–1642', *TRHS*, 5th series, 23 (1973), 95–103.

9 *Ibid.*, 102.

10 Bacon insisted that Smyth must continue as he was bound to pay £5 per annum to his sister's son at Cambridge. J. Bruce and T.T. Perowne (eds), *The Correspondence of Matthew Parker* (Parker Society, Cambridge, 1853), pp. 312–13.

11 *Ibid.*, p. 310.

12 J. Craig, 'John Walker', *ODNB*.

13 CP 26, fo. 65r: 09/05/1594. The *Liber Cleri* of 1594 notes that a Richard Webster held the living of Markbie (Markby) in the deanery of Calcewaith, which may suggest a specific Lincolnshire connection to Mildred. See C.W. Foster (ed.), *The State of the Church in the Reigns of Elizabeth and James I* (Lincoln Record Society, 23; Lincoln, 1926), p. 388.

14   NA, SP 12/195, fo. 21r: 16/11/1586.

15   P. Collinson, 'Godly Master Dering', in Collinson, *Godly People*, pp. 303–5.

16   CUL Ii.v.37.

17   *Ibid.*, fos 2r–4v.

18   L. Schleiner, *Tudor and Stuart Women Writers* (Bloomington, 1994), p. 40; Stevenson, 'Mildred Cecil', p. 65.

19   Schleiner, *Women Writers*, p. 39; CUL Ii.v.37, fo. 5r.

20   CUL Ii.v.37, fo. 105v.

21   The final numeral 'i' in the date has been changed into a '2' in arabic numbers. This is Old Style dating, therefore with my convention of starting the year on 1 January, not 25 March, the first date was February 1572. All other dates continue to be given according to Old Style dating, except with the year beginning on 1 January. The same hand which altered the date corrected Anne Locke Dering's name on fo. 5v from 'Anna Derin' to 'Anna Dering'.

22   NA, SP 12/85, fo. 173r.

23   J. Strype, *Annals of the Reformation and Establishment of Religion* (4 vols in 7, Oxford, 1824), II, ii, p. 484.

24   *Ibid.*, II, ii, pp. 487–91.

25   By December 1573, Leicester was acting as Dering's patron. See *A parte of a register, contayninge sundrie memorable matters, written by divers godly and learned in our time* (Middleberg, 1593), p. 85 and Collinson, 'Dering', p. 310. For Leicester's support of the godly, see S.L. Adams, 'A godly peer? Leicester and the Puritans', in S.L. Adams (ed.), *Leicester and the Court* (Manchester, 2002), pp. 225–34.

26   CUL Ii.v.37, fo. 5r. Translations of the Greek poems are by L. Roller, cited in Schleiner, *Women Writers*, pp. 255–7.

27   *Ibid.*

28   CUL Ii.v.37, fo. 5r. The translation of Elizabeth's poem by L. Roller is again from Schleiner, *Women Writers*, p. 41.

29   CUL Ii.v.37, fos 5v, 8r.

30   BL, Lansdowne MS 17, fo. 100v: 28/08/1573.

31   Collinson, 'Dering', p. 309.

32   *Ibid.*, pp. 309–11.

33   *Ibid.*, p. 314.

34   *Ibid.*, pp. 309–10; Tittler, *Nicholas Bacon*, pp. 168–86.

35   CUL Ii.v.37, fo. 8r.

36   Strype, *Annals*, II, ii, pp. 58–9; C.H. Cooper, *Athenae Cantabrigienses* (3 vols, Cambridge, 1858–1913), II, p. 242.

37   NA, SP 12/77, fo. 20r.

38   LPL 647, fo. 145r: 12/04/1584.

39   Nicholas Faunt wrote to Anthony Bacon on 20 November 1583, describing meeting Anne at one of Travers's lectures at the Temple Church. See LPL 647, fo. 162r. For

Anne's connections with Travers in the 1590s, see also BL, Lansdowne MS 79, fo. 79r: 22/05/1595.

40 The longer history of women listening to parliamentary debates is discussed in E. Chalus, *Elite Women in English Political Life, c. 1754–1790* (Oxford, 2005), pp. 47–52. For an alternative view, see L. Magnusson, 'Imagining a national church: election and education in the works of Anne Cooke Bacon', in J. Harris and E. Scott-Baumann (eds), *The Intellectual Culture of Puritan Women, 1558–1680* (Basingstoke, 2010), pp. 42–56.

41 BL, Lansdowne MS 43, fo. 119r: 26/02/1585.

42 *Ibid.*

43 Collinson, *Elizabethan Puritan Movement*, p. 269.

44 BL, Lansdowne MS 43, fo. 119r.

45 *Ibid.* Anne echoes this line in a later letter to Anthony describing Archbishop Whitgift. See chapter 3 and LPL 653, fo. 343r: 03/02/1592.

46 BL, Lansdowne MS 43, fo. 120r.

47 A. Pearson, *Thomas Cartwright and Elizabethan Puritanism 1535–1603* (Cambridge, 1925), pp. 464–5.

48 *Ibid.*, p. 465.

49 *Ibid.*, p. 464.

50 Thomas Cartwright had visited Elizabeth Russell in 1586, when he met her two daughters, Anne and Elizabeth. According to his letter of 23 May 1591, their mother recommended Cartwright to them as 'a man whom for good respects [she] favoured'; Cartwright also referred to Elizabeth's pleasure in his previous 'mention of your worthie father in my letters I wrote unto you'. See BL Lansdowne MS 68, fo. 131r: 13/08/1591.

51 *Ibid.*

52 *Ibid.*

53 *Ibid.*, fo. 132v.

54 BL, Lansdowne MS 68, fo. 135r: 04/12/1591.

55 BL, Additional MS 28571, fo. 172r.

56 Morrice cited in J.E. Neale, *Elizabeth I and her Parliaments, 1584–1601* (1957), p. 268.

57 T.E. Hartley (ed.), *Proceedings in the Parliaments of Elizabeth I* (3 vols, Leicester, 1981–85) III, pp. 30–44.

58 CP 170, fo. 53r: 05/1593.

59 *Ibid.*

60 CP 25, fo. 51r: 24/02/1595.

61 CP 24, fo. 97r: 14/01/1595.

62 CP 25, fo. 51r.

63 See chapter 4.

64 CP 118, fo. 159r: 1606; CP 109, fo. 27r: 1604.

65 LPL 649, fo. 153r: 26/06/1593.

66 C.S. Knighton, 'P. Wiburn', *ODNB*.

67 NA, SP 12/77, fo. 20r: 31/01/1571.

68 G. Fenton, *Actes of conference in religion holden at Paris betweene two papist doctours of Sorbone, and two godlie ministers of the Church* (1571), sig. A2v.

69 LPL 648, fo. 167r: 17/05/1592. Wilblood is also known as Wildblood.

70 See LPL 648, fo. 167r: 17/05/1592; LPL 649, fo. 121r: 25/05/1593; LPL 653, fo. 246r: n.d.; fo. 303r: 14/08/n.y.; fo. 316r: 13/12/1596; fo. 323r: 08/1595; LPL 654, fo. 297r: 12/01/1596/7; LPL 660, fo. 124r: 13/12/1596.

71 LPL 654, fo. 297r: 12/01/1597.

72 LPL 653, fo. 316r: 13/12/1596.

73 LPL 649, fo. 37r: 22/02/1593.

74 Such efforts did not always immediately yield a deeper spiritual understanding. Anne admitted to Anthony in June 1592 that one kitchen servant was 'A shrewd witted boy & pretely caterchised: but yet An untowarde crafty boy'. However, she believed 'he wyll mende I warrantt yow throwghly'. See LPL 648, fo. 177r. and LPL 649, fo. 39r.

75 LPL 650, fo. 117r: 03/1594.

76 LPL 653, fo. 323r: 02/08/1595. See also LPL 653, fos 303r, 333r.

77 LPL 647, fo. 145r: 12/04/1584.

78 NA, PROB 11/61.

79 Hertfordshire Archives and Local Studies, Hertford (HALS) ASA 5/2, p. 300 [ASA 5/1–4 numbered on consecutive pages, rather than by leaf].

80 HALS ASA 5/1, p. 227.

81 BL, Lansdowne MS 61, fo. 71r. For Wetherhead's inability to preach, see also HALS ASA 5/2, p. 454.

82 J. Strype, *Historical Collections of the Life and Acts of ... John Aylmer, Lord Bp. of London in the Reign of Queen Elizabeth* (Oxford, 1821), p. 204; HALS ASA 5/2, p. 351.

83 Dike had previously been a minister at Cogshill, Essex. See A. Peel (ed.), *A Second Parte of a Register* (2 vols, Cambridge, 1915), I, pp. 225–6 and II, p. 163.

84 BL, Lansdowne MS 61, fo. 74r.

85 *Ibid.*, fos 72r–v.

86 *Ibid.*, fo. 74r.

87 *Ibid.*, fo. 71r.

88 W. Urwick, *Nonconformity in Herts. Being Lectures upon the Non-Conforming Worthies of St Albans and Memorials of Puritanism and Nonconformity in all the Parishes of the County of Hertford* (1884) (Urwick), p.106. Dike was also described as being the long-term 'preacher' at St Michael's by Innocent Read on 22 September 1589: BL, Lansdowne MS 61, fo. 73r.

89 BL, Lansdowne MS 61, fo. 74r.

90 *Ibid.*

91 *Ibid.*, fos 72v, 73r. For Dike's preaching at St Albans' Church, see LPL 650, fo. 347v.

92 BL, Lansdowne MS 61, fo. 73r.

93 *Ibid.*, fo. 75r.

94 *Ibid.*, fos 72r, 73v.

95 *Ibid.*, fo. 74r.

96 *Ibid.*, fo. 71r.

97 *Ibid.*

98 Urwick, p. 113.

99 Strype, *Alymer*, p. 204.

100 London Metropolitan Archives, London (LMA), DL/C/335, fo. 29r.

101 HALS ASA 5/3, p. 557. It is unclear whether or not Cooke was a distant relation of Anne's.

102 J. Venn, *Alumni Cantabrigienses* (4 vols, Cambridge, 1922–26), I, i, p. 143; HALS ASA 5/3, p. 557.

103 LPL 649, fo. 414r: 06/12/1593.

104 *Ibid.* The edges of the letter are damaged, but the missing parts of words are supplied in square brackets.

105 HALS ASA 5/5, part 2, no. 291: 21/06/1596; HALS ASA 7/20, fo. 5v.

106 Guildhall MS 9531/13, fo. 237v.

107 J. Foster, *Alumni Oxoniensis ... 1500–1714* (4 vols, Oxford, 1891–92), IV, p. 1399.

108 LMA, DL/C/334, fo. 312v; HALS ASA 5/2, pp. 411, 417, 455.

109 Peel (ed.), *Second Parte of a Register*, II, p. 92.

110 Guildhall MS 9531/ 13, fo. 246v. Unlike the previous candidates, Wilblood was not a graduate. HALS ASA 7/13, fo. 8v.

111 *Ibid.*, fo. 34r.

112 LPL 648, fo. 167r: 17/05/1592.

113 LPL 653, fo. 335r: n.d.; R. Newcourt, *Repertorium Ecclesiasticum Parochiale Londinense* (2 vols, 1708–10), I, p. 638.

114 LPL 653, fo. 335r.

115 HALS ASA 7/17, fo. 2v; HALS ASA 7/16, fo. 5r.

116 Urwick, p. 294.

117 HALS ASA 7/15, fo. 8v.

118 LPL 655, fo. 95r: 14/02/1598.

119 LPL 653, fo. 366r: 25/12/n.y.

120 HALS ASA 5/3, pp. 551, 560.

121 LPL 655, fo. 1r: 16/02/1597.

122 W. Pierce (ed.), *The Marprelate Tracts, 1588–1589* (1911), p. 32.

123 LPL 655, fo. 95r: 14/02/1597.

124 *Ibid.*

125 Anne's letter now exists only as a copy made by Anthony's secretary, suggesting that he saw his mother's letter to Stanhope. Bradley had already written to Anthony Bacon about the matter. See LPL 655, fo. 33r: 10/02/97. Bradley had long called upon him

to act as his patron, both in curbing the wrath of Stanhope and in obtaining him a prebendaryship. For Bradley's appeals to Anthony Bacon over Stanhope, see LPL 648, fo. 159r: 20/03/1594; LPL 649, fo. 35r: 06/02/1593. For Bradley's appeals for a prebendaryship, see LPL 651, fo. 139r: 07/05/1595; LPL 654, fo. 32r: 10/01/1597; LPL 655, fo. 25r: 23/02/1597; LPL 660, fo. 25r: 18/11/1596; LPL 661, fo. 162r: 02/04/1597.

126 LPL 655, fo. 1r: 16/02/1597.

127 LPL 653, fo. 248r: n.d.

128 Guildhall MS 9531/14, fo. 27r.

129 Gawton had counted himself as one of Thomas Cartwright's 'brethren' since at least 1577. The 'brethren' also included other members of Anne's circle, such as John Field and Thomas Wilcox. See Peel (ed.), *Second Parte of a Register*, I, pp. 136–8.

130 Urwick, p. 115.

131 *Ibid.*

132 LPL 658, fo. 27r: 15/07/1596.

133 Gawton's close relationship with Anne is demonstrated by a letter written to him in March 1605, whilst he was rector of Redbourne. He has copied out on the back the Latin verse that Katherine Cooke Killigrew wrote to Mildred Cooke Cecil. See NA, SP 46/23, fo. 225d: 03/04/1605 and chapter 4, above, for the verse.

134 HALS ASA 5/3, p. 727.

135 R. Gawton, 'The troubles of M. Richard Gawton of late preacher at Norwich', in *A parte of a register*, sig. Ddd3r.

136 HALS ASA 7/26, fo. 3v.

137 BL, Lansdowne MS 61, fo. 71r.

138 Spencer's letters are discussed more fully in chapter 6.

139 LPL 650, fo. 253r: 16/08/1594.

140 Collinson, *Elizabethan Puritan Movement*, p. 446.

141 BL, Lansdowne MS 103, fo. 118v.

142 LPL 651, fo. 328r.

143 R. Peters, *Oculus Episcopi: Administration in the Archdeaconry of St Albans 1580–1625* (Manchester, 1963), p. 95.

144 Venn, *Alumni Cantabrigienses*, I, iv, p. 347; HALS ASA 5/3, p. 725.

145 HALS ASA 7/13, fos 36v, 39r; HALS ASA 7/17, fos 29v, 49r, 50v, 51v, 53v, 54v, 56v, 58v.

146 LPL 654, fo. 47r: 25/01/1597.

147 LPL 650, fo. 347v.

148 *Ibid.*

149 LPL 653, fo. 362r: n.d.

150 LPL 650, fos 347v–348r.

151 E. Powell (ed.), *The Register of Bisham: Baptisms 1560–1812, Burials 1560–1812, Marriages 1560–1812* (Parish Register Society, 15; London, 1898), p. 8; Wiltshire and Swindon Record Office, D1/2/16; D1/2/19.

152 M. Hoby, *The Diary of Lady Margaret Hoby, 1599–1605*, ed. J. Moody (Stroud, 1998), p. 189.

153 NA, PROB 11/113: 23/04/1609.

154 *Diary of Lady Margaret Hoby*, ed. Moody, pp. 119, 120, 124, 134, 136. She also attended communion at St Anne's on 5 March 1600, as she received a letter from Robert Cecil whilst at the church. See CP 178, fo. 132r.

155 NA, SP 12/260, fo. 176r: c. 11/1596. The following year, Elizabeth wrote to her nephew Robert Cecil, acting as an intermediary to apply for a steward to be appointed in the Blackfriars, who would likewise bring order to the parish. See CP 53, fo. 88r: 07/1597.

156 LPL 651, fo. 310r: 03/08/1595. For Anne's support of the French Stranger Church, see also LPL 651, fo. 326r; LPL 653, fo. 343r.

157 *Actes du consistoire de l'Église française ... vol. I*, ed. E. Johnson (Huguenot Society of London, 38, 1937), pp. 22, 124.

158 Ballard, p. 207. Robert Masson's presentation of his 1583 edition of *Loci Communes* to Mildred Cecil may also have been a means of seeking support for the French Church. See chapter 1.

159 Ballard, p. 207. *Correspondance de Théodore de Bèze*, ed. H. Aubert *et al.* (38 vols, Geneva, 1970), XXII, pp. 108–10, 128–30. See also *ibid.*, pp. 185–7.

160 J. Malliet, 'Memoires et procedures de ma negociation en Angleterre', in I. Archer *et al.* (eds), *Religion, Politics, and Society in Sixteenth-Century England* (CS, 5th series, 22, 2003), p. 194. For contributions by Anne's clergy at Redbourn and St Michael's in 1583 see HALS ASA 5/1, pp. 153, 161.

161 F. de Schickler, *Les Eglises du Refuge en Angleterre* (3 vols, Paris, 1892), III, p. 144.

162 S. Citron and M.C. Junod (eds), *Registres de la Compagnie des Pasteurs, VI (1589–1594)* (Geneva, 1980), p. 63.

163 H. Robinson (ed.), *The Zurich Letters* (2 vols, Parker Society, Cambridge, 1842), I, p. 190: 25/02/1568.

164 T. de Bèze and G. Buchanan, *Sacratiss. psalmi Davidis* (Geneva, 1593). The volume also contained George Buchanan's psalm paraphrases.

165 T. de Bèze, *Chrestienes meditations sur huict pseaumes du prophete David composees et nouvellement mises en lumiere par Theodore de Besze* (Geneva, 1581); LPL 649, fo. 190r: 02/06/1593.

166 LPL 649, fo. 190r.

167 LPL 649, fo. 187r: 08/06/1593.

168 *Ibid.*

169 LPL 653, fo. 318r: 17/04/1593. Also see LPL 651, fos 310r, 328r; LPL 653, fos 203r, 337r.

170 LPL 650, fo. 253r: 16/08/1594.

171 LPL MS 652, fo. 20r. Fletcher's brother was the Latin poet Giles Fletcher, who sought Mildred Cecil as a patron for his eclogues in 1571. See chapter 1.

172 R.C. Barnett, *Place, Profit and Power: A Study of the Servants of William Cecil, Elizabethan Statesman* (Chapel Hill, 1969), p. 68.

173 P. Collinson, J. Craig and B. Usher (eds), *Conferences and Combination Lectures in the*

Elizabethan Church: Dedham and Bury St Edmunds, 1582–90 (Church of England Record Society, 10, Woodbridge, 2003), p. xlvii; J. Merritt, 'The cradle of Laudianism? Westminster Abbey, 1558–1630', *JEH*, 52 (2001), 627–9; J. Merritt, 'The Cecils and Westminster 1558–1612: the development of an urban power base', in Croft (ed.), *Patronage, Culture and Power*, pp. 235–6.

174 Strype, *Annals*, III, ii, p. 126.

175 L. Tanner, *Westminster School* (1951), p. 26.

176 Mildred also gave money to the College for the bodily comfort of its scholars; she paid for fires to be lit in hall on Sundays and holy days from All Saints' Day to Candlemas, when no other provision was made by the College, as well as secretly giving money to build a new pathway from the College to lectures. See BL, Lansdowne MS 103, fo. 118v.

177 See chapter 1.

178 BL, Lansdowne MS 103, fo. 118v.

179 Venn, *Alumni Cantabrigiensis*, IV, p. 1657.

180 NA, PROB 11/113.

181 Tittler, *Nicholas Bacon*, p. 61.

182 Urwick, p. 82.

183 LPL 654, fo. 47r: 25/01/1597.

184 *Ibid.*

185 Urwick, p. 83, n. 1.

186 BL, Lansdowne MS 79, fo. 79r: 22/05/1595.

187 P. Collinson, 'John Field and Elizabethan Puritanism', in P. Collinson (ed.), *Godly People* (1983), p. 354.

188 Urwick, p. 86; Collinson, *Elizabethan Puritan Movement*, p. 440.

189 Collinson, *Elizabethan Puritan Movement*, p. 238.

190 T. Wilcox and J. Field [T.W. and J.F.], 'The copie of a Letter, with a confession of Faith, written by two faithfull servants of God, unto an Honourable, and vertuous Ladie', in *A parte of a register*, p. 528.

191 Wilcox, *A short, yet sound commentarie*, sigs A3r, A4r–v.

192 My italics.

193 'The copie of a Letter', p. 528.

194 *Ibid.*, p. 529.

195 *Apologie*, sig. A4v. See chapter 2.

196 *Ibid.*, sig. E2v.

197 *Ibid.*, sig. M2r.

198 *Ibid.*, sig. B7v. See chapter 2 for discussion of the credal emphasis in Anne's translation.

199 For previous Christian creeds, see H. Bullinger, *The Decades of Henry Bullinger*, trans. H.I., ed. T. Harding (5 vols in 4, Parker Society, Cambridge, 1849–52), I, pp. 12–35.

200 'The copie of a Letter', pp. 533–4.

201 *Apologie*, sig. C7r; 'The copie of a Letter', p. 535

202 *Apologie*, sig. C1v.

203 'The copie of a Letter', p. 540.

204 *Apologie*, sig. C8v; 'The copie of a Letter', p. 542.

205 Collinson, *Elizabethan Puritan Movement*; Collinson, *Godly People*; Lake, *Moderate Puritanism*.

206 *Diary of Lady Margaret Hoby*, ed. Moody, p. 137.

Chapter 6

'Of more learning than is necessary for that sex': responses to learned women

Two of the Cooke sisters, Anne and Elizabeth, are held by legend still to haunt the world as ghosts. Anne Bacon's ghost is reported to haunt Gray's Inn, where her two sons studied, protesting loudly against the revelry that occurs on Call Night, an annual festivity.[1] The story of her sister's ghost is more elaborate. According to local legend, the ghost of 'wicked Lady Hoby' still haunts her former home at Bisham. Elizabeth is said to be condemned to this state through causing the death of one of her sons, William, who apparently was intellectually backward, having a tendency to smudge and drop ink on his copybooks. The legend is confused as to how Elizabeth actually killed the boy. In one version, after William failed to learn his lessons, she administered a fatal blow to her son with a ruler.[2] Another account of the tale suggests that a schoolroom for the children was built near the river at Bisham Abbey, in which Elizabeth was seen from the towpath opposite, ill-treating her son: 'one gossip related in a nearby inn ... that he had seen "my lady's boy" being beaten about the head till he collapsed with blood streaming from his eyes, nose and mouth, and saturating the grass'.[3] In the final version, William so angered his mother during his lessons that she tied him to his chair until he improved his work. She then supposedly went riding to assuage her anger, where she was met by the Queen, who persuaded Elizabeth to accompany her to Windsor. Unbeknownst to the servants at Bisham, William was left tied to his chair in the schoolroom; by the time his mother returned, the child had apparently starved to death.[4] The various versions of the Bisham ghost story are, without doubt, fiction; the earliest references to the tales are Victorian.[5] Yet these ghost stories shed light on the representations of the Cooke sisters and, more generally, on the representations of learned women. Anne is characterised by legend as the outspoken mother, whilst Elizabeth's ghost highlights negative stereotypes which have long been associated with learned women: high levels of education drive women to unnatural acts and madness.

Such prejudices were articulated by the male contemporaries of early modern learned women; education was thought to bring women into the risk of sin. Vives discussed these negative connotations surrounding women's eloquence in his *De institutione foeminae christianae* (1523), suggesting that educated women demonstrating their rhetorical abilities ran the risk of being labelled proud, shrewish, dissembling, foolish and, worse, over common and potentially unchaste.[6] In his preface to Margaret Roper's translation of Erasmus's *Precatio Dominica* (1524), Richard Hyrde discussed at length contemporary suspicions of women's classical learning:

I have heard men put great doubt whether it should be expedient and requisite or not, a women to have learning in books of Latin and Greek. And some utterly affirm that it is not only nother necessary nor profitable, but also very noisome and jeopardous. Alleging for their opinion that the frail kind of women, being inclined of their own courage unto vice, and mutable at every newelty, if they should have skill in many things that be written in Latin and Greek tongue ... it would of likelihood both inflame their stomachs a great the more unto that vice, that men say they be too much given unto of their own nature already and instruct them also with more subtilty and conveyance, to set forward and accomplish their froward intent and purpose.[7]

The connection between learning and sexual promiscuity could be levelled at female scholars, including Mary Sidney Herbert, the countess of Pembroke.[8] By the beginning of the seventeenth century, a high level of reading by women was even associated with madness.[9] These negative representations have largely informed the scholarly stereotype of the early modern learned woman as an 'oddity' or a 'threat'.[10]

There were, however, more positive contemporary representations of the learned woman. For Vives, learned women should follow the model of the Virgin Mary. Both Vives and Richard Hyrde argued that the female scholar should thus aspire to the greatest virtue; through learning she could overcome her sinful nature rather than become more vulnerable to vice, as argued by their opponents.[11] Renaissance Italian female humanists have received the most detailed scholarly analysis of the overtly positive representations accorded them by their male contemporaries. Margaret King has argued that Italian female scholars were celebrated as creatures beyond the sex of womankind, praised as members of a third sex, in terms that destroyed their gendered identity; they were lauded as female warriors of myth, such as Athena or the Amazons.[12] Moreover, King suggested that learned Italian women were celebrated for withdrawal from the world, from any public profession of their learning, into 'studious solitude'.[13] Lisa Jardine has detailed how fifteenth-century scholarly women were mythologised by their male contemporaries, in terms either of an abstract intellectual ideal, such as the warrior virgin, or of a social ideal, in terms of chastity, modesty or beauty.[14] Jardine's argument is that this process of representation was a coping mechanism for male humanists, faced with women desiring to join their ranks. Unlike their male contemporaries, Renaissance Italian female humanists were excluded from the active, civic profession which was the usual outcome of the acquisition of humanist skills; Jardine has argued that therefore their male contemporaries had recourse to mythologising women, so that they could be celebrated without calling into question the ultimate aim of their education.

In this chapter, I argue that a very different explanation lies behind the contemporary representations of the Cooke sisters. Like their Italian sisters, they too were mythologised, primarily in comparison with the classical Muses. However, for the Cookes this mythologising was a response to their political abilities in light of their public agency, rather than a reaction to their exclusion from public engagement; they were extravagantly praised precisely because of their abilities to act as brokers to their husbands on behalf of male humanists. This mythologising process happened not during their virginal years, as with fifteenth-century female scholars, but after marriage, at the height of their political influence. This was occasioned in many ways by the upward social trajectory of the sisters, the result of their high-profile marriages.[15] The greatest praise, as we shall see, was reserved for the most well-connected sister, Mildred, the result of her marriage to the influential William Cecil. Moreover, the longevity of both Anne and Elizabeth also allows an exploration of the effects of declining status and old age upon the representations of learned women: for these sisters, widowhood left them vulnerable to critique as outspoken women. Yet I suggest that these representations are again a response to the perceived power of the sisters. Whilst in relative decline due to their widowed status, Anne and Elizabeth still had political connections, and the complex representations of the aged sisters respond to their perceived influence.

In many ways, this chapter therefore offers a warning against the methodology of past research on the stereotype of the learned woman. It contends that the Cooke sisters, as is the case with too much scholarly work on the gendered representations of early modern women, have been subject to the practice of 'mining' for apt quotations, which obscures the overall impression presented by a text. Clapham's *Certain Observations*, written after the death of Elizabeth I, has previously been cited as evidence of Mildred Cecil's 'bad press' and of contemporary hostility to her learning.[16] Admittedly, Clapham commented in his memoir that Mildred was 'as some persons may suppose, of more learning than is necessary for that sex'. Yet I would suggest that it is important to note that in the same sentence Clapham balanced his critique, describing her also as 'a woman of great wit'.[17] Clapham himself was not necessarily condemning Mildred's learning, although he was, of course, suggesting that negative contemporary opinions of female learning were in circulation. This chapter therefore considers the representations of the Cookes in context, and with awareness of the motivations behind certain representations of the sisters. Only by taking this approach can we hope to understand more fully the contemporary reactions to learned women. Ultimately, this chapter reveals that there is no one judgement on the value of education for early modern women. Each representation is a response not simply to the learned woman herself, but to her perceived power and influence in early modern society.

FROM MAIDENS TO MATRONS

There are very few extant representations of the Cooke sisters before marriage, unlike their learned female contemporaries, such as Lady Jane Grey and the Seymour sisters.[18] Walter Haddon described their childhood education in the Cooke household as akin to a Tuscan humanist academy, and they receive brief mention in surveys of learned women of the period.[19] The least-known of the sisters, Margaret, was certainly recognised for her learning before her marriage, whilst she was serving Mary I.[20] In a verse by Richard Edwards, written before 1555, he celebrates eight women, including Margaret Cooke, who 'nowe serves one noble Quene': 'Coke is cumly and thereto in books setes all her care/ in lernyng with the romayne dames of ryghte she may compare.'[21] The verse reveals two aspects of Margaret's reputation. Firstly, that Margaret's educated status was well known in the courtly circle and her continued pursuit of learning was not discouraged at Mary's court. Secondly, there is the suggestion that Margaret's beauty leaves her in danger of seduction at the court, thus she rightly puts all 'her care' in scholarship.[22] Here the association between women's learning and sexual promiscuity is inverted. However, this association is reinstated in the most detailed description of one of the sisters before marriage, deriving again from the pen of Walter Haddon. He had wanted to marry Anne Cooke and even sought the assistance of both William and Mildred Cecil in his suit, but Anne eventually chose Nicholas Bacon instead.[23] The situation prompted Haddon to write a final epistle to Anne. Whereas most learned virgins in this period are lauded for their combination of scholarship and virginity, Anne is here represented in far more contentious terms. Haddon tells her that whilst he will never contact her again, she will 'tamen colenda semper et admiranda et congitanda ut desyderanda' (nevertheless, always be cherished and admired and regretted and desired); the inclusion of 'desyderanda' moves the tribute into dangerous, sexual territory. Her learning is paramount in this letter: he compares her betrayal to ancient Greek legend, namely that of Cressida, who pledged to love Troilus, only to change her affections to Diomedes. Anne is presented as faithless and Haddon says that, like Troilus, he hopes for an early death.[24] Thus, there are hints as to the negative, sexual aspects of learned women in these virginal representations of the sisters, a reaction to their unmarried status and relative vulnerability.

Such allusions disappear from the representations of the Cookes after marriage. In their iconographical representations, which exist for the sisters only after marriage, their learning goes almost unnoticed. The dynastic aspect of their marriages is now paramount. Their portraits and tombs, like those of their contemporaries, are emblazoned with family arms, emphasising the connections brought by their marriages. Burghley noted that at Mildred's funeral her family ancestry would be shown 'by the sondry Cotes of Noble howses joined by blood with hirs', and both her final tomb and the earlier sketches by Burghley incorporate the heraldic connections.[25] John Clapham's first reference to Mildred in his *Certain Observations* emphasises the political importance of her marriage, before his much later comment on her learning, revealing its primary status in his representation of Mildred. She is described as 'Sir Anthony Coke's daughter', and he suggests that, like Cecil's earlier marriage to Mary Cheke, the connections brought by this match proved 'a great help and strength to his further purposes'.[26]

The sisters' fertility is also highlighted in iconographical representations. A portrait of Mildred Cecil, attributed to Hans Eworth in 1563, is a rare example of a sixteenth-century image of a pregnant woman, marking her carrying her son Robert (Figure 4). The bunch of cherries that Mildred holds in her right hand symbolises innocence, in this instance the innocent fruitfulness of marriage.[27] Yet there is more to this portrait than first meets the eye. Childbearing proved difficult for Mildred and no children were born for the first nine years of the marriage, until the birth of Francisca on 6 July 1554; the child, however, died shortly after birth.[28] Previous important work on the portrait by Pauline Croft and Karen Hearn noted the 'deep concern' the Cecils must have felt regarding their childless state, but the pressure Mildred was under was intense and is worth exploring in more detail.[29] By January 1551, just over five years into their marriage, Richard Morison expressed surprise that Mildred had not yet become pregnant, writing to her husband 'I wyshe yow helth & my lady your wyfe sick of chyld'.[30] The birth of Francisca was followed in December 1556 by that of Anne, who lived to maturity. Mildred's father wrote to William Cecil, pleased that she had come through the delivery and saying that whilst a son would have been a greater blessing, it boded well that Mildred had given birth twice in such close duration and at her age; he offered that thought as comfort for his daughter, who apparently was 'not happy' at giving birth to another girl.[31] Two boys were then born to Mildred, both named William; the first died a few hours after birth in October 1559 and the second lived for 19 months, dying in December 1562. Their father was highly concerned about having a single male heir, his son, Thomas, from his first marriage. In May 1561 he told Nicholas Throckmorton that he had allowed Thomas permission to travel to Paris at that time only because another son, William, had been born; after his namesake died, he forbade Thomas to travel through Italy because of the

Figure 4 Mildred Cooke Cecil, Lady Burghley, attributed to Hans Eworth

dangers to which it would expose his now only male heir.[32] Mildred's continued fertility and the possibility of another male heir was therefore highly significant for the family and worth celebrating through the 1563 portrait.

The monuments of both Mildred and Elizabeth feature not only images of the sisters, but also of their children. Elizabeth designed her Bisham monument to depict her surrounded by her offspring, with the deceased Russell heir, Francis, at her feet. In her completed Westminster Abbey monument, Mildred

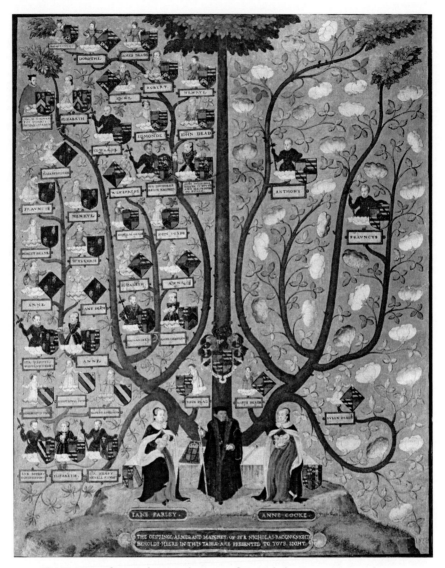

Figure 5 Tree of Jesse, showing the issue of Sir Nicholas Bacon, artist unknown

shares a tomb with her daughter, Anne, whilst the monument itself incorporates images of Anne and her brother, Robert Cecil, as well as Mildred's de
Vere grandchildren, Elizabeth, Bridget and Susan. Not all the visual images of
the sisters, however, celebrated their fertility. The issue of Sir Nicholas Bacon
are depicted in a Tree of Jesse but, compared to the fecundity of Bacon's first
wife, Anne is shown to have produced only two living offshoots, each as yet
producing no children themselves (Figure 5).

208

MARRIED LOVE AND INTELLECTUAL UNION

The sisters' marriages seem to have been happy unions. To Burghley, writing upon his wife's death, Mildred was a 'deare wiff', amended on her Westminster monument to 'dearest above all' and 'far beyond the race of womankind'.[33] When defending her funeral to Alexander Nowell, the dean of St Paul's, against any accusations of 'corrupt abuse', he argued that it would instead be 'a testimony of my harty love which I did beare hir, with whom I lyved in the state of matrimony forty and three yers contynually without any unkyndnes to move separation'.[34] On Mildred's monument, Burghley's epitaph noted that she had shared with him 'all my fortunes in times good and bad'. Anne was a 'wife most dear' to Nicholas Bacon. The success of the union of Thomas Hoby and Elizabeth Cooke meant that they were loath to be parted when the former undertook his Parisian embassy; despite the expense entailed, the whole family journeyed to France together.[35] In comparison, less is known about the success of Elizabeth's second marriage, although she lamented John Russell's death, both in private correspondence and in verse.[36] Similarly, Henry Killigrew's repeated concern in his letters for his wife, Katherine, would seem to testify to a happy match.[37]

Erasmus argued that educated women made better wives, for 'what makes wedlock delightful and lasting is more the good will between mind and mind than any physical passion'.[38] There is evidence that this belief was borne out by the Cooke sisters. For Burghley, writing Mildred's epitaph for her tomb, her learning was central to their happy marriage. He recorded her classical education at the hands of her father, 'a noble Maecenas to all men of letters', and praised her meditation, throughout her life, on Scripture and the writings of Greek Church Fathers.[39] A poem written during the Marian period by Nicholas Bacon paints a rosy picture of his marriage to Anne, founded upon their shared intellectual interests, as shown by two of the stanzas:

> Thinkeinge alsoe with howe good will
> The Idle tymes whiche yrkesome be
> You have made shorte throwe your good skill
> In readeinge pleasante thinges to me.
> Whereof profitte we bothe did se,
> As wittenes can if they could speake
> Bothe your Tullye and my Senecke.
>
> ... In doeinge this I hadd respecte
> As reason woulde to your delighte,
> And knoweinge as in moste women's sighte
> Thoughe vayne in dede semes moste of mighte,
> Therefore for you I coulde not fynde
> A more depe thinge then frutes of mynde.[40]

There was a wider recognition of the intellectual aspect to the sisters' marriages. The French humanist Jean-Antoine de Baïf owned a copy of Elizabeth's Latin verse commemorating her marriage to Thomas Hoby, written after the latter's death in 1566. As we have seen, the poem shows Elizabeth as a widow confined to unceasing grief, praising the late Thomas as 'O chare consors, coniugum ô dulcissime' (O dear husband, o sweetest of spouses).[41] The copy of the poem owned by Baïf is in the hand of Daniel Rogers. Rogers would serve Thomas Hoby's successor to the Parisian embassy, Sir Henry Norris, later in 1566, but he was already close to members of the *Pléiade*, a group of French humanist poets including Pierre de Ronsard, Joachim du Bellay and Jean-Antoine de Baïf.[42] The interest of Rogers and Baïf in this verse reveals the wider awareness of the marriage of the Hobys as an intellectual union. Matthew Parker similarly referred to Anne as Nicholas Bacon's 'other self' in a letter written to her on 6 February 1568, and it is surely no coincidence that he expressed his sentiment in Latin, writing that she was an 'alter ipse to him, unus spiritus, una caro' (other self to him, one spirit, one flesh).[43] Here, though, we need to be aware of evidentiary context. Parker's letter detailed an argument between himself and Nicholas Bacon, as has been discussed, over the latter's dismissal of two unlicensed prebendaries whom the Lord Keeper had installed in Norwich cathedral.[44] Parker appealed to Anne to intervene with her husband. This is therefore primarily a petitionary letter, designed to please its recipient with its representation of a learned union between Anne and Nicholas.

LEARNED REPRESENTATIONS OF THE SISTERS

All the sisters were influential intermediaries to their husbands and brothers-in-law and as such received many dedicatory verses, particularly from male humanists. George Buchanan, the Scottish neo-Latin poet, wrote several verses describing the sisters. His epigram 'Ad Antonium Cucum Equitem Anglum, et filias doctissimas' (To Anthony Cooke, English Knight, and his very learned daughters) casts their father as Apollo, with the sisters as the Muses.[45] Hadrianus Junius, the Dutch humanist, wrote a poem praising Mildred's birth and learning in the form of a dialogue between the poet and the Muses. Junius tells the Muses not to overlook Mildred Cecil; they agree that her poetry is worthy to be read by them, and so vote to make her one of their number, stating that now it is not only Sappho who is worth their praise. The verse ends with Junius declaring that 'Proinde Cecilleidi iam thura paremus et aras/ Vates cuncti, aucto Pierdum numero' (Therefore let all of us poets prepare incense and altars for Cecil's wife, who has been added to the number of the Muses).[46] An epitaph written for Katherine Killigrew after her death in 1583 by the Scottish humanist Andrew Melville similarly described her as a mother and sister to the Muses and as 'Palladis et Phoebi comes una' (The one companion of Athena [Pallas] and Apollo [Phoebe]), as a friend of the goddess of wisdom and the leader of the Muses. In the same vein, William Chark's epitaph on Katherine describes her as 'Sororem Musarum' (sister of the Muses).[47] Christopher Ockland's dedicatory verse, appended to his *EIPHNAPXIA, sive Elizabetha* (1582) and translated into English in 1585 by John Sharrock, compares Mildred to Athena, referring to her as 'like an other Pallas'.[48]

Two things are striking about the association of the Muses with the Cookes. Firstly, given that the sisters were all married when the subjects of these verses, the comparison to the virginal Muses is unusual. Secondly, although other early modern female writers attempted to defend their activities with references to the female Muses, the association between the Muses and women writers by men is often a negative formulation, one that Frances Teague has shown to be commonly 'sexually ambiguous and contemptible'.[49] Why, then, are all these verses on the Cooke sisters so overtly positive regarding their learning? I suggest these optimistic representations of the Cookes as female scholars are influenced by their political status as wives of key members of the Elizabethan elite. Buchanan's epigram 'To Anthony Cooke ... and his very learned daughters' makes this link explicit. In the verse, Buchanan equates the 'Cucides', the descendants of Cooke, solely with his daughters; no mention is made of his sons. The reason is provided later in the verse: the sisters are of practical use to Buchanan, more so than their unmentioned brothers and more so than their father. The poet seeks 'gleanings' from their 'harvest' in return for his poetry: the verse is a bid for patronage from the Cooke sisters.[50]

Buchanan also sent at least four poems to Mildred herself, in just such a bid for preferment. The first was a New Year's gift, probably dating from the period between 1568 and 1569 that Buchanan spent in England. He explains in his verse that if Mildred greatly enjoys his poem, then she could return the favour with patronage; if she esteems the gift as a small present, then she should be pleased that Buchanan seeks so little from her.[51] Buchanan seems uncertain as to what reception his verse will receive from Mildred, finishing his poem with the line: 'Quocunque optaris tu mihi, id opto tibi' (Whatever you wish to me, I wish that to you).[52] Her response is revealed by Buchanan's second verse, which thanks Mildred not only for the money she sent him but also for the poem which she composed: 'Quod, Mildreda, mihi carmen precio- sius auro/ Miseris, ingenio gratulor usque tuo' (Mildred, since you sent me a poem more precious than gold/ I rejoice continually in your wit).[53] Mildred's verse apparently suggested that wealth was a sickness, which she could relieve through her patronage of poets. In his second verse, therefore, Buchanan agreed to an exchange: he would send Mildred verses, in return for gold. The third and fourth poems to Mildred testify to this arrangement, with Buchanan thanking Mildred in his fourth verse for the money she sent in return for a bad, inept and ungraceful poem.[54]

Similarly, whilst one of the two verses written by Hadrianus Junius for Mildred in July 1568 concentrates only on her status as a Muse, the other piece presents Mildred solely as an influential intermediary for patronage. She is portrayed in verse as having great power over her husband, suggesting that she could influence her husband to commend Junius's services to the Queen.[55] Junius was attempting to gain support for his edition of *Eunapius Sardianus*, and the poems he addressed to William Cecil at this time all stress his desire for patronage from the Queen; he finally published the work, dedicated to Queen Elizabeth, in 1568.[56] Other writers were even more explicit as to their desire for patronage. Mildred is similarly described as a 'friendly Muse' by Ulpian Fulwell in the dedicatory verse appended to his 1576 work, *Ars adulandi, the art of Flattery*. Fulwell makes plain his desire for patronage in an acrostic on Mildred's name:

> MY friendly Muse leave Parnas hill a while,
> I crave thy ayde and counsayle now at neede:
> Lend mee thy laurel crown to guide my stile,
> DRED drives my minde to doubt of lucky speed.[57]

Christopher Ockland explicitly characterises himself as Mildred's 'Clyent' in a dedicatory verse appended to his *EIPHNAPXIA, sive Elizabetha*:

> O Nymphes, O noble Sisters foure, but (Myldred) unto thine
> High favour, as the chiefest, I appeale, be thou mine aide,
> And like an other Pallas, let thine Aegis strong be laide.[58]

His description of Mildred as the Greek goddess of wisdom is overtly related to her role as a potential patron, underlined by his explicit reference to Athena's *aegis*, her protective shield.

EUROPEAN FAME?

The sisters were lauded, too, in European humanist circles. William Chark's epitaph to Katherine after her death in 1583 described her fame in Europe as known throughout the stretch of the Rhine and Rhone rivers.[59] In many cases, the desire for patronage was again behind the representations of the sisters' European fame. Roger Ascham detailed Mildred's erudition in a letter to Johann Sturm on 14 December 1550. After discussing his favourite theme, the Princess Elizabeth's learning, Ascham admitted 'I cannot skip over two English women, nor should I want you, my Sturm, to skip over them if you are considering cultivating English friends, than which I can think of nothing more desirable'.[60] The first was Lady Jane Grey, the second, Mildred herself: 'The other woman is Mildred Cecil, who speaks and understands Greek about as well as English. It is difficult to decide whether she is happier in this superior knowledge because she was born to that noble man Anthony Cooke, her father and teacher ... or because she married William Cecil, a young man, to be sure, but a young man with the prudence of an old man and a great understanding of life and letters.'[61] Ascham is often cited by scholars as an influential supporter of female humanist learning, representative of the Edwardian *zeitgeist*, yet the close proximity between his descriptions of Mildred's learning and her marriage to William Cecil is significant: Mildred's scholarship is worthy of praise because of her political usefulness, both to Ascham and potentially to Sturm, highlighted by Ascham's telling reference to the value of 'cultivating English friends'. By 1550, Ascham's career as a member of Princess Elizabeth's circle had been badly affected by events at court and he soon turned to William Cecil for patronage.[62] It is also known that Ascham provided Mildred with copies of his letters to Sturm at this time, so his tribute may have come directly to her attention.[63] This is not to suggest that Ascham's praise of Mildred's education is necessarily insincere; however, it is to argue for an awareness of context in analysing the praise of learned women within European circles.[64] A letter sent by Richard Morison, the Edwardian diplomat, to William Cecil in January 1553 should be read in the same light. Morison included the following message for Mildred in his letter: 'I do send my lady your bedfellow, a few verses, made by a woman bornn in Italie, & for the Gospels' sake, glad to dwel in germanie. I can no skyl, but I wold my lady your bedfelow, wold with som epistle in Greek, pick som quarel of acquayntance to her.'[65] The verses are no longer included with the letter, so the identity of the female poet has never been previously identified. However, from the information included by Morison, it is clear that she must have been Olympia Morata. The Italian poet was born in Italy and received a humanist education from her father, Fulvio Morata, before fleeing to religious exile in Germany with her Protestant husband, Andreas Grunthler, in 1550. The verses were probably in Greek, as Morison urged Mildred to respond in that language. It is very possible that one of the verses was Ὀλυμπίας τῆς Μωράτης εἰς Εὐτυχὸν Ποντανὸν Κέλτην (To Eutychus Pontanus Gallus), which discusses Morata's distinctiveness from other women and their pursuits, due to her humanist learning.[66] Unfortunately it is not known whether Mildred ever began an acquaintance with Morata; however, Morison's attempt to connect these learned women was politically astute.[67] Flattering Mildred through the presentation of Greek verse would have surely made her more likely to support Morison's calls upon her husband for greater financial support of his embassy.[68]

Such factors need to be taken into account when considering the celebration of Mildred's sister Elizabeth, again in European circles. Her diplomatic visit to France in 1566 brought her into contact with the French humanist poets in the *Pléiade*.[69] As we have seen, Jean-Antoine de Baïf owned a manuscript copy by Daniel Rogers of a verse written by Elizabeth on the death of Thomas Hoby in 1566. The neo-Latin verse not only celebrates the Hobys' intellectual union, but also highlights Elizabeth's educated status through its Latin verse and classical allusions.[70] However, such interest in Elizabeth's learning should not be accepted without awareness of Baïf's role as a secretary of the royal chamber of Charles IX. Courtesy to Elizabeth on the death of her ambassador husband in 1566 was politicised, as has already been suggested, with Charles IX stating that 'that yf there were any thinge in his realme that might stand her in steed, she might as well comand yt as yf she were in England'.[71] It is highly likely, then, that interest in this tributary verse by the royal secretary, whilst recognising and celebrating Elizabeth's learned status, reflects the political nature of her status as a diplomatic wife and widow.

An epigram addressed by George Buchanan to Katherine Cooke Killigrew highlights the difficulty of evaluating the representations of learned women in poetry. He presented her with an epigram on her marriage in 1565, yet an earlier version of the same poem was addressed to the French female humanist Camille de Morel; Buchanan simply exchanged Killigrew for her Continental contemporary.[72] The piece was then renamed 'Nomine Henrici Kilgraei Angli ad Antonii Cocii doctissimi filiam egregie doctam, quae postea Kiligraeo nupsit' (In Name of Henry Killigrew, Englishman; To a very Learned Daughter, of the Learned Anthony Cooke, whom Killigrew afterwards Married). The epigram's title highlights Katherine's learned status, linking it to that of her father, but her scholarly nature is still secondary to her marital status. The poem itself is startlingly unspecific as to its recipient's qualities:

> Et decor et facies cum simplicitate venusta,
> Insidiosa oculis, imperiosa animis:
> Et motura feras docti vox pectoris index
> Pene parem superis te facit esse deis.
> Si par eximiam decoret constantia formam
> Efficiet superos haec tibi pene pares.[73]

> (Both your beauty and your face are simply charming,
> Dangerous to the eyes and over-powering to the mind.
> Your voice, proof of your learned heart, which would move even wild beasts,
> Makes you almost the equal of the gods above.
> If an equal constancy might crown your outstanding beauty,
> Then this would make the gods above almost your equal.)

The epigram alludes to Katherine's learning only implicitly, through its language and with its reference to the power of her voice. Her beauty, as with Camille's before her, is instead the focus of this interchangeable epigram. Another couplet by Buchanan on Katherine, appended to her manuscript volume of his poetry, is similarly commendatory yet vague: 'Haec tua te virtus diis immortalibus aequum,/ efficit atque hominum supra fastigia tollit' (This virtue of yours makes you equal to the immortal gods, and raises you above the most exalted of men).[74] Its context, however, highlights the motive behind Buchanan's verses on Katherine. The manuscript was a gift to Katherine, designed, like these pieces of verse, to gain her goodwill and friendship. Her diplomat husband, Henry, was a useful contact for Buchanan, dating from the latter's earlier stay in England in 1563–64, and particularly upon Killigrew's embassy to Scotland between 1572 and 1575. As much as Katherine might cement Buchanan's goodwill through her verses for him, it was equally important for Buchanan to do the same in return.[75] Katherine's erudition was, for Buchanan, less important than her marital status, and hence her representation in his poetry is positive, yet, now understandably, vague.

The impact of political status upon the representations of learned women is demonstrated by the writings of the Cookes themselves. When presenting her with a volume of St Basil in 1552, Mildred praised Lady Jane Grey in an accompanying letter for her education and piety.[76] Mildred recognised their bond as learned women and testified to her great fondness for Jane, yet the connection between the women would have been useful for the career of Mildred's husband, William Cecil, hence Jane's learned qualities were worth praising. Conversely, Elizabeth was still in contact with one of the younger Seymour sisters, Mary, in 1599, when she wrote to her nephew Robert Cecil on behalf of Mary's husband. Although Mary's eldest sisters were most famous for their learning, Elizabeth does not mention the educational status she shared with Mary to her nephew, writing that he should act upon the suit either out of remembrance of his father's debt to the family, or else not at all.[77]

A particular type of client, however, was less moved to praise the sisters' learning. Edward Dering, the evangelical preacher, was a client of the Cooke sisters, yet his letters to Katherine Cooke Killigrew make no reference to her learning, presumably understanding that Katherine ranked the assurance of her election above praise of her education.[78] Her epitaph by Robert Masson, minister to the French Stranger Church in London, similarly highlights her elect status, with no mention of her scholarship.[79] Thomas Cartwright explained to Elizabeth Russell why overt celebration of learning could be spiritually problematic. In 1591 he praised her 'mark of learning' as one 'rare in your sex', as well as her patronage of scholars, before adding 'yet this is not that wherein your praise doeth or ought to consist'. For Cartwright, 'Godlines only is that which endureth and maketh to endure such as have gotten possession of it'. He therefore argued that to praise Elizabeth for her learning would not be 'safe', unless he added reproof of what was still amiss in her, for all men should work towards godliness: 'I easilie see a law of silence layd upon me in that thing which men suters especially doe willinglie pursue.'[80]

OUTSPOKEN WOMEN

A humanist education theoretically provided women with the skills of oratory, and in his dedicatory verse to Mildred, appended to his *EIPHNAPXIA*, Christopher Ockland hints at the public speaking of learned 'English Ladies':

> Who joyne, like learned men, the Greekish tong, with Latine phrase.
> Yea which is more, like skilfull Poets, in dulcet verse they floe,
> Wherewith Homerus frought his bookes, or Mantuan Maro.
> If cause requirde, ex tempore, their meeters framing fine.[81]

Whilst such outspokenness could be condemned, Mildred's marriage to Burghley guaranteed a favourable presentation. Ulpian Fulwell's decision to render the dedicatory verse to Mildred, appended to his *Ars adulandi*, in the form of a dialogue suggests too a recognition of her verbal skills. Yet there are still hints that, as a learned woman, she was more headstrong and outspoken than was encouraged in her female contemporaries. Fulwell has Mildred in his dialogue call him 'simple sot', and an epigram by Karel Utenhove, the Dutch poet, also presents a picture of a similarly strong-willed Mildred.[82] Entitled 'Pro. Mild. Ce.', it was published with his 1568 *Xenia*:

> Sollicitis quid agam tua quaerit epistola verbis
> Verba sed à factis sunt aliena tuis.
> Vix tibi vix digner redituro dicere Salve,
> Quem piguit blanda dicere voce Vale.[83]

> (I will do what your letter asks in anxious words,
> But the words are divorced from your actions.
> Scarcely, to you, scarcely shall I stoop to say 'Hail' to you in return,
> Whom it disgusts to say 'Farewell' in a pleasant voice.)[84]

Jane Stevenson has rightly noted that the 'pro' of the title means that this was an epigram written by Utenhove on behalf of Mildred, rather than written about her, suggesting that Mildred commissioned Utenhove to write the verse for her.[85] Yet Utenhove's characterisation of Mildred here is significant and deserves greater analysis. The epigram seems to be directed to a suitor of Mildred's, who has written asking for her patronage with 'anxious words'. The letter was apparently full of praise and love for Mildred, no doubt calling on the language of friendship and reciprocity, yet the verse suggests that those 'words are divorced from your actions'. Mildred therefore disdains to act as patron for this suitor and, more significantly, she is unafraid to voice her refusal, albeit through Utenhove's verse. Instead of disguising her rejection with empty promises, Mildred commissioned a piece to be sent to the suitor, clearly stating her anger at their past actions and her rejection of their request.

There is a similar suggestion of Mildred's strong opinions in a verse by George Buchanan, this time explicitly about Mildred's daughter, Anne Cecil, the countess of Oxford: 'Quod tibi vis tacito voto, quod mater aperto,/ Hoc tibi fors cito det, filia Caecilii.'[86] (What you wish for in silence, and what your mother wishes for quite openly/ Fortune will speedily grant you, o daughter of Cecil.) Mildred is presented here as exercising ultimate control over her daughter. This accords with the representation advanced by the earl of Oxford, Mildred's son-in-law. When Burghley tried to mediate in the marital difficulties between Oxford and his daughter, Anne, in April 1575, he noted down one of the former's grievances: 'my wiff hath ever drawen his wiffe's love from hym, and that she hath wished hym dead'.[87] Oxford's description of Mildred not only highlights her control over Anne, but again her outspokenness to her son-in-law, however understandable given the circumstances.

In *The Rocke of Regard* (1576), George Whetstone included two verses on Mildred and Elizabeth, which again consider the sisters' speech. They are both described as beautiful and virtuous, yet Mildred, whilst still professing her thoughts in 'words', is characterised as less demonstrative of her learning than her younger sister: 'Her wit, her weedes, her words, her workes and all,/ So modest are, as slaunder yealdes her thrall.'[88] In comparison, Elizabeth is presented as virtuously outspoken: 'Her words of worth, doth win her toung such praise,/ As when she speakes, the wisest silent stayes.'[89] For Whetstone, beginning his literary career and in search of patrons, there was no suggestion of the inappropriateness of Elizabeth's outspokenness, as was also the case with the verses by Utenhove and Buchanan. Significantly, both Mildred and Elizabeth were married women at the time they were immortalised by Whetstone; Elizabeth had married her second husband, John Russell, two years previously. Widowhood, however, left both Elizabeth and her sister Anne far more open to attack on the grounds of outspokenness.

WELL-CONNECTED WIDOWS

Two different accounts of Anne's outspokenness during her widowhood deserve close attention. The first is a testimony by Captain Francis Allen. He visited Anne at the request of her son Anthony in August 1589. Anne apparently treated Allen 'curtiusly', until he broached the reason for his visit; he was to move her to help secure the release of Thomas Lawson from prison, at the request of her son.[90] Lawson, a Catholic, had been acting as a messenger to England for Anthony, then still in France, but had been imprisoned by Anthony's uncle, Lord Burghley. According to Anthony, this had been done at his mother's request.[91] From the start of the interview between Francis Allen and Anne, the latter was therefore recognised as wielding political influence. In his letter, Allen reported that Anne's response to her son's request was as follows:

she let not to say you ar a traitre to god and your contry. you have undone her, you
sieke her death, and when you hav that you sieke for you shall have but on hundered
pounds mor then you hav now. She is resolut to procure her magistis lettre for to
force to you to retourne, and when that shalbe if her Magesty gave you your right, or
desart, she shuld clap you up in prison. She cannot abid to hir of you, as she saith;
nor of the other [Lawson] espetially, and tould me plainly she shuld be the worse
this month for my comming without you, and axed me why you could not hav come
from thence as well as myself. She saith you ar hatted of all the Chiffest on that sid
and Curst of god in all your actions since Mr Lauson's being with you.[92]

In light of Anne's speech, Allen counselled Anthony to cease to seek for
Lawson's release, citing more of Anne's words: 'no no, saith she, I hav learned
not to imploy il, to do good, and if ther were no more men in Ingland, and
altogether you shuld nevar com home, he shalbe hindered from comming to
you'.[93] In light of Anne's arguments, Allen was silenced, writing 'It is unpos-
sible to perswad my Lady ... as my self to send you Pouls-stiple'. Yet what is
striking about Allen's account of Anne is that he does not characterise her as
crazed or even unreasonable in her speech. He judges her to have overstepped
the boundaries of acceptable speech on only one occasion: 'My Lady said
she had rather you made the wars with the King of Nither [Navarre] to hav
staid so long Idle in Montoban and with great ernestnes, also ters in her eys,
she wished that when she heard of Mr Selvin's imprisonement you had bin
fairly buried provided you had died in the Lord – by my simple jugment she
spoke it in her passion, and repentid immediatly her words.'[94] Allen softens
the impact of Anne's actual words by referencing her tears and by suggesting
that she regretted her most controversial comment, that of wishing for Anthony's death. According to Allen, Anne was simply playing the role of a loving
mother; he argues that he will never see 'a wis lady, an honorable woman, a
Mother mor perplexsed for her son's absence, then I hav sien that honorable
Dame for yours'.[95]

Whilst Allen did not interpret Anne's outspokenness as unreasonable
or mad, Anthony Standen, another close friend of Anthony Bacon's, was
convinced only two years later that madness was the only explanation for her
behaviour. Standen was arrested as a Spanish spy in Bordeaux, and news of
his friendship with her son had reached Anne via her English agents in the
French town. Anne feared Standen, as an English Catholic, would undermine
Anthony's faith; Standen alleged that Anne used contacts with merchants in
Bordeaux to convince the authorities not to release him.[96] Standen delivered
his opinion of Lady Anne to Edward Selwin, accusing her of outspokenness,
having 'forbydden all kynde of speches of [Anthony] in her precence, giving
him owte for Illegitymate and not to be borne of her body, that she hath
enjoyned all Englishe marchants, yea, and his owne brothers, not to administer
any support or succor unto him, and in syne that she doth not acknowledge

him any way to appartayne unto her'. His conclusion was to question Anne's sanity: 'When therfor I enter into consideration of that good lady, her education, nobylitie of her house, her lerninge & good nature whereof in tymes paste I have byne better acquaynted, I can not but muze at sutch a change'.[97] Anthony wrote to his mother at this time, protesting his fidelity. He showed the letter to Standen and, in response, Standen was explicit as to his mother's irrationality:

> yow have done excedynge well to be playne and specially withe a woman, whiche is a vessell so frayle and variable as every wynde wavereth as yow knowe. And althoughe I well knowe my ladye your mother to be one of the sufficientest without comparaison of that Sex, yett att the ende of the Carriere il y a toujours de la femme (women are still women), even with the perfytttest of them all. Accordinge to a sentence the late Quene of Scotland ones alledged to me when in talkynge of the Quene's Majestie, our present Mystres, and I extollinge to the sayde Quene our Soveraygne's rare parts, she sayed these words, Escuyer quand vous parles en louange de nostre sexe en voulant louer quelqu'une femme advisee et sage, mais dittes qu'elle est moyns folle que les autres, car touttes en tiennent de la follie (When praising our sex, avoid commending a woman for her intelligence and wisdom. Rather say that she is less mad than the rest, for all of them are a little mad).[98]

The very different conclusions reached by Francis Allen and Anthony Standen are striking, yet they both report Anne's outspokenness in similar terms. The explanation, I suggest, again derives from the perception of Anne's political influence. To Standen, frustrated and personally disadvantaged by Anne's continued sway and power over her eldest son, orchestrated through her political networks, her outspokenness is inexplicable and read as madness. Yet for Francis Allen, a former soldier with a desire to rise in the world, Anne was a potentially useful intermediary; she had underlined her political connections to Allen on his visit. Moreover, Allen believed Anne's brother-in-law, Lord Burghley, to have a long-held vendetta against his family, preventing his advancement.[99] Given such a context, it is unsurprising that Anne was treated more sympathetically by Allen and, moreover, that Allen counselled in favour of her greatest desire: Anthony's return from France.

EDWARD SPENCER ON ANNE BACON'S 'UNQUIETNESS'

It is the conclusion of Anthony Standen as to Anne's madness that has long gained credence with historians. This follows the line of Godfrey Goodman, bishop of Gloucester, who wrote that Anne was 'little better than frantic in her age'.[100] Modern scholars have taken Goodman's representation at face value, with no reference to the inexactness of the comment, nor noting that it was written in the 1650s, at least forty years after Anne's death; the religious difference between the godly Anne and the Catholic sympathies of Goodman likewise goes unaddressed. Francis Bacon's Victorian biographer, James Spedding, thus wrote of the 'peculiar condition of her mind and spirits' in later life, 'suffering more than usually from anxieties and jealousies'.[101] Patrick Collinson has written of her 'dottiness', wondering if it was the result of intellectual frustration.[102] For Jardine and Stewart, Anne was little short of mad in her later years: 'Lady Bacon's opinions were increasingly ignored by her family, who were starting to doubt her judgment on many matters'.[103]

The most conclusive evidence of Anne's madness has long been seen to be the letters of Edward Spencer.[104] Here, too, however, close analysis reveals Spencer's reaction to Anne's outspokenness to be conditioned by a perception of her power and influence, although in this case the response is to the declining status and vulnerability resulting from her widowhood. Spencer, a servant of Anthony Bacon, was sent to stay with the latter's mother at Gorhambury at various times in 1593 and 1594.[105] Spencer relayed to his master in July 1594 how 'unquiet my Lady is with all her household', a phrase which reoccurs in his letter of 16 August.[106] Spencer's great problem was with Anne's speech: 'And to yield my duty, what I am able I will, but not willing to be here unless she would be quiet. She make me to buy starch and soap to wash my linen withal: more than was wont to be; yet I care not so she would be quiet.'[107] Anne's unruly speech against Anthony's circle was again condemned by Spencer in August: 'She have fallen out with Crossby and bid him get him out of her sight. – Now for your Doctor at Redbourn, she saith he is a Papist or some sorcerer or conjurer or some vild name or other. – She is as far out with Mr. Lawson as ever she was, and call him villain and whoremaster with other vild words.'[108] Spencer's letters focused on two incidents at Gorhambury, which he used to illustrate Anne's 'unquietness' and her quickness to anger. The first involved a greyhound, sent to Spencer by another of Anthony's servants, the aforementioned Catholic, Thomas Lawson:

> And as soon as my Lady did see her, she sent me word she should be hanged. Now I had thought to sent her to kepein.[109] Now by-and-by she sent word by Cros[by] that if I did not make her away she should not sleep in her bed; so indeed I hung her up; whereat she was very angry, and said I was fransey [frenzied], and bade me go home to my master and make him a fool, I should make none of her. 'There is a company of ye: I marvel where he picked ye out. There is Mr. Lawson, who have gotten away my brewer, and your master together: but he shall hear of it one day. My comen shall be served when your master and the brewer will.' The bitch was good for nothing, else I would not a hung her. My Lady do not speak to me as yet.[110]

Spencer's narrative implies that, rather than his own actions being 'fransey', those of Anne instead are crazed, a conclusion that he builds on in his letter of 16 August. This incident relates to Spencer's staying out late with his sparrow-hawk, returning only after the rest of the household had had supper. According to his testimony, Anne met Spencer with the following words:

'What, come you home now? I would you and your hawk would keep you away altogether. You have been a-breaking of hedges between neighbour and neighbour: and now you come home out of order and show an ill example in my house. Well you shall keep no hawk here.' – 'I am the more sorrier. I have given no acause that your Ladyship should be offended, nor I will not. To please your Ladyship, I will pull off her head.' – Whereat she stamped, and said I would do by her as I did by the bitch. Insomuch she would let me have no supper. So truly I went to bed without my supper.[111]

These letters have been taken by previous scholars at face value as evidence of Anne's increasingly questionable mental state. The context of her verbal outbursts against Spencer has, however, received no attention. Firstly, it should be noted that this was not the first dispute between Anne and Spencer. In May 1593 Spencer was already serving Anne on her son's behalf and she stated to Anthony that 'I care not For his servyce, let him do lyke A prowd ignorant verlet. let him be talking & stepp abroad unseasonably & cloake it with lyes'.[112] Spencer is portrayed as the outspoken one, rather than Anne herself; she added that Spencer was particularly difficult if reproved for his behaviour, writing an 'Irefull pevish Fellow yf he be looked into & checked For his loose demeanour'.[113] By the end of May 1593, there had been another falling out between Anne and Spencer, over both his drinking and his ill-treatment of the horses in his care. Anne relayed the end of the dispute to her son: 'he both lyed & wrangled disgracefully with me. Wherupon loth to troble my selff I bad with these wordes, A man master wolde go ny to breake thy head For this speach, but I byd the gett the owt of my syght lyke A lying prowde verlet. Wherupon glad belyke he went Immediatly to the stable & took his cloake & sword & jetted away lyke A jack. he was here both christianly & too well used here.'[114] Anne's contention was that it was Spencer's unruly speech which provoked her own verbal outburst. Moreover, she argued the necessity of such recourse through her own vulnerability as a widow, without a husband to discipline Spencer.

In his letter of 16 August 1594, Spencer had suggested that he was not the only one who felt that Anne was outspoken to the point of madness: 'There is not one man in the house but she fall out withal,' he wrote to Anthony Bacon, 'She put away Winter a fortnight, and took away his cloak, and then sent for him again. She have fallen out with both the Knights, and they do not mean to continue with her. There is not one in the house but she fall out withal, and is not in charity one day in a week; but with priests, which will undo her.'[115] Here too, however, context needs to be provided for Anne's actions. Thomas Knight continued with Anne long after Spencer suggested he meant to leave her service, although Anne continually complained to Anthony regarding his insubordination to her and the slackness of his behaviour.[116] There is also a need to provide context over Anne's previous dealings with Goodman Winter.

An altercation had already occurred between Anne and Winter in January 1594. Winter had acted towards Anne with 'undewteyfull demeanour and speeches', according to Anthony Bacon, who came to hear of his mother's treatment. He urged his mother that Winter should 'be called [to] account' for his words and actions; as he was at Redbourn, Anthony proposed sending Richard Lockey from St Albans to intervene on his behalf.[117] Anne's response was to reject his offer, entreating her son not to call upon Lockey:

> as For Winter's wordes, Fond inowgh to me. it is the man's custom they say, I make no great reasoning of such person's speches. I have such usage often where I owght not & have learned not to make A matter of every such & wold not have Mister Lockey deale in eny thing concerinng my selff. he is an open mowthed man with owt discretion, Full of Foolysh babling. he wold make all the town Ryng of his Foolyshnes. I pray yow defend not me thus way, I nether lyke it ner nede. prowd speaches [are] common & I am acqwanted with them & do rather contemn then regard.[118]

Anne attributed Winter's outburst to his personality, which accords with her son's judgement of 'winter's insolency', which 'beinge in things ordinary with him is or shalbe so much knowne and spoken of by his own braggs'.[119] His mother's disdain for loose speech is demonstrated not only by her treatment of Winter, but also by her rejection of Lockey's intervention, due to his reputation for indiscretion. Anne has accepted that such 'prowd speaches' will regularly be made to her by men, yet her response was to ignore them rather than to seek retribution.

The central issue underlying Spencer's representations of Anne and her interactions with Thomas Knight and Winter is power and influence. Whilst Anne's status did decline after her being widowed in 1579, she was left well provided for by her husband, receiving a life interest in Gorhambury and in the lease and copyhold lands surrounding the estate.[120] Thus whilst Anthony did receive properties directly from his father in his will, he would not gain control of Gorhambury and the nearby lands until his mother's death.[121] Yet Anne's authority over Gorhambury was contested, not least by her son's example.[122] She pleaded with her son not to make decisions on her behalf which would affect Gorhambury.[123] Anthony's servants, including Edward Spencer and Thomas Lawson, clearly rejected her authority as life mistress of Gorhambury. Edward Spencer's letter from 16 August 1594 centres on Thomas Lawson's role in sending a dog to Gorhambury against Anne's wishes, yet it was not the first time her authority had been contested in such a way. Earlier in 1594, Anne had complained to Anthony that men from his Redbourn estate visited Gorhambury 'allmost dayly' with their dogs, disordering her property.[124] In 1595 Anne again complained to Anthony regarding Lawson and Spencer's attitude towards Gorhambury, when they tried to leave their lame horses at the estate.[125] Anne was angered by servants repeatedly going to her son, either for decisions contrary to her wishes, or to complain of her.[126] She told Anthony on one occasion to reprimand a servant, writing 'goodram must not make my men his underlyngss to check & command'.[127] She complained that her son sent servants to take horses from Gorhambury without arrangement, which she could not abide: 'elce I geve over my Authyrite to my Inferiors which I think is A discreadit to eny of accompt that knows Rightly their place'.[128] The vulnerability of her position was even acknowledged by Anne herself, for she recognised that hers was only a life-interest and that the property would ultimately go to her son. She told Anthony that she bore to keep 'servannts of that sorte with Edward & such lyke', who have a tendency to 'brake of owt of order with me' for her son's good: 'I have it as I myght not, greving liberly to their hurt & my discredit, because I wold yow shuld every way be well & comfortably here.'[129]

The range of options available to Anne to counteract the infractions of Edward Spencer, Thomas Lawson and Anthony's other men was in actuality very limited. When Anne complained that Anthony's 'lavish' and 'idle' men from Redbourn plagued the Gorhambury estate, her answer was simple. 'I wolde owt my selff with all kind of Doggs Against them & kyll theirs', but she recognised that that was an impossibility, due to her physical vulnerability, as one 'syckly & weak'.[130] She appealed to Anthony to discipline them: 'I pray yow in my tyme tell my servaunts loke to me.'[131] Speech acts, such as that directed at Edward Spencer, were her only recourse and in reality Anne's speech often had little effect on the behaviour of the men of Gorhambury. One of her tenants sub-let some of his lands to Mr Rockett in 1596, whom Anne met coming onto the land carrying a hawk. Rockett exchanged 'prowd wordes' and 'qwarellpiking' with Anne, so much so that she was forced to send for the mayor as her only recourse.[132] Widowhood, for Anne, meant a contested independence, and it is the ambiguity of her status which lies at the heart of Spencer's condemnation of her as one so 'unquiet'.

ELIZABETH RUSSELL AND THE DONNINGTON CASTLE DISPUTE

Whilst the widowed Anne's 'unquietness' was perceived as madness, for her sister Elizabeth, outspokenness during her second widowhood was reported instead as 'more then womanlike'.[133] One of the most extreme examples of Elizabeth's outspokenness was demonstrated in 1606 at the first Star Chamber hearing over the Donnington Castle dispute. Elizabeth claimed to have held keepership of the castle since a grant in 1590, whilst in 1601 Donnington Castle was settled on Charles Howard, the Lord Admiral and earl of Nottingham, and his wife.[134] The dispute concerned the repossession of the Castle by Nottingham's men in 1603 and their refusal to allow Elizabeth Russell entry in person, which led to their being charged with riot and affray.

From the point of denying her entrance to Donnington, to the first Star Chamber hearing, issues were raised as to the widowed Elizabeth's outspokenness. James Bellingham, one of Nottingham's followers, testified in the Star Chamber that he spoke respectfully to Elizabeth whilst barring her entrance to Donnington Castle Lodge. Elizabeth instead told Robert Cecil that she remembered Bellingham taunting her, in response to her silence. She said that she then told Bellingham that she would not answer his baiting questions.[35] Bellingham apparently offered the following response to Elizabeth: 'Oh, sayth he, Belike yow think me like somme of your kin, that delight to heere them selves speake. He sayth in his awnser that I called him knave, which on my fayth I did not, skorning to 'fyle my mowth with a servant who did but his Duty for matter, thogh not in manner.'[36] Elizabeth protested her silence against Bellingham's accusations in that instance, but by the time the case reached the Star Chamber, she certainly expressed her opinions forcefully. Elizabeth looked unlikely to win her prosecution of a nobleman for trespassing on his own property.[37] The law reporter Hawarde noted that, faced with defeat, Elizabeth decided to intervene: 'the Judges ... began to moove the Courte; but the Ladye, interruptinge them, desyred to be hearde, & after many denyalls by the Courte, vyolentelye & with greate audacitie beganne a large discourse, and woulde not by nay meanes be stayed nor interrupted, but wente one for the space of halfe an howre or more'.[38] Despite the negative reaction to her speech, including the response from her own counsel, Elizabeth would not be stopped. She was determined to defend her honour and nobility through speech, as she did through her verse on the family's funeral monuments.[39] Hawarde then described Elizabeth's manner of speech and her supposed aim from such actions, arguing that she spoke,

> in a verye boulde & stoute manner, withoute any shewe of any distemparature, or any loude speakinge, but shewing a very great spirite & an undaunted Courage, or rather will, more then womanlike, whose revenge by her tounge semed to be the summe of her desyre ... in an meaner personage, it is usuallye termed 'mallice' & 'envye', but in her, beinge honorable, learned, & indued with many excellente guyftes, wee grace it with 'a great spirite', which I feare the worlde conceavethe to be more then blemyshed, if not utterlye extinguyshed, with extreame pryde.[40]

Hawarde's representation of Elizabeth in these passages deserves close analysis. Whilst she spoke in a 'boulde & stoute manner', Hawarde admitted that her speech was without 'distemparature, or any loude speakinge': Elizabeth's speech was calm and controlled, an act of oration conditioned by her education. Yet for Hawarde, such speech acts took her beyond appropriate activity for a woman, ungendering her and making her 'more then womanlike'. Hawarde's rhetorical argument protested, rather hollowly, that her familial connections saved Elizabeth from complete condemnation, yet her political vulnerability was apparent to the participants at the hearing. She had asked her nephew Robert Cecil to be present at the hearing to 'Censure according to Justice and Equity'; as a privy councillor, Cecil would have sat among the judges of the case.[41] Yet he did not attend that hearing, or the second hearing, ignoring his aunt's request.[42] Aware of her vulnerable position as a widow, Elizabeth was forced to resort to speech. With her political isolation apparent to the hearing, Hawarde joined the rest in 'condemning greatly' her outspokenness, going so far as to label her as a woman without virtue: envious, malicious and full of pride. In this instance, without defenders or political influence, the widowed Elizabeth Russell was open to censure as an early modern learned woman.

CONCLUSION

This chapter has looked in more detail at the reputations of the Cooke sisters, seeking in all cases to gain an awareness of the circumstances in which their representations originated. In many instances, the sisters' learning did not feature at all in their images or descriptions, yet when their erudition was mentioned, a more complex picture emerges of the early modern learned woman than previous research has acknowledged. The sisters were lauded as akin to the classical Muses, yet, unlike fifteenth-century Italian women, such mythologising was not the result of their exclusion from the world of politics, rather it was a response to their influence and power. The sisters' marriages had made them desirable intermediaries for clients, and the imagery of their many dedicatory verses and other positive representations reflects this fact. Only when their political influence began to fade were they increasingly at risk of critique, due to the outspokenness that resulted from their rhetorical education. Ultimately, the representations of the Cookes reveal how very difficult it is to assess the worth of female education in early modern England. Female scholarship in the sixteenth century was limited to women from elite families and as such was desirable as long as their social status remained. The example of the widowhoods of Elizabeth and Anne reveal that it is only when political power and influence starts to wane that learned women are labelled with any certainty as mad, bad and, worse, 'more than womanlike'.

NOTES

1 G. DuCann, 'Ghosts at Gray's Inn', *Graya*, 1 (1927), 27; R. Tittler, *Nicholas Bacon: The Making of a Tudor Statesman* (1976), p. 51.

2 P. Compton, *The Story of Bisham Abbey* (Maidenhead and Trowbridge, 1973), p. 104.

3 *Ibid.*, p. 105.

4 *Ibid.*, p. 104.

5 The earliest references appear to be connected to a discovery in 1840 noted by Mrs

General Vansittart, the then owner of Bisham Abbey. She recalled finding a collection of old copybooks under the floorboards when completing some renovations at Bisham. She remembered that the copybooks were 'all signed by various names of the Hobby family and corrected by Lady Russell', adding, 'In one of William Hobby, I think, every leaf had some blot'. Mrs General Vansittart lamented that the copybooks went missing soon after their discovery, presumed sold by the workmen. For her recollections, see E. Dormer, 'Bisham', *Berks, Bucks and Oxon Archaeological Journal*, 12 (1909), 94–5. There are various problems with this tale. There are no records of Elizabeth having a son named William Hoby or William Russell. Even in Mrs General Vansittart's recollections she seems unsure if the name on the blotted copybooks was William. It may be that the story of the doomed 'William Hoby' developed in the Vansittart family after the discovery of the copybooks, fuelled by the presence of the striking portrait and tomb of Lady Elizabeth Hoby Russell at Bisham. A later 'sighting' of Elizabeth's ghost comes from Mrs General Vansittart's son Edward and Victorian retellings of the story afford prominence to the discovery of the copybooks. See Compton, *Bisham Abbey*, p. 106; R. Chambers, *The Book of Days: A Miscellany of Popular Antiquities* (2 vols, 1879), I, p. 475. As with many legends, the ghost tales built on allusions to fact. Elizabeth certainly was not overly fond of her youngest Hoby son, Thomas Posthumous, whom she criticised to Burghley for 'insufficiency by want of stature, learning and otherwise'. Thomas, however, lived to the grand age of 78. For Elizabeth's criticisms of Thomas Posthumous, see BL, Lansdowne MS 10, fo. 136v: 25/08/1584. For another early modern ghost story and its refashioning by subsequent generations, see P. Marshall, *Mother Leakey and the Bishop* (Oxford, 2007).

6 Vives, pp. 94–5.

7 Richard Hyrde quoted in Vives, p. 162–3.

8 For Mary Herbert, see J. Aubrey, *Brief Lives*, ed. R. Barber (1982), pp. 139–40. For attacks on the sexual promiscuity of Isotta Nogarola, see M. King, 'Book-lined cells: women and humanism in the early Italian Renaissance', in P. Labalme (ed.), *Beyond Their Sex: Learned Women of the European Past* (New York, 1980), pp. 76–7.

9 For example, reading is shown as triggering the mental instability of Dol Common in Jonson's play, *The Alchemist* (1610). See R. O'Day, *Women's Agency in Early Modern Britain and the American Colonies* (Harlow, 2007), p. 411. See also J. Pearson, 'Women reading, reading women', in H. Wilcox (ed.), *Women and Literature in Britain 1500–1700* (Cambridge, 1996), pp. 85–6; R. Porter, 'Reading is bad for your health', *History Today*, 48/3 (March 1998), 12.

10 See, for example, J.R. Brink, 'Introduction', in J.R. Brink (ed.), *Female Scholars: A Tradition of Learned Women before 1800* (Montreal, 1980), p. 5; P. Labalme, 'Introduction', in P. Labalme (ed.), *Beyond Their Sex: Learned Women of the European Past* (New York, 1980), pp. 4–6; M.E. Lamb, 'The Cooke sisters: attitudes toward learned women in the Renaissance', in M.P. Hannay (ed.), *Silent But for the Word* (Kent, Ohio, 1985), pp. 114–15.

11 Vives, pp. 87–8, 92, 166–7.

12 King, 'Book-lined cells', pp. 75–80.

13 *Ibid.*, p. 74.

14 L. Jardine '"O Decus Italiae Virgo", or the myth of the learned lady in the Renaissance', *HJ*, 28 (1985), 815–16.

15 This, for example, compares with their contemporaries, the Seymour sisters, whose

political worth was strongest during their virginal years, whilst their father was Lord Protector.

16 P. Croft, 'Mildred, Lady Burghley: the matriarch', in P. Croft (ed.), *Patronage, Culture and Power: The Early Cecils* (2002), p. 283.

17 J. Clapham, *Elizabeth of England: Certain Observations concerning of Life and Reign of Queen Elizabeth*, ed. E. Plummer Read and C. Read (Oxford, 1951), pp. 84–5.

18 For the Seymour sisters, see B.M. Hosington, 'England's first female-authored encomium: the Seymour sisters' *Hecatodistichon* (1550)', *Studies in Philology*, 93 (1996), 117–63. For Lady Jane Grey, see J.S. Edwards, '"Jane the Quene": A New Consideration of Lady Jane Grey, England's Nine-Days Queen' (PhD thesis, University of Colorado at Boulder, 2007), pp. 48–53.

19 See chapter 1 for discussion of these references.

20 For Margaret's service for Mary, see NA, LC 5/31, fo. 107r and C 66/932/m3.

21 BL, Cotton MS Titus A.XXIV, fo. 79r. Ros King suggests the poem must have been written before the marriage of Katherine Bridges in December 1555. See R. Edwards, *The Works of Richard Edwards*, ed. R. King (Manchester, 2001), p. 231.

22 The allusion to Margaret's comeliness may be misleading. Edwards's poem is based around finding a 'flattering, yet teasing' adjective to alliterate with each of the ladies' names; Arundel is therefore 'aunciaunte in thes her tender yeare'. See Edwards, *The Works of Richard Edwards*, ed. King, p. 231.

23 For Haddon's letter to William Cecil, see BL, Lansdowne MS 3, fo. 19r: 11/11/1552. For Mildred's letter advancing the match, see BL, Lansdowne MS 104, fo. 156r: n.d.

24 BL, Lansdowne MS 98, fo. 252r: n.d.

25 BL, Lansdowne MS 103, fo. 67r: 21/04/1589; Bodl., Gough Maps 44.249; CP Maps II/14.

26 Clapham, *Elizabeth of England*, p. 73.

27 P. Croft and K. Hearn, '"Only matrimony maketh children to be certain ...": Two Elizabethan pregnancy portraits', *British Art Journal*, 3 (2002), 24.

28 Cecil's memorandum book noted all of Mildred's births, beginning with Francisca. See BL, Lansdowne MS 118, fo. 82v.

29 Croft and Hearn, 'Two Elizabethan pregnancy portraits', 22.

30 NA, SP 68/6, fo. 4r: 07/01/1551.

31 CP 151, fo. 141r: 10/01/1556. See also CP 152, fo. 8r: 27/03/1557.

32 NA, SP 70/26, fo. 62r: 08/05/1561; NA, SP 12/26, fo. 22r: 15/12/1562.

33 BL, Lansdowne MS 103, fo. 117r. Inscription on Mildred's tomb, Chapel of St Nicholas, Westminster Abbey, London. Translation by Margaret Stewardson from an unpublished text held at Westminster Abbey Library.

34 BL, Lansdowne MS 103, fo. 167r: 21/04/1589.

35 N. Bacon, *The Recreations of His Age* (Oxford, 1919), p. 27. For Thomas Hoby's expenses in taking his whole family to Paris, see NA, SP 70/84, fo. 172r.

36 BL, Lansdowne MS 10, fo. 137r. For Elizabeth's commemorative verse for John Russell, see chapter 2.

37 A. Miller, *Sir Henry Killigrew: Elizabethan Soldier and Diplomat* (Leicester, 1963), pp.

98–9.

38 D. Erasmus, *The Correspondence of Erasmus*, ed. R.A.B. Mynors *et al.*, *Collected Works of Erasmus*, 8 (Toronto, 1988), p. 298.

39 Translation by Margaret Stewardson. Burghley's *Precepts* also cite the importance of choosing a wife wisely and disdaining foolish women. 'For it wyll like thee to heare her talke, and thou shalt finde (to thy great griefe) that there is nothying so fulsome as a shee foole': W. Cecil, *The Counsell of a Father to his Sonne, in ten severall Precepts* (1611), single-page sheet.

40 Bacon, *Recreations of His Age*, p. 27.

41 BN, Dupuy 951, fo. 122v.

42 M. Loudon, 'Daniel Rogers', *ODNB*.

43 J. Bruce and T.T. Perowne (eds), *The Correspondence of Matthew Parker* (Parker Society, Cambridge, 1853), p. 316.

44 See chapter 5 for a discussion of the disagreement between Bacon and Parker.

45 G. Buchanan, *Georgii Buchanani Scoti poemata in tres partes digesta* (1686), p. 438.

46 NA, SP 12/47, fo. 18r: 09/07/1568. The poem was also copied out by Jan Dousa, which, as Jane Stevenson has rightly argued, suggests it was circulating in European humanist circles. See BN, Dupuy 951, fo. 291r and J. Stevenson, 'Mildred Cecil, Lady Burleigh: poetry, politics and Protestantism', in V. Burke and J. Gibson (eds), *Early Modern Manuscript Writing: Selected Papers from the Trinity/Trent Colloquium* (Aldershot, 2004), p. 69.

47 Ballard, p. 207.

48 C. Ockland, 'To the noble and most vertuous Lady ... Myldred', in C. Ockland, *Elizabeth Queene*, trans. J. Sharrock (1585), sig. 3r. See also C. Ockland, *EIPHNAPXIA, sive Elizabetha* (1582), sigs A3r–v.

49 F. Teague, 'Early modern women and "the muses ffemall"', in R. Evans and A. Little (eds), *'The muses females are': Martha Moulsworth and other Women Writers of the English Renaissance* (West Cornwall, CT, 1995), pp. 173–9.

50 Buchanan, *Scoti poemata*, p. 438.

51 *Ibid.*, p. 236.

52 *Ibid.*

53 *Ibid.*, pp. 236–7.

54 *Ibid.*, pp. 237–8.

55 NA, SP 12/47, fo. 17r.

56 For Junius's verse for William Cecil, see *ibid.*, fos 15r–16v, 20r. For *Eunapius Sardianus*, see J. Stevenson, *Women Latin Poets: Language, Gender and Authority, from Antiquity to the Eighteenth Century* (Oxford, 2005), p. 264; I.M. Veldman, 'Hadrianus Junius', *ODNB*.

57 My italics. U. Fulwell, 'A Dialogue betweene the Author and his Muse', in U. Fulwell, *Ars adulandi, the art of Flattery* (1576), sig. 2r.

58 C. Ockland, 'To the noble and most vertuous Lady ... Myldred', sig. 3r.

59 Ballard, p. 207.

60 *Ascham Letters*, p. 182.

61 *Ibid.*, p. 183.

62 R. O'Day, 'Roger Ascham', *ODNB*. For Ascham's seeking preferment from William Cecil, see BL, Lansdowne MS 3, fo. 3r: 27/09/1552; fo. 5r: 28/11/1552; fo. 77r: 24/03/1553; fo. 61r: 09/07/1553.

63 NA, SP 68/6, fo. 28v: 03/02/1551. See also chapter 1.

64 Ascham's fairness is demonstrated by his descriptions of the learning of the Princess Elizabeth. He praises the latter's erudition in another letter to Johann Sturm in 1550 and then again after her accession to the throne in *The Schoolmaster* (1570); in both instances, however, he celebrates her command of Greek far less than her facility in Latin, French and Italian, despite wishing to remain close to his former pupil. See *Elizabeth I: Translations, 1544–1589*, ed. J. Mueller and J. Scodel (Chicago, 2009), p. 11.

65 NA, SP 68/11, fo. 8v: 01/1553.

66 See O. Morata, *The Complete Writings of an Italian Heretic*, ed. H.N. Parker (Chicago, 2003), p. 179.

67 There is also no evidence as to the outcome of Karel Utenhove's suggestion in 1564 to Jean de Morel that his highly educated daughter Camille should start a correspondence with Mildred. Stevenson, *Women Latin Poets*, p. 190.

68 For Morison's demands for his diplomatic diets, see NA, SP 68/11, fo. 8v.

69 The group had formerly celebrated the verses of the Seymour sisters in the 1551 edition of their *Hecatodistichon*, published in Paris by the girls' tutor, Nicolas Denisot. See Hosington, 'England's first female-authored encomium', 118.

70 BN, Dupuy 951, fo. 122v. See chapter 2 for detailed analysis of the poem.

71 NA, SP 70/85, fo. 41r: 17/07/1566.

72 I. McFarlane, *Buchanan* (1981), p. 236.

73 Buchanan, *Scoti poemata*, sig. T5r.

74 BN, NAL 106, p. 152.

75 For Katherine's poems to Buchanan, see chapter 2.

76 NA, SP 10/15, fo. 178a: c. 1552. See chapter 1 for a more detailed discussion of this letter.

77 CP 59, fo. 93r: 22/02/1599.

78 E. Dering, *Certaine godly and comfortable Letters* (1614), sigs C3r–C5v.

79 Ballard, p. 207.

80 BL, Lansdowne MS 68, fo. 131r: 13/08/1591. The rejection of the praise of female learning for an exhortation to piety is also evidenced by John Calvin in writing to the Seymour sisters. See J. Calvin, *Joannis Calvini opera quae supersunt omnia*, ed. J. Baum *et al.* (59 vols, Brunswick, 1863–1901), XIII, cols. 300–302, no. 1207.

81 C. Ockland, 'To the noble and most vertuous Lady ... Myldred', sig. 3r.

82 Fulwell, 'A Dialogue betweene the Author and his Muse', sig. 2r.

83 K. Utenhove, *Xenia, seu ad illustrium aliquot Europæ hominum nomina allusionum* (Basel, 1568), pp. 69–70.

84 Translation from Stevenson, 'Mildred Cecil, Lady Burleigh', p. 58.

85 If the piece were about Mildred, then the pronoun would have been ad or in. See Stevenson, 'Mildred Cecil, Lady Burghley', p. 59.

86 Buchanan, *Scoti poemata*, sig. U3v.

87 CP 146, fo. 11r: 29/04/?1575.

88 G. Whetstone, *The Rocke of Regard* (1576), p. 124.

89 *Ibid.*, p. 123.

90 LPL 647, fo. 245r: 17/08/1589.

91 See LPL 659, fos 24v–25r.

92 LPL 647, fo. 245r.

93 *Ibid.*, fo. 245v.

94 *Ibid.*, fo. 246r.

95 *Ibid.*

96 T. Birch, *Memoirs of the Reign of Queen Elizabeth* (2 vols, 1754), I, pp. 67–8; L. Jardine and A. Stewart, *Hostage to Fortune: The Troubled Life of Francis Bacon, 1561–1626* (1998), p. 126.

97 LPL 648, fos 86r–v: 05/09/1591.

98 LPL 648, fo. 94r: 01/09/1591.

99 See LPL 650, fos 50r–v; P. Hammer, 'Patronage at court, faction and the earl of Essex', in J. Guy (ed.), *The Reign of Elizabeth I: Court and Culture in the Last Decade* (Cambridge, 1995), p. 72.

100 Goodman instead described Mildred as a 'most virtuous and good lady'. See G. Goodman, *The Court of King James the First*, ed. J.S. Brewer (2 vols, 1839), I, p. 285.

101 Spedding, p. 310.

102 P. Collinson, 'Sir Nicholas Bacon and the Elizabethan *via media*', *HJ*, 23 (1980), 151.

103 Jardine and Stewart, *Francis Bacon*, p. 166. See also A. Stewart, 'The voices of Anne Cooke, Lady Anne and Lady Bacon', in D. and E. Clarke (eds), *This Double Voice: Gendered Writing in Early Modern England* (Basingstoke, 2000), pp. 89, 99.

104 Spedding, p. 310; D. du Maurier, *Golden Lads: A Study of Anthony Bacon, Francis and their Friends* (1975), pp. 121–2; Jardine and Stewart, *Francis Bacon*, pp. 166–7; Stewart, 'The voices of Anne Cooke', pp. 89, 99.

105 It is often suggested that Spencer was only with Anne during the summer of 1594, however the first mention of his service for Anne comes in May 1593. See LPL 649, fo. 121r: 25/05/1593.

106 Spencer's letters are here quoted from the modernised version in Spedding for the reader's convenience, due to Spencer's eccentric spelling. The reference to the original letter is, however, also given in each case. Spedding, pp. 310–11; LPL 651, fo. 229r: 07/1594; LPL 651, fo. 253r: 16/08/1594.

107 Spedding, p. 312; LPL 651, fo. 254r.

108 *Ibid.*

109 Spedding suggested that the word meant may have been 'keeping'. Spedding, p. 310.

110 Spedding, p. 310; LPL 651, fo. 229r.

111 Spedding, p. 311; LPL 651, fo. 253r.

112 LPL 649, fo. 121r: 25/05/1593.

113 *Ibid.*

114 LPL 653, fo. 363r: 31/05/1593.

115 Spedding, p. 312; LPL 651, fo. 253r.

116 See LPL 651, fo. 110r: 26/04/1595; 653, fo. 328r: n.d.; fo. 333r: 20/08/n.y.

117 LPL 649, fo. 22r: 10/01/1594.

118 LPL 653, fo. 365r: n.d.

119 LPL 649, fo. 22r.

120 She also was bequeathed the remnant of the lease of York House in London and she was to receive sheep stocks from her stepson Nicholas, from Ingham and Tymworth in Suffolk, properties related to her jointure. She also received plate, jewels, horses, coaches, litters and the household stuff from York House, as well as half the household contents at Gorhambury. See A. Hassell Smith, G. Baker and R. Kenny (eds), *The Papers of Nathaniel Bacon of Stiffkey* (4 vols, Norfolk Record Society, 46, 49, 53, 64, Norwich, 1979–2000), II, pp. 25–9.

121 Anthony received Redbourne and Barley in Hertfordshire and Pinner Park in Middlesex. See *ibid.*

122 For example, she resisted attempts to override her authority in January 1597 by both her nephew Edward Hoby and William Brooke, Lord Cobham. See LPL 654, fo. 45r: 01/1597.

123 In October 1593 Anthony promised not 'to medle with ought els that concerneth your Ladyship livinge ^withowt your leave^'. The addition of 'withowt your leave' makes clear the difficulty of Anne's position as a widow. See LPL 649, fo. 337r: 19/10/1593.

124 LPL 649, fo. 37r: 25/02/1594.

125 LPL 651, fo. 165r: 15/05/1595.

126 See LPL 651, fo. 310r; 652, fo. 129r; 653, fos 256r, 366r.

127 LPL 653, fo. 254r: n.d.

128 LPL 656, fo. 47r: 18/03/1597.

129 LPL 653, fo. 252r: n.d.

130 LPL 648, fo. 37r: 25/02/1594.

131 *Ibid.* On occasion, Anthony protested to his mother that he had indeed disciplined her servants. See, for example, LPL 657, fo. 154r: 07/09/1596.

132 LPL 653, fo. 354r: 03/08/1596. This was most likely the same Rockett who served as the official and registrar to the archdeacon of St Albans, which would suggest religious differences were at the heart of the quarrel.

133 J. Hawarde, *Les Reportes del Cases in Camera Stellata 1593 to 1609*, ed. T.P. Baildon (1894), p. 275.

134 For more on this dispute, see *ibid*, pp. 434–5.

135 CP 119, fo. 73r: 06/11/1606.

136 *Ibid.*

137 F. Heal, 'Reputation and honour in court and country: Lady Elizabeth Russell and Sir Thomas Hoby', *TRHS*, 6th series, 6 (1996), 167.

138 Hawarde, *Les Reportes del Cases*, p. 275.

139 See chapter 2 for Elizabeth's commemorative verse.

140 Hawarde, *Les Reportes del Cases*, p. 275.

141 CP 119, fo. 74r: 13/05/1606.

142 CP 119, fo. 73r: 06/11/1606.

Conclusion

———◆———

Elizabeth Russell returned repeatedly to the same line in her commemorative verse: 'Quod licuit feci, vellum mihi plura licere' (I have done what was allowed, I wish more were allowed of me).[1] Her meditation has already been considered for its relation to her funerary verse, but it has a more general significance for what it tells us about Elizabeth and her sisters as examples of sixteenth-century womanhood. Her acknowledgement of the restrictions placed upon her by a patriarchal society was justified: she could not study at educational institutions, hold political office or take holy orders, unlike her male contemporaries.[2] However, this book has concentrated on the implications of the phrase 'Quod licuit feci' and on uncovering exactly what Elizabeth and her sisters were able to achieve, particularly in the fields of education, piety and politics. It has not concentrated solely on the prescriptive context, but instead has also paid close attention to what the writings of the Cooke sisters themselves reveal about the agency of sixteenth-century elite women. Burghley himself confessed in 1589 that he discovered the extent of Mildred's activities as a patron only after her death, through study of the 'ernest wrytyngs' she left behind.[3]

The Cooke sisters' education has been at the centre of their posthumous reputation, but by reconstructing their libraries, the breadth of their scholarship has been revealed for the first time. The sisters' reading went far beyond even the considerable list set by Juan Luis Vives for Princess Mary and reveals the limitations of relying solely on the prescriptive context. Moreover, rather than using their learning primarily to read religious works, the Cookes were familiar with a wide variety of classical and contemporary texts, including those which were often thought unsuitable for women, such as Terence and Boccaccio. Many of the texts owned by the sisters were first editions, showing the impact that print had on the education of women. Print allowed them access, within the household, to texts previously only accessible in manuscript form and books normally found only within educational institutions. Working on the late medieval period, Mary Erler has emphasised the continuities of women's popular religious reading across the advent of print, yet the example of the Cooke sisters reveals the difference that print made to the reading of one set of learned women.[4] Print enabled the sisters to continue to educate themselves throughout their lives.

Their humanist education also had a practical utility, as it provided them

233

with opportunities to communicate through the written word. The act of translation offered the Cooke sisters the chance not only to bolster their political networks, but also to contribute to strengthening the faith of their contemporaries. Close engagement with Anne Cooke Bacon's widely disseminated 1564 translation of Jewel's *Apologia Ecclesiae Anglicanae* has revealed her involvement with issues of national importance to the reformed faith, far beyond the rhetorical stance portrayed in the dedicatory material to her work and in tandem with the priorities of her husband and her brother-in-law William Cecil. For her sister Elizabeth, classical learning too allowed her opportunities with the written word. Through neo-Latin and Greek verse, she could advance her self-image as an educated woman and speak clearly about issues close to her heart, legitimated by classical ideas concerning feminine mourning. Through correspondence, the sisters could use the written word to offer political and religious counsel to men. As women, the Cookes were aware of the vulnerability of their counsel within a patriarchal society; however, they turned their humanist training to good effect in providing strategies to bolster their advice-giving. They strategically utilised rhetorical appeals to their own political and religious experience in their correspondence, whilst also making considerable reference to their classical and scriptural learning. This allowed them to conceal, emphasise and legitimate their epistolary counsel, particularly through recourse to their reading in the form of *sententiae*, highlighting their shared educational background to their male correspondents. Through their *sententiae*, we also have an insight into the practical use that the sisters made of their reading. This evidence of the Cookes as active readers can be placed aside their extant marginalia. Although the sisters' Greek marginalia do not allow a full exploration of their reading practices, it reveals that they were not silenced in the margins of their texts, although their interaction was limited to the highly educated within their households. These scholarly endeavours were part of their married lives and later the widowhoods of Anne and Elizabeth. Marriage, rather than restricting their learned activities, was a period in which they could pursue their intellectual interests.

Family connections through marriage were also of paramount importance to the considerable influence the sisters held as intermediaries and brokers of political and religious patronage; the influence of their marital relationships was, however, more complex than previous work on women's kin networks has acknowledged. The sisters' marriages allowed them the political agency to act as intermediaries for men at the highest levels of Elizabethan government. This was most obviously true in the case of Mildred Cooke Cecil, who worked alongside her husband in the pursuit of 'British' security in the 1560s and 1570s, as another facet in the intelligence-gathering web that Stephen Alford has shown as being centred on William Cecil.[5] Yet Mildred has also been revealed as capable of working against her husband over the controversial godly preacher Edward Dering, demonstrating that Conyers Read's argument that Mildred was silenced as a political figure from 1570 onwards is simply not borne out by the evidence.[6] Widowhood is also shown as a period of considerable influence for Elizabeth and Anne. Their kin networks meant that they were still recognised as influential intermediaries through their familial access to William and Robert Cecil. Here analysis of Elizabeth's role as an intermediary between the Cecils and the Essex circle has revealed her to be a more substantial and less inept broker than has been acknowledged by previous research on the political culture of the 1590s. Moreover, widowhood allowed the sisters greater freedom to work on behalf of godly figures; the limits of Anne's influence for godly clerics during the life of Nicholas Bacon are revealed by the erasure of her name in the Sylva manuscript. Exploration of the differences between the sisters' godly identities demonstrates in another way the complexity of the family bonds at the heart of this study.

The arenas in which the sisters were empowered as agents have also been a central concern of this book. Previous research on women's political and religious agency has tended to focus on the spaces of the household and the court. This study has shown that the sisters were influential not only within the setting of the English court, but also at the French court, in the case of Elizabeth, and in other arenas of 'high politics'. Elizabeth's interest in the activities of Parliament was testified to by her description of herself as a 'parlament woman', whilst Anne attended the session in the House of Commons on 25 February 1585; in both cases, there is evidence that the sisters' parliamentary activities were facilitated by their private connections, with Robert Cecil and his father, Lord Burghley, respectively.[7] Moreover, through their correspondence, the sisters' influence was felt across English borders, as demonstrated by Mildred's involvement in Anglo-Scottish and Irish politics. The case of Anne's godly patronage has shown that the household, rather than representing the bounds of her religious agency, instead was a microcosm of her activities as an ecclesiastical patron in her local community. The evidence of the spatial dimensions of the Cookes' agency rejects a simple dichotomy of gendered separation between the private, domestic and female sphere and the public, political and male sphere.[8] Instead their activities emphasise the complexity of the boundaries between 'public' and 'private' in this period. Their writings too engage with the contested nature of these concepts, shown by Anne's frequent and varied rhetorical use of the terms in her letters, as we have seen.[9] Created within the private household, her translation of the *Apologia* was intended to be a method of mobilising public Protestant opinion, which in itself generated Catholic hostility. Both the activities and the writings of the Cooke sisters thus reveal that there is further work to done in order to elucidate the relationship between women and conceptions of 'public' and 'private' in the later sixteenth century.

The sisters' agency was grounded in a combination of their formal, humanist education and their political and religious networks, engendered by their high-profile marriages. Anne herself recognised the potency of this combination when describing herself to her son as one of the 'few preclarae feminae meae sortis' (distinguished women of my sort).[10] Anne's implicit reference to her educational background in her Latin phrase makes apparent that the agency she derived from her scholarship was unusual, shared by only a small number of their female contemporaries. The sisters' learning informed their political and religious agency at many points, as demonstrated explicitly through their use of their classical language skills, or more incidentally, for example through Elizabeth's recourse to her knowledge of judicial oration when questioning her nephew Anthony Bacon. This book has therefore questioned previous research which has argued that early modern women were excluded from using their humanist education to political ends. However, it also has a wider import for further study on early modern elite women, as the evidence from the detailed reconstruction of the Cooke sisters' political and religious networks highlights new areas for future research. Elizabeth's involvement in her husband's 1566 embassy to Paris raises the issue of the influence of wives in diplomatic culture, a result of the Tudor development of resident embassies, as does Mildred's participation in matters of international diplomacy. Similarly, more work on women's lay ecclesiastical patronage throughout the later sixteenth century is surely overdue in order to integrate women more fully into the narrative of the Protestantisation of England.

Finally, the representations of the Cooke sisters in verse and correspondence reveal how their agency was perceived by their contemporaries. Previous research has explored condemnatory images of learned early modern women, but the language and ideas used in the contemporary descriptions of the Cookes is more complex. The considerable number of dedicatory verses, from clients across Europe, demonstrates the extent of their perceived influence as intermediaries for patronage. Moreover, it is apparent that positive representations of the Cookes' learning, and thus the value ascribed to their high-level of education, were dependent upon this perceived power; only during the widowhoods of Elizabeth and Anne, when that influence starts to wane, are they open to critique as educated women.

Such negative representations highlight the ever-present issue of the patriarchal restrictions upon the sisters' agency. Ultimately, this study argues for the flexibility of such codes. At many points during their lives, the sisters were confronted with restrictive social conventions, yet their political connections and their sense of godly election empowered them to negotiate such constraints, armed as they were with the tools of a male scholar. By exploring the evidence from the Cookes' own libraries and writings, a more complex and detailed picture is gained of the power of these sisters as educated, pious and political women within a patriarchal society.

NOTES

1 See chapter 2 for a more detailed discussion of the line.

2 Unusually, Elizabeth was appointed to a crown office in 1590, as Keeper of the Queen's Castle of Donnington and Baliff of the Honour, Lordship and Manor of Donnington. As we have seen, her claim to the keepership was, however, disputed on various grounds; one of the issues discussed was whether a woman could hold this office because 'it appertains to the war, and is to be executed by men only'. See chapter 6 for details of the dispute. For discussion of the holding of the office by a woman, see J. Hawarde, *Les Reportes del Cases in Camera Stellata 1593 to 1609*, ed. T.P. Baildon (1894), p. 435; G. Croke, *Reports of Sir George Croke, Knight* (3 vols, Dublin, 1791–93), II, p. 18.

3 BL, Lansdowne MS 103, fo. 117r.

4 M. Erler, *Women, Reading and Piety in Late Medieval England* (Cambridge, 2002), p. 135.

5 S. Alford, *The Early Elizabethan Polity: William Cecil and the British Succession Crisis, 1558–1569* (Cambridge, 1998).

6 C. Read, *Lord Burghley and Queen Elizabeth* (1960), pp. 446, 448.

7 CP 90, fo. 151r; BL, Lansdowne MS 43, fo. 119r.

8 Important contributions to the separate spheres debate include A. Vickery, 'Golden age to separate spheres? A review of the categories and chronology of English women's history', *HJ*, 36 (1993), 383–414; L. Klein, 'Gender and the public/private distinction in the eighteenth century: some questions about evidence and analytic procedure', *Eighteenth Century Studies*, 29 (1995), 97–109; L. Davidoff, 'Regarding some old husbands' tales: public and private in feminist history', in L. Davidoff, *Worlds Between: Historical Perspectives on Gender and Class* (Oxford, 1995), pp. 227–76; L. Davidoff, 'Gender and the "Great Divide": public and private in British gender history', *Journal of Women's History*, 15 (2003), 11–27.

9 For Anne's use of 'public' and 'private', see chapter 3. For use of the terms by early modern men, see N. Mears, *Queenship and Political Discourse in the Elizabethan Realms* (Cambridge, 2005), pp. 86–7; A. Hughes, 'Men, the "public" and the "private" in the English revolution', in P. Lake and S. Pincus (eds), *The Politics of the Public Sphere in Early Modern England* (Manchester, 2007), pp. 191–212.

10 LPL 651, fo. 156r.

Bibliography

MANUSCRIPT SOURCES

BERKSHIRE RECORD OFFICE, READING
D1/A2 Archdeaconry of Berkshire records

BIBLIOTHÈQUE NATIONALE, PARIS
fonds Dupuy
951
Fonds Latin
18592
Nouvelles acquisitions latines (NAL)
106 Volume of poetry by George Buchanan

BODLEIAN LIBRARY, OXFORD
Carte
LVI, LVII, LVIII, CXXXI Papers of Sir William Fitzwilliam
Maps
Gough 44
MS. Eng.
c. 7065.
Rawlinson
B 146

BRITISH LIBRARY, LONDON
Additional
35830
36294
4115
18764
19400
28571
29546
38823
Cotton
Nero B.I.
Titus B.II
Vespasian C.VII
Egerton

1671
2148
2713
Harleian
871
1877
7017
Lansdowne
3
5
9–10
12
18–20
23
25
28
31
33
38
40
43
51
61
68
76
79
83
91
98
102–4
109
118
Royal
5 E.XVII Anthony Cooke, Latin translation of St Gregory Nazianzen's *Theophania*
12 A.I–IV Volumes of *sententiae* collected by Mary Fitzalan
17 B.XVIII Mildred Cecil's translation of a sermon by St Basil
Sloane
2063

CAMBRIDGE UNIVERSITY LIBRARY, CAMBRIDGE

MS Ff.v.14 Commonplace book of W. Kytton
MS Ii.v.37 *Giardino Cosmografico Da Bartholo Sylva*

UNIVERSITY OF EDINBURGH LIBRARY, EDINBURGH

Laing MS III/193 Anthony Bacon's commonplace book

Bibliography

ESSEX RECORD OFFICE, CHELMSFORD

D/DMS/T12/4
D/DMS/Q3
D/DMY/15M50/328
Sage collection 773

FOLGER SHAKESPEARE LIBRARY, WASHINGTON DC

L.d. Bacon/Townshend MSS
X.c.87

GUILDHALL LIBRARY, LONDON

GL 9531/13 Registers of the bishop of London, 1559–1627
GL 9531/14 Registers of the bishop of London, 1600–1632

HATFIELD HOUSE, HERTFORDSHIRE

Cecil Papers
25
27–8
30–3
35
37
41
43
49
52–3
57–9
63
68
73–4
82
86–88
90
106
114
118–19
126
128
140
143
146
152–3
155
157
170
175–6

178–80
186
197
226
298
1949
Maps II/14 Sketch for Cecil tomb, 1562

HERTFORDSHIRE ARCHIVES AND LOCAL STUDIES, HERTFORD
Records of the Archdeaconry of St Albans
Act Books
ASA 7/10, 26 May 1574–January 1619
Miscellaneous Papers
ASA 5/1–5, 1575–1637

HUNTINGTON LIBRARY, SAN MARINO, CALIFORNIA
HM 1340 Commonplace book of Nicholas Bacon

LAMBETH PALACE LIBRARY, LONDON
Anthony Bacon Papers
647
648
649
650
651
652
653
654
655
656
657
658
659
660
661
Talbot MS
3203

LINCOLNSHIRE ARCHIVES, LINCOLN
10ANC/333

LONDON METROPOLITAN ARCHIVES, LONDON
DL/C/334–335 Vicar General's Act Books

MERTOUN HOUSE, ROXBURGHSHIRE
Egerton MS 45–7

Bibliography

NATIONAL ARCHIVES, LONDON
Records of the Lord Chamberlain
LC 5/31
LC 5/49
Records of the Prerogative Court of Canterbury
PROB 11/113, will of Elizabeth Russell
PROB 11/48, will of Thomas Hoby
PROB 11/59, will of Anthony Cooke
PROB 11/61, will of Nicholas Bacon
State Papers
SP 6 Theological Tracts, Henry VIII
SP 10 State Papers, Domestic, Edward VI
SP 11 State Papers, Domestic, Mary I
SP 12 State Papers, Domestic, Elizabeth
SP 14 State Papers, Domestic, James I
SP 15 State Papers, Domestic, Addenda
SP 46 State Papers, Domestic, Supplementary
SP 63 State Papers, Ireland, Elizabeth I to George III
SP 68 State Papers, Foreign, Edward VI
SP 69 State Papers, Foreign, Mary I
SP 70 State Papers, Foreign, Elizabeth I
SP 81 State Papers, German states, 1577–1784
SP 83 State Papers, Holland and Flanders, 1577–1584

PARKER LIBRARY, CORPUS CHRISTI COLLEGE, CAMBRIDGE
109/9
114/39
122/9

PIERPONT MORGAN LIBRARY, NEW YORK
81707/MA 1209

SURREY HISTORY CENTRE, WOKING
6729/6/98 More Molyneux family correspondence
LM/COR/3/595

WILTSHIRE AND SWINDON HISTORY CENTRE, CHIPPENHAM
D1/2/16 Register of bishops of Salisbury, 1535–1571
D1/2/17 Register of bishops of Salisbury, 1571–1589
D1/2/18 Register of bishops of Salisbury, 1591–1596
D1/2/19 Register of bishops of Salisbury, 1598–1615

PRINTED PRIMARY SOURCES

(The place of publication is London, unless otherwise stated.)

Actes du consistoire de l'Église française ... vol. I, ed. E. Johnson (Huguenot Society of London, 38, 1937).

Aeschylus, *Tragoediae VII* (Paris, 1557) [Westminster School].

Alston, R.C., *Books with Manuscript: A Short Title Catalogue of Books with Manuscript Notes in the British Library* (1994).

Apollinaris, *Apollinarii interpretatio Psalmorum, versibus heroicis* (Paris, 1552) [Balliol College, Oxford].

Archer, I. *et al.* (eds), *Religion, Politics, and Society in Sixteenth-Century England*, (CS, 5th series, 22, 2003).

Aristotle, *Organon* (Basel, 1545) [Hatfield House].

Aristotle, *The Art of Rhetoric*, trans. J.H. Freese (1926).

Ascham, R., *Apologia doctissimi viri Rogeri Aschami Angli pro caena Dominica, contra Missam et eius praestigias* (1577) [Hatfield House]. *STC* 825.

Ascham, R., *The Schoolmaster*, ed. L.V. Ryan (New York, 1967).

Ascham, R., *Letters of Roger Ascham*, trans. M. Hatch and A. Vos, ed. A. Vos (New York, 1989).

Ashmole, E., *The Antiquities of Berkshire* (3 vols, 1719).

Askew, A., *The Examinations of Anne Askew*, ed. E. Beilin (Oxford, 1996).

Aubrey, J., *Brief Lives*, ed. R. Barber (1982).

Bacon, F., *Letters and Life of Francis Bacon, including all his occasional works*, ed. J. Spedding (7 vols, 1861–74).

Bacon, F., *The Works of Francis Bacon*, ed. J. Spedding, R.L. Ellis and D.D. Heath (14 vols, 1861–79).

Bacon, N., *The Recreations of His Age* (Oxford, 1919).

Ballard, G., *Memoirs of Several Ladies of Great Britain*, ed. R. Perry (Detroit, 1985).

Barnes, J., *Speeches delivered to Her Majestie this last progresse, at the Right Honorable the Lady Russels at Bissam ...* (Oxford, 1592). *STC* 7600.

Basil, St, *Divi Basilii Magni Opera Graeca quae ad nos extant omnia* (Basel, 1551) [Pierpont Morgan Library, New York].

Basil, St, *Orationes de moribus XXIIII* (Paris, 1556) [Hatfield House].

Basil, St, and Gregory Nazianzen, St, *Basilii Magni et Gregorii Nazanzeni, Epistolae Graecae* (Haguenau, 1528) [British Library].

Beilin, E., (ed.), *Protestant Translators: Anne Lock Prowse and Elizabeth Russell*, The Early Modern Englishwoman (Aldershot, 1998).

Bèze, T. de, *Chrestienes meditations sur huict pseaumes du prophete David composees et nouvellement mises en lumiere par Theodore de Besze* (Geneva, 1581).

Bèze, T. de, *Christian meditations upon eight Psalmes of the prophet David*, trans. I.S. (London, 1582). *STC* 2004.

Bèze, T. de, *Correspondance de Théodore de Bèze*, ed. H. Aubert, F. Aubert and H. Meylan (38 vols, Geneva, 1970).

Bèze, T. de, and Buchanan, G., *Sacratiss. psalmi Davidis: duplici poetica metaphrasi altera alteri e regione opposita vario genere carminum latine expressi* (Geneva, 1593).

The Bible and Holy Scriptures conteyned in the Olde and Newe Testament (Geneva, 1560).

Biblia Sacra Hebraice, Chaldaice, Graece et Latine (8 vols, Antwerp, 1569–72) [St John's College, Cambridge].

Birch, T., *Memoirs of the reign of Queen Elizabeth, from the year 1581 till her death* (2 vols, 1754).

Boccaccio, G., *Le Philocope ... contenant l'histoire de Fleury et Blanchefleur* (Paris, 1555) [Hatfield House].

Bodin, J., *Les six livres de la République* (Lyons, 1580) [Hatfield House].

Bruce, J. and Perowne, T.T. (eds), *The Correspondence of Matthew Parker* (Parker Society, Cambridge, 1853).

Buchanan, G., *Georgii Buchanani Scoti poemata in tres partes digesta* (1686). Wing B5292.

Bullinger, H., *The Decades of Henry Bullinger*, trans. H.I., ed. T. Harding (5 vols in 4, Parker Society, Cambridge, 1849–52).

The Byble in Englyshe ... all the holy scrypture, both of the olde and newe testament (1539). STC 2068.

Caesar, J., *The eyght bookes of Caius Julius Caesar conteyning his martiall exploytes*, trans. A. Golding (1565) [Hatfield House]. STC 4335.

Calendar of Letters and State Papers relating to English affairs preserved principally in the Archives of Simancas, 1558–1603, ed. M.A.S. Hume (4 vols, 1892–99).

Calendar of State Papers, Domestic Series, of the Reign of Edward VI, 1547–1553, ed. C.S. Knighton (1992).

Calendar of State Papers, Foreign Series, of the Reign of Elizabeth I, 1558–1603, ed. J. Stevenson (23 vols, 1863–1950).

Calendar of State Papers relating to Ireland in the Reigns of Henry VIII, Edward VI, Mary, and Elizabeth, 1509–1573, ed. H.C. Hamilton (1860).

Callimachus, *Cyrenaei Hymni, cum scholiis nunc primum aeditis sententiae ex diversis poetis oratoribusque ac philosophis collectae, non ante excusae* (Basel, 1532) [Westminster School].

Calvin, J., *Joannis Calvini opera quae supersunt omnia*, ed. J. Baum, *et al.* (59 vols, Brunswick, 1863–1901).

Camden, W., *Reges, reginae, nobiles, & alii in ecclesia collegiata B. Petri Westmonasterii sepulti* (1606). STC 4520.

Camden, W., *The history of the most renowned and victorious Princess Elizabeth* (1688). Wing C363A.

Castiglione, B., *The courtyer of Count Baldessar Castilio divided into foure bookes*, trans. T. Hoby (1561). STC 4778.

Catalogue of Books in Theology, Ecclesiastical History and Canon Law ... On Sale, at the Prices affixed by Thomas Rodd (1848).

Catalogue of the Library: Manuscripts, Autograph Letters, Maps and Prints, forming the collection of G.E. Hart (Boston, 1890).

Cecil, W. *The Counsell of a Father to his Sonne, in ten severall Precepts* (1611). STC 4900.5.

Cheke, J., *Joannis Cheki Angli De pronuntiatione Graecae potissimum linguae disputations cum Stephano Vuintoniensi Episcopo*, ed. C.S. Curio (Basel, 1555).

Cheke, J., *The Gospel according to St Matthew*, ed. J. Goodwin (1843).

Child, H., and Greg, W. (eds), *Iphigenia at Aulis, Translated by Lady Lumley* (1909).

Chrysostom, St John, *Divi Joannis Chyrsostomi in omnes Pauli apostoli epistolas accuratissima vereque aurea et divina interpretation* (Verona, 1529) [CUL].

Chrysostom, St John, *De orando Deum libri duo* (Louvain, 1551) [Hatfield House].

Cicero, *Brutus. Orator*, trans. G.L. Hendrickson and H.M. Hubbell (1939).

Cicero, *Tusculanae disputationes*, trans. J.E. King (1945).

Cicero, *De officiis*, trans. W. Miller (1968).

Citron, S. and Junod, M.C. (eds), *Registres de la Compagnie des Pasteurs, VI (1589–1594)* (Geneva, 1980).

Clapham, J., *Elizabeth of England: Certain Observations concerning the Life and Reign of Queen Elizabeth*, ed. E. Plummer Read and C. Read (Philadelphia, 1951).

Coke, J., *The debate betweene the Heraldes of Englande and Fraunce* (1550). STC 5530.

Collins, A., *Letters and Memorials of State, in the Reigns of Queen Mary, Queen Elizabeth, King James, King Charles the First, part of the reign of King Charles the Second, and Oliver's usurpation* (2 vols, 1746).

Collinson, P., Craig, J. and Usher, B. (eds), *Conferences and Combination Lectures in the Elizabethan Church: Dedham and Bury St Edmunds, 1582–90* (Church of England Record Society, 10; Woodbridge, 2003).

Cooke, A., *Diallacticon, c'est-à-dire réconciliatoire d'un bon et sainct personage touchant la vérité, nature et Substance du corps et sang de Jésus Christ en l'Eucharistie (par A. Cooke)* (Paris, 1566).

Croke, G., *Reports of Sir George Croke, Knight* (3 vols, Dublin, 1791–93).

Dering, E., *A briefe and necessary Instruction, verye needefull to bee knowen of all housholders* (1572). STC 6679.

Dering, E., *Certaine godly and comfortable Letters* (1614). STC 6683.3.

Diallacticon de veritate, natura atque substantia corporis & sanguinis Christi in eucharistia (Unknown, 1576).

Diallacticon viri boni et literati, de veritate, natura atque substantia corporis & sanguinis Christi in Eucharistia (Strasbourg, 1557).

Dietz, B. (ed.), *The Port and Trade of Early Elizabethan London: Documents* (London Records Society, 8; Leicester, 1972).

Dionysius of Halicarnassus, *Antiquitatum Romanarum lib. X* (Paris, 1546–47) [St John's College, Oxford].

Divinae Scripturae, Veteris ac Novi Testimenti, omnia (Basle, 1545) [Pembroke College, Cambridge].

Drant, T. (trans.), *A medicinable morall, that is two books of Horace his satyres* (1566).

Edwards, R., *The Works of Richard Edwards*, ed. R. King (Manchester, 2001).

Elizabeth I, *Collected Works*, ed. L. Marcus, J.M. Mueller and M.B. Rose (Chicago, 2000).

Elizabeth I, *Elizabeth I: Translations, 1544–1589*, ed. J. Mueller and J. Scodel (Chicago, 2009).

Elizabeth I, *Elizabeth I: Translations, 1592–1598*, ed. J. Mueller and J. Scodel (Chicago, 2009).

Elyot, T., *The boke named the Governour* (1531). STC 7635.

Elyot, T., *The Education or bringinge up of children, translated oute of Plutarche* (1532). *STC* 20057.

Elyot, T., *The Book Named The Governor*, ed. S.E. Lehmberg (London, 1962).

Epistola cuiusdam Angli qua afferitur consensus verae religionis doctrinae & caeremoniarum in Anglia (Paris?, 1561). STC 18332.

Erasmus, D., *Erasmi Roterodami Paraphrasis in Evangelium secundum Joannem* (Basel, 1523) [Folger Shakespeare Library].

Erasmus, D., *The first tome or volume of the Paraphrase of Erasmus upon the Newe Testamente* (1548). *STC* 2854.4.

Erasmus, D., *Opus de conscribendis epistolis, ex postrema auctoris recognitione emendatius editum* (Antwerp, 1564) [Hatfield House].

Erasmus, D., *De duplici copia verborum ac rerum commentarii duo multa accessione novisque formulis locupletati. Una cum commentaries M. Veltkirchii* (1573) [Hatfield House]. *STC* 10473.

Erasmus, D., *De conscribendis epistolis*, ed. J.K. Sowards, *Collected Works of Erasmus*, 25 (Toronto, 1985).

Erasmus, D., *The Right Way of Speaking Latin and Greek*, trans. M. Pope, *Collected Works*, 26 (Toronto, 1985).

Erasmus, D., *The Correspondence of Erasmus*, ed. R.A.B. Mynors *et al.*, *Collected Works of Erasmus*, 8 (Toronto, 1988).

Erasmus, D., *Spiritualia*, ed. J. O'Malley, *Collected Works of Erasmus*, 66 (Toronto, 1988).

Euclid, *The elements of geometrie of the most aunciant philosopher Euclide of Megara* (1570) [Colgate University].

Eusebius, *Ecclesiasticae historiae libri decem* (Paris, 1544) [Westminster Abbey Library].

Eusebius, *Pamphili evangelicae praeparationis lib. XV* (Paris, 1544) [Westminster Abbey Library].

Eutropius, *A briefe chronicle, where in are described shortlye the originall, and the successive estate of the Romaine weale publique*, trans. T. Haward (1564). *STC* 10579.

Fénélon, B. de Salignac, *Correspondance diplomatique* (7 vols, Paris, 1838–40).

Fenton, G., *Actes of conference in religion, holden at Paris betweene two papist doctours of Sorbone, and two godlie ministers of the Church* (1571). *STC* 24726.5.

Fenton, G., *Monophylo* (1572). *STC* 10797.

Fernel, J., *Medicina* (Paris, 1554) [Hatfield House].

Foster, C.W. (ed.), *The State of the Church in the Reigns of Elizabeth and James I* (Lincoln Record Society, 23; Lincoln, 1926).

Foxe, J., *The Acts and Monuments of John Foxe*, ed. S.R. Cattley (8 vols, 1837–41).

Fulwell, U., *Tee [sic] first part of the eighth liberall science: entituled, Ars adulandi, the art of Flattery* (1576). *STC* 11471.

Galen, *Opera omnia* (Basel, 1538) [Christ Church, Oxford].

Galen, *De sanitate tuenda, libri sex, Thoma Linacro Anglo interprete* (Lyons, 1559) [Hatfield House].

Galen, *Opera omnia* (Venice, 1562–63) [Christ Church, Oxford].

Gardiner, S.R. (ed.), *The Fortescue Papers* (CS, new series, 1, 1871).

The Geneva Bible: A Facismile of the 1560 Edition (Madison, Wisc., 1969).

Goodman, G., *The Court of King James the First*, ed. J.S. Brewer (2 vols, 1839).

Gregory of Nyssa, *Opus admirandum Gregorii Nysseni antistitis de hominis opificio* (Basel, 1567) [Westminster Abbey Library].

Haddon, W., *G. Haddoni Legum Doctoris, s. Reginae Elisabethae à supplicum libellis, lucubrationes passim collectae, & editae* (1567). *STC* 12596.

Haddon, W., *Poematum Gualteri Haddoni, Legum Doctoris, sparsim collectorum, libri duo* (1576). *STC* 12597.

Haddon, W., *Contra Hieron. Osorium, eiusque odiosas insectationes pro evangelicae veritatis necessaria defensione, responsio apologetica* (1577) [Hatfield House]. *STC* 12593.

Harrington, J., *A New Discourse of a Stale Subject, called the Metamorphosis of Ajax* (1596). *STC* 12780.

Harrington, J., *Ludovico Ariosto's 'Orlando Furioso'*, ed. R. McNulty (Oxford, 1972).

Hartley, T.E. (ed.), *Proceedings in the Parliaments of Elizabeth I* (3 vols, Leicester, 1981–85).

Hassell Smith, A., Baker, G. and Kenny, R. (eds), *The Papers of Nathaniel Bacon of Stiffkey* (4 vols, Norfolk Record Society, 46, 49, 53, 64, Norwich, 1979–2000).

Hawarde, J., *Les Reportes del Cases in Camera Stellata, 1593 to 1609, from the original MS. of J. Hawarde*, ed. T.P. Baildon (1894).

Haynes, S., *A collection of State papers, relating to affairs in the reigns of King Henry VIII. ... Queen Elizabeth, from the year 1542 to 1570* (1740).

Hemmingsen, N., *Commentarius in epistolam Pauli ad Ephesios* (1576) [Hatfield House]. *STC* 13057.5.

Hentzner, P., *Itinerarium Germaniae, Galliae, Angliae, Italiae* (Nuremberg, 1612).

Herodotus, *Herodoti Halicarnassei Historia, sive historiarum libri IX., qui inscribuntur Musae* (Geneva, 1570) [Royal Library, Windsor Castle].

Hoby, M., *The Private Life of an Elizabethan Lady: The Diary of Lady Margaret Hoby, 1599–1605*, ed. J. Moody (Stroud, 1998).

Hoby, T., *The Travels and Life of Sir Thomas Hoby, Kt of Bisham Abbey, written by himself: 1547–1564*, ed. E. Powell (*Camden Miscellany* 10, CS, 3rd series, 4, 1902).

The holie Bible, conteynyng the olde Testament and the newe (1568). *STC* 2099.

Horace, *Satires, Epistles and Ars poetica*, trans. H.R. Fairclough (1929).

Horace, *Vatis amici: Horace Odes II*, trans. D.A. West (Oxford, 1998).

Horace, *Odes and Epodes*, trans. N. Rudd (2004).

A Huguenot Family in the XVI Century: The Memoirs of Philippe de Mornay Sieur du Plessis Marly Written by his Wife, trans. L. Crump (1926).

Jewel, J., *The copie of a Sermon pronounced by the Bisshop of Salisburie at Paules Crosse* (1560). *STC* 14612.

Jewel, J., *Apologia Ecclesiae Anglicanae* (1562). *STC* 14581.

Jewel, J., *An Apologie, or aunswer in defence of the Church of England, concerning the state of Religion used in the same*, trans. anon (1562). *STC* 14590.

Jewel, J., *An Apologie or answere in defence of the Churche of Englande, with a briefe and plaine declaration of the true Religion professed and used in the same*, trans. A. Bacon (1564). *STC* 14591.

Jewel, J., *The Apologie of the Church of England. With a briefe and plaine declaration of the true Religion professed and used in the same*, trans. A. Bacon (1600). STC 14592.

Jewel, J., *The Apologie of the Church of England. With a briefe and plaine declaration of the true Religion professed and used in the same*, trans. A. Bacon (1635). STC 14593.

Josephus, F., *Flavii Josephi Antiquitatum Judaicarum libri XX* (Basel, 1544) [Westminster Abbey Library].

Justin Martyr, *Opera Graeca* (Paris, 1551) [Westminster Abbey Library].

Kempis, T. à, *De Christo imitando, contemnendisque mundi vanitatibus libellus authore Thoma Kempisio ... interprete Sebastiano Castellione* (Basel, 1563) [Hatfield House].

Leedham-Green, E.S., *Books in Cambridge Inventories* (2 vols, Cambridge, 1986).

Leedham-Green, E.S. and Fehrenbach, R.J., *Private Libraries in Renaissance England: A Collection and Catalogue of Tudor and Early Stuart Book-Lists* (6 vols, Marlborough, 1992–2004).

Lloyd, D., *State-worthies: or, the statesmen and favourites of England from the Reformation to the Revolution*, ed. C. Whitworth (2 vols, 1766).

Locke, A., *A Meditation of a Penitent Sinner: Anne Locke's Sonnet Sequence*, ed. K. Morin-Parsons (Waterloo, Ont., 1997).

MacCulloch, D. (ed.), 'The *Vita Mariae Angliae Reginae* of Robert Wingfield of Brantham' (*Camden Miscellany* 28, CS, 4th series, 29, 1984), pp. 181–300.

MacCulloch, D. (ed.), *Letters from Redgrave Hall: The Bacon Family, 1340–1744* (Suffolk Record Society, 50; Woodbridge, 2007).

Machyn, H., *Diary of Henry Machyn, Citizen and Merchant Taylor of London, from A.D. 1550 to A.D. 1563*, ed. J.G. Nichols (CS, old series, 42, 1848).

Manutius, A., *Orationes horum rhetorum* (Venice, 1513) [Westminster School].

Monumenta S. Patrum orthodoxographa, ed. J.J. Grynaeus (2 vols, Basel, 1569) [St John's College, Oxford].

Morata, O., *The Complete Writings of an Italian Heretic*, ed. H.N. Parker (Chicago, 2003).

More, T., *The workes of Sir Thomas More Knyght* (1557). STC 18076.

Moschopulus, M., *De ratione examinandae orationis libellus* (Paris, 1545).

Murdin, W. (ed.), *A collection of state papers relating to affairs in the reign of Queen Elizabeth from the year 1571–1596* (1759).

Newcourt, R., *Repertorium Ecclesiasticum Parochiale Londinense* (2 vols, 1708–10).

Obsopoeus, V., *Castigationes ac diversae lectiones in orationes Demosthenis* (Nuremburg, 1534) [Hatfield House].

Ochino, B., *Sermons of Barnadine Ochine of Sena godlye, frutefull, and very necessarye for all true Christians*, trans. anon (1548). STC 18764.

Ochino, B., *Sermons of the ryght famous and excellent clerke Master Bernardine Ochine*, trans. R. Argentine (Ipswich, 1548). STC 18765.

Ochino, B., *Certayne Sermons of the ryghte famous and excellente Clerk Master Barnadine Ochine*, trans. anon (1551). STC 18766.

Ochino, B., *Fouretene sermons of Barnadine Ochyne, concernyng the predestinacion and eleccion of god*, trans. A[nne] C[ooke] (?1551). STC 18767.

Ochino, B., *Prediche, novellamente ristampate & corrette* (5 vols, Basel, 1562).

Ochino, B., *Sermons of Barnadine Ochyne (to the number of 25) concerning the predestinacion and eleccion of god*, trans. A[nne] C[ooke] (1570). STC 18768.

Ockland, C., *EIPHNAPXIA, sive Elizabetha* (1582). *STC* 18775a.

Ockland, C., *Elizabeth Queene or a short and compendious declaration of the peaceable state of England*, trans. J. Sharrock (1585). *STC* 18777.

Osorius, *De rebus Emmanuelis Regis Lusitaniae invictissimi* (Cologne, 1576) [British Library].

Ovid, *Fasti*, trans. J.G. Frazer (1931).

A parte of a register, contayninge sundrie memorable matters, written by divers godly and learned in our time (Middleberg, 1593). *STC* 10400.

Payne, M. and Hunter, J. (eds), *Renaissance Literature* (Oxford, 2003).

Peacham, H., *The Garden of Eloquence* (1577). *STC* 19498.

Peacham, H., *The Compleat Gentleman* (1634). *STC* 19504.

Peck, F., *Desiderata curiosa: or, a collection of divers scarce and curious pieces* (2 vols, 1732–35).

Peel, A. (ed.), *A Second Parte of a Register, being a calendar of manuscripts under that title intended for publication by the Puritans about 1593* (2 vols, Cambridge, 1915).

Pierce, W. (ed.), *The Marprelate Tracts, 1588–1589* (1911).

Pindar, *Olympia, Pythia, Nemea, Isthmia* (Rome, 1515) [Westminster Abbey Library].

Plato, *Laws*, trans. R. Bury (2 vols, 1984).

Powell, E. (ed.), *The Register of Bisham, co. Berks: Baptisms 1560–1812, Burials 1560–1812, Marriages 1560–1812* (Parish Register Society, 15; London, 1898).

Publilius Syrus, *Publilii Syri Sententiae*, ed. R.A.H. Bickford Smith (1895).

Quaritch, B., *Examples of Book-Binding and Volumes bearing Marks of Distinguished Ownership* (1897).

Quintilian, *Institutio Oratoria*, trans. H.E. Butler (4 vols, 1920–22).

Robinson, H. (ed.), *The Zurich Letters* (2 vols, Parker Society, Cambridge, 1842).

Robinson, H. (ed.), *Original Letters Relative to the English Reformation* (2 vols, Parker Society, Cambridge, 1846–47).

Scrinia Ceciliana, Mysteries of State & Government in Letters of the Late Famous Lord Burghley (1663). Wing S2109.

Seneca, *Ad Lucilium epistulae morales*, trans. R.M. Gummere (3 vols, 1917–25).

Seneca, *Moral Essays*, trans. J. Basore (3 vols, 1958).

Sidney, M., *The Collected Works of Mary Sidney, The Countess of Pembroke*, ed. M. Hannay, N. Kinnamon and M. Brennan (Oxford, 1998).

Sophocles, *Antigone, Women of Trachis, Philoctetes, Oedipus at Colonus*, trans. H. Lloyd-Jones (1994).

Stephanus, R. and H. (eds), *Fragmenta poetarum veterum Latinorum quorum opera non extant* (Paris, 1564).

Stevenson, J. and Davidson, P. (eds), *Early Modern Women Poets (1520–1700): An Anthology* (Oxford, 2001).

Stowe, J., *The Survey of London* (1633). *STC* 23345.5.

Taffin, J., *Of the markes of the children of God, and of their comforts in afflictions*, trans. A. [Locke Dering] Prowse (1590). *STC* 23652.3.

Terence, *Phormio, The Mother-in-law, The Brothers*, trans. J. Barsby (2001).

Terence, *The Woman of Andros, The Self-Tormentor, The Eunuch*, trans. J. Barsby (2001).

Utenhove, K., *Xenia, seu ad illustrium aliquot Europæ hominum nomina allusionum ... liber primus* (Basel, 1568).

Valerius, C., *Tabulae totius dialectices* (Cologne, 1573) [Hatfield House].

Velcurio, J., *Commentariorum libri iiii. In universam Aristotelis Physicen: nunc recens summa fide exactaque diligentia castigati et excusi* (Lyons, 1573) [Hatfield House].

Vermigli, P.M., *Most learned and fruitfull Commentaries ... upon the Epistle of S. Paul to the Romanes*, trans. H. Billingsley (1568). *STC* 24672.

Vermigli, P.M., *Petri Marytis Vermilii, Florentini praestantissimi nostra aetate theologi, Loci communes*, ed. R. Masson (1576) [Kingston Lacey House, Dorset]. *STC* 24667.

Vermigli, P.M., *Loci communes D. Petri Martyris Vermilii*, ed. R. Masson (1583) [Hatfield House]. *STC* 24668.

Verstegan, R., *A Declaration of the True Causes of the Great Troubles, Presupposed to be Intended against the Realm of England* (Antwerp, 1592). *STC* 10005.

Virgil, *Aeneid*, trans. H.R. Fairclough (1999).

Vives, J.L., *Vives and the Renascence Education of Women*, ed. F. Watson (New York, 1912).

Vives, J.L., *The Education of a Christian Woman: A Sixteenth Century Manual*, trans. C. Fantazzi (Chicago, 2000).

Walsall, J., *A Sermon Preached at Pauls Crosse by John Walsal, one of the Preachers of Christ his Church in Canterburie* (1578). *STC* 24995.

Warmington, E.H. (ed.), *The Remains of Old Latin* (4 vols, Cambridge, Mass., 1935).

A Way of Reconciliation of a good and learned man touching the Trueth, Nature and Substance of the Body and Blood of Christ in the Sacrament, trans. E. Russell (1605). *STC* 21456.

Whetstone, G., *The Rocke of Regard* (1576). *STC* 25348.

Whitgift, J., *The defense of the Aunswere to the Admonition against the Replie of T[homas] C[artwright]* (1574) [Hatfield House] *STC* 25430.

Wilcox, T., [T.W.] *A short, yet sound Commentarie; written on that woorthie worke called; the Proverbes of Salomon ...* (1589). *STC* 25627.

Wilson, T., *Arte of Rhetorique*, ed. G.H. Mair (Oxford, 1909).

PRINTED SECONDARY SOURCES

(The place of publication is London, unless otherwise stated.)

Adams. S., *Leicester and the Court: Essays on Elizabethan Politics* (Manchester, 2002).

Alexiou, M., Yatromanolakis, D. and Roilos, P., *The Ritual Lament in Greek Tradition* (Oxford, 2002).

Alford, S., *The Early Elizabethan Polity: William Cecil and the British Succession Crisis, 1558–1569* (Cambridge, 1998).

Alford, S., *Burghley: William Cecil at the Court of Elizabeth I* (2008).

Anderson, M.S., *The Rise of Modern Diplomacy, 1450–1919* (1993).

Anselment, R., 'Katherine Paston and Brilliana Harley: maternal letters and the genre of mother's advice', *Studies in Philology*, 101 (2004), 431–53.

Ashworth, E.J., 'Traditional logic', in C.B. Schmitt, Q. Skinner, E. Kessler and J. Kraye, *The Cambridge History of Renaissance Philosophy* (Cambridge, 1998), pp. 143–72.

Ashworth, E.J., 'Text-books: a case study – logic', in L. Hellinga and J.B. Trapp (eds), *The Cambridge History of the Book in Britain, III, 1400–1557* (Cambridge, 1999), pp. 380–6.

Backus, I., *Historical Method and Confessional Identity in the Era of the Reformation* (Leiden, 2003).

Barnett, R.C., *Place, Profit and Power: A Study of the Servants of William Cecil, Elizabethan Statesman* (Chapel Hill, NC, 1969).

Beilin, E., 'Current bibliography of English women writers, 1500–1640', in A.M. Haselkorn and B.S. Travitsky (eds), *The Renaissance Englishwoman in Print: Counterbalancing the Canon* (Amherst, Mass., 1990), pp. 347–60.

Bell, G.M., 'Elizabethan diplomacy: the subtle revolution', in M. Thorp and A. Slavin (eds), *Politics, Religion and Diplomacy in Early Modern Europe* (Kirksville, 1994), pp. 267–87.

Bell, G.M., 'Tudor–Stuart diplomatic history and the Henrician experience', in C. Carlton, R. Woods, M. Robertson and J. Block (eds), *State, Sovereigns and Society in Early Modern England* (Stroud, 1998), pp. 25–43.

Ben-Amos, I.K., *Adolescence and Youth in Early Modern England* (New Haven, 1994).

Berry, L., 'Five Latin poems by Giles Fletcher, the elder', *Anglia*, 79 (1962), 338–77.

Bindoff, S.T., *The House of Commons, 1509–1558* (3 vols, 1982).

Binns, J.W., *Intellectual Culture in Elizabethan and Jacobean England* (Leeds, 1990).

Boissevain, J., *Friends of Friends: Networks, Manipulators and Coalitions* (Oxford, 1974).

Booty, J.E., *John Jewel as Apologist of the Church of England* (1963).

Bornstein, D., 'The style of the Countess of Pembroke's translation of Philippe de Mornay's *Discours de la vie et de la mort*', in M.P. Hannay (ed.), *Silent But for the Word* (Kent, Ohio, 1985), pp. 126–48.

Bowden, C., 'The library of Mildred Cooke Cecil, Lady Burghley', *The Library*, 7th series, 6 (2005), 3–29.

Braddick, M. and Walter, J., 'Grids of power: order, hierarchy and subordination in early modern society', in M. Braddick and J. Walter (eds), *Negotiating Power in Early Modern Society: Order, Hierarchy and Subordination in Britain and Ireland* (Cambridge, 2001), pp. 1–42.

Brady, C., *The Chief Governors: The Rise and Fall of Reform Government in Tudor Ireland, 1536–1588* (Cambridge, 1994).

Brayman Hackel, H., 'The Countess of Bridgewater's London library', in J. Andersen and E. Sauer (eds), *Books and Readers in Early Modern England* (Philadelphia, 2002), pp. 138–59.

Brayman Hackel, H., '"Boasting of silence": women readers in a patriarchal state', in K. Sharpe and S. Zwicker (eds), *Reading, Society and Politics in Early Modern England* (Cambridge, 2003), pp. 101–21.

Brayman Hackel, H., *Reading Material in Early Modern England: Print, Gender and Literacy* (Cambridge, 2005).

Brink, J.R. (ed.), *Female Scholars: A Tradition of Learned Women before 1800* (Montreal, 1980).

Burke, V. and Gibson, J. (eds), *Early Modern Manuscript Writing: Selected Papers from the Trinity/Trent Colloquium* (Aldershot, 2004).

Byrne, M. St C., 'The first Lady Burghley', *The National Review*, 103 (1934), 356–63.

Byrne, M. St C., 'The mother of Francis Bacon', *Blackwood's Magazine*, 236 (1934), 758–71.

Cambers, A., 'Readers' marks and religious practice: Margaret Hoby's marginalia', in J.L. King (ed.), *Tudor Books and Readers: Materiality and the Construction of Meaning* (Cambridge, 2010), pp. 211–31.

Capp, B., 'Separate domains? Women and authority in early modern England', in P. Griffiths, A. Fox and S. Hindle (eds), *The Experience of Authority in Early Modern England* (1996), pp. 117–45.

Carley, J., *The Books of King Henry VIII and his Wives* (2004).

Chadwick, H., *The Cambridge History of Later Greek and Early Medieval Philosophy* (Cambridge, 1967).

Chalus, E., *Elite Women in English Political Life, c. 1754–1790* (Oxford, 2005).

Chambers, R., *The Book of Days: A Miscellany of Popular Antiquities* (2 vols, 1879).

Clark, P., 'The ownership of books in England, 1560–1640: an example of some Kentish townsfolk', in L. Stone (ed.), *Schooling and Society* (Baltimore, 1976), pp. 95–111.

Clarke, D., 'The politics of translation and gender in the Countess of Pembroke's *Antonie*', *Translation and Literature*, 6 (1997), 149–66.

Collinson, P., *The Elizabethan Puritan Movement* (1967).

Collinson, P., 'Sir Nicholas Bacon and the Elizabethan *via media*', *HJ*, 23 (1980), 255–73.

Collinson, P., *Godly People: Essays on English Protestantism and Puritantism* (1983).

Collinson, P., 'The monarchical republic of Elizabeth I', *Bulletin of the John Rylands Library*, 69 (1987), 394–424.

Collinson, P., 'The Elizabethan exclusion crisis and the English polity', *Proceedings of the British Academy*, 84 (1995), 51–92.

Compton, P., *The Story of Bisham Abbey* (Maidenhead and Trowbridge, 1973).

Considine, J., *Dictionaries in Early Modern Europe* (Cambridge, 2008).

Cooper, C.H., *Athenae Cantabrigienses* (3 vols, Cambridge, 1858–1913).

Croft, P., 'Mildred, Lady Burghley: the matriarch', in P. Croft (ed.), *Patronage, Culture and Power: The Early Cecils* (2002), pp. 283–300.

Croft, P. (ed.), *Patronage, Culture and Power: The Early Cecils* (2002).

Croft, P. 'The new English church in one family: William, Mildred and Robert Cecil, 1547–1612', in S. Platten (ed.), *Anglicanism and the Western Christian Tradition* (Norwich, 2003), pp. 163–88.

Croft, P. and Hearn, K., '"Only matrimony maketh children to be certain ...": two Elizabethan pregnancy portraits', *British Art Journal*, 3 (2002), 19–24.

Daintith, J. *et al.*, *Biographical Encyclopedia of Scientists* (2nd edn, 2 vols, Abingdon, 1994).

Daston, L., and Stolleis, M., *Natural Law and the Laws of Nature in Early Modern Europe* (Aldershot, 2008).

Davidoff, L., 'Regarding some old husbands' tales: public and private in feminist history', in L. Davidoff, *Worlds Between: Historical Perspectives on Gender and Class* (Oxford, 1995), pp. 227–76.

Davidoff, L., 'Gender and the "Great Divide": public and private in British gender history', *Journal of Women's History*, 15 (2003), 11–27.

Davidson, P. and Stevenson, J., 'Elizabeth I's reception at Bisham (1592): elite women as writers and devisers', in J.E. Archer, E. Goldring and S. Knight (eds), *The Progresses, Pageants and Entertainments of Queen Elizabeth I* (Oxford, 2007), pp. 207–26.

Dawson, J., 'William Cecil and the British dimension of early Elizabethan foreign policy', *History*, 74 (1989), 196–216.

Daybell, J., '"Suche news as on Quenes hye wayes we have met": the news and intelligence networks of Elizabeth Talbot, countess of Shrewsbury (c. 1527–1608)', in J. Daybell (ed.), *Women and Politics in Early Modern England, 1450–1700* (Aldershot, 2004), pp. 114–31.

Daybell, J. (ed.), *Women and Politics in Early Modern England, 1450–1700* (Aldershot: 2004).

Daybell, J., 'Scripting a female voice: women's epistolary rhetoric in sixteenth-century letters of petition', *Women's Writing*, 13 (2006), 3–20.

Daybell, J., *Women Letter-Writers in Tudor England* (Oxford, 2006).

Daybell, J., 'Women, news and intelligence networks in Elizabethan England', in R.J. Adams and R. Cox (eds), *Diplomacy and Early Modern Culture* (Basingstoke, 2010), pp. 101–19.

Dear, P., 'The meanings of experience', in K. Park and L. Daston (eds), *The Cambridge History of Science, III: Early Modern Science* (Cambridge, 2006), pp. 106–31.

Demers, P., *Women's Writing in English: Early Modern England* (Toronto, 2005).

Dibdin, T., *An Introduction to the Knowledge of the Rare and Valuable Editions of the Greek and Latin Classics* (1827).

Donawerth, J., 'Women's reading practices in seventeenth-century England: Margaret Fell's *Women's Speaking Justified*', *The Sixteenth Century Journal*, 37 (2006), 985–1005.

Doran, S., *England and Europe 1485–1603* (1996).

Doran, S., *Monarchy and Matrimony: The Courtships of Elizabeth I* (1996).

Dormer, E., 'Bisham', *Berks, Bucks and Oxon Archaeological Journal*, 12 (1909), 94–5.

Dowling, M., *Humanism in the Age of Henry VIII* (1986).

DuCann, G., 'Ghosts at Gray's Inn', *Graya*, I, (1927), 27–30.

Du Maurier, D., *Golden Lads: A Study of Anthony Bacon, Francis and their Friends* (1975).

Durant, D.N., *Bess of Hardwick: Portrait of an Elizabethan Dynast* (rev. edn, 1999).

Ellis, R., 'Translation for and by the young in 16th-century England: Erasmus and the Arundel children', in G. Iamartino, M. Maggioni and R. Facchinetti (eds), *Thou Sittest at another Boke ... English Studies in Honour of Domenico Pezzini* (Milan, 2008).

Elston, T., 'Transformation or continuity? Sixteenth-century education and the legacy of Catherine of Aragon, Mary I, and Juan Luis Vives', in C. Levin, J. Carney and D. Barrett-Graves (eds), *High and Mighty Queens of Early Modern England: Realities and Representations* (Basingstoke, 2003), pp. 11–26.

Erler, M., *Women, Reading and Piety in Late Medieval England* (Cambridge, 2002).

Evenden, E., *Patents, Pictures and Patronage: John Day and the Tudor Book Trade* (Aldershot, 2008).

Ezell, M., *The Patriarch's Wife: Literary Evidence and the History of the Family* (Chapel Hill, 1987).

Ezell, M., *Writing Women's Literary History* (Baltimore, 1992).

Ezell, M., *Social Authorship and the Advent of Print* (Baltimore, 1999).

Fincham, K., and N. Tyacke, *The Altars Restored: The Changing Face of English Religious Worship, 1547–c.1700* (Oxford, 2007).

Foster, J., *Alumni Oxonienses: The Members of the University of Oxford, 1500–1714* (4 vols, Oxford, 1891–92).

Foyster, E., *Manhood in Early Modern England: Honour, Sex and Marriage* (Harlow, 1999).

Franklin Harkrider, M., *Women, Reform and Community in Early Modern England: Katherine Willoughby, Duchess of Suffolk and Lincolnshire's Godly Aristocracy, 1519–1580* (Woodbridge, 2008).

Freeman, T., '"The good ministrye of godlye and vertuouse women": the Elizabethan martyrologists and the female supporters of the Marian martyrs', *Journal of British Studies*, 39 (2000), 8–33.

Friedman, A.T., 'The influence of humanism on the education of girls and boys in Tudor England', *History of Education Quarterly*, 25 (1985), 57–70.

Furdell, E., *Publishing and Medicine in Early Modern England* (Rochester, NY, 2002).

Gaukroger, S., *Francis Bacon and the Transformation of Early-Modern Philosophy* (Cambridge, 2001).

Gibson, J., 'Letters', in M. Hattaway (ed.), *A Companion to English Renaissance Literature and Culture* (Oxford, 2000), pp. 615–19.

Greaves, R.L., 'The role of women in early English nonconformity', *Church History*, 52 (1983), 299–311.

Guy, J., (ed.), *The Reign of Elizabeth I: Court and Culture in the Last Decade* (Cambridge, 1995).

Guy, J., 'The rhetoric of counsel in early modern England', in D. Hoak (ed.), *Tudor Political Culture* (Cambridge, 1995), pp. 292–310.

Guy, J., *A Daughter's Love: Thomas and Margaret More* (2008).

Haigh, C., *English Reformations: Religion, Politics and Society under the Tudors* (Oxford, 1993).

Hamlin, H., *Psalm Culture and Early Modern Literature* (Cambridge, 2004).

Hammer, P., 'Patronage at court, faction and the earl of Essex', in J. Guy (ed.), *The Reign of Elizabeth I: Court and Culture in the Last Decade* (Cambridge, 1995), pp. 65–86.

Hammer, P., *The Polarisation of Elizabethan Politics: The Political Career of Robert Devereux, Second Earl of Essex, 1585–1597* (Cambridge, 1999).

Hannay, M.P. (ed.), *Silent But for the Word: Tudor Women as Patrons, Translators, and Writers of Religious Works* (Kent, Ohio, 1985).

Hannay, R.K., 'The earl of Arran and Queen Mary', *Scottish Historical Review*, 18 (1920–21), 258–76.

Harris, B., 'Women and politics in early Tudor England, *HJ*, 33 (1990), 259–81.

Harris, B., 'The view from my lady's chamber: new perspectives on the early Tudor monarchy', *Huntington Library Quarterly*, 60 (1997), 215–47.

Harris, B., *English Aristocratic Women, 1450–1550: Marriage and Family, Property and Careers* (Oxford, 2002).

Heal, F., 'Reputation and honour in court and country: Lady Elizabeth Russell and Sir Thomas Hoby', *TRHS*, 6th series, 6 (1996), 161–78.

Heal, F., *Reformation in Britain and Ireland* (Oxford, 2003).

Hickman, K., *Daughters of Britannia: The Lives and Times of Diplomatic Wives* (1999).

Higgins, P., 'The reactions of women, with special reference to women petitioners', in B. Manning (ed.), *Politics, Religion and the English Civil War* (1973), pp. 177–222.

Hoak, D., (ed.), *Tudor Political Culture* (Cambridge, 1995).

Hosington, B.M., 'England's first female-authored encomium: the Seymour sisters' *Hecatodistichon* (1550)', *Studies in Philology*, 93 (1996), 117–63.

Hosington, B.M., 'Translation in the service of politics and religion: a family tradition for Thomas More, Margaret Roper and Mary Clarke Basset', in J. de Landstheer and H. Nellen (eds), *Between Scylla and Charybdis: Learned Letter Writers Navigating the Reefs of Religious and Political Controversy in Early Modern Europe* (Leiden, 2010), pp. 93–108.

Hudson, W.S., *John Ponet, 1516?–1556* (Chicago, 1942).

Hufton, O., 'Reflections on the role of women in the early modern court', *The Court Historian*, 5 (2000), 1–13.

Hughes, A., 'Gender and politics in Leveller literature', in S. Amussen and M. Kishlansky (eds), *Political Culture and Cultural Politics in Early Modern Europe* (1995), pp. 162–88.

Hughes, A., 'Men, the "public" and the "private", in the English revolution', in P. Lake and S. Pincus (eds), *The Politics of the Public Sphere in Early Modern England* (Manchester, 2007), pp. 191–212.

Hurstfield, J., *The Queen's Wards: Wardship and Marriage under Elizabeth I* (1958).

Ives, E., *The Life and Death of Anne Boleyn: 'The Most Happy'* (Oxford, 2004).

James, S.E., *Kateryn Parr: The Making of a Queen* (Aldershot, 1999).

Jardine, L., '"O Decus Italiae Virgo", or the myth of the learned lady in the Renaissance', *HJ*, 28 (1985), 799–819.

Jardine, L. and Grafton, A., *From Humanism to the Humanities: Education and the Liberal Arts in Fifteenth and Sixteenth-Century Europe* (1986).

Jardine, L. and Grafton, A., '"Studied for action": how Gabriel Harvey read his Livy', *Past and Present*, 129 (1990), 30–78.

Jardine, L. and Stewart, A., *Hostage to Fortune: The Troubled Life of Francis Bacon, 1561–1626* (1998).

Jayne, S.R., *Library Catalogues of the English Renaissance* (Berkeley, 1956).

Johnston, A.F., 'The "Lady of the farme": the context of Lady Russell's entertainment of Elizabeth at Bisham, 1592', *Early Theatre*, 5 (2002), 71–85.

Keaney, J., 'Moschopoulos and Harpocration', *Transactions and Proceedings of the American Philological Association*, 100 (1969), 201–7.

Kennedy, W., *Elizabethan Episcopal Administration: An Essay in Sociology and Politics* (3 vols, 1924).

Kinder, D., 'Clement of Alexandria: conflicting views on women', in E. Ferguson (ed.), *Christianity and Society* (1999), pp. 213–20.

King, J.N., 'Patronage and piety: the influence of Catherine Parr', in M. Hannay (ed.), *Silent But for the Word* (Kent, Ohio, 1985), pp. 43–60.

King, J.N., 'John Day: master printer of the English Reformation', in P. Marshall and A. Ryrie (eds), *The Beginnings of English Protestantism* (Cambridge, 2002), pp. 180–208.

King, M., 'Book-lined cells: women and humanism in the early Italian Renaissance', in P. Labalme (ed.), *Beyond Their Sex: Learned Women of the European Past* (New York, 1980), pp. 66–90.

Klein, L., 'Gender and the public/private distinction in the eighteenth century: some questions about evidence and analytic procedure', *Eighteenth Century Studies*, 29 (1995), 97–109.

Kolkovich, E.Z., 'Lady Russell, Elizabeth I and female political alliances through performance', *English Literary Renaissance*, 39 (2009), 290–314.

Labalme, P.H. (ed.), *Beyond Their Sex: Learned Women of the European Past* (New York, 1980).

Lake, P., *Moderate Puritans and the Elizabethan Church* (Cambridge, 1982).

Lamb, M.E., 'The Cooke sisters: attitudes toward learned women in the Renaissance', in M.P. Hannay (ed.), *Silent But for the Word* (Kent, Ohio, 1985), pp. 107–25.

Lewis, C.S., *English Literature in the Sixteenth Century* (Oxford, 1954).

Llewellyn, N., 'Honour in life, death and the memory: funeral monuments in early modern England', *TRHS*, 6th series, 6 (1996), 179–200.

Lloyd-Jones, G., *The Discovery of Hebrew in Tudor England* (Manchester, 1983).

McArthur, E., 'Women petitioners and the Long Parliament', *English Historical Review*, 24 (1909), 698–709.

McCutcheon, E., *Sir Nicholas Bacon's Great House Sententiae* (Amherst, Mass., 1977).

McEntee, A., '"The [un]civill-sisterhood of oranges and lemons": female petitioners and demonstrators, 1642–53', in J. Holstun (ed.), *Pamphlet Wars: Prose in the English Revolution* (1992), pp. 92–111.

MacFarlane, I.D., *Buchanan* (1981).

McIntosh, M.K., 'Sir Anthony Cooke: Tudor humanist, educator, and religious reformer', *PAPS*, 119 (1975), 233–50.

McKitterick, D., 'Women and their books in seventeenth-century England: the case of Elizabeth Puckering', *The Library*, 7th series, 1 (2000), 359–80.

McLaren, A.N., *Political Culture in the Reign of Elizabeth I: Queen and Commonwealth, 1558–1585* (Cambridge, 1999).

Mack, P., *Elizabethan Rhetoric: Theory and Practice* (Cambridge, 2002).

Magnusson, L., 'Widowhood and linguistic capital: the rhetoric and reception of Anne Bacon's epistolary advice', *English Literary Renaissance*, 31 (2001), 3–33.

Magnusson, L., 'A rhetoric of requests: genre and linguistic scripts in Elizabethan women's suitors' letters', in J. Daybell (ed.), *Women and Politics in Early Modern England, 1450–1700* (Aldershot: 2004), pp. 51–66.

Magnusson, L., 'Imagining a national church: election and education in the works of Anne Cooke Bacon', in J. Harris and E. Scott-Baumann (eds), *The Intellectual Culture of Puritan Women, 1558–1680* (Basingstoke, 2010), pp. 42–56.

Malay, J., 'Thomas Sackville's elegy to Thomas and Philip Hoby: the discovery of a draft manuscript', *Notes and Queries*, 56 (2009), 513–15.

Marshall, P., *Mother Leakey and the Bishop* (Oxford, 2007).

Matthew, A.R. (ed.), *The Oxford Dictionary of National Biography* (Oxford, 2004).

Mattingly, G., *Renaissance Diplomacy* (1955).

May, S., *Elizabethan Courtier Poets: The Poems and Their Contexts* (Columbia, 1991).

Meale, C. and Boffey, J., 'Gentlewomen's Reading', in L. Hellinga and J.B. Trapp (eds), *The Cambridge History of the Book in Britain, III, 1400–1557* (Cambridge, 1999), pp. 526–40.

Mears, N., 'Regnum Cecilianum? A Cecilian perspective of the court', in J. Guy (ed.), *The Reign of Elizabeth I: Court and Culture in the Last Decade* (Cambridge, 1995), pp. 46–64.

Mears, N., 'Politics in the Elizabethan Privy Chamber: Lady Mary Sidney and Kat Ashley', in J. Daybell (ed.), *Women and Politics in Early Modern England, 1450–1700* (Aldershot, 2004), pp. 67–82.

Mears, N., *Queenship and Political Discourse in the Elizabethan Realms* (Cambridge, 2005).

Merritt, J., 'The cradle of Laudianism? Westminster Abbey, 1558–1630', *JEH*, 52 (2001), 623–46.

Merritt, J., 'The Cecils and Westminster 1558–1612: the development of an urban power base', in P. Croft (ed.), *Patronage, Culture and Power: The Early Cecils* (2002), pp. 230–46.

Miller, A., *Sir Henry Killigrew: Elizabethan Soldier and Diplomat* (Leicester, 1963).

Milne, K., 'The forgotten Greek books of Elizabethan England', *Literature Compass*, 4 (2007), 677–87.

Mn, J.H., 'Lord Bacon's mother', *Notes and Queries*, 95 (1857), 327.

Morant, P., *The History and Antiquities of the County of Essex* (2 vols, 1823).

Morgan, P., 'Frances Wolfreston and "Hor Bouks": a seventeenth-century woman book-collector', *The Library*, 6th series, 11 (1989), 197–219.

Morini, M., *Tudor Translation in Theory and Practice* (Aldershot, 2006).

Morrissey, M., 'Scripture, style and persuasion in seventeenth-century English theories of preaching', *JEH*, 53 (2002), 689–90.

Morrissey, M. and Wright, G., 'Piety and sociability in early modern women's letters', *Women's Writing*, 13 (2006), 38–50.

Mukherjeee, N., 'Thomas Drant's rewriting of Horace', *Studies in English Literature, 1500–1900*, 40 (2000), 1–20.

Nares, E., *Memoirs of the Life and Administration of Lord Burghley* (1831).

Neale, J.E., *Elizabeth I and her Parliaments, 1584–1601* (1957).

Norland, H., *Drama in Early Tudor England, 1485–1558* (1995).

O'Day, R., 'The ecclesiastical patronage of the Lord Keeper, 1558–1642', *TRHS*, 5th series, 23 (1973), 95–103.

O'Day, R., *Women's Agency in Early Modern Britain and the American Colonies: Patriarchy, Partnership and Patronage* (Harlow, 2007).

Orgel, S., 'Marginal maternity: reading Lady Anne Clifford's *A Mirror for Magistrates*', in D. Brooks (ed.), *Printing and Parenting in Early Modern England* (Aldershot, 2005), pp. 267–90.

Orme, N., *Education in the West of England, 1066–1548* (Exeter, 1976).

Overell, M.A., *Italian Reform and English Reformations, c.1535–c.1585* (Aldershot, 2008).

Parker, P., *Shakespeare from the Margins: Language, Culture, Context* (1996).

Payne, H., 'The Cecil women at court', in P. Croft (ed.), *Patronage, Culture and Power: The Early Cecils, 1558–1612* (2002), pp. 265–82.

Payne, H., 'Aristocratic women, power, patronage and family networks at the Jacobean court, 1603–1625', in J. Daybell (ed.), *Women and Politics in Early Modern England, 1450–1650* (Aldershot, 2004), pp. 164–80.

Pearson, A., *Thomas Cartwright and Elizabethan Puritanism 1535–1603* (Cambridge, 1925).

Pearson, J., 'Women reading, reading women', in H. Wilcox (ed.), *Women and Literature in Britain 1500–1700* (Cambridge, 1996), pp. 80–99.

Peltonen, M., *Classical Humanism and Republicanism in English Political Thought, 1570–1640* (Cambridge, 2004).

Peters, R., *Oculus Episcopi: Administration in the Archdeaconry of St Albans 1580–1625* (Manchester, 1963).

Phillippy, P., *Women, Death and Literature in Post-Reformation England* (Cambridge, 2002).

Pièpho, L., 'The ecclesiastical eclogues of Giles Fletcher the elder', in A. Moss *et al.* (eds), *Acta Conventus Neo-Latini Hafniensis* (Binghamton, 1994), pp. 817–29.

Pollock, L.A., '"Teach her to live under obedience": the making of women in the upper ranks of early modern England', *Continuity and Change*, 4 (1989), 231–58.

Pollock, L.A., *With Faith and Physic: The Life of a Tudor Gentlewoman* (1993).

Pollock, L.A., 'Rethinking patriarchy and the family in seventeenth-century England', *Journal of Family History*, 23 (1998), 3–27.

Porter, R., 'Reading is bad for your health', *History Today*, 48/3 (March 1998), 11–16.

Prescott, A.L., 'The pearl of the Valois and Elizabeth I: Marguerite of Navarre's *Mirroir* and Tudor England', in M.P. Hannay (ed.), *Silent But for the Word* (Kent, Ohio, 1985), pp. 61–76.

Price, R., 'Are there holy pagans in Justin Martyr', in E. Peters and E. Livingstone (eds), *Studia Patristica*, 31 (1997), 167–71.

Read, C., *Mr. Secretary Cecil and Queen Elizabeth* (1955).

Read, C., *Lord Burghley and Queen Elizabeth* (1960).

Roberts, S., *Reading Shakespeare's Poems in Early Modern England* (Basingstoke, 2003).

Ryan, L.V., 'The Haddon-Osorio controversy (1563–1583)', *Church History*, 22 (1953), 142–54.

Sandys, J., *A Short History of Classical Scholarship* (Cambridge, 1915).

Schleiner, L., *Tudor and Stuart Women Writers* (Bloomington, Ind., 1994).

Schlickler, F. de, *Les Eglises du refuge en Angleterre* (3 vols, Paris, 1892).

Scott-Warren, J., *Sir John Harrington and the Book as Gift* (Oxford, 2001).

Sharpe, K., *Reading Revolutions: The Politics of Reading in Early Modern England* (2000).

Sheils, W.J., *The Puritans in the Diocese of Peterborough, 1558–1610* (Northampton Record Society, 30; Northampton, 1979).

Shenk, L., 'Turning learned authority into royal supremacy: Elizabeth I's learned persona and her university orations', in C. Levin, J. Carney and D. Barrett-Graves (eds), *Elizabeth I: Always Her Own Free Woman* (Burlington, 2003), pp. 78–96.

Shenk, L., *Learned Queen: The Image of Elizabeth I in Politics and Poetry* (Basingstoke, 2010).

Sherman, W., *John Dee: The Politics of Reading and Writing in the English Renaissance* (Amherst, 1995).

Siraisi, N.G., *History, Medicine and the Traditions of Renaissance Learning* (Ann Arbor, 2007).

Skinner, Q., *Reason and Rhetoric in the Philosophy of Hobbes* (Cambridge, 1996).

Smith, H., 'Humanist education and the Renaissance concept of women', in H. Wilcox (ed.), *Women and Literature in Britain 1500–1700* (Cambridge, 1996), pp. 9–29.

Smith, H., 'Women as sextons and electors: King's Bench and precedents for women's citizenship', in H. Smith (ed.), *Women Writers and the Early Modern British Political Tradition* (Cambridge, 1998), pp. 324–42.

Smith, W., *Dictionary of Greek and Roman Mythology and Biography* (1870).

Sotheby's, *The Library of the Earls of Macclesfield removed from Shirburn Castle. Part Seven: Bibles 1477–1739* (2006).

Stears, K., 'Death beomes her: gender and Athenian death ritual', in S. Blundell and M. Williamson (eds), *The Sacred and the Feminine in Ancient Greece* (1998), pp. 113–27.

Stevenson, J., 'Women, writing and scribal publication', *English Manuscript Studies 1100–1700*, 9 (2000), 1–32.

Stevenson, J., 'Mildred Cecil, Lady Burleigh: poetry, politics and Protestantism', in V. Burke and J. Gibson (eds), *Early Modern Manuscript Writing: Selected Papers from the Trinity/Trent Colloquium* (Aldershot, 2004), pp. 51–73.

Stevenson, J., *Women Latin Poets: Language, Gender and Authority, from Antiquity to the Eighteenth Century* (Oxford, 2005).

Stewart, A., 'The voices of Anne Cooke, Lady Anne and Lady Bacon', in D. Clarke and E. Clarke (eds), *This Double Voice: Gendered Writing in Early Modern England* (Basingstoke, 2000), pp. 88–102.

Strype, J., *The Life and Acts of Matthew Parker, the first Archbishop of Canterbury in the Reign of Queen Elizabeth* (4 vols, 1711).

Strype, J., *Historical Collections of the Life and Acts of the Right Reverend Father in God, John Aylmer, Lord Bp. of London in the Reign of Queen Elizabeth* (Oxford, 1821).

Strype, J., *Annals of the Reformation and Establishment of Religion ... during Queen Elizabeth's happy Reign* (4 vols in 7, Oxford, 1824).

Tanner, L., *Westminster School* (1951).

Teague, F., 'Early modern women and "the muses ffemall"', in R. Evans and A. Little (eds), *'The muses females are': Martha Moulsworth and Other Women Writers of the English Renaissance* (West Cornwall, CT, 1995), pp. 173–9.

Tittler, R., *Nicholas Bacon: The Making of a Tudor Statesman* (1976).

Urwick, W., *Nonconformity in Herts. Being Lectures upon the Non-Conforming*

Worthies of St Albans and Memorials of Puritanism and Nonconformity in all the Parishes of the County of Hertford (1884).

Venn, J. and Venn, J.A., *Alumni Cantabrigienses* (4 vols, Cambridge, 1922–26).

Vickery, A., 'Golden age to separate spheres? A review of the categories and chronology of English women's history', *HJ*, 36 (1993), 383–414.

Vosevich, K., 'The education of a prince(ss): tutoring the Tudors', in M. Burke, J. Donawerth, L. Dove and K. Nelson (eds), *Women, Writing, and the Reproduction of Culture in Tudor and Stuart Britain* (New York, 2000), pp. 61–76.

Wabuda, S., 'Shunamites and nurses of the English Reformation: the activities of Mary Glover, niece of Hugh Latimer', in W.J. Sheils and D. Wood (eds), *Women in the Church* (Studies in Church History, 27; Oxford, 1990), 335–44.

Wabuda, S., 'The woman and the rock: the controversy on women and Bible reading', in S. Wabuda and C. Litzenberger (eds), *Belief and Practice in Reformation England* (Aldershot, 1998), pp. 46–59.

Wall, A., 'Elizabethan precept and feminine practice: the Thynne family of Longleat', *History*, 75 (1990), 23–38.

Warnicke, R., 'Women and humanism in England', in A. Rabil (ed.), *Renaissance Humanism: Foundations, Forms and Legacy* (3 vols, Philadelphia, 1988), II, pp. 66–93.

White, M., 'Renaissance Englishwomen and religious translations: the case of Anne Lock's *Of the Markes of the Children of God* (1590)', *English Literary Renaissance*, 29 (1999), 375–400.

White, P., *Predestination, Policy and Polemic* (Cambridge, 2002).

Whiting, M.B., 'Anne, Lady Bacon', *Contemporary Review*, 122 (1922), 497–508.

Whiting, M.B., 'The learned and virtuous Lady Bacon', *Hibbert Journal*, 29 (1931), 270–83.

Wiles, G., *Paul's Intercessory Prayers* (Cambridge, 1974).

Willen, D., 'Godly women in early modern England: Puritanism and gender', *JEH*, 43 (1992), 561–80.

Wing, D. (comp.), *A short-title catalogue of books printed in England, Scotland, Ireland, Wales and British America and of English books printed in other countries, 1641–1700* (4 vols, New York, 1982–98).

Wray, R., 'Recovering the reading of Renaissance Englishwomen: deployments of autobiography', *Critical Survey*, 12 (2000), 33–48.

Wright, P., 'A change in direction: the ramifications of a female household, 1558–1603', in D. Starkey (ed.), *The English Court from the Wars of the Roses to the Civil War* (1987), pp. 147–72.

Zemon Davis, N., '"Women's history" in transition: the European case', *Feminist Studies*, 3 (1976), 83–103.

UNPUBLISHED THESES

Clarke, C.M., 'Patronage and Literature: The Women of the Russell Family, 1520–1617' (PhD thesis, Reading University, 1992).

Edwards, J.S. '"Jane the Quene": A New Consideration of Lady Jane Grey, England's Nine-Days Queen' (PhD thesis, University of Colorado at Boulder, 2007).

Farber, E., 'The Letters of Lady Elizabeth Russell (1540–1609)' (PhD thesis, Columbia University, 1977).

Gladstone, H., 'Building an Identity: Two Noblewomen in England, 1566–1666' (PhD thesis, Open University, UK, 1989).

Greenbaum Goldsmith, J.B., 'All the Queen's Women: The Changing Place and Perception of Aristocratic Women in Elizabethan England, 1558–1620' (PhD thesis, Northwestern University, Illinois, 1987).

Hammer, P.J., '"The bright shininge sparke": The Political Career of Robert Devereux, 2nd Earl of Essex, c.1585–c.1597' (PhD thesis, Cambridge University, 1991).

Harvey, S. 'The Cooke Sisters: A Study of Tudor Gentlewomen' (PhD thesis, Indiana University, 1981).

King, S., 'The Daughters of Sir Anthony Cooke (1505–1576) of Gidea Hall, Essex' (MPhil. thesis, Birmingham University, 1998).

McIntosh, M.K., 'The Cooke Family of Gidea Hall, Essex, 1460–1661' (PhD thesis, Harvard University, 1967).

Mair, K., 'Anne, Lady Bacon: A Life in Letters' (PhD thesis, Queen Mary, University of London, 2009).

Merton, C., 'The Women Who Served Queen Mary and Queen Elizabeth: Ladies, Gentlewomen and Maids of the Privy Chamber, 1553–1603' (PhD thesis, Cambridge University, 1992).

Index

Note: 'n.' after a page reference indicates the number of a note on that page and page numbers in italic refer to illustrations.

Lightning Source UK Ltd.
Milton Keynes UK
UKOW04f2329140116

266334UK00001B/4/P